JUN 2 6 2015

TESOL: A Guide

D1291084

JUN 2 5 2015

ALSO AVAILABLE FROM BLOOMSBURY

TESOL: A Guide

JUN LIU
AND CYNTHIA M. BERGER

Bloomsbury Academic
An imprint of Bloomsbury Publishing Plc

B L O O M S B U R Y
LONDON • NEW DELHI • NEW YORK • SYDNEY

Bloomsbury Academic

An imprint of Bloomsbury Publishing Plc

50 Bedford Square	1385 Broadway
London	New York
WC1B 3DP	NY 10018
UK	USA

www.bloomsbury.com

BLOOMSBURY and the Diana logo are trademarks of Bloomsbury Publishing Plc

First published 2015

© Jun Liu and Cynthia M. Berger, 2015

Jun Liu and Cynthia M. Berger have asserted their right under the Copyright, Designs and Patents Act, 1988, to be identified as Authors of this work.

All rights reserved. No part of this publication may be reproduced or transmitted in any form or by any means, electronic or mechanical, including photocopying, recording, or any information storage or retrieval system, without prior permission in writing from the publishers.

No responsibility for loss caused to any individual or organization acting on or refraining from action as a result of the material in this publication can be accepted by Bloomsbury or the author.

British Library Cataloguing in Publication Data
A catalogue record for this book is available from the British Library.

ISBN:	HB:	978-1-4411-7479-6
	PB:	978-1-4742-2866-4
	ePDF:	978-1-4411-6882-5
	ePub:	978-1-4411-2713-6

Library of Congress Cataloging-in-Publication Data
Liu, Jun, 1959-
TESOL : a guide / Jun Liu and Cynthia M. Berger.
p. cm.– (Bloomsbury companions)
Includes bibliographical references and index.
ISBN 978-1-4411-7479-6 (hardback)– ISBN 978-1-4742-2866-4 (paperback)–
ISBN 978-1-4411-6882-5 (epdf)
1. Test of English as a Foreign Language–Evaluation. 2. English language–Study and teaching–Foreign speakers. 3. English language–Ability testing. I. Berger, Cynthia M. (Linquist) author. II. Title.
PE1128.A2L5336 2015
428.0071–dc23
2014037400

Typeset by Fakenham Prepress Solutions, Fakenham, Norfolk NR21 8NN
Printed and bound in Great Britain

Contents

3 0053
01078
1105

List of figures

List of tables

Acknowledgements

This book has taken us a few years to write. In the process of writing this book, we have consulted many people, and we are indebted to our colleagues, friends, and the many individuals who shared their resources, offered their advice, and made invaluable suggestions to help us shape and reshape the book.

We would like to begin by thanking the following past Presidents of TESOL International Association who contributed written reflections of their time with the association so that Chapter 4 could be more instructive to readers: John Fanselow, Joy Reid, Denise E. Murray, Mary Ann Christison, Kathleen M. Bailey, David C. Nunan, Neil J. Anderson, Amy Schlessman, Sandy Briggs, Mark Algren, Christina Coombe and Suzanne Panferov. In particular, we are honoured to have the original contribution from the 'father of TESOL', James E. Alatis, who provided first-hand narratives of the history of TESOL since its inception via the thoughtful interview responses at the beginning of Chapter 4 of this book. Although we did not receive direct contribution from all previous past presidents and TESOL leaders, their encouragement and occasional comments throughout the writing process also encouraged us to think and rethink what the book would become.

We are also grateful to TESOL Central Office staff in Alexandria, Virginia who provided valuable resources and were willing to be interviewed for this book. These enthusiastic and invaluable staff members include: Dr Rosa Aronson, Executive Director of TESOL International Association; Carol Edwards, Publishing Manager; John J. Segota, Associate Executive Director for Public Policy & Professional Relations; Craig A. Triplett, Digital Content Manager; Barry S. Pilson, Director of Marketing and Membership; and Sarah Sahr, Director of Education Programs. Special thanks also go to former TESOL Central Office staff, in particular: Chuck Amorosino, former Executive Director; Pam Williams, Former Director of TESOL Membership; and John Donaldson, former Director of Professional Development. These individuals spent quite a number of years with TESOL and continue to serve as its institutional memory.

Numerous colleagues offered feedback at various points in the evolution of this manuscript. These include Diane Belcher, Alan Hirvela, Viviana Cortes, Eric Friginal, and John M. Murphy. We also wish to thank Jun's previous graduate assistants at University of Arizona, Karen Barto and Autumn Witt, for their help with early versions of the glossary of TESOL-related terms. Cynthia wishes to acknowledge the faculty and staff at Georgia State University's Department of Applied Linguistics & ESL for their indirect contribution to this book, as well as the faculty and employees at Nashville State Community College and the Tennessee Foreign Language Institute.

Last, but not least, we thank Bloomsbury Publishing for allowing us the time and flexibility to shape this book into its final version. Since TESOL is an ever growing field, an expanding global association, and a profession with increasing visibility and respect, we feel the information we provide and the issues we discuss here are ultimately as dynamic as TESOL itself. Still, we offer *TESOL: A Guide* as a snapshot of a field in motion, and we promise to begin our notes for a future edition as soon as this one is published.

Foreword

David Nunan Ph.D.
President Emeritus, Anaheim University California
Professor Emeritus, University of Hong Kong

Some years ago, as a Past President of TESOL Inc. (now TESOL International Association), I received an invitation from the editors of the present volume to write a chapter for a proposed volume on TESOL. This proposed book had a laudable aim. As TESOL the Association approached its 50th anniversary, the book would capture the reflections, memories, and experiences of those of us who had led the Association before we all went gaga. I thought the idea was entirely praiseworthy and rushed into print, assembling my memories before I went gaga myself, something which my daughters had been telling me for some time was imminent. For one reason or another, the book never made it past the enthusiasm stage. It may have been that by that stage, too many of my fellow Past Presidents had already entered Gagaland. (Something I doubt. I know most of them, and as they age they are as mentally acute as they have ever been. Eccentric as they have ever been of course, but definitely not gaga.)

Then, several months prior to the 2010 TESOL convention in Boston, Kathleen M. Bailey, who had preceded me as President, Andy Curtis, who would become a future president (and, in fact, is President as I write this piece), and I were asked to give a plenary on the history of the Association. We had fun and frustration in equal measure putting together this plenary, harassing Central office for photographs and archival information. We presented a decade-by-decade snapshot of the evolution of TESOL as a profession and as an association. For each decade, we took a tripartite approach, looking first at what major events were shaping the world at large, then at what trends were preoccupying the profession, and finally at how events in the world at large and in the field of TESOL in general were shaping the association. Sadly, the video version of our plenary never made it out of the convention. That was a pity. We dug up a lot of archival footage for that plenary. According to feedback, it wasn't a bad plenary as plenaries go, and as plenaries go, it went.

I was therefore more than delighted to receive an invitation to contribute a foreword to this collection, which has, it seems, been inspired in part by the desire to do what the Past Presidential volume never achieved – mainly because it never got published. One of the good things about TESOL the acronym is its chameleon-like character. Eavesdrop on any conversation in which the acronym is used and you have to figure out first of all in what sense the term is being used: to refer to the profession, to the association, or the field of study? Or are the interlocutors referring to all three? More likely than not, the answer is the latter.

TESOL: A Guide is aptly named. It offers the neophyte (and I'm sure many post-neophytes) the three dimensions of TESOL covered by the term. The reader is provided with a basic overview of the profession, the association, and the field of study. It is particularly useful as an overview of the Association, and of the role that the Association has played, through its various activities: its publications, most notably *TESOL Quarterly*; its Annual Convention; its outreach to the profession through professional development activities, actual and virtual, around the world; its work in developing and promoting professional standards of practice; its political advocacy to protect and preserve the interests of the constituencies it represents; its work in developing professional standards of practice; and its promotion of an active research agenda. All of these aspects and more are captured within these pages.

One thing that makes this volume special is the fact that it is co-authored by two TESOL members who represent different generations of the profession and the association. Past-President Jun Liu brings institutional memory and the unique perspective of being the first Asian president of the association. Cynthia Berger brings the freshness and energy of the new generation.

This book needs to find a place on the bookshelf, or on the desktop, of every practicing TESOL teacher and of those teachers who are currently contemplating entering the field.

Preface

Introduction

This book project, *TESOL: A Guide*, has gone through several phases in its formation. It started as a book of reflection from past presidents of TESOL to reflect on their own TESOL experiences as they embarked on the journey of TESOL Association leadership. It then went through a phase of audience reconsideration – would the book be for future leaders in TESOL or for its membership? If the latter, what benefits might TESOL members get from such a book? It took a few more rounds of hesitancy before the framework of the current book came into being. Eventually, what began as a research project about the nature of TESOL merged with the past presidents' reflections and grew into the book before you: a three-dimensional introduction to TESOL as a field of study, as a profession, and as an association. It is our hope that our dual perspectives as a professor and as a graduate student resonate with the purpose of the book – to bring to aspiring TESOL professionals, or TESOLers, particularly the novice, a guide full of resources, information, strategies, and suggestions for an exciting and rewarding career in TESOL.

Introductions

In the section below, we take a moment to introduce ourselves and then to speak in our own respective voices about our unique experience with TESOL and how it has shaped our journey towards writing *TESOL: A Guide*.

Jun Liu, the first author of this book, also a long-term TESOL member and leader, has been inspired by the transformation of many TESOLers like himself who went from being a learner of English as a Foreign Language to a Professor of English in a major research university in the United States. In other words, he has gone from enjoying the benefits of TESOL to contributing to TESOL himself.

Cynthia Berger, the second author of the book, a novice TESOL member and a PhD student in Applied Linguistics and ESL, still remembers how her own initial untrained teaching experience as a native English speaker prompted her to seek out theories, research studies, and principles-based practices in TESOL.

Part I: Stories from Cynthia

My first experience with TESOL was as a young college student studying abroad several years ago. As I left my apartment building in southern Spain one morning, I was approached by two men in business suits who explained that they worked in an office nearby. They'd noticed me speaking English with my Swiss roommate and asked if I would be interested in providing them with English lessons once a week. I was thrilled at the idea of having a few extra euros per month and enthusiastically agreed. The naivety with which I entered into this initial teaching arrangement parallels the way many first-time, untrained English language teachers enter the classroom: I didn't know the learners' background (though I'm glad to report that they did not turn out to be kidnappers); I didn't know how or where they used English in their everyday lives; I had no intention of assessing the students' current competence in English; nor did I stop to consider their specific objectives for learning English in the first place. I did assume, however, as many still do, that speaking English fluently was the only prerequisite to teaching it (a notion that still makes me cringe today). Anytime I stop to reflect on this experience as a novice English teacher, I realize how far I've come. After working on this book, I realize how far I have to go.

By the time I entered the graduate programme in the Department of Applied Linguistics and ESL at Georgia State University, I was passionate about teaching English and had accumulated a considerable amount of teaching experience in a variety of contexts. Still, I had no background in research, knew little about the most pressing issues and controversies in the field, cared little about the professional dimension of TESOL, and certainly had never considered investing my hard-earned money on conference attendance or for membership in a professional association. Furthermore, after my first week of course reading, I was utterly overwhelmed by the plethora of terminology, acronyms, and concepts referred to in TESOL literature, no doubt written by scholars who assumed that readers would share their knowledge base. In other words, I was still a novice.

Two years later, when I was considering whether or not to pursue a PhD in the field, I found myself in novice territory once again, as I attempted to navigate the PhD application process, to understand the variety of research specializations within the field, and to grasp the nature of the TESOL profession as a whole. Which research agenda interested me the most?

Where would I best fit in the field professionally? What role might a professional association play in helping me to develop individually while gaining access to resources, cutting-edge research, and networks within the TESOL community at large?

In a way, this book is written for all of my past selves: newcomers, essentially, either to TESOL as a whole, or to a particular aspect of TESOL as a body of research, a profession, or an association. I should also acknowledge that writing this book has been valuable to my present self, a PhD student seeking to gain a better understanding of the sheer breadth of TESOL at the same time that she refines her perspective towards key issues within TESOL and develops a clear sense of the history of TESOL International Association and the role it has played and continues to play in the growth of the field.

In this regard, it is my hope that *TESOL: A Guide* will serve as a valuable resource to 'newcomers' at all stage of experience, from novice teachers to incoming graduate students, to seasoned practitioners and researchers in the field. One thing I've realized about the TESOL profession is that it is constantly changing, an ongoing process of development that demands continual adaptation and learning. In other words, I have grown accustomed to the feeling of being a novice, both as a researcher and within my teaching practice, and I hope that you, too, will experience the enthusiasm and curiosity of a newcomer as you explore this book.

Part II: Stories from Jun

It must have been around 2 a.m. on a crisp morning on 12 January 2005 in China when I received a call from Washington, DC. It was Chuck Amorosino, TESOL's Executive Director at the time:

'Jun, are you ready for the election results?' Chuck asked calmly.

'Yes, please,' I said, eagerly awaiting the answer. After a prolonged pause, which was almost torture, I heard,

'You won! You're the next President of TESOL. Congratulations!'

'What?' I uttered quietly, for fear of waking up my neighbours. 'You mean I was elected by TESOL members to be their president for the next three years?'

'Yes, Jun, now I hope you can get some sleep.' Did I sleep afterwards? No. Not that night for sure, nor for many nights after that until the very day when my presidential tenure ended in 2008.

My mind has always been full of TESOL-related issues and people. From being unable to comprehend *TESOL Quarterly* articles as a young college English teacher in China to becoming one of its contributors; from self-learning TESOL methods and techniques to teaching such courses in graduate programmes in the US; from being an emerging NNEST caucus leader to serving on the TESOL Board of Directors as member at large; and from positioning myself in US academia to bouncing back to China and larger TESOL communities outside North America – I now realize how I have come such a long way over the last four decades from being a learner of English as a foreign language to a professor teaching English to American students.

After that phone call, I both day-dreamed and night-dreamed, but I knew for sure that it was real, and that I was ready to step up and serve the association we are all so passionate about. Among all of the responsibilities that I had as TESOL President, one thing for sure is that I travelled constantly to reach out to TESOL members around the world. From Dubai to Mexico, from Turkey to Greece, from the Philippines to Cambodia, from South Korea to China, from France to Thailand, I enjoyed meeting with current and future TESOLers around the world, speaking at affiliates' conferences, and in particular, I enjoyed bringing TESOL to these international communities. I walked the TESOL walk, danced the TESOL dance, and smelled like a TESOLer. But it was not until my keynote speech at the 27th ThaiTESOL Annual convention and the 6th Pan Asia Conference that I realized how well TESOL had finally been received by our international communities. As the first Asian TESOL President at their conference, I delivered my prepared speech 'Promising Asia and Unlimited Boundaries'. During the post-plenary interview, I was asked by a reporter from *Bangkok Post* how I felt being the first Asian President of TESOL. I replied with 4 Ss: *Special, Significant, Splendid, and Smooth.*

It was SPECIAL because having an Asian president is a symbol of the association reaching outside the US. TESOL's claim of being a global association is now validated by its leadership, its membership, as well as its partnership. With global outreach as one of the goals of TESOL's strategic plan, I feel TESOL has come a long way to reach this status. I am truly happy that TESOL is global, and that a few years after my presidency, the name TESOL Inc. has officially been changed to TESOL International Association.

It was SIGNIFICANT that wherever I went and whomever I met in different countries, I was seen as a role model for hundreds and thousands of non-native English teachers and learners. By listening to my speeches and stories, they found their own identities, their own shadows, and their own voices, which permeate their lives and workplaces. The fact of the matter is that more than 80 per cent of English language teachers are non-native speakers and it is significant that they understand that TESOL respects, values, and represents them.

It was SPLENDID in that TESOL had come a long way, through four decades of innovation, creativity, and reconfiguration, to reach the point where we were recognized by English language teachers for the professional resources we provide; we were and continue to be consulted by govern-ments and agencies for expert opinions regarding language policy, standards, curriculum, teaching and testing; we have had contracts with publishers such as Thomson Learning, McGraw-Hill, and Harcourt Assessment to launch joint products for the profession, and we have partnered with sister associations to discuss joint projects.

It was SMOOTH in that, however complicated and complex matters were, the TESOL Board of Directors always worked with TESOL Central Office staff collaboratively and collegially. TESOL members were always consulted, and voices from different entities and constituents were always heard loud and clear.

In a word, TESOL has spanned the globe through tides of change over decades, for the better. For years, I have had the desire to write a book dedicated to TESOL not only as a field of study and a profession, but as an international association and a global community of English language teaching professionals. I have sought to inspire and inform younger TESOL genera-tions to better understand where TESOL comes from, who its members are, what they do, and how they develop their TESOL professional identify over decades.

To me, *TESOL: A Guide* is a book I needed when I first began teaching English in China more than three decades ago, when I studied in the Second and Foreign Language PhD programme at The Ohio State University more than two decades ago, and when I started teaching and advising graduate students in the English Language/Linguistics (ELL) and Second Language Acquisition and Teaching (SLAT) Interdisciplinary PhD programme more than 16 years ago.

1

Introduction: What is TESOL?

The three dimensions of TESOL

The term *TESOL*, an acronym for *Teaching English to Speakers of Other Languages*, has been used over the last 100 years to refer to English language teaching as a broad endeavour, as well as to various aspects of English language teaching specifically. For the purposes of this book, we intend to reference three primary dimensions of teaching English to speakers of other languages in our use of the acronym *TESOL*: TESOL as profession, as a field of study, and as an international association (i.e. TESOL International Association). Let us begin by briefly explaining what each of these dimensions represents before more thoroughly exploring each in the remainder of the book.

TESOL as a profession

When we use the phrase *TESOL as a profession*, we refer to the community of skilled practitioners who are actively involved in the teaching of English as a second or foreign language. It is not surprising then that English instructors probably comprise the largest portion of TESOL professionals. That said, *TESOL professional* may also include researchers, curriculum designers, materials developers, teacher trainers, tutors, test developers, etc. – in other words, anyone who makes or directly influences pedagogical choices in the language classroom.

Important to note is our use of the term *skilled* to qualify the TESOL practitioner. This is, admittedly, an aspirational quality. Anyone who has spent considerable time in countries where English is not a predominant language has probably encountered opportunities for paid yet unskilled English teaching, often accompanied by the assumption that being a native speaker is the only prerequisite one needs to teach English well. However, the goal of cultivating and supporting truly skilled English language teaching is one that has shaped the TESOL profession since the mid-twentieth century. As evidence of the progress that the TESOL profession has made, Allen (1966) cites a 1964 survey of teachers of non-English speakers in the US which revealed that 85 per cent of the elementary and secondary school teachers had no formal study in methods of teaching ESL, 75 per cent had no formal training in English phonetics, morphemics, or syntax, and 61.8 per cent had no training in general linguistics (for a detailed account of this survey, see Chapter 4). Today, TESOL has emerged as a legitimate global professional community of practice (Wenger, 1998), one that is constantly evolving to better meet the needs of English language learners in a rapidly changing world.

Chapter 2 will further explore the nature of the TESOL profession. We will begin by examining what it means to have a 'profession', and then discuss what is unique about the TESOL profession specifically. For new and/or peripheral members of the TESOL professional community, we will also discuss the potential benefits (and pitfalls) of pursuing a TESOL certificate or degree, how to go about doing so, and where/how to begin researching potential programmes of study to meet one's professional goals. For readers who already consider themselves TESOL professionals and who may have already found employment in the field, these sections of Chapter 2 will be useful in gaining a better understanding of the challenges and opportunities that novices to the field experience, and may serve as a helpful resource for more experienced professionals who wish to mentor newcomers. The remainder of Chapter 2 focuses on TESOL professional standards and the importance of professional development for all TESOL professionals, regardless of their level of experience. We will also present a sampling of some of the many opportunities for professional development that exist for current TESOL professionals.

TESOL as a field of study

TESOL as a field of study is used in this book to refer to any research, scholarship, publication, etc., which seeks to inform decisions regarding the teaching and learning of English as an additional language. TESOL as a field of study is, by necessity, multidisciplinary. Though many assume that applied linguistics aligns most readily with the research interests and objectives of TESOL as a field of study, there are many other disciplines which have contributed to the diversity and sophistication of TESOL scholarship as well: these include linguistics (i.e. theoretical linguistics, sociolinguistics, psycholinguistics, and neurolinguistics), education, psychology, sociology, anthropology, second language acquisition and learning, intercultural communication, and language policy and planning, among others.

Our ontological understanding of a field or discipline can serve to predetermine the discipline itself (Seargeant, 2010). This happens in two ways: first, the very description of the field itself may exclude other possibilities or directions for the field; and second, the disciplinary framework of the field may influence the structure, diffusion, and application of research and knowledge that the field produces. Thus, Seargeant has argued that a historic-ontological analysis of a field can have 'an emancipatory effect ... as the boundaries of the object of study are being pushed backwards, and explanation of that object of study is expanded into unpredicted areas' (p. 12). In a later section of this chapter, we will attempt to examine nearly 50 years of TESOL as a field of study so as to better understand the boundaries of our object of study, i.e. TESOL), and to ensure that we offer an expansive description of our field, including its most 'unpredicted areas'.

Chapter 3 of this book will continue our examination of TESOL as a field of study by exploring the diversity of TESOL research, methodologies, and controversies. We will begin by describing the unique nature of TESOL research, along with suggestions for newcomers to the field wishing to conduct their own research for the first time. After a brief glimpse of the TESOL Association research agenda and the insight it provides, we will turn our attention to methodological considerations and options in TESOL research, before examining action research specifically. Author Jun Liu then offers three of his own cases studies illustrating why action research is best considered a methodological option rather than a research method. Finally, Chapter 3 will offer an annotated selection of ten key issues in TESOL research that we feel all TESOL practitioners should be aware of, regardless of whether or not they identify primarily as researchers or instructors.

TESOL as an International Association

TESOL International Association is currently the largest association of English language professionals in the world. Founded in 1966 to 'advance professional expertise in English language teaching and learning for speakers of other languages worldwide' (TESOL International Association, n.d. 2), TESOL's current credo includes the following:

professionalism in language education; interaction of research and practice for educational improvement; accessible, high quality instruction; respect for diversity, multilingualism, and multiculturalism; respect for individual language rights; and collaboration in the global community. (TESOL International Association, n.d.)

In recent years, TESOL International Association has also undertaken an impressive global initiative, which included renaming the organization itself (from TESOL, Inc.) in order to suggest a more global orientation towards English language teaching and learning. As further proof of its global influence and appeal, TESOL International Association boasts a diverse membership of over 13,000 members representing 170 distinct countries, over 3,500 of whom live outside the United States (TESOL International Association, 2014, April).

As TESOL International Association nears its 50th anniversary, we feel that it is both appropriate and necessary to reflect on the association's history and on its continuing influence to both the TESOL profession and the field of study. Chapter 4 will explore the breadth and depth of TESOL International Association, beginning with a brief history of the professional association as told through an interview with the 'father of TESOL', James Alatis. We will also read reflections from several of TESOL International Association's past presidents, including their professional and personal thoughts on associational leadership, the state of the field, and the directions they believe TESOL will take in the future. Next, Chapter 4 will describe the scope of TESOL International Association and discuss the many resources made available by the association to its members, as well as to non-members.

Of course, while TESOL International Association is certainly the largest association of English language professionals in existence today (and arguably the most influential), numerous other TESOL-related associations exist regionally, nationally, and globally. We will provide a sampling of these in Chapter 5, in addition to several other resources relevant to readers, including common TESOL acronyms and abbreviations, job placement resources, and academic journals, for both scholarly reading and publication. Finally, Chapter 5 concludes with in-depth explanations of TESOL-related terminology combined with key readings for each to comprise an encyclopaedic glossary for novice and experienced TESOL practitioners alike.

The TESOL study: A historical perspective

The objectives of the section below are threefold: to further examine TESOL as a field of study, as a profession, and as a professional association; to consider the ways in which these three dimensions of TESOL have evolved; and to acknowledge the changes that are currently taking place so as to better predict and prepare for the future.

It is clear by now that globalization and technological innovation are changing our world at breakneck speed. New instructional technology, changing learner demographics, multidisciplinary approaches, evolving and occasionally conflicting ideologies, and more market-driven approaches and innovations are influencing and redefining the multiple dimensions of TESOL. As with any other discipline or profession, it is imperative that TESOL reflects on the current state of affairs and responds proactively.

Such an imperative can, in fact, be invigorating. Change can be celebrated as the welcome result of professional movements, of the advancement and accessibility of technology, and the implementation of innovative approaches to problems, new and old. TESOL researchers, practitioners, and leaders today are quite different from their counterparts 50 years ago, and the same will undoubtedly be said of TESOL researchers, practitioners, and leaders to come. This inevitability is indicative of the ongoing reflection, flexibility, and innovation that characterize our vibrant profession.

In order to better reflect on the past, understand the present, and predict the future in the field of TESOL, we conducted a diachronic study which looked closely at the publications of TESOL's flagship academic journal, *TESOL Quarterly*, coupled with the organization's policymaking position statements and a survey targeted at professionals representing the three dimensions of TESOL described above. Assuming that research guides practice and is thus indicative of current and future development, we posited *TESOL Quarterly* research as our primary means to better understand what has already been accomplished in the field of TESOL, to examine current trends and themes within the context of this understanding, and to anticipate and prepare for challenges to come.

The remainder of Chapter 1 details the study described above. We begin by explaining the purpose of our study, including its core research questions and an explanation of our methodology. We then describe our findings, using a variety of tables, charts, and figures to illustrate the trends that emerged in our analysis. Finally, we propose and discuss the key issues we believe are most salient to the future of TESOL and recommend six habits and abilities that TESOL practitioners should adopt in light of our conclusions.

Methodology

In order to better understand TESOL in all of its dimensions, but especially as a field of study, the authors of this book conducted the following study. As the primary objective of our study, we sought to answer the following questions:

● What trends are evident in past and current TESOL research?

● How can we use them to predict the future of TESOL?

With these specific questions in mind, we conducted a thorough document analysis of TESOL's flagship journal, *TESOL Quarterly*.[1] Using the themes and categories derived from this document analysis (described further below), we triangulated our initial results with data derived from TESOL International Association position statements and from a survey questionnaire administered to various TESOL professionals representing the three dimensions of TESOL. Our methodology and results are explained further below.

TESOL Quarterly

Founded in 1967, *TQ* has consistently served as a bridge for English language teaching theory and practice. A refereed and research-based journal publishing articles concerned with English language teaching and learning, *TQ* also solicits and publishes submissions from around the world. In doing so, *TQ* serves as a venue for international perspectives and the application of a diverse body of research on language teaching and learning.

We began our document analysis by collecting the titles and abstracts from each of the major articles published by *TQ* from 1967 to 2011. Our goal was to capture the most salient issues in the field of TESOL at the time of each volume's publication. We deliberately did not include reviews, reports, summaries, forums, reflections, editor's notes, etc., as we wanted to be consistent in data collection by featuring the main articles in each issue as the basis for analysis.

Once we had collected all 1,121 major article titles and abstracts published from 1967 to 2011, we applied open coding methods (see Glaser and Strauss, 1967) to conceptualize and categorize our data. Goulding (2009) explains that in the early stages of open coding, the process is 'unstructured and hundreds of codes may be identified. Inevitably these need to be reduced as coding moves on to a more abstract level in the search for patterns and themes that suggest a relationship' (p. 383). Using key words from article titles as an initial indicator, we began our analysis of *TQ* by assigning labels to each article according to its most salient issue(s). At this point, the specificity of the label was primarily determined by the scope of the article, as we hadn't yet begun the comparative analysis of phenomena that would allow us to identify relationships and develop broader categories (Glaser, 1978; Glaser and Strauss, 1967; Goulding, 2009). Thus, there was considerable overlap at this stage in the coding, and several articles were assigned multiple labels. Where applicable, we also applied a parallel layer of coding which pertained to the need and context of language learning and/or teaching. For example, the article 'Narrating America: Socializing adult ESL learners into idealized views of the United States during citizenship preparation classes' (Griswold, 2010) was coded as 'Language context: ESL: North America', while 'A total approach to the high school English-as-a-second-language program' (Wissot, 1970) was coded as 'Language need: Secondary'.

Once we had amassed a considerable amount of preliminary data in the form of issues, contexts, and need collected from article titles, we began the process of grouping these concepts into broader categories, which might themselves contain other concepts or subcategories. From this process, several key categories began to emerge which both subsumed lesser categorizations and differentiated themselves from others. Not infrequently, certain articles still required multiple labels. For example, the article 'Composition correctness scores' (Brodkey and Young, 1981) called for primary categorization under 'Assessment' and secondary categorization under 'Language skills: writing'. It should be noted that in our final data analysis, we did not distinguish between primary and secondary coding but considered all label categories as having equal weight in the analysis. Since an article's title sometimes did not provide enough key words for reliable coding, we often referred to the article's abstract for further information that enabled us to classify the article correctly. Occasionally, we read articles, or portions of the article itself, though in most cases the title and abstract were sufficient for coding.

Upon completion of our initial round of coding, we had assigned 243 different labels to the 1,121 major articles we reviewed. After several more rounds of analysis, during which categories surfaced, merged, subsumed other categories, or differentiated themselves from previous subcategories, 12 issues-related categories and seven subcategories emerged. These are listed below in order of descending frequency:

1 Language skills:

- Listening

- Speaking/Oral communication

- Reading

- Writing.

2 Language knowledge:

- Vocabulary

- Grammar

- Pronunciation.

3 Methodology.

4 Language learning and learners.

5 Language policy/standards.

6 Language use/sociolinguistics.

7 Assessment.

8 Teacher development.

9 Curriculum and materials.

10 SLA.

11 Research.

12 Corpus.

In addition to these categories, articles received parallel coding according to context and need:

Language context:

● EFL: Asia, Europe, North America, Latin America, Middle East, Africa

● ESL: North America, other

● ELF.

Language need:

● Tertiary education/EAP (university level)

● Secondary education (middle school/high school)

● Primary education/Young learners (elementary school)

● ESP/Workplace English.

As mentioned previously, these 12 issues-related categories contain within them numerous, more precise subcategories (or labels). For example, the category 'Methodology' contained within it several subcategories, including (but not limited to) classroom management, content-based instruction, task-based instruction, group work/collaborative learning, media in the classroom, reflective teaching, scaffolding, tutoring, and general classroom techniques, whereas the category 'Language Policy/Standards' was applied to articles that may have included the following: English as a Lingua Franca, World Englishes, language ecology, bilingual education, native speaker vs. non-native speaker debates, language varieties, the English Only movement, etc.

Findings

TESOL Quarterly analysis

Language context. For the purposes of this study, the term 'Language context' was used to refer to any described or anticipated environment in which an article's focus of research took place. For coding purposes, we recorded both the geographical location of the research, and whether such an environment would be considered English as a second language (ESL) or English as a foreign language (EFL). The distribution of articles involving English as a second language (ESL) and English as a foreign language (EFL) in *TQ* between 1967 and 2011 was fairly evenly: 46 per cent and 50 per cent, respectively (see Figure 1.1). Figure 1.2, however, which indicates language context in *TQ* by decade, reveals a gradual trend away from articles focusing on ESL and a substantial increase in EFL contexts, especially in the last 20 years. Although a relatively small portion of articles have specifically addressed English as a lingua franca[2] (ELF) (Jenkins, 2006) since 1967 (4 per cent), Figure 1.2 suggests that the incidence of research and publication pertaining to ELF is indeed more relevant today. While we see considerably less focus on ESL since the late 1980s, greater awareness of the expanding role of English and its resultant pedagogical implications may be partially responsible for the increase in articles written for/within an EFL context in the same time period, as discussions of ELF seem most relevant to learners and practitioners living outside regions in which English is the primary language (i.e. ESL contexts). Furthermore, this trend towards an ELF understanding of English challenges the manner in which ESL and EFL models have been traditionally defined for the last 50 years.

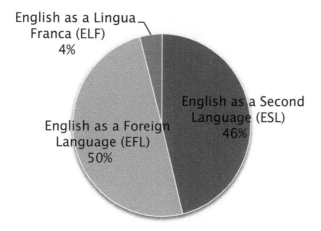

FIGURE 1.1 *Language context.* TESOL Quarterly, *1967–2011*

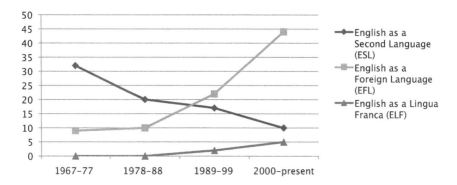

FIGURE 1.2 *Language context by decade.* TESOL Quarterly, *1967–2011*

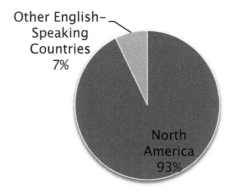

FIGURE 1.3 *ESL context.* TESOL Quarterly, *1967–2011*

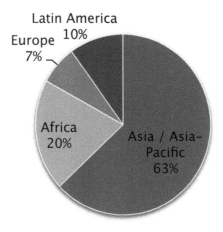

FIGURE 1.4 *EFL context.* TESOL Quarterly, *1967–2011*

Assuming the more traditional distinction between ESL and EFL for the sake of analysis, we can hone in on each of these categories and gain a better understanding of where TESOL research has been focused geographically within the last 45 years. Figure 1.3 indicates that the vast majority of ESL-focused research has occurred within the context of North America. This is less surprising than one might imagine, given the fact that the TESOL International Association was founded within the United States and only became known as TESOL International Association[3] in September 2011.

Of particular interest is the distribution of EFL contexts represented in *TQ*, as represented in Figure 1.4, which indicates that a majority of *TQ* articles incorporated an Asia/Asia-Pacific context. One potential reason for such a trend is the very high population of English language learners in Asia, in part due to its dense population. Another factor that may be contributing to this trend is the tendency for many countries in Asia to now include English as a subject in school as a requirement for most college entrance exams. Due to complex internal, external, geopolitical, socio-economic, and pedagogical factors, Asian learners are now being taught English at an earlier age and for an extensive amount of time, resulting in more and more focus on Asia/Asia-Pacific in TESOL research derived from and/or affecting this context.[4.]

Language needs. For the purposes of our study, language need was determined by learners' language objectives rather than their proficiency level. Thus, the sub-coding of language needs to be included in *ESP/workplace*, *tertiary/EAP*, *secondary*, and *primary/young learner* (see Figure 1.5) rather than *beginner*, *intermediate*, etc. Although learners in tertiary-level education and EAP programmes have received the greatest focus from *TQ* researchers since the inception of *TQ* (see Figure 1.5), a gradual rise in research addressing younger learners' needs is suggested by Figure 1.6, which indicates the distribution of language need in *TQ* per decade. In fact, the cumulative amount of articles pertaining to primary/young learners in the last ten years is almost at the same level it was during *TQ*'s first decade of publication (see Figure 1.6). It is likely that the majority of articles pertaining to young learners in the first decade of *TQ*'s existence were fuelled by interest in the critical period and the so-called natural approach to language acquisition (Lenneberg, 1967). While the majority of this early research took place within an ESL context (see Figure 1.2), the renewed scholarship we see pertaining to primary/young learners today is predominantly addressing EFL/ELF learning contexts. These findings are corroborated by the fact that evidence of students learning English at a much younger age can be found in the language policies of the Ministry of Education in many Asian countries, such as China, Korea, Japan, and Thailand (Liu, 2005). For example, it is estimated that at the turn of the century China alone had 300 million students learning English, more than half of whom were in elementary schools.

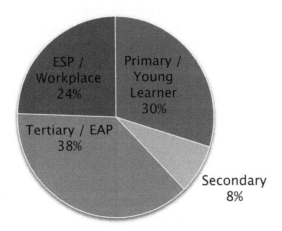

FIGURE 1.5 *Distribution of language needs.* TESOL Quarterly, *1967–2011*

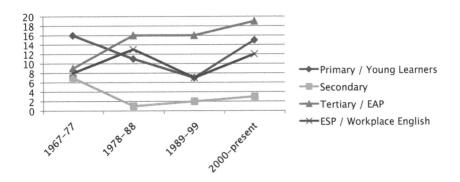

FIGURE 1.6 *Distribution of language needs by decade.* TESOL Quarterly, *1967–2011*

Since the inception of ESP in the early 1960s (Halliday, McIntosh and Strevens, 1964), ESP/Workplace English has experienced fluctuations in the level of attention it received from *TQ* researchers. Following considerable interest in the early 1980s, ESP/Workplace English received relatively little attention again in *TQ* until the turn of the century, when the incidence of articles relating to this language need increased (see section entitled 'Discussion' on page 17 for further reflection on ESP/Workplace English). At the same time, interest in tertiary/EAP-level TESOL issues is as high as it has ever been. Taken as whole, Figure 1.6 suggests that in the last 10–15 years, *TQ* articles have begun to more specifically address the needs of all learners and practitioners in the field based on context- and need-specific particulars.

Emerging issues

Independent of language context and level, ten issues-based categories emerged which subsumed the most frequently recurring issues observed during our analysis of *TQ* articles published from 1967 to 2011. These categories were as follows, in order of descending frequency (also see Figure 1.7): language skills, language elements, methodology, language learning and learners, language policy/standards, language use/sociolinguistics, assessment, teacher development, curriculum and materials, and second language acquisition (SLA).

Figures 1.8 and 1.9 demonstrate the issues which are currently upward trending and downward trending respectively, whereas Figure 1.10 isolates the four trends with the greatest degree of fluctuation overall. These include language skills, language elements, methodology, and language use/sociolinguistics. Both Figures 1.9 and 1.10 indicate increased attention to language skills relative to other issues from the mid-1970s to the mid-1990s, followed by a relatively dramatic decline. (See 'Language skills' below for further attention to this phenomenon; language elements will be addressed below as well.) With regard to methodology, it is clear that *TQ* was founded at the height of a great deal of field-wide discussion and research regarding language teaching methodology. The gradual decline in articles pertaining to *methodology* as illustrated in Figures 1.9 and 1.10 is likely to be indicative of a departure from an earlier obsession with method in the field of TESOL and greater attention to developing diverse, contextually appropriate approaches to language teaching, as well as to enhancing practitioners' more 'subjective understanding of the teaching they do' (Prabhu, 1990, p. 172).

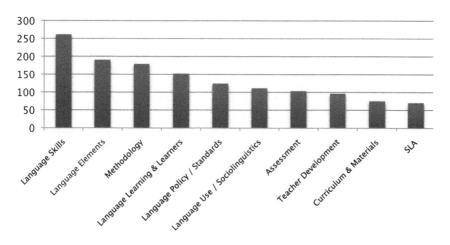

FIGURE 1.7 *Top ten issues.* TESOL Quarterly, *1967–2011*

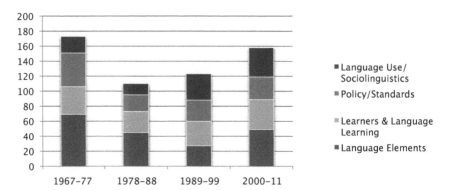

FIGURE 1.8 *Upward trends.* TESOL Quarterly, *1967–2011*

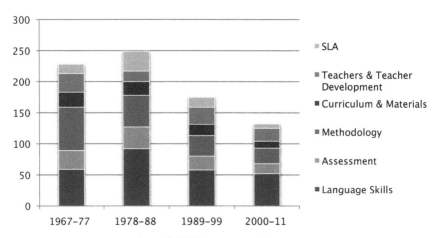

FIGURE 1.9 *Downward trends.* TESOL Quarterly, *1967–2011*

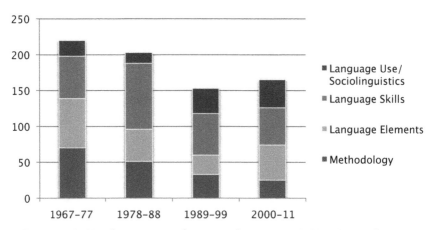

FIGURE 1.10 *Top four issues with greatest fluctuation.* TESOL Quarterly, *1967–2011*

Language skills. Our analysis of attention to the four macro-language skills[5] (i.e. reading, writing, speaking, and listening) in *TQ* revealed a principal focus on literacy (i.e. reading and writing) over the entirety of *TQ*'s history (Figure 1.11). This is not surprising given the high concentration of *TQ* articles published within a tertiary/EAP context (see Figure 1.5). However, our analysis of skills by decade (Figures 1.9 and 1.10) suggested that *TQ*'s attention to language skills as discrete units has decreased in the last 25–30 years. This may be indicative of the movement towards communicative language teaching and the resultant integration of the four skills, which gained popularity in the 1980s and 1990s. Figure 1.12 also reveals the degree to which contemporary perspectives on language curricula associate writing with reading, and speaking with listening (and vice versa, respectively) (Hinkel, 1999).

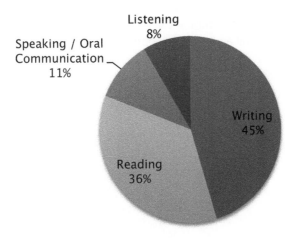

FIGURE 1.11 *Language skills*

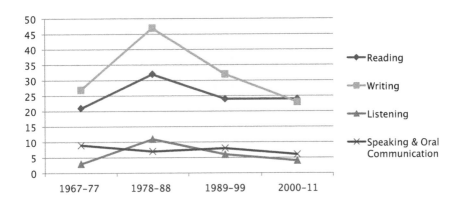

FIGURE 1.12 *Language skills by decade*

Language elements. Our examination of *TQ* articles by language element (grammar, vocabulary, or speaking and oral communication) from 1967 to 2011 revealed a principal focus on grammar (Figure 1.13). Of further interest is Figure 1.14, which demonstrates greater initial disparity between language elements at the inception of *TQ*, with grammar receiving by far the most attention, followed by a gradual decrease in overt research pertaining to language elements over the first three decades of *TQ*'s existence, and finally, a gradual pattern of increase with regard to all three elements, suggesting a potential convergence of the three. Similar to our discussion of language skills, this convergence of language elements may be indicative of a move away from treating grammatical and lexical items as discrete, isolable units (Conrad, 2000). Another explanation is that the decreasing emphasis on language elements from 1967 to the late 1990s was prompted by the stress on overall communicative competence, diverging from the traditional focus on accuracy over fluency, and the expansion of communicative competence to include sociocultural and global competences[6] (Liu, 2007c). As the role of English becomes more global, the acceptance of more varieties of English at the comprehensive level has also played a role in reassessing what it means to be communicatively competent as an overall goal of language learning (see further discussion of this phenomenon below).

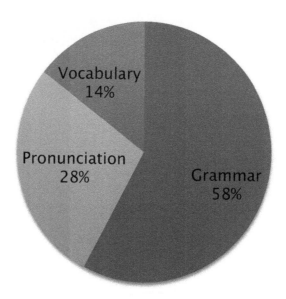

FIGURE 1.13 *Language elements*

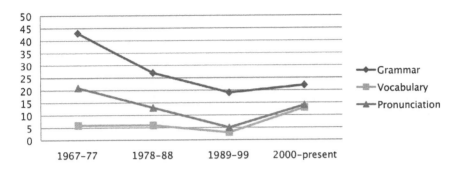

FIGURE 1.14 *Language elements by decade*

Overview of findings

These findings suggest that TESOL has undergone many transitions in the last 50 years – some dramatic, others quite gradual. In particular, our results indicate that issues surrounding *language skills, methodology, assessment, curriculum and materials, teacher development*, and *SLA* are no longer as salient to the TESOL research community as they were during the first two decades of *TQ*'s existence (see Figure 1.9). For example, analysis reveals that interest in *methodology* peaked in the first decade of *TQ*'s publication but reached an all-time low in the most recent decade. Attention to the four *language skills* was most relevant to *TQ* researchers, readers, and editors between 1978 and 1988; however, like *methodology*, articles published pertaining to *language skills* are at an all-time low.

At the same time, attention to *language use/sociolinguistics, policy/ standards, language elements*, and *learners and language learning* has gradually risen since the 1980s. In fact, by comparing these upward trending issues to those that are currently downward trending (compare Figures 1.8 to Figure 1.9), one notices an almost complementary distribution between the years 1978 and 1988. At the same time that *language skills* was peaking from 1978 to 1988, *language use/sociolinguistics* was at an all-time low. Similarly, publications relating to *policy/standards* were at their lowest between 1978 and 1988, while articles pertaining to *assessment* were at their highest.

Although *language/standards* is currently upward trending, our results indicate that frequency of publication relating to *language policy/standards* actually climaxed between 1967 and 1977, followed by rapid decline over the next 10 years. After this period of relative neglect, *policy/standards* publication began to gradually increase again, reaching its highest post-1976 results in the last decade. It would seem that the early interest in *language policy/standards* may have been primarily focused on the actual *creation* of standards. Past TESOL International Association president James Alatis (personal communication) explains how early founders of TESOL International Association saw a clear need to professionalize the field of English language teaching; one result of this mission was the creation of the first national guidelines for preparation and certification of ESOL teachers in the United States between the years 1967 and 1975. Renewed interest in *language policy/standards* is likely to be more complex, discussion of which will inform a later section in this chapter.

Comparative analysis

In order to validate and substantiate the trends and themes that emerged from our *TQ* analysis, we also triangulated our data by comparing it to both TESOL Association International position papers[7] (see Chapter 4) and a TESOL professional questionnaire.[8] Doing so allowed us to detect parallel or contradictory trending between the three sources of analyses. For example, three issues that ranked most salient in TESOL position papers actually revealed downward trending in our *TQ* analysis: *teachers and teacher development*, *curriculum and materials*, and *assessment*. Similarly, our survey questionnaire indicated that TESOL professionals consider issues such as *teachers and teacher development* and *curriculum and materials* to be significant to the future of TESOL, despite their downward trending in the field's flagship journal. Due to space limitations, we have not included tables or figures for this comparative data.

Emergent issues

Based on the results of our *TQ* study, combined with the comparative analysis provided by TESOL position papers and the TESOL professional questionnaire, we propose the emergence of the following four issues which we foresee as the most relevant to future TESOL practitioners and researchers, as well as to TESOL International Association as the leading professional association in our field:

1 Language policy/standards
2 Language learners and learning
3 Curricula and teaching materials
4 Teacher learning and development.

These issues were among the top four themes most frequently addressed in TESOL Association position papers and were each referenced by at least one of the three survey respondent groups as an issue that would most affect the future of TESOL. *Language policy/standards* and *language learners and learning* have remained consistently represented throughout the history of *TQ* (see Figure 1.8) and are both currently exhibiting an upward trend in research publication. While we might thus anticipate continued scholarship on these two issues, *curricula and teaching materials* and *teacher learning and development* do not currently indicate upward trending in recent *TQ* articles. However, due to the ever-evolving role of English in the world, as well as rapid changes in technology, learner age, and digital learning styles, we predict complex challenges to language policy, curriculum design, practitioners, and learners alike. Thus, like the respondents in our survey, we call for greater attention to curricula, materials development, and teacher learning, particularly as the role of English in an increasingly globalized world – and in the classroom – erodes the native vs. non-native speaker divide, redefines language learners as 'users', and expands our notion of communicative competence.

In the section below, we review these four issues more thoroughly, analysing different aspects of each that we believe are particularly relevant to TESOL professionals today and to the future of TESOL as a whole. We also suggest challenges posed to the field by these issues and, in some cases, make explicit recommendations. In such cases, the opinions presented are our own, though we believe that they are rooted in a nuanced understanding of the socio-historical context in which English language learning is situated and the potential for TESOL to affect change.

1 Language policy/standards

As issues pertaining to *language policy and standards* gain renewed interest (Figure 1.8), it is imperative that present and future research acknowledges the ideological backdrops and diverse sociopolitical contexts in which policy and standards decisions are made. In doing so, one must also recognize the impossibility of setting universal standards that are applicable in a variety of contexts. One way to address this problem is for local authorities and consultants to develop their own culturally appropriate standards that acknowledge the 'unique sociocultural, political, economic, and historical aspects of each individual country or setting' (Mahboob and Tilakaratna, 2010, p. 2). Reminiscent of Canagarajah's (2006b) call for greater disciplinary collaboration, Mahboob and Tilakaratna (2010) have argued that language policy should be bidirectional and involve communication and collaboration at multiple levels with a variety of stakeholders, including local practitioners, experts, researchers, students, industry, textbook writers, syllabus developers, etc.

It is from the perspective of English as the current language of globalization[9] and its complex, critical implications for local varieties, standards, non-native speakers, etc., that we predict the most substantive changes in TESOL *language policy/standards* in the future. Especially, policy and standards will be governed by an evolving redefinition of the role of English. Moreover, the very notion of global suggests not only the linking of economies, cultures, and language, but also the migration of people, the consequences of which carry complex implications for language policymakers in predominantly English-speaking countries as well.

Redefining the role of English. The story of English depends entirely on who is telling it. While the British might be tempted to call their own story 'The Triumph of English', we would argue that even the notion of 'Global English' (Graddol, 2006) lacks the complexity necessary to describe not only the ways in which English is affecting the global world but also how an increasingly global world is affecting English. This is the paradox of English today: although the residual effects of colonialism still sway ideological and political attitudes towards English, British and American influence on English has been waning and is currently confronted by native varieties of English spoken all over the globe (e.g. Indian English, Singaporean English, etc.). As a result of such phenomena, two divergent perspectives have emerged: the first concerns itself with the unified regularity, standardization and codification of English, while the second perspective stresses the legitimization of nativized varieties, intelligibility, and cross-cultural appropriateness (Sifakis, 2004). Typically, this second approach has also endorsed the World Englishes (WE) paradigm (Kachru, 1992). Kachru, typically considered the catalyst behind the WE framework (Thumboo, 2009), has argued for WE language policy and pedagogical models in which students' local varieties would be accepted as legitimate norms at the same time that said students are given knowledge about standard varieties. In this way, English users can make their own contextually dependent decisions regarding which variety of English to use. As proponents of WE ourselves, we advocate for approaches to teaching and language testing which prioritize accommodating skills and avoid penalizing or stigmatizing frequent, systematic native varieties considered intelligible among proficient speakers.

Still, the fact remains that the 'uses' of Standard English are often established by professional communities of practice and may continue to take priority over local varieties in many contexts (Mahboob and Tilakaratna, 2012). Thus, a principled WE approach should accept local varieties as legitimate norms at the same time that language students are given knowledge about standard varieties. In this way, English users can make their own contextually dependent decisions regarding which variety of English to use (Thumboo, 2009). This issue of standards vs. varieties will have immediate implications in many arenas of language policy and pedagogy: the hiring of native (NEST) vs. non-native teachers (NNEST) (Liu, 1999); whether to base assessment on local or international standards; how varieties of cultural learning should inform pedagogical approaches (Berns, 2009); to what extent local, target, and/or international cultural content should be included in materials and the teaching of pragmatic knowledge (McKay, 2002; Cortazzi and Jin, 1999; Berns, 2009; Thomas, 2006) and teacher preparation (Kachru, 1992; Brown, 2007).

Migration and globalization. It has been suggested that migrants to English-speaking countries should have two essential rights with regard to language: the right to maintain their first language, if they so desire, and the right to learn the language of the country they are entering[10] (Cooke and Simpson, 2008). Because the authors of this book currently live in the United States, and because the majority of current TESOL International Association members are from the US, we will briefly discuss what Batalova and Fix (2010) explain as an adult English education system in the US which is underfunded, plagued by low retention rates, lacking in high quality teachers, and failing to adequately integrate multiple skills in its approach to language education. Founding these problems, the National Center for ESL Literacy Education has suggested that immigration patterns in the US are shifting: states such as Tennessee, Nebraska, and Arkansas, which historically have not seen a great deal of international immigration, are now receiving significant growth in their immigrant populations (Van Duzer and Florez, 2003). Furthermore, even those states with a history of delivering ESOL instruction typically report class sizes which 'are too large to be effective' (p.18). Significantly, some adult ESL students in the US have either limited literacy in their first language or L1 literacy in a non-Roman alphabetic script (Crandall, 1993), posing obvious challenges to pedagogical decision-making and the development of curricula. At the same time, studies in the US have suggested that the ability to speak proficient English is often linked to higher wages and job security (Batalova and Fix, 2010).

While numerous factors may influence a host country's language policies towards migration, underlying these factors in the US is the reality that 'language is often a byword for race, class, or ethnicity' (Cooke and Simpson, 2008, pp. 164–5). Despite the complexity of immigration and language policy, it is clear that the future of TESOL as an altruistic community that seeks to serve the public (Judd, 2006) includes the obligation to advocate for equitable policy, sophisticated research, nuanced curricula, and adequate resources in order to meet the needs of non-English-speaking immigrants to English-dominant countries.

2. Language learners and learning

As TESOL research has shifted away from the perception of language learning as the internal adoption of a static system, what remains is 'the notion of complex and embodied language learners living in socially stratified worlds' (Toohey and Norton, 2010, p. 188). Thus, as indicated by our *TQ* analysis, increased attention to *language learners and learning* has emerged, not only in the research field of second language acquisition but in second language teaching as well. Conceiving of language – as well as language communities – as dynamic processes expands our notions of English language learners, the communities to which they belong, and the challenges presented by the sheer variety and complexity of English language learners today, especially young learners. Given this trend in research and the shifting focus to younger learners (prompted by demographic change and indicated in our *TQ* analysis), we believe that the following two aspects of *language learners and learning* will be most salient to the future of the TESOL field: (1) the reconception of language 'learners' as language 'users'; and (2) the challenges posed by teaching English to young(er) learners (TEYL).

Treating language 'learners' as 'users'. The relatively recent shift in our field's ontological conception of language from that of a fixed, static system to one that is dynamic, emergent, and variable (Larsen-Freeman, 2006) has direct implications for the ways in which we conceive of L2 speakers. While past SLA frameworks traditionally posited second language speakers as 'learners' for whom native-like proficiency is the ultimate standard, we follow Cook (1991, 2002a, 2007) in arguing that the term 'language learner' implies dependent status: within such a framework, language learners are considered 'defective native speakers' (Cook, 2002a, p. 20) who will never actually arrive at the acquisition of the L2. Rather, Cook (2007) has suggested that all L2 users have a diverse set of first and second languages which exist in the same mind as an 'integration continuum' and which may be static, developing, or reducing at any given point of time (Cook *et al.*, 2006). Unlike a language 'learner', who is 'acquiring a system for later use' (Cook, 2002a, p. 2),the term language 'users' should be used to refer to anyone who uses a second language for real-life purposes, regardless of their proficiency level.[11] In this regard, language users exploit the linguistic resources available to them and are thus empowered by their L2 user status, rather than made dependent by it.

Regardless of the actual term used to describe an L2 speaker, the field as a whole would do well to critically examine the assumptions that notions such as 'learner' imply. In particular, we believe that future TESOL research should carefully consider the goals of language users and the supposition that all L2 users hope to gain access to a native speaker community, as there are multiple, diverse L2 user communities that a speaker may wish to join instead (Cook, 2007). The pedagogical implications of applying L2 user concepts to teaching include: adapting goals to the L2 user specifically, rather than to the native L1 user; positing successful L2 users as role models rather than low-level L2 or native L1 users (see Murphy, 2014 for an excellent example of this); and promoting the value of the L1 in the classroom (Cook, 2002b).

Teaching English to young(er) learners (TEYL). Canton (2006) has described the following demographic phenomenon as a 'tidal wave' which will shape the future of globalization:

- Half of the world's population today – more than three billion people – is younger than 25 years old.

- 2.4 billion of today's total population of 6.5 billion people are children and teenagers.

- Today, almost two billion young people under the age of 15 live in the developing world.

- By 2020, the number of children under the age of 15 will be close to three billion (p. 206).

Across the globe, these same children are learning English younger and younger. For example, in China children have been learning English beginning at age 9 (Grade 3) in nearly all primary schools across the country since 2011 (Liu, 2007d). While the advocates of such compulsory early English learning often cite a critical period[12] for L2 learning (Marinova-Todd, Marshall and Snow, 2000), compulsory early English in foreign language settings may be problematic for two reasons: first, the critical period is still quite controversial in the field of SLA (Scovel, 2000). Second, most research on the critical period has been conducted in ESL settings, rather than EFL. In the former, learners are immersed in the target language; in the latter, learners have very little exposure to the target language outside the classroom and may benefit more from early L1 literacy training with L2 language study introduced later in learners' studies (Liu, 2007a; Liu, 2007b; Nunan, 2010). Given the fact that young learners' internal motivation, attitude, anxiety, etc., towards English may easily be influenced by external conditions, policymakers should take several factors into consideration before instituting compulsory English learning at an early age: available facilities (both at home and at school), attitudes towards English, the socio-economic status of students' families, quality of teaching, class size, and accessibility/availability of additional tutoring services (Liu, 2007a).

Despite the evidence that early English learning may be problematic, it would seem irresponsible for ELT researchers and practitioners to ignore the likelihood of young learners and the need for greater research-informed TEYL. In order to better understand young learners, Pinter (2006) has detailed the distinct qualities of younger vs. older learners (as cited by Nunan, 2010, pp. 2–3) suggesting that younger learners will take a more holistic approach to language learning (versus analytical); enjoy learning that is punctuated by imagination and movement rather than contextualized by the real-world; and be more concerned with their own experience than others students'. Others advocate a topic- or theme-based approach to TEYL (Moon, 2005) in order to acknowledge the unique ways in which children learn by integrating 'language learning with children's subject learning across the curriculum' (p. 119). Finally, the degree to which younger learners may interface with language and learning in unique ways due to their being digital natives is a topic we discuss under 'Digital Everything' (p. 25).

3. Curricula and teaching materials

As the role of English in the world is changing, and as our conception of language learners – as well as the demographic realities of those learners – evolves, so too will our curricula and teaching materials require innovation and subsequent reform. In order to meet the complex challenges that globalization and World Englishes phenomena present, future ELT curricula and materials should be not only innovative but flexible as well.

Due to the current predominance of generic ELT materials produced by native speakers, we argue for localized and context-specific materials, without which both practitioners and learners may have difficulty connecting with material. At the same time, greater collaboration between practitioners, publishers, researchers, etc. (Tomlinson, 1998) and student-generated content (Cooke and Simpson, 2008) may offer solutions to the inadequacies of more generic, global materials.[13] In order for curricular innovation to take root, the involvement of all participants will also be required, including policymakers, specialists, teachers, students, and mediators (Medgyes and Nikolov, 2010, pp. 265–6). Importantly, the consideration of learner needs should compel us to guarantee that the promotion of a particular culture or ideology neither overshadows minority cultures nor disregards the global texts students may need exposure to in order to become members of certain professional communities (Mahboob and Tilakaratna, 2010).

We predict that the following phenomena related to curricula and teaching materials will drive reform and future research in the field of TESOL as a whole: (1) acknowledgement of the inevitable digitization of nearly every aspect of ELT; (2) a move towards English as a medium of communication; (3) the importance of English for Specific Purposes (ESP); and (4) opportunities (technological or otherwise) for alternative forms of assessment.

Digital everything. While it took centuries for the invention of the Gutenberg printing press to result in widespread access to printed materials, digital technologies have spread to over a billion users in mere decades (Palfrey and Gasser, 2008). The term 'digital natives' (Palfrey and Gasser, 2008) is frequently used to define young people born in 1980 or later, after the advent of the first social digital technologies. Unlike 'digital settlers' (somewhat older digital users who grew up in an analogue world but have learned to use new technologies in fairly sophisticated ways) and 'digital immigrants' (who have only learned to use email and very limited social technologies late in life), digital natives have been immersed in digital technologies for their entire lives. As a result, digital natives have emerged as a generation of language learners with unique learning habits and preferences. Among them, most digital natives will share the following characteristics: a great deal of time spent using digital technologies; a penchant for multitasking;[14] a tendency to express themselves and relate to others through digital technologies; and the ability to use technology both to access information and to create new knowledge (Palfrey and Gasser, 2008).

As a result of the above, children raised with digital media and its capabilities may have less tolerance for completing worksheets by hand, listening to lectures (Collins and Halverson, 2009), or participating in any pedagogical activity which does 'not match the average computer game's exciting presentation of information' (Beatty, 2003, p. 55, as cited by Nunan, 2011, p. 215). Unlike the predominant pedagogical paradigms of the industrial era, the digitally influenced knowledge-age will result in learner preferences for 'customization, interaction, and user-control' (Collins and Halverson, 2009, p. 4). Additionally, as twenty-first century technological development continues to blur the line between traditional literacy practices and 'more applied production and presentation practices' (Collins and Halverson, 2009, p. 133), digital natives will become proficient in evolving forms of literacy made possible by technology development. Cooke and Simpson (2008) have delineated the following four aspects of emergent electronic literacy as they relate to English language learners:[15]

- reading online, which includes the potential for nonlinear texts to interact with video, graphics, etc.;

- computer-mediated communication (CMC), i.e. communication between humans made possible by computers;

- virtual communities and the malleability of identity in global, online communities; and

- barriers to gaining access to new technologies (more about barriers to access below).

Among the myriad ways in which the digital revolution will influence the field of TESOL is the inevitable breakdown of educators' and policymakers' tendency to associate learning with schooling (Collins and Halverson, 2009). Like Collins and Halverson (2009), we envisage a broadening of the ways in which our field conceives of learning. Furthermore, while 'hybrid experiences' may originate in the classroom, they will quickly migrate into other contexts (p. 129). Nunan (2010) has envisioned four different models of learning that might occur with computer-assisted language learning (CALL), both within and beyond the bricks and mortar classroom:

1   The 'traditional' classroom is supplemented and supported by technology.

2   Technology delivers the content and is supported by web-based live instruction.

3   Technology delivers the content and is supported by supplemental face-to-face instruction.

4   The fully integrated classroom (pp. 213–14).

In this final model, the fully integrated classroom, Nunan (2010) argues that technology and teachers will work collaboratively, as '[t]eachers do what they do best, such as facilitating interaction in the target language, and technology does what it does best' (p. 214). It is possible that CALL may actually exceed conventional pedagogical materials to the degree that CALL can provide instruction which is individualized, immediate, private, patient, and self-paced (Nunan, 2010).

The digital era presents challenges as well as opportunities. Clearly a problem arises when teachers themselves are only digital 'pilgrims' or 'immigrants'. TESOL practitioners should keep in mind the interactive potential of new digital technologies when faced with the daunting task of having to learn how to use them. Another problem surrounds the divide between learners with access and exposure to digital technology and those without. Critically, Palfrey and Gasser (2008) have acknowledged the importance of referring to digital natives as a *population* rather than an entire *generation* due to a 'yawning participation gap', of which 'the costs of leaving unaddressed over time will be higher than we should be willing to bear' (pp. 14–15). In particular, the consequences of 'technological exclusion' will result in a lack of access to digital technology that could further marginalize L2 learners and users from developing nations (Hyland and Hamp-Lyons, 2002).

English as a medium of instruction. Content-based instruction (CBI) – a 'pedagogical anchor to language education' (Kaufman and Crandall, 2006, p. 6) – has gained national and international popularity with widespread application across a variety of different academic contexts (Kaufman and Crandall, 2005). Specifically, CBI is becoming more prevalent in university-level settings due to a number of factors, including changing demographics, the rise of English as an international language in academic contexts worldwide, and growing acknowledgement of the need to better prepare students for future discipline-specific study (Crandall and Kaufman, 2002).

CBI, also referred to as *content and language integrated learning* (CLIL), has the potential to offer motivational incentive for learners while offering a 'fundamental difference in the use of language between the language class and the content class' (Deller and Price, 2007, p. 6). This fundamental difference reconceives of English as a subject in its own right, 'linked to the cognitive development of learners, rather than as something isolated from the rest of the curriculum' (McLean, 2012, p. 32). Furthermore, CBI/CLIL may provide a more equitable balance with regard to multiple intelligences, allowing for the participation and achievement of learners with kinaesthetic or mathematical intelligences, for example, in addition to those with high linguistic intelligence (Deller and Price, 2007).

One of the ongoing challenges of primary and secondary CBI has been the relative lack of content-specific knowledge among language teachers (Kaufman and Crandall, 2005). TESOL International Association attempted to address this issue by suggesting that teacher training programmes foster language instructors who are able to do the following:

- construct learning environments that support ESOL students' language and literacy development and content-area achievement;

- construct learning environments that support ESOL students' cultural identities, language and literacy development, and content-area achievement;

- know, understand, and use standards-based practices and strategies related to planning, implementing, and managing ESL and content instruction;

- collaborate with their colleagues across disciplines and serve as a resource to all staff ... to improve learning for all ESOL students (TESOL, 2002, as cited by Kaufman and Crandall, 2005, pp. 2–3).

Of course, we suggest that the above skills should serve as objectives for all TESOL practitioners, regardless of learner age or proficiency level. There is a further need for primary and secondary content-area teachers to be prepared to meet the needs of English language learners in their classrooms, as well as for assessment practices which take CLIL into account (Kaufman and Crandall, 2005; Deller and Price, 2007).

English for specific purposes (ESP). Thanks to corpus linguistics and genre studies, English for specific purposes (ESP) has progressed significantly from its early focus on the teaching of 'specialist registers' and the premise that linguistic features of language are completely independent from their subject (Paltridge, 2009, p. 289). Furthermore, more and more ESP scholars are questioning native-like competence as an appropriate target (Nickerson, 2005). As Paltridge (2009) explains, 'What this leads us to, then, is a very situated view of the use of language for specific purposes and one that is tightly bound up with the community of practice in which the language is used' (p. 292).

It is fitting to reiterate the increasing popularity of corpus linguistics and the data it provides regarding the nuances of the domain-specific language ESP specialists describe. Analyses of language corpora[16] make possible data-driven descriptions of domain-specific language use far more accurate than native-speaker intuition can offer researchers or practitioners. With regard to ESP, language corpora and corpus-based tools allow researchers to more accurately describe a particular genre or register, while precluding the need for instructors to be experts in the particular genre in which their students may need guidance (see McEnery, Xiao and Tono, 2006, for a thorough treatment of *corpus linguistics* and a variety of corpus-based studies).

While EAP as a sub-discipline of TESOL may have emerged from university-level learning, its role is changing. Past assumptions regarding the socio-economic and educational background of EAP students will no longer hold true, especially as more and more refugees with little-to-no previous education enter high school level courses in English-dominated countries (Hyland and Hamp-Lyons, 2002). At the same time, EAP specialists have begun to acknowledge the need for training which goes beyond undergraduate education and to focus on academic English necessary for postgraduate work and for international non-native-English academics speaking (Braine, 2002; Sengupta, Foray and Hamp-Lyons, 1999).

In English for occupational purposes (EOP), a sub-field of ESP, research has indicated that English is no longer seen as a skill completely separate from other subjects (Fitzpatrick and O'Down, 2012). Fitzpatrick and O'Down (2012) have suggested that twenty-first-century workforce skills will require 'innovative abilities, technological knowledge, and career skills' (p. 4), in addition to 'the ability to communicate in foreign languages, digital competence, and social and civic competence, as well as cultural awareness and expression' (p. 4). Current EAP course design and methods are focusing more and more on the integration of language with professional and cultural competence, based on the shared assumption that English is a tool which will enable users to develop and utilize other skills at work.

Alternative assessment. Assessment in the twenty-first century will prove challenging for two reasons in particular: (1) the high number of English test takers globally and the often high-stakes nature of such tests; and (2) the difficulty in designing English tests when World English phenomena have led to a lack of a uniform target variety (i.e. Standard English). Large-scale assessment poses a particular challenge, as many written, standardized tests continue to prioritize grammar, despite the fact that local varieties of English may use grammar in unique ways (Canagarajah, 2006a). Even localized assessment is complicated by the plethora of English varieties, as local administrators must choose the most appropriate variety and anxious learners are unsure what to study. Furthermore, in some contexts, the prioritization of communicative competence in assessment may ignore low proficiency in reading and writing, and researchers have yet to agree upon a measure for 'intelligibility' (Derwing and Munro, 2005; Jenkins, 2000).

Technology may offer answers. Collins and Halverson (2009) look forward to technological advances which would make 'embedded assessment' possible (pp. 98–9). Unlike standardized testing, which separates formative and summative assessment, embedded assessment would allow the two to converge as learners receive real-time, ongoing support (e.g. feedback, suggestions, hints, etc.) throughout the learning process. Chalhoub-Deville (2010) has suggested that computer-based testing (CBT) is already quite common in L2 assessment; however, it has been used primarily to facilitate current assessment practices rather than to 'disrupt' them (see Christensen, 1997, as cited by Chalhoub-Deville, 2010, pp. 511–12). Chalhoub-Deville (2010) calls for a 'radical transformation of assessment practices' driven by CBT which would 'expand test developers' thinking beyond the realm of P&P testing' (p. 522).

Most importantly, assessment in the twenty-first century demands a more 'humanistic' approach to assessment which would develop from an awareness that achieving native-like proficiency may be neither possible nor relevant to learners' actual needs (e.g. learners may be far more likely to communicate with non-native speakers of English in the future than native speakers). Greater collaboration between local practitioners and policymakers will also be needed when devising tests, in addition to better training of teachers with regard to a variety of assessment approaches (Mahboob and Tilakaratna, 2012).

4 Teacher learning and development

None of the above is of value without the engagement of TESOL practitioners (specifically, teachers) as active participants, action-researchers, informants, and, ultimately, stakeholders. In order to further the development of teachers as reflective TESOL stakeholders, we advocate the final dissolution of the native speaker vs. non-native speaker dichotomy, which has influenced TESOL research, curriculum design, teacher training, and hiring practices for nearly a century. Next, we suggest that globalization and the reframing of the NS vs. NNS debate should expand our traditional notion of communicative competence and thus impact teacher development, as well as practitioners' decisions in the classroom.

Breaking the native speaker and non-native speaker dichotomy. Aside from the inevitable use of terms like 'native' and 'non-native' speaker for pragmatic research purposes, we believe that the NS–NSS dichotomy is a theoretically unsound and intuitive construct based on perceived differences that do not reflect the complexity of conditions or the diversity of language use and expertise by English speakers worldwide (Moussu and Llurda, 2008). Up to 80 per cent of all communication that occurs in English takes place between non-native speakers (Prodromou, 1997) and the majority of English teachers in the world today are non-native English speakers (Liu, 1999). Despite these facts, and the supposed breakdown of the NSE vs. NNES false dichotomy (Canagarajah, 2005; Liu, 2007b), research on non-native speakers – and on non-native English-speaking teachers (NNESTs) specifically – is still relatively recent. Worse, there is evidence that some non-native speakers still are not taken into consideration for English teaching positions[17] (Clark and Paran, 2007). A native-speaker pedagogic model is particularly problematic for local teachers who are required to teach a variety that is not their own (Kirkpatrick, 2007) and who subsequently suffer from lack of confidence and self-respect (Medgyes, 1994).

In their state-of-the-art exploration of the history and research of NNESTs, Moussu and Llurda (2008) cite three arguments widely used to delegitimize the NS vs. NNS dichotomy:

1   Everyone is a native speaker of some language. Basing native-speaker designation on a person's relationship to English is indicative of Anglo-centrism and linguistic imperialism.

2   The NS vs. NNS dichotomy ignores the preponderance of English varieties (i.e. World Englishes, indigenized/nativized varieties, etc.) spoken all over the world (Higgins, 2003). Dismissing such speakers of English is akin to arguing that Australian English speakers are 'non-native' because their language variety is not the same as the English spoken in Great Britain or the United States.

3   The lack of contextualization inherent to the NS vs. NNS dichotomy ignores the degree to which language teaching and local context are intertwined. Moussu and Llurda cite case studies in which

individuals themselves could not clearly position themselves as native or non-native speakers, suggesting a continuum of speaker identity rather than the traditional NS–NNS dichotomy.

While some work has been done to counteract the unfair burden that a traditional native-speaker pedagogic model places on NNESTs, more is needed. Many researchers have lauded the unique qualities of NNESTS (Phillipson, 1992; Medgyes, 1994; Liu, 2007), suggesting that NESTs and NNESTs 'have skills and competences that complement each other' (Liu, 2007, p. 112). Moussu and Llurda (2008) have even suggested that some so-called native speakers of English may actually be less intelligible in global contexts than well-educated speakers of English as a second language. There remains a need for more research and classroom-observation studies to investigate NNS teachers' classroom performance, as well more quantitative empirical studies on NNS teachers to complement the qualitative work that has been conducted within the last decade (Moussu and Llurda, 2008). At the same time, we argue that NNESTs themselves can be empowered through teacher development which focuses on language proficiency, both content and cultural knowledge, a redefinition of the concept of research, skills development, greater investment, and critical thinking.

Beyond communicative competence. The notion of communicative competence originated with Hymes (1972) and was developed further by SLA researchers in the 1980s (see Breen and Candlin, 1980; Canale and Swain, 1980). Defined as 'the ability to produce situationally acceptable, and more especially socially acceptable, utterances, which … would normally be held to be part of a native speaker's competence' (Lyons, 1996, p. 24), communicative competence has often resulted in pedagogical approaches which value speaking and interaction with native speakers over the established focus on reading and writing, the latter of which traditionally involved a great deal of translation and memorization. However, in a rapidly changing, increasingly globalized world, neither grammatical accuracy nor pragmatic competence can guarantee social acceptability anymore (Kramsch, 2007). In place of communicative competence, a view of language competence has emerged which is more appropriate for a global world in which challenges such as social mobility, diverse speech communities, unpredictability, and a global 'communication culture' require a high level of contextual awareness and the ability to adapt language use (Kramsch, 2007). Similarly, any new pedagogical model of competence should rethink the native speaker as a reference point and acknowledge the 'mutual recognition of interlocutor's social identities' in language use (Liu, 2007c, p. 333). Such a model would help learners develop culture-sensitive knowledge, mindful reflexivity, and social identity negotiation skills (see Liu, 2001), in addition to communicative competence. Furthermore, the expansion of communicative competence will require greater instructional competence. ELT practitioners should be both cognizant of students' awareness of their own communicative incompetence, empathetic towards learners' experiences, and mindful of cross-cultural differences (Liu, 2007c).

We offer a final example that illustrates one way in which the field's notion of communicative competence may require rethinking: in the globalized business world, having a proper translation of your website into other languages is no longer enough. It has been recommended that 'digital marketers' adapt the content and format of their websites in order to cater to local markets, as '[a] truly global organization has its own modified website in each country, or region, in which it has a presence' (Charlesworth, 2012, p. 48). In the attempt to adjust to local cultures, marketers are even urged to research the significance of *colours* around the world (Charlesworth, 2012). Thus, in expanding our conception of communicative competence, we are reminded of the value of multiculturalism and Adler's (1974) notion of 'culture brokers', i.e. people who have a multiplicity of realities and are thus able to facilitate cross-cultural interactions and reduce conflict. Hong *et al.* (2010) define *multiculturalism* as a dynamic process in which individuals choose between different cultural lenses to construct reality, depending on their needs at the moment. This capacity for intercultural interaction and reflexivity is an ability beyond mere communicative competence: one that will determine the success of individuals – regardless of their native language – in the twenty-first century.

The habits and abilities of a future TESOL professional

Globalization, migration, and advances in technology and transportation continue to impact the field of TESOL in myriad ways. The 'ever-increasing connectedness in the social, political, economic, cultural, and technological spheres of life' (Cooke and Simpson, 2008, p. 2) has resulted in shifting learner demographics and a global context for learning and language use which have redefined the role of English, triggered the emergence of *nativized* varieties of English, and sparked a shift from traditional to communicative orientations. At the same time, we believe that there is the continuing potential for TESOL (in all of its dimensions) to achieve greater tolerance of pronunciation and language varieties, to reimagine standards and assessment, regard English learners as users, and broaden attitudes towards celebration of communication rather than penalizing lack of accuracy. Moreover, it is nearly impossible to overestimate the role that computer technology will play in the future of TESOL. Novel, digitally influenced and enhanced styles of learning will demand accommodation, spur future research, and affect learner expectations. Practitioners, administrators, and researchers alike should also prepare for new modes of learning that will extend beyond the classroom. Finally, geopolitical and civil unrest, poverty, war, economic deprivation, and the pursuit of better opportunities have led to global patterns of migration that are redefining the needs and experiences of language users in unique ways. Our field has an obligation to these learners' needs that goes beyond the provision of resources and language instruction that many English-dominant countries currently offer.

In the midst of all of these changes, TESOL professionals should be prepared to equip themselves with new knowledge, new approaches to pedagogy and/or research, and a fuller, more informed awareness of the very learners whose needs we serve. Clearly, the qualities and abilities that may have exemplified a good language teacher in the past will not be sufficient in the near future. This certainty carries strong implications for future teacher certificate programmes, MA teacher training, professional development, continued education curricula design, etc. In light of the need to better understand what will constitute a good language professional in the future, we believe that there are certain skills and abilities that every future TESOL professional should aspire to obtain.

In this final section of Chapter 1, we propose the six habits and abilities for future success in the TESOL profession. While none are particularly revolutionary in isolation, we believe that a simple list like the one below can provide TESOL practitioners with an accessible framework for principled action and innovative practice within their particular teaching context.

Make constant and effective changes. The world is currently experiencing its fifth stage of civilization – the Innovation Economy, preceded by the Hunter/Gatherer, Agricultural, Industrial, and Information Revolution (Canton, 2006). It is innovation that will drive the success (or lack thereof) of the globalizing world. Clearly, TESOL professionals who wish to survive and thrive in a globalizing world should be innovators as well. The qualities and skills that define a successful language teacher, researcher, or administrator today may be entirely different by 2025. Thus, TESOL professionals should strive to cultivate adaptability, reflectiveness, and the ability to resist relying on pedagogical practices or theoretical assumptions merely because they were acceptable in the past. The relationship between beliefs about language learning and actual practices is reciprocal: as we experiment with new practices, we are led to question our underlying beliefs and assumptions, which can itself lead to trying out new practice again in the future (Fullan, 1982b, p. 247, as cited by Markee, 1997, p. 54).

Learn to speak another language. The following understatement bears repeating: learning to speak another language is not an easy task. The process of attempting to do so too often leaves learners feeling frustrated and emotionally and intellectually overwhelmed. One purpose of TESOL professionals learning another language is to cultivate empathy for their students: without empathy for learners or the ability to reflect upon the experience of learning itself, TESOL pedagogy, research, and administration will fail to recognize the nuanced needs of learners or the complex and dynamic nature of language learning. Another reason why TESOL professionals should learn another language is to provide them with a new perspective from which to experience and reflect on the learning process itself. In fact, we suggest that those instructors who already speak more than one language should occasionally revisit the learner's perspective by attempting another. In this way, teachers can develop and maintain their understanding of what it is to be a learner and their appreciation for the cognitive and affective demands of the learning process. They will also be reminded that everyone is a native speaker of at least one language, regardless of whether or not that language is English.

Teach less to maximize learning. In a reprint of McLean's 1980 article in *English Teaching Forum*, beneath the heading 'Good Teaching is Timeless' (2012), readers are reminded that '[l]earning is most effective when the learner is the initiator of the learning process' (p. 33). Several decades later, Brown (2007) reiterated the notion that '[l]earner-centered, cooperative teaching is intrinsically motivating' (p. 94), and is superior to any extrinsic (i.e. externally imposed) motivation. Citing Vygotsky's (1962, 1978) 'zones of proximal development', Dörnyei and Murphy (2003) suggest that language instructors can foster learning by shifting incrementally from directive to non-directive teaching as 'students internalize more and more of the processes and as teachers learn to let go' (p. 98). In the attempt to teach less in order to maximize learning, language teachers, curricula designers, material developers, etc., should also remember the unique challenges posed by digital natives who may 'have their own imperatives of customization, interaction, and user-control' (Collins and Halverson, 2009, p. 4), resulting in more learners who favour learner-centred, non-directive approaches more than ever before.

Teach English in at least one subject area. This is perhaps our most pragmatic recommendation, emerging from undeniable trends in the TESOL employment marketplace. As more and more learners begin studying English at a younger age, and as the popularity of content and language integrated learning (CLIL), or content-based instruction (CBI), increases in Europe and North America, TESOL practitioners with background expertise in other subject areas are likely to be more competitive. In fact, it has been suggested that the lack of language instructors who can provide content-based instruction is one of the most persistent challenges facing CBI today (Wesche, 2010). Like McLean (2012), we encourage TESOL researchers and practitioners to 'see English as essentially an educative subject, linked to the cognitive development of learners, rather than as something isolated from the rest of the curriculum' (p. 32). Simply put, instructors who are knowledgeable in at least one subject will be better, more competitive English teachers.

Familiarize oneself with new learning and teaching modes. Innovation is dependent upon curiosity and exploration. Undoubtedly, as technology advances, more and more available pedagogical modes will require the mastery of technologies which are unfamiliar to even the youngest and savviest of instructors. Thus, language teachers and researchers must be fearless in the face of an admittedly daunting task – to continually make themselves aware of and amenable to new approaches, whether they be pedagogical, theoretical, or technological. TESOL professionals should always be cognizant of the degree to which modes of learning and learning preferences will be influenced by demographic, sociocultural, and technological factors. The good news is that no one is alone. Professional organizations, such as TESOL Association International, continue to offer numerous resources through which practitioners can become aware of new developments in pedagogical modes and receive support from experts and other practitioners (see Chapter 4 and Chapter 5). Of course, even as technology changes how TESOL professionals achieve their goals, it will never replace what they do, which is to facilitate the successful learning of English.

Ensure that learning takes place outside the classroom. Even language teachers are forced to admit that a great deal of language learning takes place outside the classroom. Beyond merely encouraging learners to use English outside coursework, there are a multitude of pedagogically structured learning opportunities teachers can create to ensure learning beyond the classroom. In the absence of technological resources, these have included activities such as journaling, dialogue journals, or conversation partners. However, greater access to technology now allows for internet-based assignments, online learning, multimedia presentations, and structured interaction via social media and/or handheld devices. Some instructors are even introducing podcasts into the classroom (Chinnery, 2006). Regardless of what technology is available in various teaching contexts, it is imperative that future ELT professionals begin to dissociate *learning* from *schooling* as they explore ways to foster learning outside the language classroom itself.

The list below recommends approaches to ensuring learning outside the classroom. For more in-depth discussion of these options, see our section on technology in Chapter 3, as well as individual glossary entries in Chapter 5:

- Online learning
- Self-paced learning

- One-to-one learning

- Handheld learning

- Mobile learning

- Collaborative learning

- Time-shifted learning (anytime, anywhere)

- Synchronous/asynchronous learning

- Blended learning.

Conclusion

It is only by *re-examining* our past and contextualizing our present that we are able to anticipate future directions and move forward as a field. The study described in this chapter sought to *analyse* the trends evident in TESOL research – both past and current – and use them to predict the future of TESOL. The six habits and abilities we've presented reflect the changes and adaptations that we believe TESOL professionals should strive towards in order to meet the needs of a complex, changing world in which the role of English is a dynamic one.

We do not intend to imply that these six discrete abilities represent a comprehensive description of the changes that will be necessary as the TESOL profession is forced to adapt to change. Rather, we have chosen these particular habits and abilities in the attempt to momentarily isolate – and thus more easily illustrate – the otherwise dynamic nature of TESOL and of the increasingly globalized and digitalized world in which we all live and work.

It is our hope that these six habits and abilities will enable TESOL professionals to move forward with confidence as they strive to meet the needs of a complex world in which the role of English, and indeed our field's very conception of learners, is ever-evolving. Reflection on the future of TESOL should not be overwhelming. Rather, it is our hope that this chapter will leave both experienced and novice TESOL professionals energized – while at the same time mindful of the temptation to remain idle. Let there be no mistake: TESOL cannot simply rely on what has worked well in the past. However, with greater awareness of current trends and a willingness to innovate, the TESOL profession will be well-poised to embrace the coming change and move forward as a field, as a research body, and as a professional community.

2

TESOL as a Profession

Introduction: What is the TESOL profession?

What exactly constitutes the TESOL profession is so complex that no simple answer can capture the degree to which TESOL professionals are shaping their own identities and exploring new possibilities. TESOL professionals usually perceive themselves as (or are perceived as) ESL/EFL teachers, researchers, material writers, curriculum designers, and programme administrators, among others, depending on their educational background, teaching context, access to resources, learner population, and so forth. Instead of focusing solely on educational and/or career accomplishments as stepping-stones towards becoming a professional, we prefer to think that the TESOL profession constitutes an ongoing process of professional development – one that does not necessarily begin with one's first teaching job nor end with retirement. Furthermore, like Lorimer and Shulte (2011), we would argue that the notion of a TESOL professional is a 'shifting construct' that is 'continually defined and redefined by all members of the field' (p. 34).

Still, there are certain fundamentals requisite to any profession that relate to TESOL as well. For example, it has been suggested that in order to be considered a professional, one needs to possess the appropriate 'theoretical background, mentored experience, professional affiliations, and certifications to meet the standards of excellence in the chosen field' (Wong, 2011, p. 142). In honour of TESOL International's fortieth anniversary, then-president Elliot Judd (2006) delineated several attributes of a legitimate profession in his presidential plenary. According to Judd, a profession should have a body of knowledge; a prescribed regimen of licensing for members; a code of ethics and standards; and the authority, autonomy, and status that a profession provides. He also argued that a profession is also a full-time commitment to a community that serves the public and is, among other things, altruistic. Finally, Judd observed that a profession forms professional associations. We add to this list Nunan's (1999) suggestion that responsible professionalism involves advocacy.

Which professionalism are we talking about?

Whenever professionalism is discussed, it is important to distinguish between conceptions of professionalism that exist at the institutional level and those that occur at a more personal level. In this regard, we would like to take a moment to distinguish between two types of professionalism in second language teaching – *sponsored* and *independent* (Leung, 2009) – as the two may not always coincide. While the former is established by regulatory bodies and professional associations (such as TESOL International Association), the latter develops over time as individuals engage in reflexive examination and become socially and politically aware of the impact of their profession in a particular teaching context.

Sponsored second language teacher professionalism is typically composed of standards or qualificatory frameworks imposed by teacher-training programmes, educational institutes, regulatory agencies, or professional associations. Publicly sponsored professionalism helps make explicit the 'epistemic and value preferences' (Leung, 2009, p. 51) of such institutions. Still, like *independent* professionalism, *sponsored* professionalism is ultimately context-sensitive: Leung (2009) notes that 'there is no single publicly espoused definition of ELT teacher professionalism that would apply in all educational contexts' (p. 51). Furthermore, as our field's traditionally held assumptions about language learners and their specific language needs are becoming more and more difficult to predict in advance, it's important to note the degree to which professionalism, like language and language learning, is a dynamic process that changes and adapts in response to historical, political, and contextual factors.

Another type of professionalism, *independent professionalism*, occurs when an individual teacher reflects critically on her own beliefs and on the regulatory requirements handed down to her before making principled decisions that reflect her individual values and the social, political, and pedagogical impact of her actions (Leung, 2009). It is this type of profes-sionalism that is the most essential to the vitality of the teaching profession, especially if TESOL practitioners are to be seen as more than the mere imple-menters of teaching techniques prescribed by researchers.

Because there is always potential for tension between the two types of professionalism, we believe all TESOL practitioners should work towards culti-vating a level of professional awareness that combines specialist knowledge

with critical reflection. Thus, we argue that any definition of TESOL professionalism should acknowledge the degree to which it is:

- ongoing;

- multidimensional in nature (i.e. it involves knowledge, proficiency, personality, environment, materials, and hands-on experience);

- includes a combination of discipline-based knowledge and ethical awareness; and requires reflective, responsive, and context-specific practice.

What qualifications are needed to be a TESOL professional?

One important aspect of sponsored professionalism is the notion that a teacher is qualified to begin employment in a profession due to a certain threshold of training and education. A great deal of such professionalization has occurred in ELT over the last 30 years, with an expansion from theoretical linguistics as the subject matter of language teacher education to topics as diverse as classroom-based research and syllabus design (Barduhn and Johnson, 2009). Yet the sheer range of certification and qualification require-ments for English language teaching worldwide is vast and complex. For example, while a bachelor's degree is typically considered the highest qualification for teaching internationally, there are still places in the world in which having completed a few workshops or merely being a native speaker is considered qualification enough, particularly in underdeveloped areas where compensation for teachers is low (Richards, 1990b).

A general trend in ELT qualification is for regulatory bodies to issue initial certificates for instructors to teach, followed by more extensive qualification that results from further professional development, often in the form of supervised teaching or an apprenticeship experience (Barduhn and Johnson, 2009). (In some places, such as the United States, this period of internship is followed by the completion of further education and the receipt of a state teaching licence, which legally allows a person to teach.) Importantly, initial certification is no longer seen as the last step in becoming qualified to teach; rather, teacher training is viewed as an ongoing process that develops over time and evolves as teachers gain more varied teaching experience.

Some of the ways that teachers pursue further professional development beyond receiving initial permission to teach is through receiving more advanced certification (e.g. CELTA or DELTA), completing teacher-training courses recognized by governmental agencies, or pursuing advanced degrees

(Barduhn and Johnson, 2009). Of course, professional development itself includes a greater variety of practices than those qualificatory pursuits listed above. In the remainder of the current chapter, we will focus more specifically on certificate programmes, degree programmes (BAs, MAs, PhDs), and the role of standards in the TESOL profession, in addition to reviewing the ongoing professional development that language teachers can participate in regardless of their level of experience or professional qualification.

Certificate programmes

A bachelor of arts (BA) or a bachelor of science (BS, or BSc, as it is commonly referred to in the United Kingdom) (in any major) is typically considered the most basic prerequisite for receiving a permit to teaching English in any country (see TESOL, 2014b). Still there are numerous certificate programmes that can further prepare a proficient speaker of English for teaching. In general, certificate programmes fall into two broad categories: common certificates and endorsement (or 'add-on') certificates (TESOL, 2014b). Below, we discuss what these certificates mean, whom they benefit, what participants can expect from each type of course, and what sort of further development might follow the completion of a certificate programme.

Common certificates

Whom are they for? Common certificates are generally recommended for teachers with an undergraduate degree who wish to teach English but do not have a TESL/TEFL/TESOL endorsement and choose not to immediately pursue a master's degree. Individuals who take ELT/TESOL certificate courses may also be looking to change careers, move to a different country, find employment in a foreign country where one is already located (perhaps due to a partner who works overseas), or pursue more flexible, part-time work (Brandt, 2006). While individuals who live in the United States and wish to begin working with adult ESL learners for the first time may also benefit from a common certificate, we recommend Crandall, Ingersoll and Lopez's (2010) *Adult ESL Teacher Credentialing and Certification Table* for the most current information regarding credentialing requirements per state. This document was prepared through CAELA and CAL and can be accessed through the CAL website at the following web address: http://www.cal.org/adultesl/pdfs/adult-esl-teacher-credentialing-and-certification-table.pdf/

What is required to participate in a certificate programme?

Occasionally, a bachelor's degree is required for participation, in a certification programme, but this is not usually the case. Applying to a certificate course typically involves filling out an application, conducting an interview (in person or over the phone), and/or writing a personal statement explaining your reasons for seeking admission. Importantly, acceptance to common certificate programmes does not require that a candidate be a native speaker of English or an expert in linguistics. Prior teaching experience and knowledge of a language other than English are not usually requirements; however, they may make you stand out as a candidate if admission is limited.

What to expect from a certificate course?

The TESOL International Association website (TESOL International Association, 2014a, 2014b) offers helpful advice in how to evaluate such programmes, suggesting that independent TESL/TEFL certification programmes should be taught by qualified instructors (e.g. those with master's degrees and/or significant teaching experience) and include a minimum of 100 instruction hours plus supervised teaching practicum. Any reputable certificate course will also include opportunities to observe teaching, through peer observation and/or the observation of more experienced teachers. While many such certification programmes are accredited by state, national, or professional institutions, others are not. Finally, it's important to note that these certificates alone are not likely to qualify a candidate to teach English in the United States (TESOL International Association, 2014b); however, they do give teachers with a BA or BS a competitive advantage in other countries and serve as one way to further develop as an English language teacher. We recommend investigating independent TESL/TEFL certification programmes thoroughly and inquiring about qualifying standards or accreditation from prospective employers before choosing a programme.

What does it take to be successful in a common certificate course?

Common certificate courses can require a lot of work in a short amount of time. Because of their intensive nature, many common certificates require that participants spend several hours a day in class, in addition to reading regularly assigned material; generating, peer-reviewing, and revising lesson plans; participating in collaborative activities, and engaging in peer-teaching and/or classroom observation. The time commitment and level of engagement required can be overwhelming. For many participants, a common certificate programme may also be the first time that a person has taught at all, especially in front of peers or supervisors. Performance 'jitters' are normal and to be expected. We recommend that participants focus on developing the following seven strategies for success in a common certificate programme:

- Be patient – both with yourself and with others in the course.

- See everything that happens as a learning opportunity.

- Be open to feedback, both positive and constructive.

- Don't be competitive or compare yourself with others. Every instructor's teaching style is different and has evolved out of his or her past teaching environments.

- Keep up with assigned readings and assignments; if you start to get behind, talk to the instructor/facilitator.

- Keep a journal to help you reflect on the things you're learning.

- Make constant connections between the concepts you're learning and their potential application to practice.

- Always consider how the skills and strategies you're learning might need to be adapted for different learner populations and specific learning purposes.

- Ask lots of questions!

How can I find a common certificate course?

Common certificates such as Cambridge UCLES CELTA, SIT TESOL Certificate, and Trinity Certificate in TESOL (see TESOL International Association, 2014b) are widely accepted, standardized, accredited certification programmes that offer intensive, relatively short training (from four weeks to three months) combined with practical experience. In addition to the common certificates listed above, there are numerous independent TESL or TEFL certification programmes worldwide that offer further professional development for language teachers. Teachers interested in pursuing a common certificate in TESL/TEFL/TESOL are encouraged to consult the online *The English Language Professional's Resource Guide* maintained by TESOL International Association (http://englishlanguageprofessionalsresourceguide.com/). Another excellent source for people considering a common certificate is Caroline Brandt's (2006b) *Success on Your Certificate Course in English Language Teaching: A Guide to Becoming a Teacher in ELT/TESOL*

What's next after obtaining a certificate?

Typically, individuals who complete common certificates are interested in teaching right away. Sometimes, a teacher might complete a certificate course so that he or she will be eligible for teaching positions in a non-English speaking country. Others take common certificates so that they can work with ESL learners in their own community. The type of work a course participant is looking for will determine where he or she begins looking for employment. As a first step, job candidates should ask their certificate programme itself for assistance, especially if the programme happens to be located in the same country/region where the candidate wishes to find employment. Otherwise, we recommend consulting job postings on TESOL International Association's online career centre (http://careers.tesol.org/). Teaching positions that would be attractive to recipients of common certificates can be also be found at Dave's ESL Cafe (http://www.eslcafe.com/), which has special 'job boards' for ESL positions, positions in Korea and China, and international positions in general.

Endorsement certificates[1]

Whom are they for?

In the United States, teachers pursuing a degree in K-12 education may choose to include an ESL endorsement or add-on certification offered by their college or university. Alternatively, in-service teachers who live in cities with a college or university may be able to obtain an ESL endorsement certificate while actively teaching (either through evening, weekend, and/or summer courses). The advantage of an ESL endorsement or add-on certificate is that it qualifies a teacher to teach ESL in the United States, as well as internationally (recall that independent TESL/TEFL certificates typically aren't recognized by institutions in the United States) (TESOL International Association, 2014b). However, not everyone who pursues an ESL endorsement certificate does so because they want to be an ESL instructor, per se. For example, some mainstream educators in school districts with large numbers of international students are encouraged (or even required) to obtain an endorsement certif-icate to better prepare them for the challenges (and benefits!) of having so many non-native English speaking students in the classroom.

What is required to participate in an endorsement certificate?

The requirements for an endorsement certificate are similar to those for a common certificate (see above). However, given the fact that endorsement certificates are geared towards teaching K-12 ESL in the United States, admission into such a programme typically requires either the completion of an undergraduate degree or that a candidate be currently pursuing an undergraduate degree.

What to expect from an endorsement certificate?

ESL endorsements and add-on certificates typically involve 2–4 semesters of university-level study. Their curricula are determined by state departments of education, though some states' endorsements are interchangeable. As a random example of one such endorsement curriculum, the four courses included in Arkansas Tech University's ESL endorsement are listed below:

- second language acquisition
- teaching English as a second language
- ESL assessment
- teaching people of other cultures.

In addition to these courses, participants in Arkansas Tech University's endorsement programme are required to complete a praxis.

For another random example, we can look at Oakland University in Michigan, which offers a 20-credit hour ESL endorsement that is completed over four successive semesters. The following courses are required, some of which are offered online:

- linguistic structures
- language, culture, and society
- language pedagogy
- curriculum material design
- assessment and compliance
- language acquisition
- ESL practicum.

Clearly the range and mode of course offerings will vary from programme to programme. These two examples were selected randomly merely to illustrate the diversity of such endorsement certificates.

What does it take to be successful in an endorsement certificate course?

Endorsement certificate courses require strategies for success similar to those suggested (above) for a common certificate course. However, because endorsement certificate courses are often offered by colleges and universities, we recommend that participants approach them the same way they would other college-level courses. This means that a person enrolled in an endorsement certificate course can expect the same workload per course as they would any other course for college credit. When there is a noticeable difference between an endorsement certificate course and other university pedagogy courses, it will likely be the degree to which the endorsement certificate attempts to tie the concepts learned in the course to actual practice in a language classroom. For example, rather than reading and talking about a particular pedagogical concept, an endorsement certificate course will require participants to enact that concept by generating a lesson plan, micro-teaching, peer-teaching, etc.

In addition to the strategies listed above regarding common certificate courses, we recommend the following for achieving success in an endorsement certificate course:

- Make sure you read the syllabus clearly and understand the expectations of the course.

- Be sure you are aware of all assessment procedures and how your mastery of course objectives will be evaluated.

- Ask questions about how the particular endorsement certificate course you're enrolled in serves as credentialing in your state/region of intended employment.

- If a concept seems too abstract, ask your instructor to provide examples of how it might apply to daily classroom practice.

- As always, consider how the skills and strategies you're learning might need to be adapted for different learner populations and learning purposes.

- Have fun!

How can I find an endorsement certificate course?

Current undergraduate and graduate students interested in pursuing an ESL endorsement or add-on certificate are encouraged to consult their adviser or the department director of their college or university for further information. TESOL International Association's *The English Language Professional's Resource Guide* will also be helpful in locating colleges and university departments that offer this option (http://englishlanguageprofessionalsres ourceguide.com/). In-service K-12 educators in the United States who are seeking an ESL endorsement will find the above website helpful as well; we also recommend that they speak with their principal, superintendent, or immediate supervisor about ESL endorsement opportunities in their state.

What's next after obtaining an endorsement certificate course?

Typically an individual completes an endorsement certificate course in order to begin teaching ESL or to better prepare himself or herself to meet the needs of non-native English speaking students in mainstream classrooms. Students completing an endorsement certificate course at a college or university in the United States will likely seek employment within that state (given that their teaching licence will be specific to the state in which they attended college or university). However, ESL endorsements will certainly make job candidates seeking teaching positions in other countries more competitive than those without a similar certificate and candidates are encouraged to emphasize this endorsement during the job application process.

Degree programmes

Bachelor of Arts or Science (BA/BS) in TESOL

While master's degrees in TESOL have been and continue to be more prevalent than bachelor's degrees (http://graduate-school.phds.org/education-index/bachelors-in-tesol-degree-programmes), an increasing number of undergraduate programmes are also beginning to offer bachelor of arts (BA) and bachelor of science (BS) degrees that prepare students to teach English. The most common bachelor's degrees that prepare a candidate to teach English are BAs in TESOL, ESL, or applied linguistics, while BAs in linguistics, education, or English may offer helpful training and/or a TESOL endorsement or minor as well (see above).

Whom is it for?

Increasingly, an undergraduate bachelor's degree is necessary if an individual wishes to meet the most basic prerequisite for teaching the English language professionally, while a BA/BS specifically in TESOL is ideal for anyone who knows early on in their academic career that they would like to become a TESOL professional. However, readers are reminded that in the United States, a BA/BS in TESOL alone, in the absence of a state-recognized endorsement and/or teaching licence, will not qualify an instructor to teach at certain institutions.

What is required to participate in a BA/BS in TESOL?

Anyone who obtains general admission to a college or university should be eligible to study in an undergraduate TESOL programme. Readers are reminded that a BA/BS in TESOL, as with any bachelor's degree at a college or university, will require a number of general education courses that aren't directly related to TESOL.

What to expect from a BA/BS in TESOL

A bachelor's degree in TESOL (or a related degree) is likely to include some combination of the following courses, though probably not all of them (and of course, programmes may title their courses differently):

- Knowledge about language:
    - introduction to linguistics
    - phonetics/phonology
    - grammar for TESOL/pedagogical grammar
    - second language acquisition
    - sociolinguistics
    - intercultural communication/language and culture.
- Pedagogical knowledge:
    - teaching second languages
    - methods/approaches in TESOL
    - materials design
    - course/syllabus design

● assessment/testing

● practicum.

A bachelor's degree in TESOL (or an equivalent degree) should also include some sort of supervised teaching experience, which may involve practice teaching and/or classroom-based experience. The above may take the form of a practicum course, an apprenticeship with a mentor-teacher, tutoring, micro-teaching, etc. Prospective students interested in a BA/BS in TESOL are encouraged to consult university departments regarding course offerings and the potential for supervised teaching practice before making a selection.

What does it take to be successful in a BA/BS degree programme?

Success in a BA/BS degree programme will be largely determined by the time, energy, and interest you are able to commit to the *endeavour*, as is the case with any undergraduate or graduate degree. We recommend the following strategies for success in a BA/BS degree programme:

● Once you know that you would like to major in TESOL, speak to an adviser immediately about a plan of study to ensure that you are taking the correct courses and can graduate in a timely manner.

● Make sure you read all course syllabuses clearly and understand the expectations of the courses, including how you will be evaluated.

● It's not too early to join a professional association or attend a conference. A good place to start is to look up your state or regional chapter of TESOL.

● If a course presents concepts that seem too abstract, ask your instructor to provide examples of how they might apply to daily classroom practice.

● Carefully consider how the skills and strategies you're learning might need to be adapted for different learner populations and learning purposes.

● Pursue opportunities to practise teaching in and/or observe language classrooms.

● Explore opportunities to study abroad. If you live in an English speaking country, seek study experiences abroad in a non-English speaking country, and vice versa.

- Speak to career services in your department/college early on about the types of employment your BA/BS in TESOL will prepare you for.

- If you wish to teach in the United States, talk to your adviser right away about any additional credentialing you might need (e.g. a state teaching licence) for your intended teaching context.

- As you near graduation, ask an adviser or instructor to guide you in the completion of a teaching philosophy, as well as a résumé and/or CV.

How can I find a BA/BS degree in TESOL?

As we mentioned previously, BA/BS degrees in TESOL are not offered everywhere. *The English Language Professional's Resource Guide*, sponsored by TESOL International Association, is a good resource for prospective students interested in studying TESOL at the undergraduate level: http://englishlanguageprofessionalsresourceguide.com/.

What's next after obtaining a BA/BS in TESOL?

Because a BA/MA in TESOL does not necessarily qualify a person to teach K-12 ESL at institutions in the United States, most individuals who pursue this degree may have plans to teach internationally or to work with adult ESL learners. Those who are interested in working with adult ESL learners in the United States are encouraged to consult Crandall, Ingersoll and Lopez's (2010) *Adult ESL Teacher Credentialing and Certification Table* for the most current information regarding credentialing requirements per state. For graduates interested in teaching positions abroad, TESOL International Association's online career centre (http://careers.tesol.org/) and Dave's ESL Cafe's various job boards (http://www.eslcafe.com/) are good places to start (see Chapter 5 for a full list of TESOL job market and job placement resources).

MA or MEd in TESOL

The vast majority of TESOL degree programmes in the United States and Canada are offered at the master's level. Master of Arts (MA) or Master of Education (MEd) in TESOL has traditionally been designed to prepare graduates to teach English to adults at colleges and universities or private institutions domestically or abroad. (Prospective graduates who wish to teach English to children in the United States are typically recommended to pursue degrees from education departments so that they can receive a state teaching licence, enabling them to teach K-12 ESL students at public schools in the United States.) In addition to MA TESOL programmes, teachers may also gain valuable knowledge, skills, and experience from an MA in applied linguistics, an MEd in TESOL, or an MA in English with an emphasis in TESOL or with a TESOL endorsement. Still other universities offer MATs (master's in teaching) in TESOL or ESL (TESOL, 2014b).

Whom are they for?

MAs or MEds in TESOL are for individuals who are very serious about pursing TESOL as a career. MA TESOL graduates typically wish to work with adult learners, while MEds in TESOL are more likely to prepare students for both adult and child language teaching. MA/MEd TESOL graduates are very competitive in the international job market and are often hired to teach in Intensive English Programmes (IEPs) and community colleges in the United States and Canada.

What is required to participate in an MA or MEd in TESOL?

As with any master's degree, an MA/MEd in TESOL requires a prior undergraduate degree. Most MA/MEd TESOL programmes also prefer that a candidate has obtained a threshold of proficiency in a language other than English. Evidence of such attainment is typically offered through an assessment procedure or through proof of several semesters of language study at college level. Furthermore, prior teaching experience is likely to make one candidate more competitive than another if admission to an MA/MEd programme is limited.

Most MA or MEd TESOL programmes will require an application package that involves a statement of purpose (sometimes called a 'personal statement') and two to four letters of recommendation. The best letters of recommendation usually come from former or current college professors and/or former or current teacher supervisors (especially if they have observed a candidate teach and can comment on their abilities specifically). For those candidates who haven't yet worked in the TESOL profession, former or current college professors are usually best, followed by bosses or supervisors in whatever prior employment the candidate has worked. Mainly, programmes are looking for letters that demonstrate a candidate's ability to succeed in study at the master's level, so qualities like work ethic and responsibility – even from a referee who hasn't seen a candidate teach – are still of value. Candidates are encouraged to read each programme's application carefully for variations in the requirements for letters of recommendation and to provide references at least one month prior to the date at which letters of recommendation are due.

What to expect from a MA or MEd in TESOL?

We would like to remind prospective graduate students that the MA/MEd TESOL programme is not designed to provide language teachers with ready-made techniques that will guarantee success in any teaching context (nor are certificate courses, though owing to time constraints they do tend to be a bit more prescriptive). While such a strategy may have traditionally been taken in past approaches to teacher training, the nature of teacher training (especially at the master's level) has evolved to include much more context-dependent and reflective aspects of becoming a language teaching professional. Furthermore, in Nancy Bell's (2009) *A Student's Guide to the MA TESOL*, she reminds prospective graduate students that their MA TESOL will vary depending on the programme they attend: 'The agendas of specific professors, of the department, of the university, and of the wider society will all influence what is discussed in the classroom, how it is discussed, and what is excluded' (p. 16).

To give readers a better grasp of the type of MA/MEd TESOL programmes available, we will very briefly describe three well-known programmes in the United States that offer master's-level degrees in TESOL or TESOL-related fields: these include Michigan State University, Northern Arizona State University, and University of Illinois at Urbana-Champaign. Their inclusion in this chapter is in no way intended to be an official endorsement of any of these programmes. Rather, we believe that a brief description of each gives readers a better understanding of the types of MA TESOL programmes available:

● Michigan State University (MSU) offers an MA TESOL (Teaching English to Speakers of Other Languages) that requires 36 credit hours and the completion of either a thesis or a certifying exam to graduate. The MA TESOL is offered through the Department of Linguistics and Germanic, Slavic, Asian, and African Languages (LGSAAL). Courses are taught by eight different faculty members. MSU is able to offer some accepted MA TESOL students teaching assistantships in their English Language Center, in addition to a handful of research assistantships through the LGSAAL department. MSU does not offer a PhD in TESOL, but it does offer a PhD in linguistics through the LGSAAL department (Michigan State University, 2014). For more

information, visit MSU's MA TESOL website directly: http://linglang.
msu.edu/tesol/.

- Northern Arizona University (NAU) offers an MA TESL (Teaching of
  English as a Second Language) with three separate tracks: the first in
  applied linguistics, the second in language teaching, and the third in
  language teaching for practising teachers (which includes an Arizona
  ESL endorsement). The MA TESL is offered through NAU's English
  department. There are 11 core TESL and applied linguistics faculty
  members, plus several affiliated professors in related departments.
  Highly qualified MA TESL students are chosen for teaching
  assistantships in several different programmes, including the English
  composition programme or NAU's Program in Intensive English.
  Prospective students who are interested in pursuing a PhD in applied
  linguistics or TESOL are encouraged to consider the applied linguistics
  track. NAU also offers a PhD in applied linguistics (Arizona Board of
  Regents, 2014). For further information and to see how the above
  three tracks differ, visit their website directly (http://nau.edu/CAL/
  English/Degrees-Programs/Graduate/MA-TESL/).

- University of Illinois at Urbana-Champaign's Department of Linguistics
  offers an MA TESL (Teaching of English as a Second Language).
  In addition to required coursework, graduation is contingent
  upon completing a master's thesis or passing a comprehensive
  examination. Teaching assistantships are available in the programme's
  Intensive English Institute and ESL courses for matriculated
  undergraduate and graduate students, in addition to less readily
  available laboratory and library assistantships. There are 16 ESL and
  language faculty members listed for this programme, in addition to
  the large number of faculty members specializing in linguistics and
  those from affiliated departments (Department of Linguistics, 2014).
  For more information about the MA TESL at University of Illinois at
  Urbana-Champaign, visit their website directly (http://www.linguistics.
  illinois.edu/students/grad/matesl/).

Regardless of the programme an individual attends, an important component
of any master's-level programme designed to prepare candidates for profes-
sions in TESOL is the inclusion of supervised teaching and actual classroom
experience. For this reason, prospective students are encouraged to ask
colleges and universities about opportunities such as practicum, practice
teaching, classroom observation, micro-teaching, etc. In addition to practical
experience, master's-level TESOL programmes should include some combination of the following courses, though it's unlikely that any department will

offer all of them (and of course, programmes are likely to title their courses differently):

- Knowledge about language:
  - introduction to linguistics
  - pedagogical grammar
  - second language acquisition
  - sociolinguistics
  - intercultural communication
  - psycholinguistics/language learning.
- Pedagogical knowledge:
  - teaching second languages
  - methods/approaches in TESOL
  - materials writing and teaching resources
  - syllabus design and curriculum development
  - assessment/testing
  - practicum.
- Potential electives in TESOL/applied linguistics:
  - discourse analysis
  - corpus linguistics
  - phonology and phonetics
  - morphology
  - syntax
  - semantics
  - pragmatics
  - L2/ESL/EFL writing
  - research methods in TESOL
  - computer-assisted language learning (CALL)/language and technology
  - psycholinguistics

- bilingualism/multilingualism

- teaching English to younger learners (TEYL)

- L2 reading/literacy

- genre

- English for specific purposes

- English as an international language

- intercultural rhetoric

- history of English language/historical linguistics.

Finally, depending on the degree programme and/or the candidate, some master's programmes in TESOL (or related fields) are able to offer funding to prospective students in the form of partial-to-full tuition waivers, out-of-state fee waivers, scholarships, and/or monthly stipends. Often, tuition can be waived when departments are able to offer teaching, research, or lab assistantships to their graduate students. In such cases, graduates may have the opportunity to work with TESOL/applied linguistics faculty on their current research projects, or to teach and/or tutor undergraduate ESL or IEP students. Qualified multilingual candidates may also be invited to teach foreign language courses in exchange for a tuition waiver. Applicants are encouraged to contact colleges and universities directly in order to determine the specific types of funding available. Prospective students are also encouraged to investigate the partnerships that university departments have with other language institutions, either within the nearby community or abroad, as such partnerships offer invaluable opportunities for engagement with the larger TESOL professional community, as well as for potential teaching experience. One such partnership that may help candidates finance their education is the Peace Corps programme's Master's International, which pairs graduate students at select institutions in the US with volunteer opportunities abroad. For more information and to see a list of Master's International partner schools, visit the Master's International website directly (http://www.peacecorps.gov/ volunteer/graduate/mastersint/).

What does it take to be successful in an MA or MEd TESOL programme?

One difference between an MA or MEd TESOL programme and a BA/BS in TESOL is that while the latter involves a great many general education classes in a variety of different subjects, the former focuses entirely on

TESOL. Another difference lies in the greater amount of reading and writing required of graduate students and the higher calibre of scholarship expected as a whole. MA or MEd TESOL students should expect to encounter a considerable amount of scholarly writing (e.g. academic journal articles), to engage with theory on a level that they probably would not in a certificate course or at the BA/BS level, and to produce a significant amount of scholarly writing themselves. Some MA/MEd TESOL programmes require the completion of a master's thesis before graduation, while others may ask students to develop a teaching portfolio during their time in the programme. Either way, prospective MA/MEd TESOL students should be aware of the level of academic work that will be required of them.

The following strategies are recommended for a successful experience in an MA or MEd TESOL programme:

- Speak to your adviser early on about a plan of study to ensure that you are taking the correct courses and can graduate in a timely manner.

- Make sure you read all course syllabuses clearly and understand the expectations of the course, including how you will be evaluated.

- Make sure you understand what is expected of a graduate beyond completing required courses (e.g. hours spent observing in a classroom, hours spent teaching in a classroom with or without supervision, completion of a master's thesis, the creation of a teaching portfolio, composing a teaching philosophy, etc.).

- Ask about study abroad opportunities, either for teaching and/or learning in another part of the world. For example, some programmes have sister universities in other countries that offer equivalent credit for required courses.

- Seek out teaching opportunities. If your programme doesn't offer immediate options for teaching, look beyond the college or university for volunteer teaching in community centres or for non-profits. The more opportunities you have to apply what you're learning, the more successful you will be.

- The genre of texts you will be asked to produce and engage with at this level of study may be unfamiliar to you. This is to be expected. Remember that it may take a while for you to become accustomed to the conventions of reporting research results, for example, or to the rhetorical devices used to organize literature reviews, as another example.

- Go to local, regional, or national conferences as much as possible. At this stage in your career, it's perfectly acceptable to attend a conference, even if you're not presenting. Conferences are excellent opportunities to learn more about the field and to network with other TESOL professionals (see a more thorough discussion of conferences later in this chapter).

- Join at least one professional organization. While your local or regional TESOL organization is a good place to start, the American Association of Applied Linguistics and TESOL International Association both have active graduate student committees.

- Speak to your adviser and/or career services about a plan for obtaining employment after graduation. Begin compiling a teaching portfolio that contains (at a minimum) a curriculum vitae/résumé, sample lesson plans you generated during your time in the master's programme, a teaching philosophy, any teaching evaluations or observation notes you may have received, and an audio or video (video is preferred) recording of your teaching.

- Make friends! Your peers in the master's programme will probably be your professional colleagues for many years to come. You will lean on them for both emotional and professional support. Conferences and professional associations are another great way to begin networking outside your programme.

- Keep up with all readings and assignments. If you find yourself struggling, talk to your instructor and/or adviser immediately.

- Be a critical consumer of everything that you hear and read in your courses. Remember that an important component of becoming a TESOL professional is the ability to reflect critically on the principles and underlying assumptions handed down to you and whether they align with your own individual values and the (future) social, political, and pedagogical impact of your actions as a language teacher (Leung, 2009).

For a more thorough discussion of how to be successful as a student of TESOL at the master's level, as well as what to expect, we highly recommend Nancy Bell's (2009) book-length treatment on the topic, *A Student's Guide to the MA TESOL*.

How can I find an MA or MEd in TESOL?

The English Language Professional's Resource Guide is one of the best sources we know of prospective students interested in studying TESOL at the graduate level (http://englishlanguageprofessionalsresourceguide.com/). Local and regional professional organizations affiliated with the TESOL profession may also serve as resources for locating MA or MEd TESOL programmes within relative proximity. Remember that an MA or MEd in TESOL may be offered by a different department than one might expect. For example, linguistics or applied linguistics departments, English departments, and education departments are all good places to look for master's degrees equivalent to the MA/MEd TESOL.

What's next after obtaining an MA or MEd in TESOL?

Many graduates of MA/MEd TESOL programmes go on to work as instructors in IEP programmes, community colleges, adult education programmes, or at colleges, universities, and/or private language institutions in countries where English is not the predominant language. We strongly recommend that MA/MEd TESOL students think about *what* (EAP, English for aviation, beginning English, etc.), *where* (a Midwestern IEP, a university in China, etc.) and *whom* (adult immigrants, Mexican high school students, international teaching assistants, etc.) they would like to teach long before graduation. Once this has been determined, they should speak to an adviser about how best to go about preparing for and obtaining relevant employment. One benefit of being in a graduate programme is that many job opportunities are shared on the department email listserv. TESOL International Association's online career centre (http://careers.tesol.org/) usually hosts a variety of teaching positions both domestically and abroad.

Other graduates from MA/MEd programmes may be interested in immediately pursuing further study in a PhD programme in TESOL (see below). If this is the case, prospective PhD students are encouraged to discuss this option with their adviser at least one year prior to graduation from the master's-level programme. This is because PhD applications are typically due six to nine months before a programme begins and may require significant time to prepare. Still others who are interested in a PhD may wish to teach for a few years to gain more practical teaching experience before pursuing a PhD. We recommend speaking to an adviser to determine which option is the best for a particular candidate.

PhD in TESOL

Whom are they for?

Finally, PhD programmes in TESOL are relatively rare but becoming less so. They are more frequently offered as PhDs in Applied Linguistics rather than in TESOL or ESL/EFL specifically. Doctoral graduate study is recommended for academics who wish to conduct and publish research in a particular area of TESOL as a career and who may like to train other TESOL undergraduate and graduate professionals in the future. A PhD may also be useful to TESOL professionals who are interested in language policy planning or who wish to work in the field as assessment specialists, materials designers, or at more administrative levels.

What is required to participate in a PhD in TESOL?

As with any university-level study at the doctoral level, a candidate needs to have already completed an undergraduate degree and master's degree previously. Most PhD programmes require that applicants have received an MA or MEd in TESOL or a related field (e.g. applied linguistics, education, English, etc.). As with the MA/MEd in TESOL, most PhD programmes also prefer that applicants demonstrate proficiency in a language other than English and have some prior teaching experience. The application package for a PhD programme is typically due six to nine months before a candidate expects to begin actual study. Beyond what is usually required for master's-level admission to a TESOL programme (see above), most PhD programmes require a writing sample that demonstrates a candidate's ability to conduct research and compose scholarly texts at a level appropriate to PhD-level study. Ultimately, we believe that the best source for helping a candidate apply to a PhD programme (including choosing a writing sample) is a candidate's current or former instructors and/or advisers from their previous master's programme. These individuals can give candidates the best advice about the nature of the programme they're applying to, the quality of their writing sample, and the best direction to take with the candidate's statement of purpose.

What to expect from a PhD in TESOL?

In addition to the courses listed above for master's-level study in TEOSL, PhD degrees are likely to offer advanced courses in research methodology (qualitative, quantitative, mixed methods), second language teaching education/development, preparation for teaching undergraduate students, and other advanced topics in applied linguistics/TESOL. PhD programmes also offer advanced seminars specific to the research specialization of their faculty. For this reason, prospective students are encouraged to consider the research interests of a department's faculty when making application or acceptance decisions. Another factor to consider is the interdisciplinary nature of the PhD programme. PhD programmes in TESOL tend to fall along a continuum that constitutes purely TESOL-focused coursework and research on one end, with more interdisciplinary work on the other end.

As we did for master's-level TESOL study (above), we have included three PhD TESOL programmes in the United States that we believe will give readers a glimpse of how different programmes situate themselves in the field and how faculty tend to focus on diverse research areas. Again, these do not indicate an endorsement of these programmes per se, though it is the case that all three are ranked very highly.

- University of Hawai'i offers a PhD in Second Language Studies (SLS). In addition to SLS faculty, PhD courses may be taught by professors from the departments of Anthropology, East Asian Languages and Literatures, and Linguistics. Course content focuses on second language analysis, learning, use, and pedagogy. Courses in research methods are required as well. In addition to course and language requirements, PhD students must pass a comprehensive exam (including oral and written components) and propose and defend a dissertation. All admitted PhD students are automatically considered for assistantships within the department (Department of SLS, 2014). For more information regarding the PhD in SLS at University of Hawai'i, consult their website directly (http://www.hawaii.edu/sls/sls/programmes/doctorate/).

- The University of Arizona's PhD in Second Language Acquisition and Teaching (SLAT) is an interdisciplinary programme with 74 faculty members across 17 departments. Candidates can specialize in language analysis, use, processes and learning, or pedagogical theory and programme administration (see http://slat.arizona.edu/slat-dissertations for a list of past dissertations). Most SLAT doctoral students receive graduate teaching assistantships, either in the Center for English as a Second Language or across collaborating departments. Graduation is contingent upon required coursework, a language requirement, satisfactory completion of a qualifying exercise and a written and oral comprehensive exam, and dissertation defence (Arizona Board of Regents, 2013). For further details regarding this PhD programme, consult their website directly (http://slat.arizona.edu/home).

- Georgia State University's (GSU) Department of Applied Linguistics and ESL (ALESL) offers a PhD in applied linguistics. Courses are taught by ten ALESL faculty members, and all admitted PhD students are guaranteed teaching or research assistantships. Teaching assistant positions are typically in the Intensive English Program or

the (undergraduate and graduate) ESL programme, though some
PhD students will teach in the undergraduate ALESL programme
itself. Successful completion of the doctoral programme requires
satisfactory completion of a qualifying exam, a comprehensive exam,
and dissertation proposal and defence, in addition to course and
language requirements (Georgia State University, 2013). For further
information regarding the PhD in applied linguistics from GSU, we
recommend reviewing their website (http://www2.gsu.edu/~wwwesl/
phd_applied_linguistics.html).

Regardless of the programme an individual chooses, TESOL or applied
linguistics study at the doctoral level will include the proposal, completion,
and defence of a dissertation. The required structure, style, complexity, data
collection process, and timeline for completion of a dissertation will vary from
university to university, and from country to country, so rather than attempt
a generic description of typical dissertation requirements, we recommend
consulting individual programmes directly. To grasp the sheer range of research
agendas that a PhD dissertation may involve, we recommend perusing recent
TESOL PhD dissertations (ProQuest's Linguistics and Language Behavior
Abstracts (LLBA) is a good place to start).

Because of the full-time commitment required by PhD TESOL programmes,
many departments offer partial-to-full funding for their students. These
funding opportunities are similar to those described in our discussion of
master's-level funding (see p. 54). Prospective PhD students are encouraged
to inquire about such opportunities directly from the departments in question,
as specific opportunities and application processes will vary. Teaching assistantships that allow doctoral students to teach undergraduate or graduate
TESOL/Applied Linguistics courses are highly recommended but competitive.

How can I find a PhD in TESOL?

As for finding PhD programmes in TESOL, we believe that the best place to
start is TESOL International Association's *English Language Professional's
Resource Guide* (http://englishlanguageprofessionalsresourceguide.com/).
Also, recall that a PhD in TESOL may go by different names and be offered
by a different department depending on the university. Finally, although
the three programme examples above are all in the United States, there
are a number of PhD programmes in TESOL in other countries. The *English
Language Professional's Resource Guide* is a good way to begin exploring
such options.

What's next after obtaining a PhD in TESOL?

Most PhD students hope to gain employment as a faculty member at a college or university after graduation, though others may wish to become assessment specialists, materials developers, administrators, etc. Candidates who already know the type of work they prefer are encouraged to take this into account when choosing a programme.

Standards

What are TESOL standards?

Educational standards are usually public statements that support professional accountability by defining levels of competence in education, for both learners and instructors. The field of TESOL needs standards or benchmarks in order to assess, for instance, the qualification of language teachers, the expectation of learners, and the various kinds of language programmes. For example, it is well argued in the literature that just because someone is a native speaker of English it does not automatically qualify the person to teach English. Rather, a person has to be formally certified by a professional body and belong to a specific profession by virtue of having completed a required course of studies and/or practice. An individual's competence can also be measured against an established set of standards. Such standards are often developed by state and national institutions, as well as by professional associations. The various standards that TESOL International Association has developed in the past are discussed below.

TESOL International Association standards

As a professional association, TESOL International Association has worked hard to develop a number of standards over the years, some of which have been well received in the field. While we briefly summarize these below, we recommend consulting the TESOL International Association's website for revisions and details (http://www.tesol.org/advance-the-field/standards).

PreK-12 English language proficiency standards

Published in 2006, these standards focus on ensuring the success and achievement of all school-aged children in the United States, regardless of their native language. The PreK-12 English Language Proficiency Standards were designed to supplement existing discipline-specific standards, and take as their starting point the need for 'effective and equitable education for ESOL students' (TESOL International Association, 2014c). For an overview of the standards framework see http://www.tesol.org/docs/books/bk_prek-12elpstandards_framework_318.pdf?sfvrsn=2/.

Technology standards

Whereas the above standards focus on the proficiency outcomes of learners, TESOL's Technology Standards emphasize how technology is used by English language learners, instructors, and administrators both in and out of the classroom. They are similar to standards already developed by the National Educational Technology Standards (NETS) Project in the International Society for Technology in Education (ISTE), but focus more strongly on English language pedagogy. The Technology Standards framework is divided into two sections devoted to language learners and language teachers.

TESOL/NCATE standards for P-12 teacher education programme

These performance-based standards, also known as the *TESOL Professional Teaching Standards*, 'address the professional expertise needed by ESL educators to work with language minority students' (TESOL International Association, 2014e). They can also be used to assess institutions that train teacher educators.

Standards for adult education

These include separate sets of standards for teachers of ESL/EFL adults, adult ESL language and literacy instruction, and general standards for adult ESL. See http://www.tesol.org/advance-the-field/standards/standards-for-adult-education for a more thorough discussion of each with links for further reading.

Guidelines for developing EFL professional teaching standards

These act as guides for anyone developing standards in an EFL context. Unlike many of the standards described above, these are freely accessible online (http://www.tesol.org/docs/default-source/standards/tesol-guidelines-for-developing-efl-professional-teaching-standards.pdf?sfvrsn=4).

EFL instructors, administrators, policymakers, governmental institutions, etc., are invited by TESOL International Association to download and adapt these guidelines to suit their needs and particular EFL context.

A proposed framework of standards for teachers of English in ESL/EFL settings

For readers who are new to the concept of professional and educational standards and wish to better understand how standards might apply to their own current or future teaching context, we wish to propose an integrative framework of standards for TESOL professionals who work in either ESL or EFL settings around the world. In offering these standards, we do not intend to replace the professional standards developed by local, state, or national institutions, nor do we intend to imply that these standards surpass those offered by professional organizations, such as TESOL International Association (see above). Rather, we hope that this integrative framework serves as a starting point for newcomers to the field who wish to better understand the role that standards may play in the TESOL profession. Readers are welcome to make copies of this framework and/or adapt it for their own purposes.

Our proposed framework is organized around three domains (see Figure 2.1): *language and culture*, *instruction and assessment*, and the core, which is *professionalism*. The components of each are described below.

Domain I: Language and culture:

1 Linguistics knowledge

2 English proficiency

3 Language processes and strategies

4 Cultural and intercultural communication skills.

Domain II: Instruction and assessment:

5 Pedagogical knowledge and teaching methodology

6 Curriculum development and syllabus design

7 Knowledge and skills in technology

8 Testing and assessment.

Domain III: Professionalism:

9 Professional development and research

10 TESOL research.

FIGURE 2.1 *Domains of proposed standards framework*

These domains are further divided into ten standards, each of which is supported by performance indicators. These indicators help identify evidence of candidate performance. They can be met at three proficiency levels:

- *Approaches standard*: The documentation provided and the evidence submitted clearly establish that the candidate has knowledge about the subject content, but does not apply it adequately to the classroom.

- *Meets standard*: The documentation provided and the evidence submitted clearly establish that the teacher candidates demonstrate the dispositions, knowledge, and skills to teach English learners effectively, and that candidates apply that knowledge in the classroom and other professional teaching situations.

- *Exceeds standard*: The documentation provided and the evidence submitted clearly establish that the teacher candidates consistently demonstrate the dispositions, knowledge, and skills associated with candidates who demonstrate positive effects on student learning and go on to successful teaching.

Below, we offer in further detail the proposed framework of standards for English teachers around the world. Readers are encouraged to consider the ways in which these standards may be implemented, adopted, and adapted across a variety of teaching contexts. It is important to point out that standards are only useful and meaningful when local situations are considered.

1. Linguistic knowledge

Goal: Teachers demonstrate knowledge of the nature of human language and the phonological, morphological, lexical/semantic, and syntactic systems of English and are able to describe the similarities and differences between English and the native language in these areas.

> Objective 1: Teachers understand the nature of human language and how it is similar to and different from other communication systems humans and animals use.

> Objective 2: Teachers demonstrate knowledge of how speech sounds are produced and perceived. They demonstrate knowledge of the sound system of both English and their native language/or another language. They understand the basic concepts and tools used in the analysis and comparison of speech sounds and how sounds are combined to form large linguistic units of speech within and across languages. They understand both segmental and suprasegmental features of the two languages.

> Objective 3: Teachers understand the basic concepts and tools for morphological analysis. They are familiar with the classification of morphemes and word formation rules in English and their native language or another language. They are also familiar with the unique features each language has in the lexicalization of meaning.

> Objective 4: Teachers understand the basic concepts and tools for syntactic analysis. They are familiar with the syntactical structures of both English and their native language or another language. They demonstrate knowledge of pedagogical English grammar.

2. English proficiency

Goal: Teachers demonstrate adequate oral and written proficiency in social and academic English.

> Objective 1: Teachers will be able to communicate in English in both oral and written formats at the level required for a four-year college degree in English language and literature or the equivalent.

Objective 2: Teachers are able to communicate with native speakers of English with adequate fluency, idiomaticity, and appropriateness on topics related to daily life, current social events, and professional topics.

Objective 3: Teachers will be able to demonstrate their overall communicative competence (e.g. linguistic, discourse, pragmatic, sociocultural, and strategic) in natural or simulated communication encounters.

Objective 4: Teachers will be able to write clearly at both sentence and discourse levels, and be able to write academic papers for conference presentations and publications for both national and international journals.

3. Language-learning processes and strategies

Goal: Teachers understand the nature of human language and the psycho-linguistic and sociolinguistic processes and factors involved in native and non-native language acquisition and use.

Objective 1: Teachers demonstrate knowledge of child language development. They understand the biological foundations of human language and language acquisition, developmental stages involved in language acquisition, and theories of child language acquisition.

Objective 2: Teachers understand the similarities and differences between native and non-native language acquisition. They understand how linguistic and non-linguistic factors may affect the rate and ultimate attainment of second language acquisition. They demonstrate knowledge of theories of second language acquisition.

Objective 3: Teachers are able to identify and understand learner strategies in second and foreign language learning and are able to accommodate the diverse needs of learners in teaching.

Objective 4: Teachers are able to identify and understand different learning styles, and how the differences in learning styles can be accounted for in teaching.

4. Cultural and intercultural communication skills

Goal: Teachers understand the nature of language and culture and communicative styles and skills in various intercultural communication contexts.

Objective 1: Teachers understand how language use is influenced by social and cultural contexts. They demonstrate adequate knowledge and skills in analysing second language use in social and cultural contexts and understand the unique features involved in cross-cultural communication.

Objective 2: Teachers demonstrate their understanding in selecting, developing, and critiquing teaching materials.

Objective 3: Teachers demonstrate their cultural awareness in teaching culturally sensitive materials and topics that require cultural explanations.

Objective 4: Teachers demonstrate familiarity with different communication styles reflected in authentic teaching materials used both inside and outside regular classrooms.

5. Pedagogical knowledge and teaching methodology

Goal: Teachers are familiar with various methods for and approaches to teaching English as a foreign language. They are also familiar with basic principals in language teaching and learning.

Objective 1: Teachers demonstrate knowledge of various TESOL methods and approaches, including their theoretical foundations, pedagogical principles, and classroom procedures and activities. They understand the strengths and weaknesses of these approaches and their limitations in language classrooms in their own countries.

Objective 2: Teachers demonstrate knowledge of the processes of teaching English as a foreign language in their own contexts.

Objective 3: Teachers understand the basic concepts related to student needs analysis, lesson planning, classroom management, classroom interaction, and classroom participation.

Objective 4: Teachers are familiar with and understand the rationale of the English curriculum or syllabus and textbooks they have adopted.

6. Curriculum development and syllabus design

Goal: Teachers demonstrate adequate skills in designing and implementing effective materials and learning tasks and activities in the classroom.

Objective 1: Teachers are able to see the broad picture of their teaching goals and objectives beyond single lessons.

Objective 2: Teachers have clear and specific goals and objectives for each lesson they design and teach.

Objective 3: Teachers are able to choose and design instructional materials that are consistent with the goals and objectives of the lesson and appropriate to the need and level of the students.

Objective 4: Teachers are able to design and implement learning tasks and activities that can help best to achieve the goals and objectives of the lesson.

7. Knowledge and skills in technology

Goal: Teachers demonstrate their familiarity with, and application of, technology in their teaching.

Objective 1: Teachers are able to search for information and pedagogical resources online.

Objective 2: Teachers are able to apply available instructional technology for enhancing their instruction.

Objective 3: Teachers are able to engage teaching tasks and activities with students outside classrooms via email, chat room, blog, or other modes of computer-mediated communication and technology-enhanced devices.

Objective 4: Teachers are able to identify and utilize available computer-assisted language-learning materials, and evaluate the effects of technology applications.

8. Testing and assessment

Goal: Teachers demonstrate adequate skills in designing various kinds of quizzes, tests, and examinations.

Objective 1: Teachers demonstrate their understanding of the validity and reliability of tests.

Objective 2: Teachers understand the relationship between testing and teaching, and are able to design classroom tests which reflect students' achievement of the content covered in class.

Objective 3: Teachers are familiar with alternative assessment procedures, such as portfolio assessment and self-assessment, and are able to use them as they see fit.

Objective 4: Teachers are familiar with the grading procedures for both holistic and diagnostic purposes, and are able to incorporate testing and assessment as part of their daily teaching and evaluation.

9. Professional development

Goal: Teachers stay current on research, trends, policies, and legal mandates affecting TEFL programmes.

Objective 1: Teachers access and use current information from a variety of sources to plan and evaluate instruction and programmes.

Objective 2: Teachers know how to gather and analyse data to improve teaching and learning.

Objective 3: Teachers reflect on their practice to establish goals for professional development.

Objective 4: Teachers continue their professional growth through coursework and participation in professional organizations, training opportunities and conferences at the local, provincial, regional, national, or international level.

10. TESOL research

Goal: Teachers demonstrate their knowledge of both qualitative and quantitative research methods and how they can use these methods to reflect their teaching and improve their teaching.

Objective 1: Teachers understand the major differences between qualitative and quantitative research methods and how each can be used to enhance classroom teaching and learning.

Objective 2: Teachers understand the unique characteristics of classroom research, teacher research, or action research.

Objective 3: Teachers are able to conduct action research in their language classrooms.

Objective 4: Teachers are able to apply the results of their action research into the improvement of understanding learners and their learning difficulties, and the improvement of their own teaching.

Professional development

What is professional development?

Professional development in TESOL is best thought of as ongoing education and improvement that continues beyond the formal training period of L2 teacher education (SLTE). For example, while it's likely that MA TESOL students or students enrolled in common certificate programmes will be engaged in activities designed to facilitate their development as teachers, the need for ongoing professional development for such students does not end when their final course does. This is the case for several reasons.

First, the knowledge base of SLTE is constantly changing (Freeman and Johnson, 1998; Richards and Farrell, 2005; Burns and Richards, 2009). This is evidenced by a recent expansion in the scope of SLTE (Freeman, in Burns and Richards, 2009) from a previously exclusive focus on disciplinary knowledge (e.g. second language acquisition) and the formal properties of language (e.g. phonetics) to include teachers' pedagogical content knowledge[2] (Shulman, 1987) and attention to the actual activity of L2 teaching. Second, ongoing professional development is important because the needs of TESOL practitioners will inevitably change over time, as will the nature of the teaching contexts in which they practise (Richards and Farrell, 2005). Finally, because more recent theories of learning suggest that teacher learning emerges through interaction with a community of practice (Johnson, 2009), teacher learning is no longer seen as the translation of static knowledge into practice but as the dialogic process of 'constructing new knowledge and theory through participating in specific social contexts and engaging in particular types of activities and processes' (Burns and Richards, 2009, p. 4). This more thorough acknowledgement of the role that context plays in teaching and learning has resulted in more attention to contextualized professional development practices that arise through participation in specific settings. Such practices, many of which are described below, are by their very nature ongoing, especially as in-service teachers engage in self-directed and collaborative activities within their communities.

What are the purposes of professional development?

In the same way that professionalism itself is both *independent* and *sponsored* (Leung, 2009, see above), professional development can be considered from both an *individual* and an *institutional* perspective (Richards and Farrell, 2005). The former pertains to a teacher's personal goals (e.g. to better understand learners, to increase subject matter knowledge) while the latter typically focuses on potential benefits to the institution as a whole (e.g. increase student learning, promote collegiality). Ideally, the objectives and activities involved with these two perspectives of professional development will overlap significantly.

In the remainder of this chapter, we propose a variety of activities and practices relevant to nearly any TESOL practitioner, including both TESOL in-service teachers and teachers-in-training. We organize our discussion of these activities around eight key needs (expanded from a list of objectives for professional development originally proposed by Wong, 2011) that language educators are likely to have throughout their career. While these are primarily framed from the perspective of an individual, it is clear to see that many of the goals would overlap with institutional objectives as well. Furthermore, the proposed activities were compiled under the assumption that professional development subsumes both second language teacher education and ongoing second language teacher development (Richards and Farrell, 2005). However, because many of the activities reviewed comprise a reflective approach to professional development, we feel it is necessary to take a moment to comment on the role of reflection in second-language teacher professional development.

What is reflective teaching? Critical reflection?

Reflection is a term that has been used widely in teacher education since the 1990s. Reflection in teaching has been defined as occurring when teachers learn to 'subject their own beliefs of teaching and learning to a critical analysis, and thus, take more responsibility for their actions in the classroom' (Farrell, 2001, p. 23). Reflection allows instructors to move from being 'guided largely by impulse, intuition, or routine, to a level where their actions are guided by reflection and critical thinking' (Richards, 1990a, p. 5). Thus, the term *critical reflection* implies the conscious consideration of a previous experience 'as a basis for evaluation and decision-making, and as a source for planning and action' (Richards, 1990a, p. 5). *Reflective teaching*, then, is more than simply thinking about how a particular lesson might have been more successful. Rather, the term *reflective* with regard to teaching suggests a 'way of being' in the classroom (Goodman, 1991, p. 60). For example, it has been suggested that reflective teachers are better able to self-assess their actions, make in-the-moment decisions, and respond to evolving learner needs better than teachers who are less reflective (Mann, 2005).

Readers will notice that many of the professional development activities suggested below are designed to encourage critical reflection, especially to the degree that they foster self-awareness and prioritize self-development as an ongoing process that acknowledges one's local teaching context. At the same time, other activities, such as those engaged in for the purposes of enhancing one's career, may take an approach that enacts professional development in a more public venue (e.g. presenting at an academic conference). We suggest thinking of professional development as a continuum of highly reflective activities with personal goals on one end and more public, career-oriented action. However, as with *individual* and *institutional* professional development (Richards and Farrell, 2005), it is likely that objectives on both ends of this spectrum will overlap.

Finally, while the six questions posed below (adapted from Wong, 2011) provide a useful framework for organizing professional activities, readers should keep in mind that many professional development activities serve multiple purposes at once. For example, a teacher may participate in action research in order to raise awareness of strengths and weaknesses, solve a particular problem, and find fulfilment in his or her work simultaneously. Still, we have chosen to group activities into what we consider to be their most salient, but by no means exclusive, purpose.

How can I become more aware of my own strengths and weaknesses?

Participate in peer observation

Peer observation refers to non-hierarchical colleagues observing one another teaching a lesson or portion of a lesson. The objects of peer observation are various and may include an instructor's questioning techniques, the level of student engagement, or elements of the teaching context, such as classroom interaction (Richards and Farrell, 2005). While this professional development activity is sometimes used for assessment purposes, we believe that such a practice may lead to discord (for example, when peers provide negative feedback) or be rendered meaningless (for example, when peers only provide flattering comments to avoid negatively affecting the careers of their colleagues) (Cosh, 1998). Furthermore, because many practitioners are likely to be resistant to the comments they receive (and because so few agree on what constitutes good teaching in the first place) we suggest that the true value of peer observation lies in the self-development and increased awareness of the non-evaluative observer as he or she is encouraged to reflect upon his or her own teaching in action (Cosh, 1998; Calderhead and Gates, 2004). Peer observation can also be a valuable professional development activity in situations where resources are limited, as this professional development practice requires little in the way of resources (Cosh, 1998).

Engage in self-observation

We believe that self-observation can also play an important role in second language teacher professional development. *Self-observation*, or *self-monitoring*, involves documenting one's own teaching, evaluating it later, and making subsequent changes in the future. The benefits of self-observation include the development of teacher confidence, the identification of previously unacknowledged problems, and the discovery of potential improvements (Richards and Farrell, 2005).

Options for self-observation include completing lesson reports, making audio-recordings of oneself teaching, or video-recording a lesson (Richards and Farrell, 2005). Lesson reports may take many forms. For example, a lesson report may comprise a narrative account of what worked well and what didn't work well in a lesson, or it may involve the completion of a checklist or questionnaire following a lesson. Of course, any audio- or video-recording in the classroom will require the consent of students in the classroom. Instructors are encouraged to speak with their supervisor about the best way to obtain consent for audio- or video-recording while maintaining sensitivity to students' privacy.

Keep a teaching journal

A teaching journal is a written account of an instructor's reflections and observations about teaching. We believe it is important that teaching journals foster ongoing, active reflection, which means that they should constitute a relatively regular activity (if not daily, then at least weekly entries). While some practitioners may wish to keep a traditional paper-and-pen journal, others may find digital journaling more convenient. Beyond the mode of journaling, a teaching journal may be intrapersonal or dialogic (Burton and Carroll, 2001; Gebhard and Oprandy, 1999). In the former, the audience is primarily private: the sole audience is the writer himself or herself. In the latter, the journal is more collaborative: its audience may be another teacher, a teacher educator, or a supervisor.

Teaching journals have been linked to the development of reflective teaching (Grosse, 1991; Brock, Yu and Wong, 1992). They also provide a venue for both new and seasoned teachers to express their doubt or frustration with daily teaching experiences (Bailey, 1990) and foster teachers' abilities to solve their own problems (Grosse, 1991). In this regard, teaching journals offer a space for instructors to begin thinking about classroom research (see below).

How can I learn from colleagues?

Team teach

As the name implies, *team teaching* refers to two or more instructors undertaking to teach the same course(s) simultaneously. It is occasionally referred to as *pair teaching* or *co-teaching*, as well. However, team teaching does not imply that one instructor plans her portion of the lesson independently and then teaches it while another grades homework, and vice versa. Rather, team teaching is intended to involve multiple instructors sharing responsibility for all aspects of a course (Richards and Farrell, 2005). The specific configuration of team teaching will vary, however, and is dependent on the types of activities that different instructors engage in and their roles with respect to one another (O'Loughlin, 2011; Richards and Farrell, 2005). For example, we believe that team teaching can be especially effective when native and non-native English speaking teachers are paired, as specific activities can be undertaken that highlight the strengths of each.

Team teaching fosters collegiality, provides opportunities for teachers to share expertise, encourages creativity, and leads to increased learning (Richards and Farrell, 2005). It also may help some instructors feel less isolated (O'Loughlin, 2011). In recent years, team teaching projects have been undertaken digitally. For an example of one such online collaboration across three universities, see Kabilan, Adlina and Embi (2011).

Join a Critical Friends Group

Typically, Critical Friends Groups (CFGs) consist of regular, structured meetings between small groups of non-hierarchical colleagues from the same institution. CFGs are 'composed of peers [who constitute] a democratic, reflective, and collaborative community of learners' (Vo and Nguyen, 2010, p. 206). The ultimate goal of CFGs is to discover ways to increase student learning while collaboratively reflecting on the types of practices likely to be most effective given the affordances and constraints of participants' local context (Dunne, Nave and Lewis, 2000). A CFG is likely to organize itself around different protocols designed to focus the group's attention on a different aspect of teaching and learning and provide a format for discussion that keeps the group on track (Franzak, 2002). While different scholars recommend different sizes for CFGs (Franzak, 2002; McKenzie and Carr-Reardon, 2003), we suggest a minimum of four participants and a maximum of eight.

CFGs can influence change at the individual level, as well as on a more cultural or institutional level (Bambino, 2002). They are often considered more satisfying than other professional development initiatives because of the degree to which they cultivate trust between colleagues (Dunne, Nave and Lewis, 2000). Finally, as an inquiry-oriented approach to professional development, CFGs acknowledge the dynamic nature of student learning and the important role that both context and participation play in L2 teacher learning (Johnson, 2009).

How can I acquire new knowledge?

Attend a professional conference, convention, symposium, etc.

Professional conferences and symposia are likely to offer the most current research in the field of TESOL, even more so than scholarly articles or books, which typically take a long time to reach publication. Professional conferences occur at a local, state, regional, national, and international level. Arguably, the largest international conference in the field of TESOL is TESOL International Association's annual TESOL International Convention and English Language Expo, which boasts over 6,500 participants from all over the globe. Other large national and international conferences relevant to TESOL include the annual American Association for Applied Linguistics (AAAL) conference, the International Association of Applied Linguistics (AILA) international World Congress (held every three years), and the International Association of Teachers of English as a Foreign Language (IATFL) International Annual Conference and Exhibition, among others.

Typically, large professional conferences organize presentations by *strand*, a term used to describe the specific research area to which a presentation belongs. For example, TESOL International Association organizes the presentations given at its annual international conference into strands that represent each of the association's Interest Sections (see Chapter 4 for a list of TESOL Interest Sections and a more complete discussion of the role that the Interest Sections play in the organization). As another example, in 2014 the American Association of Applied Linguistics conference included the following 16 strands:

- assessment and evaluation
- bilingual, immersion, heritage, and language minority education
- language and cognition
- corpus linguistics
- analysis of discourse and interaction

- educational linguistics

- language and ideology

- language, culture, and socialization

- language planning and policy

- second and foreign language pedagogy

- pragmatics

- reading, writing, and literacy

- second language acquisition, language acquisition and attrition

- sociolinguistics

- language and technology

- text analysis, written discourse (AAAL, 2014, p. 5).

Clearly some of these will be more directly relevant to pedagogy than others, but there is still clear overlap between the research interests of TESOL practitioners and those of more broadly oriented applied linguists. Furthermore, while many conference participants attend presentations that pertain to a particular strand(s) of interest, newcomers to the field – especially novice teachers and/ or new graduate students – may enjoy exploring a variety of different presentations. This is one way for newcomers to better grasp the breadth of the TESOL field before focusing on specific areas of interest in greater depth.

At the same time, there are also numerous state and regional conferences that a practitioner may wish to attend. For example, TESOL also hosts numerous state and regional conferences within the United States and abroad (e.g. Georgia TESOL and Southeast (SE) TESOL), as well as one-day regional symposia hosted by TESOL's various worldwide affiliates (e.g. KOTESOL in Korea) (for more about these, see Chapter 4). Some smaller conferences focus on a particular research area within the field of applied linguistics, such as the conference organized by ECOLT (the East Coast Organization of Language Testers) or by the American Association for Corpus Linguistics. These are typically attended by those who are already somewhat specialized within the field and are less likely to be organized into a variety of different strands.

Newcomers to TESOL may wonder how best to approach their first conference. Below, we suggest several strategies for ensuring that novice conference attendees maximize the benefits of attending a professional conference or convention:

- **Do your 'homework' in advance and find out what is offered.**
  Spend some time the night before the conference looking through

the programme and planning which presentations you would like to attend. Otherwise, it's easy to become overwhelmed during the conference and miss the sessions you're most interested in.

- **Focus on a particular interest.** For those attendees who already know which aspects of TESOL most interest them, we suggest sticking to just a few strands. That way your experience at the conference will be a bit more coherent.

- **Go to plenaries to get a better sense of trends in the field.** Plenaries, another term for keynote addresses, are often attended by several hundred, if not several thousand, conference attendees. They are usually centred on topics of general interest to the field and are an excellent way to grasp the 'big picture' in TESOL.

- **Always consider conventions/conferences as opportunities for networking and socializing with colleagues.** Socializing at conferences can be just as beneficial professionally as attending actual presentations, plenaries, workshops, etc. Take time to visit former instructors, advisers, and peers. Be aware of any receptions offered during the conference, as these are designed especially for networking.

- **Try to present at conferences to gain an insider's perspective.** It's never too early in one's career to begin presenting at conferences. See our more thorough discussion of this option below.

- **Spend time at publishers' exhibitions.** Most conferences invite publishers to set up special tables exhibiting their most recent books and journals. Take time to peruse the publishers' selections. Often, books are offered at a discount rate during conferences. Regardless of whether you purchase anything, publishers' exhibits are an excellent way to see what's being published in the field and to familiarize yourself with well-known authors.

- **Reflect on your experience and follow up on any new connections.** You will remember more of what you learned at a conference if you take notes during presentations and then read those notes again when the conference is over. You may want to write up a short account of the presentations you attended and any new theories, research areas, concepts, scholars, etc., that you would like to learn more about. Similarly, it's a good idea to note any new people you met at the conference so that you'll remember their names, where they are from, and their contact information.

Join and participate in professional organizations

Nearly all the conferences above are organized by professional organizations. Professional organizations are an excellent way for TESOL practitioners to network with others; volunteer; learn about research projects, professional development opportunities, and job openings within the field; participate in advocacy initiatives; and generally become more involved with local, regional, national, and/or global communities. For example, towards its goal of helping to connect members and advance professional expertise, TESOL International Association offers numerous professional development programmes, including online symposia and certificate programmes; hosts regional, national, and international conferences (see above); publishes special interest newsletters and professional journals, including its flagship journal, *TESOL Quarterly*; provides career services; maintains an online resource centre for both members and non-members; and promotes advocacy for language teachers and learners worldwide by way of numerous special interest efforts and publication of TESOL position papers and statements.

Professional associations offer tangible benefits to members as well. For example, in addition to reduced conference registration fees and discounts on language-related books and journals, many associations, including TESOL International Association, are likely to offer grants and scholarships for research or travel funds to its members. Finally, special interest groups within associations (more about these below) provide a venue through which members have power to directly influence the policies of the association, and thus of the field as a whole.

Graduate students will be happy to learn that many professional associations feature special committees or interest groups especially for MA and PhD students. For example, the American Association for Applied Linguistics has a Graduate Student Committee and hosts a specific area of their website ('The Graduate Student Corner') dedicated to resources and professional development opportunities specifically for graduate students. Similarly, TESOL International Association's Graduate Student Forum and Doctoral Forum are special sessions at the annual conference especially for MA and PhD students, respectively, to present posters, network with one another, and discuss their ongoing research. Readers are encouraged to consult both the AAAL and TESOL International Association for further details regarding the above.

Read professional and/or academic publications

Chapter 5 contains a selected list of professional and/or academic journals relevant to the field of TESOL. The nature of the articles in this list represents a range dependent upon a particular journal's focus and readership. While there is some overlap between the discourse of research and the discourse of language teaching pedagogy, some highly research-oriented journals, for example, *Journal of Second Language Acquisition* or *Language Learning*, frequently publish experimental studies with complex statistical analyses that are less likely to be immediately accessible to language teachers with little background in empirical research. However, we do not intend to imply that research articles are somehow beyond teachers' intellectual abilities. Journals with a more pedagogical orientation are just as likely to assume prior knowledge and contain terminology that is shared among language teachers but which would be unfamiliar to applied linguistic researchers who have had little exposure to the discourse of language pedagogy scholarship.

Unfortunately, subscriptions to most academic journals are somewhat costly for individuals. If a journal is published by a professional association, access to that journal is typically included in membership fees. Most university libraries also have institutional subscriptions to academic journals. However, if a practitioner is not a student or university faculty member, this is not an option. That said, some journals allow non-subscribers to purchase individual articles or feature free-to-access sample articles online as a marketing strategy. *Language Teaching Research* is an example of a journal that offers a free electronic sample of a complete issue, while *ELT Journal* features several free-to-access 'Editor's Choice' articles. TESOL International Association usually provides a free article from *TESOL Quarterly* and/or *TESOL Journal* to non-members through their association website.

Still, there are a variety of journals published for free online that are relevant to TESOL practitioners. These include the following:

- *English Teaching Forum* (http://americanenglish.state.gov/about-english-teaching-forum): This journal is published by the US Department of State specifically for classroom English teachers worldwide. Print versions are distributed freely by US embassies and consulates, but the electronic version is always available for free online.

- *Internet TESL Journal* (http://iteslj.org/): While this journal is no longer receiving submissions, its website hosts a freely available online archive of articles about lessons, teaching techniques, and other issues of interest to English language teachers that were published by Internet TESL Journal from 1995 to 2010.

- *English Language Teaching* (http://www.ccsenet.org/journal/index.php/elt): This peer-reviewed international journal is published by the Canadian Center of Science and Education. Readers pay for print copies but digital issues are available for free online.

- **TESL-EJ (Teaching English as a Second or Foreign Language)**
  (http://www.tesl-ej.org/wordpress/): TESL-EJ is another free online
  academic journal featuring refereed articles and reviews of interest to
  ESL and EFL practitioners.

- **Reading in a Foreign Language** (http://nflrc.hawaii.edu/rfl/): This freely
  accessible refereed international online journal is co-sponsored by the
  National Foreign Language Resource Center; University of Hawai'i
  College of Languages, Linguistics and Literature; and University of
  Hawai'i Department of Second Language Studies. It covers a range of
  issues related to foreign language reading and literacy.

- **Heritage Language Journal** (http://www.heritagelanguages.org/):
  This online, refereed journal about the acquisition and pedagogy
  of heritage languages offers access to articles by way of free
  registration. It is published by the National Heritage Language
  Resource Center at UCLA.

- **English Teaching: Practice and Critique** (http://edlinked.soe.waikato.
  ac.nz/research/journal/view.php?current=trueandp=1): This online,
  refereed journal is offered freely by the University of Waikato. It
  features articles related to classroom-based research and critical
  reflective teaching, with a focus on English literacy.

- **Teaching English with Technology** (http://www.tewtjournal.org/):
  This free peer-reviewed online journal publishes current scholarship
  related to technology in TESOL. Access requires a membership, but
  registration is free.

- **TESOL Connections** (http://www.tesol.org/read-and-publish/
  newsletters-other-publications/tesol-connections): TESOL Connections
  is published as an electronic newsletter for members of TESOL
  International Association; however, current and past issues are now
  freely accessible online to members and non-members alike. Articles
  contain practical teaching tips, strategies, and resources relevant to
  classroom teaching.

- **English Language Teaching Bulletin** (http://multibriefs.com/briefs/
  TESOL/): This bi-weekly digest published by TESOL International
  Association operates as a weekly newsfeed that compiles news
  from around the world relevant to ELT, as well as a small section
  devoted to association news. Email subscriptions are free to anyone,
  and archives of past and current issues are available online. Do note,
  however, that this bulletin features news articles rather than scholarly
  articles. It also contains advertisements.

The Directory of Open Access Journals (DOAJ) is also useful in locating freely accessible, peer-reviewed academic journals. It can be accessed here: http://doaj.org/.

Join or launch a teachers' reading group

Teacher reading groups, sometimes referred to more broadly as *study groups* or *learning circles*, consist of in-service teachers meeting voluntarily to read and discuss scholarly publications collaboratively. Such an opportunity gives teachers the opportunity to engage with the field's scholarship and gain 'a deeper understanding of their practice in relationship and dialogue with each other' (Twomey, 2010, p. 50). At the same time, teachers' reading groups encourage somewhat isolated teachers to connect with their larger social world in more meaningful ways (Twomey, 2010).

Teachers' readings groups have even begun to take place online. For example, KOTESOL's (TESOL's Korean affiliate) Professional Development Special Interest Group (PD-SIG) uses Yahoo! Groups (https://groups.yahoo.com/neo) to host members' discussions of scholarly books electronically. Past books chosen by the reading group include Nation's (2013) *What Should Every EFL Teacher Know?* and Richards and Farrell's (2005) *Professional Development for Language Teachers: Strategies for Teacher Learning* (see the KOTESOL PD-SIG website for further details: http://www.koreatesol.org/content/professional-development).

Pursue an advanced degree or certificate

Teachers who wish to acquire new knowledge may make a commitment towards pursuing an advanced degree or certificate in TESOL or applied linguistics. We encourage practitioners interested in this option to review the first two sections of this chapter, which focus specifically on certificate and degree programmes.

How can I solve a particular problem in the classroom?

Analyse a critical incident

A critical incident refers to an unanticipated moment or event during a lesson that can be analysed later for the sake of gaining further insight into teaching. The use of critical incidents in professional development typically involves the documentation and subsequent analysis of such unplanned events so as to help teachers structure reflection and develop ways to further improve (Richards and Farrell, 2005). Importantly, critical incidents do not have to be negative: for example, 'teaching highs' may serve as positive critical incidents (Thiel, 1999).

In Farrell's (2008) case study of critical incidents analysis used in teacher training, he offers step-by-step guidelines for those who wish to use critical incidents for teacher development with pre-service teacher-learners. We have adapted his suggested procedures below:

1 Teacher-learners write a description of the incident that occurred during teaching practice. The account should be descriptive only, with no attempt to determine why the event occurred.

2 Next, on a separate page, teacher-learners attempt to explain why the event happened.

3 In pairs, teacher-learners exchange descriptions of their critical incidents (but not explanations) and have the opportunity to offer potential interpretations of their partner's critical incident. These are then compared with the explanations written by the teacher who experienced the critical incident.

4 Teacher-learners participate in a whole-class discussion with their peers and with the instructor regarding the incidents that occurred and the interpretations of each that emerged through individual writing and pair work. Recalling that critical incidents don't have to be negative, teacher trainers are encouraged to elicit positive incidents as well (Farrell, 2008, pp. 9–10, adapted).

The above suggestions are written for pre-service teachers, but similar steps could be taken with in-service teachers or between an in-service teacher and his or her supervisor.

For further reading, we recommend Richards and Farrell's (2005) chapter devoted to the role of critical incidents in professional development, as well as Tripp (1993), whose book-length treatment of how teachers can use critical incidents to develop includes examples of critical incidents and suggestions for how to develop a critical incident file.

Join/begin a special interest group

One feature of membership that many of the larger professional associations offer is participation in special interest groups. These typically focus on a particular aspect of TESOL, such as adult education, second language writing, or refugee teaching. Interest groups are likely to publish newsletters, host listservs, and provide spaces for online discussion. Some have even begun to collectively review conference proposals for members. Essentially, special interest groups within professional organizations offer a more direct way to connect with other members in an online community of practice.

In addition to the variety of ways in which such groups can foster a participating group member's professional development, special interest groups are essentially unofficial communities of experts (or experts-in-training) on a given topic, skills area, learner population, etc. For this reason, many of the pressing problems, questions, concerns, etc. that a practitioner has can be addressed accurately and innovatively by members of such groups. Arguably, the organization that hosts the largest and most active collection of special interest groups in our field is TESOL International Association. Readers who are interested in joining an existing TESOL interest group are encouraged to see our discussion of this topic in Chapter 4 or visit TESOL's webpage for interest sections at the following address: http://www.tesol.org/connect/interest-sections. Note that interest sections are only accessible to current members of TESOL International Association. We recommend that readers who would like to start their own special interest group with a different organization should contact the administrators of the organization directly.

Engage in a case study

In education, the term *case study* is typically used to refer to accounts of 'how practitioners carry out their practice and resolve the issues that they confront' (Richards and Farrell, 2005, p. 126). The definition of a case study may vary depending on its purpose; however, in language education, writing a case study typically involves creating a narrative account of a real-life, context-specific event or sequence of events with a focus on describing the event in such a way that the role of interpretation or evaluation is left to the reader (Messerschmitt and Hafernik, 2009). Rather than viewing a case study as an exploration of a particular *problem* (which implies a direct and obvious solution), we recommend that practitioners approach case study writing and analysis as if they were addressing a 'puzzle' (Carter, 1992). Readers who would like to better understand the methodology for writing case studies themselves may wish to consult Egbert and Petrie (2005) as a reference.

For teachers and researchers wishing to better understand a particular issue, learner population, teaching context, or policy, reading existing case studies is another way to engage with situations that are likely to occur in actual language teaching but are rarely represented in the scholarly literature. For readers, case studies 'promote the connection of theory with practice, lend themselves to the examination of literature in the field, and encourage personal and community reflection' (Messerschmitt and Hafernik, 2009, p. xix). They can also help language professionals to be more reflective and make teachers-in-training more aware of the role of context in language teaching.

For a thorough exploration of ethical dilemmas encountered in post-secondary language teaching, readers could turn to Messerschmitt and Hafernik's (2009) *Dilemmas in Teaching English to Speakers of Other Language*, which contains 40 individual cases based on actual accounts of language teaching. For those interested in the benefits and challenges of online teacher education, the International Research Foundation for English Language Education (TIRF) and Dr. Denise Murray have compiled 18 case reports that each offer a contextualized, first-hand account of issues relevant to attempts to offer language teacher education online. These are freely accessible for download via the TIRF website: http://www.tirfonline. org/english-in-the-workforce/publications/online-language-teacher-education-case-reports/. Still another recommended source for case studies of L2 teaching is Richards's (1998) edited collection entitled *Teaching in Action: Case Studies from Second Language Classrooms*.

Participate in classroom research

For the purposes of this book, we use *action research* and *classroom research* synonymously: the term *action research* is typically used to refer to 'teacher-conducted classroom research that seeks to clarify and resolve practical teaching issues and problems' (Richards and Farrell, 2005, p. 171), while the aim of *classroom research* itself has been described as developing a better understanding of 'what goes on in the classroom setting' (McKay, 2009, p. 282). The underlying premise of classroom research is the assumption that teachers are the most well-suited for pursuing classroom research, as they are the most familiar with the particular context in which they teach (McKay, 2009). Classroom research is also ongoing: it involves constantly examining and re-examining one's practice.

For those teachers wishing to engage in their own classroom research, we recommend the following steps, which are loosely adapted from Kemmis and McTaggart (1988):

- Begin with a question you have about a particular phenomenon in your classroom (e.g. group work, learner engagement, over-reliance on the L1).

- Develop a plan of action that is intended to address the question. This will probably involve action that seeks to solve a problem, but sometimes classroom research may explore the cause of a particular problem as well.

- Put your plan into action.

- Find a way to observe the effects of your action in context. Depending on your question/action, audio- or video-recording may be useful.

- Reflect on the effects of your action and use the results of your reflection in future planning.

Teachers' participation in classroom research is particularly beneficial to the degree that it helps reduce the gap between scholarly research and practical classroom application. Burns (2009) calls this 'the gap between the ideal (the most effective way of doing things) and the real (the actual ways of doing things) in the social situation' (p. 290). TESOL practitioners who are interested in action research are encouraged to read a special section of *Language Teaching Research* entitled 'Practitioner Research'. It is an excellent resource for readers to better familiarize themselves with action research and with the sheer variety of teaching contexts in which language instructors are situated today.

How can I keep my skills current with advances in technology and/or changes in the field?

Participate in a workshop

Workshops are slightly different than conference paper presentations in that workshops are typically more interactive and involve discussion and/or active participation on the part of attendees. In the field of TESOL, workshops are usually designed to introduce participants to an innovation of some sort, which could mean anything from a groundbreaking teaching technique to newly released educational software to a novel assessment strategy. Conferences that are pedagogically oriented typically offer workshops in addition to more traditional paper presentations. Note, however, that the term *workshop* can be used somewhat loosely in the field of TESOL to refer to interactive learning opportunities that vary in terms of duration and cover a range of topics. For example, the University of Pennsylvania offers 15-hour, three-day workshops during which participants receive hands-on training for ESL and EFL teaching (Penn Graduate School of Education, n.d.), whereas Georgia TESOL (Georgia TESOL, n.d.), as another example, hosts a hybrid webinar/workshop on 'ESL Classes, Culture, and Change' that has an online component, as well as a 3-hour face-to-face component during the GATESOL conference. At the same time, TESOL International Association offers required 8-hour workshops as part of its Leadership Management Certificate Program.

Opportunities for workshops related to TESOL are too numerous to mention here. For local workshop opportunities, we recommend that readers contact their local and regional professional associations. For workshops at national and international conferences, they can check the conference website and/or programme for details.

Participate in a webinar/virtual seminar

Online webinars, sometimes referred to as *virtual seminars*, are excellent ways for TESOL practitioners to acquire new skills and increase their knowledge base in a particular area, especially with regard to aspects of the TESOL profession that are constantly changing, such as curricula, standards, assessment measures, and technology.

The following list contains links to free or reasonably priced webinars relevant to English language teachers, many of which are offered by publishers in the field of TESOL and/or second language teaching:

- Macmillan (http://www.macmillanenglish.com/webinars/). These free online webinars for English language teachers consist of live talks presented by language experts, after which webinar participants are given the opportunity to submit questions electronically.

- Cambridge English Teacher (http://www.cambridgeenglishteacher. org/webinar-list). This website offers access both to live webinars and to replays of past webinars; some require paid membership to participate, others are free. Topics cover a range of subjects of interest to TESOL practitioners, including technology, curricula, assessment, lesson planning, and corpora.

- Oxford University Press (https://elt.oup.com/events?cc=globalandselL anguage=enandmode=hub). These webinars are offered at no charge with free registration to the Oxford Teachers' Club.

- Pearson (http://www.pearsonelt.com/pearsonelt/ professionaldevelopment/index.page). Pearson ELT's professional development page contains links to podcasts, videocasts, and articles relevant to English language teachers. The following web address links to a PDF that explains how to go about participating in a Pearson ELT webinar: http://www.pearsonelt.com/assets/pearsonelt/ document/how_to_attend_webinar.pdf

- Virtual Round Table (http://www.virtual-round-table.com/page/ vrtwebconprogram). Virtual Round Table is an annual web-based conference devoted to language-learning technologies. Conference recordings are recorded and posted online. The above web address links to the 5th Annual Virtual Round Table, which took place in 2012.

- TESOL Virtual Seminars (http://www.tesol.org/attend-and-learn/online-courses-seminars). These 90- to 120-minute webcasts focus on a range of issues relevant to TESOL practitioners. Each advertised virtual seminar specifies whom the seminar is intended for and what skills and knowledge will be gained by participants. They are usually free to members but cost US$45 for non-members.

- Education Connections (https://www.obaverse.net/edconnect/): Hosted by the Center for Applied Linguistics and sponsored by the University of Oregon, Education Connections offers webinars for teachers of English language learners, in addition to a variety of other resources. Registration is free.

- The Grammar Teaching Webinar Series (http://www.cambridge.org/grammarandbeyond/webinar): This series consists of six in-depth grammar presentations offered by Dr Randi Reppen from 2011 to 2014. The videos are still available online and serve as a valuable resource for English teachers of grammar.

- National Centre of Literacy and Numeracy for Adults (http://www.literacyandnumeracyforadults.com/resources/355177): This website offers a plethora of resources for teachers of adult English learners with emergent literacy and numeracy. The above site directly links to freely available webinars, though users are encouraged to explore the range of resources offered by the website as a whole.

- The International Research Foundation (TIRF) for English Language Education (http://www.tirfonline.org/about-us/slide-casts/): This link doesn't necessarily contain webinars, but it does feature several slide-casts (in the form of PowerPoint slides) of keynote addresses and plenaries offered in the past by scholars affiliated with TIRF. The slide-casts are freely accessible to anyone.

- English Language Learner University (ELL-U) online courses (http://lincs.ed.gov/programmes/ell-u/online-courses): This web address links to the Literacy Information and Communication System's ELL-U online courses, where participants have access (with free registration) to five different self-paced 2.5–3.5-hour online courses focusing on different aspects of teaching adult learners with emergent print literacy.

For general instructions on how best to participate in a webinar, we recommend reading Joe McVeigh's (2012) brief blog post on the subject (http://blog.tesol.org/try-a-webinar/).

Take advantage of online tutorials and other electronic resources

The sheer number of electronic resources available to teachers online is overwhelming. As general advice to TESOL instructors in the twenty-first century, we recommend creating a website (Google Sites is a free option: https://sites.google.com/) that organizes in one place all the online resources that an instructor compiles over the course of attending conferences, workshops, speaking with colleagues, etc. The website may be structured in such a way so that technology tutorials are on one page, electronic articles and scholarly references on another, teaching resources on a third, etc.

Because we cannot possibly even begin to offer a comprehensive list of all of the electronic resources available to TESOL practitioners, we will list only a handful of particularly excellent sources below:

- For readers who would like to be aware of the most up-to-date research in a particular area of TESOL research, we recommend making use of TIRF's extensive electronic reference lists, which compile suggested references for a variety of topics in the field. They can be freely accessed at the following web address: http://www. tirfonline.org/resources/references/.

- For more pedagogically related reading, we recommend the British Council's collection of recent articles pertaining to topics such as pronunciation, culture, teaching resources, and methodology (http:// www.teachingenglish.org.uk/articles).

- One great electronic source for general questions related to technology is The LINGUIST List's 'Ask an Expert' page, which is dedicated solely to questions about language technology (http:// emeld.org/school/ask-expert/before-submitting.html). The LINGUIST List also offers simple online tutorials about certain technology that would be helpful to TESOL practitioners who are charged with administrative tasks, such as creating databases, maintaining a website, or planning a conference (http://linguistlist.org/multimedia/ index.cfm#tutorials).

- A fabulous electronic resource for TESOL practitioners is TESOL Resource Center (http://www.tesol.org/connect/tesol-resource-center), which compiles teaching strategies, lesson plans, activities, technology tips, etc., for English language teachers. The site is free to both members and non-members of TESOL alike.

- As a simple resort for strugglers with technology, we always recommend checking YouTube (https://www.youtube.com/) to see if an organization or individual has already created a tutorial for the technology that is causing the challenge. For example, a simple YouTube search revealed numerous tutorials for teachers wishing to use Wordle (http://www.wordle.net/), a free online programme that allows users to create visual 'word clouds' based on a text's key words. Some of the tutorials were even tailored specifically for ELT.

- Another option is TeacherTube (http://www.teachertube.com/), which has similar video tutorials for teachers, in addition to a variety of other audio and visual electronic sources.

How can I advance my career?

Present at a conference

Most professional TESOL practitioners who wish to advance their career could probably benefit from presenting at a professional conference (see our discussion regarding attendance at conferences, above). Conference presentations can help a practitioner develop professionally in a number of ways. First, presenting at a conference allows other teachers and scholars to hear a person's work and 'put a name with a face.' Second, conference presentations on a professional's C.V. indicate to administrators and hiring committees that a candidate (for a job, promotion, scholarship, etc.) is engaged in the scholarly community, conducts work that is competitive (after all, the conference proposal was selected!), and is knowledgeable in one or more specialized areas of the field.

Readers wishing to submit to a conference for the first time are encouraged to carefully examine samples of successful conference proposals to serve as models for their own proposal draft. We recommend obtaining previously successful proposals from mentors, current/past instructors, or colleagues. Members of special interest sections may find that it is easy to request and obtain proposals from other members of the same group. Sometimes, members of special interest sections may even offer to review a proposal for another member before it is submitted.

For those readers interested in submitting a conference proposal for the first time, we recommend trying a smaller, local conference the first time around. While large conferences sometimes have acceptance rates as low as 50 per cent, local conferences are typically able to accept a greater percentage of the submissions they receive.

Write for academic publication

For many faculty members in higher education, academic publication is considered the currency of their profession. Undoubtedly, any curriculum vitae can be bolstered by the inclusion of one or several academic publications. The most prestigious research publications are typically featured in double-blind, peer-reviewed journals, many of which are published by universities (e.g. Cambridge), professional organizations (TESOL International Association), or major publishing outlets (e.g. Wiley).

Still, it's possible for TESOL practitioners to seek publication through less competitive outlets. For example, TESOL International Association invites members to submit articles and resources for *TESOL Connections* or for Interest Section newsletters (see http://www.tesol.org/read-and-publish/ information-for-authors for details). Local chapters of TESOL also offer opportunities for publication in newsletters, while many local/regional associations publish their own journals and seek submissions from local practitioners.

For graduate students, novices in the field, or practitioners with less of a research focus, reviewing a book for publication may also be a worthwhile endeavour. Many academic publications include a section of each issue dedicated to short reviews written by contributors. Depending on the review, these may be written about a recently published scholarly book or about a textbook for language learners or teachers-in-training. For readers who are interested in publishing their own book review, we recommend contacting a journal's editor (or book editor, if it has one) and asking if a particular book seems relevant to the journal's readership in advance. Some journals accept unsolicited reviews, while others do not. That said, it never hurts to ask.

For those seeking to write for academic publication for the first time, we recommend Casanave and Vandrick's (2003) *Writing for Scholarly Publication: Behind the Scenes in Language Education.* Non-native English speakers who are anxious about publication in English are also encouraged to read Braine (2010), which contains an entire chapter (Chapter 10) dedicated to presenting strategies specific to the needs of NNESs wishing to publishing in English.

How do I pursue an advanced degree or certification? (See our discussion of this topic above)

Document all professional development activities

In a final note regarding the advancement of one's career in TESOL through professional development, we wish to make clear that all of the professional development opportunities detailed in this chapter (as well as the many activities we were unable to list due to space restrictions) can serve to advance one's career in a number of ways. Readers are encouraged to carefully document their participation in any of the professional development activities described in this chapter, no matter how 'informal' or 'alternative' they may seem. As more socioculturally-oriented approaches to SLTD (see Johnson, 2009a, 2009b) gain influence in the field, many such approaches – namely, those that 'encourage teachers to engage in ongoing, in-depth, and reflective examinations of their teaching practices and their students' learning' (p. 25) – are being perceived as increasingly valid forms of professional development. If an individual is unsure as to whether or not a particular activity belongs on his or her curriculum vitae, he or she is encouraged to consult with a supervisor and/or colleagues in the field.

How can I prevent burnout, feel less isolated, and/or find fulfilment in my work?

Mentor less experienced teachers

The benefits of mentoring a less experienced teacher are numerous (Huling and Resta, 2001; Malderez and Bodóczky, 1999). However, mentoring novice teachers is not the same thing as supervising them. In contrast with more supervisory roles, mentoring is primarily concerned with the 'transformation or development of the mentee and of their acceptance into a professional community' (Malderez, 2009, p. 260) rather than, say, compliance with standards at a particular institution.

While some mentoring relationships may arise organically between a more experienced teacher and a novice to the profession, others are structured in advance by an institution or supervisor. Similarly, a mentor may play many roles at the same time. For example, they may act as models, acculturators, supporters, sponsors, and educators (Malderez and Bodóczky, 1999). We do not recommend, however, that mentors attempt to evaluate or assess their mentees. Instead, a mentor of a novice teacher should provide some level of material support (e.g. offering to make copies, helping a novice teacher make professional connections, listening to a teacher's frustrations) at the same time that he or she engages in the 'educationally supportive process of scaffolding the learning of the core skills of professional learning, thinking, and action' (Malderez, 2009, p. 263).

Readers who are interested in mentoring a novice teacher but don't know where to begin are encouraged to speak with their own institution about this opportunity. They may also wish to consult Jonson (2002) or Pitton (2006).

Join or create a teacher support group

Teachers' reading groups were discussed above with regard to acquiring new knowledge; however, somewhat similar collaborative meetings between language educators, more broadly conceived as *teacher support groups*, can also empower teachers and help them feel less isolated (Richards and Farrell, 2005). The following list, adapted from Richards and Farrell (2005, pp. 52–6), lists a variety of purposes for teacher support groups:

- to reflect on teaching

- to develop and evaluate materials

- to structure and discuss peer observation

- to co-write articles for academic publication

- to invite expert speakers

- to engage in collaborative research

- to develop awareness of issues in language teaching

- to increase motivation and overcome isolation.

Readers who are interested in forming their own teacher support groups are encouraged to read Richards and Farrell (2005, pp. 56–60), which contains instructions on how to form a teacher support group, as well as a description of different types of support groups (e.g. topic-based, writing groups, etc.).

Engage in online professional development

Online professional development opportunities are particularly helpful for teachers who are teaching in isolated contexts and/or may not be able to afford to attend professional conferences, workshops, etc. Many of the professional development activities already described involve online opportunities (e.g. webinars/virtual seminars, special interest groups, etc.). We will not restate them here, but readers who feel overwhelmed and/or isolated in their teaching careers are encouraged to consider online opportunities for development, learning, and networking, in addition to seeking out local and regional opportunities with other practitioners and/or professional associations.

Engage in volunteering and advocacy

We believe that maintaining a critical perspective towards the role of English in an increasingly globalized world is an integral component of being a TESOL professional. Despite the obvious potential for English to empower learners, critically aware TESOL professionals cannot deny the fact that English also has the potential to marginalize non-English speakers, privilege native speakers over proficient speakers of English, and endanger minority languages worldwide. In acknowledgement of this potential, we believe that the TESOL profession has an especially urgent mandate to serve its public altruistically and to engage in advocacy efforts that prevent and/or address such power differentials (Judd, 2006; Nunan, 1999).

TESOL professionals can participate in advocacy both as members of professional associations and as individuals. The degree to which professional associations engage in advocacy varies, though some may include advocacy-related goals as part of their mission statement and thus devote a considerable amount of energy and association resources to select concerns. For example, larger organizations may issue resolutions or position statements and/or work to influence policy at the national level by lobbying and educating voters. They may also fund research of under-served populations, subsidize professional development activities for language teachers in less economically developed areas of the world, and address the reality of international varieties of English in published standards. For smaller associations, advocacy efforts may take the form of offering free workshops or resources to teachers who work with less privileged students, organizing volunteering, or ensuring that members are fully aware of policies already in place at the local and national level. Some associations have special interest groups devoted entirely to social advocacy. For example, TESOL International Association's 'Social Responsibility' special interest section aims to 'promote social responsibility within the TESOL profession and to advance social equity, respect for differences, and multi-cultural understanding through education' (TESOL International Association, 2014d).

Individuals who wish to serve as advocates can begin by developing a critical awareness of issues surrounding the role of language and inequitable relations of power (Hawkins and Norton, 2009). In their classroom, practitioner-advocates can avoid proscribing learners' principled use of their L1, develop a greater awareness of the power dynamic inherent to classroom interaction and work to mitigate it, encourage learners to value themselves as multilingual, and critically challenge any curricula or assessment tools that assume attainment of native-like proficiency as the ultimate goal. Individuals who are able may also consider volunteering. In particular, teachers who have worked with more privileged learner populations for a number of years may find it refreshing to teach less-advantaged students for a change (Wong, 2011). For teachers who are interested in volunteering within their communities, we recommend contacting local chapters of professional associations, community centres, and non-profit organizations. For readers who wish to learn more about advocacy initiatives at the policy level, we recommend reviewing TESOL International Association's Advocacy Resources website for helpful resources and further information about the type of efforts underway in our field (http://www.tesol.org/advance-the-field/advocacy-resources). *TESOL Connections* also features a regular column on policy issues that can serve to keep readers informed.

Graduate student professional development

But what can I do as a graduate student?

While we recommend the above activities for nearly any professional in the field of TESOL, the remaining section of this chapter will focus specifically on ways that graduate students of TESOL might take steps towards becoming professional members of the vibrant community that constitutes/comprises TESOL. We have formatted these as a list of suggested strategies that graduate students can implement/adopt in order to foster their own professionalization. Many of the strategies below incorporate activities that have already been described in detail in earlier sections of this chapter; when this is not the case, we have attempted to provide guidance in the form of suggestions for further reading, and/or brief description.

- With the consultation of your adviser, draft and maintain a Professional Development Plan (PDP) to set short- and long-term goals and to track your professional development from graduate school and beyond (Lorimer and Shulte, 2011; Wong, 2011).

- Document all of your professional development activities for inclusion in a teaching portfolio and/or curriculum vitae.

- Take advantage of any local professional development activities offered/promoted by your department.

- Pursue professional development activities (conferences, workshops, etc.) outside your programme as well; doing so will help you to better grasp the breadth of the field beyond your school or department.

- Join a professional association (see above); even better, join an association and become involved with its graduate student members (graduate student committees or special interest groups are a good place to start).

- Join any local student associations, especially if they are relevant to TESOL in any way.
- If you are teaching, keep a teaching journal (see above) to structure and document your own reflection.
- Participate in peer observation (see above).
- Begin or join a reading group (see above) with peers and/or faculty.
- Present at a local or national conference (see above); we suggest that graduate students interested in presenting at a conference for the first time consider collaborating with a peer.
- Write for academic publication (see above).
- Ask faculty and/or advisers to share their experiences in the TESOL job market.
- Make connections with fellow graduate students at other universities; these are your future colleagues!
- Be willing to take risks, maintain a spirit of curiosity throughout your academic career, and stay engaged (Lorimer and Shulte, 2011).

3

TESOL as a Field of Study

TESOL research

Research can mean different things to different people, and there are already numerous books and literature on the various types of research and research methodology. Given the nature of this book, we will only discuss research relevant to the field of TESOL specifically. That is, the following discussion on research has TESOL as a focus, with teacher-researchers or practitioners in mind. The information we share, the examples we use, and the recommendations we make are all for teachers, practitioners, teacher-researchers, and novice researchers (such as graduate students) in TESOL.

Too often, we are either driven or threatened by research because we either love or are intimidated by it. We love research because we find it relevant to what we do and we enjoy the dissemination of research results in publications or at conferences to be reassured and appreciated by our colleagues. We are also satisfied when we see the research results bear immediate pedagogical implications. Conversely, we may not be thrilled by research as we are too busy to do research on the one hand, or too disappointed that our research can rarely get published. It is true that not many research studies can be published owing to the lack of journals in our field coupled with the fierce competition and low acceptance rate for journal article publication.

Nevertheless, any sound study that is research-based deserves to be shared through publication. Research, by its nature, is twofold: it is process-oriented on the one hand, and it is product-driven on the other. As a process, research seeks to employ formal, systematic, intensive processes of the scientific method to make careful inquiry or examination. It is usually considered systematic and data driven, and involves critical investigation of a phenomenon or pattern in order to make sense out of it. Therefore, research-as-process usually requires persistent effort to think straight and to plan ahead. As a product, research aims to discover new information or relationships, expand

and verify existing knowledge, gather and provide new knowledge, discover general principles, increase our understanding and/or predict an event by relating it empirically to antecedents in time, and sometimes control an event by manipulating the independent variables to which it is functionally related.

Research usually involves gathering new data or using existing data for a new purpose from primary or first-hand sources. It is directed towards the solution of a problem and often characterized by carefully designed procedures that require observation, analysis, and interpretation. Research in the field of TESOL is no exception. However, owing to the purpose of TESOL research specifically, which serves to enhance language learning and teaching, TESOL research has its own uniqueness, characteristics, as well as methods and techniques.

What is TESOL research?

As a field of study, TESOL has unique characteristics when it comes to research. Traditional second language acquisition research tends to emphasize empirical evidence by way of experimental research or in-depth case studies that are sometimes considered remote or irrelevant to English language classroom teachers. Action research or classroom research, though more relevant to TESOLers, lacks the venue for publication, and is often considered less rigorous or too anecdotal. For years, TESOL professionals have been searching for their own identity as researchers. While there has still been no completely satisfactory result, TESOL research is commonly perceived today as research for practical purposes. That is, scholarship is not considered TESOL research if there are no immediate implications for language learners and teachers, and if it lacks relevance to classroom practice or does not have immediate impact on language learning processes, learning outcomes, learners, and teachers. Therefore, TESOL research, in a way, is associated with best practices that are driven by theory and yet lead to better results in language learning and teaching.

What are some characteristics of TESOL research?

1. TESOL research is classroom-based or classroom-oriented

Research in general can be longitudinal, experimental, lab-based, qualitative, quantitative, or classroom-based. TESOL research is usually associated with classroom practice directly or indirectly, regardless of the research methods. The purpose of TESOL research is to enhance language learning and teaching and solve problems theoretically and practically that are related to language learning and teaching. Perhaps that is what differentiates TESOL research from other research. Because it is based in or related to the classroom, research cannot be controlled as many experimental research studies are, nor can it be longitudinal, as each course usually lasts one semester and changes occur all the time. Given the ad hoc nature of TESOL research, it is realistic not to expect astonishing findings.

2. TESOL research is done by or with classroom teachers

There is a perception that researchers and teachers have different respon-sibilities. Sometimes they have clearly articulated but different goals in their work. While we encourage teachers to be researchers, we cannot expect researchers to be teachers, as the two are likely to appear in the same classroom doing different things. Researchers care more about *how* something is done while teachers focus on *what* is done. Meanwhile, researchers look at issues more objectively while teachers cannot hide their own subjectivity. The ideal scenario is collaboration between the teacher and the researcher, and in many instances successful and insightful research is the result of teacher–researcher collaboration. TESOL research, however, empowers teachers to become researchers as they are encouraged to think outside the box from time to time and to question what they are doing and why they are doing it in order to understand what is taken for granted and to bring change to their usual practice.

3. TESOL research is outcome-based

TESOL research seeks to identify an issue or problem, devise strategies to address it, and then observe the results before employing new strategies or providing reinforcement to sustain the results. Trial and error is usually the best way to test the effectiveness of the intervention. Many experienced teachers know where problems are and how to fix them, though there are different ways to fix problems depending on teachers' own choices and judgement. Just as there is no best method of teaching, there is no best solution to a problem. The effort it takes to identify a problem and solve the problem itself is research, and this happens constantly in the classroom. What differentiates TESOL research from a language classroom technique or strategy is the persistence and consistence used in research, thus bringing sustainable results over time.

4. TESOL research is flexible in design

Whenever we talk about research, we talk about research design. It seems that a well thought out research design is fundamental to the success of research. Whenever doctoral students propose their research, whether qualitative or quantitative in nature, an expected chapter or component in their proposal is research design – what their research question is, what data they are going to collect, how they plan to analyse their data, and what their expected outcome is as the result of their data analysis. We almost take it for granted that a research design should be established before research takes place and thus our profession upholds this requirement in the field. But the reality for classroom teachers, or TESOL teacher-researchers, is just the opposite. They simply do not have time to have a thorough plan ahead of time. Sometimes problems occur instantly and they have to find ready solutions or change their intervention several times during the class. The interpretation of research design for teacher-researchers is not the same as what is expected for experimental or quasi-experimental research. To many, TESOL research design is situation-driven and flexible during the course of action. Having a big picture of what needs to be accomplished is usually considered sufficient guidance in searching for multifaceted strategies in dealing with complex situations at work. In sum, TESOL research requires more flexibility in design or planning.

5. TESOL research is context-driven and case-based

TESOL research is highly dependent on context and on the educational settings and cultures in which the research takes place. It is not meant to be generalizable to other contexts, therefore replicability of the research results is not necessarily expected. Because of this constraint, sometimes the value of TESOL research is left to the interpretation of the individual. The context where the research takes place varies according to cultural background, the proficiency level of leaners, teacher factors, curricula, as well as learning and teaching objectives. The more explanation and background that is provided, the better understanding for readers or consumers of research.

6. TESOL research is reflective

One goal of TESOL researchers is their own professional development. Inquiry can be extremely valuable to teachers who wish to reflect and improve on their own teaching and thus grow in personal professionalism. What instructors learn from research can affect their practice in specific ways: it may affect their attitudes, motivation, or expectations about students' abilities and growth, or it may affect teachers and students in unexpected ways that manifest themselves immediately or over time. Beyond personal growth, the value of TESOL research can be multiple. Not only can one's own classroom be improved, but projects can also result in much larger changes, such as innovations in curriculum, teaching methodology, assessment, and administration. On a broader level, school districts, language institutes, and the TESOL profession in general can expect to benefit from the most insightful of such research when teachers share it with broader communities through conferences, symposia, workshops, or other professional development activities.

7. TESOL research is self-empowered

Research sometimes becomes an isolated world where teachers do not feel they belong, mainly because of the use of unfamiliar jargon and the expectation for rigid design. By conducting their own research, TESOL researchers can contribute to knowledge in their own way. A related but stronger rationale for teacher inquiry is that of emancipating teachers. By asking their own questions and exploring them in their own ways, many teachers have gained a new sense of their own creative power. They come to see themselves as challengers and creators rather than just transmitters and receivers of others' construction of knowledge. Bolstered with a new confidence through knowledge gained in their own research, teachers then play a strong role in initiating critical dialogues and changing structures they find oppressive to themselves, to their colleagues, and to their students. Having said that, we must be mindful that the meanings, values, and outcomes of TESOL research, including its role in emancipating teachers, must be determined by teachers themselves in their own sociocultural settings.

What are the steps in doing TESOL research?

Doing TESOL research involves a series of steps, from identifying a problem and formulating a research question to determining the methodology of how to go about beginning research at the initial phase. Once the study is completed, it is only half done, as there are many other steps to follow including synthesizing, analysing, and interpreting data, and writing it up for presentation or publication. Below, we offer ten recommended steps for readers interested in conducting their own TESOL research for the first time.

1. Identify the problem and state it succinctly

TESOL research usually begins with a problem, a question, or an issue that needs attention. Frequently, problems, questions, or issues are mixed or blurred. For instance, it is often the case that students are not making progress in language learning over a period of time no matter how much effort the instructor puts into teaching. In this case, the problem is that students are not learning, while the research question is 'What are the factors preventing students from learning?' At the same time, the issue itself is the lack of learning on the part of the students causing great concern for parents. As a TESOL researcher, an instructor faced with such a concern will determine where to begin research by first identifying the problem. A clear problem statement is then needed in order to match the research question(s) with research methods. Sometimes it is not easy to describe or articulate the problem without contextualizing it. Therefore, it is important to provide context or background to situate the problem. It is equally important to succinctly describe the problem without any ambiguity.

2. Review literature comprehensively

Once a problem is clearly identified and articulated, it is important to know what research has already been done to address the identified problem, from what contexts existing research has been conducted, from what angle the problem is addressed in research methodology, what the research findings actually are, and how these findings shed light on improving the practice. This is an essential step for any research endeavour, as our field has already produced so much research and has published so many papers in the various domains of language learning and teaching over the last several decades. Sometimes, the research we do will be more or less the same as an existing research design only with different research settings or research goals. Knowing the literature can also help us understand what has been done and identify the newness in the current research in order to make an original contribution to the field.

Most of the research we do in TESOL builds on what has been done previously, thus validating the previous research methods or challenging previous research results. Often we label this kind of research a *replication study*. In the field of TESOL, exact replication is often impossible, as we are constantly dealing with different learners in different learning environments and with different learning objectives. However, in TESOL research, general replication is relatively easy as TESOL researchers can constantly try something new in their classrooms to test its effectiveness and to make adjustment until effectiveness is achieved.

3. Design the research holistically

Once a problem has been identified, and what has been done to address the problem previously has been reviewed, research is ready to be designed. The next step is to come up with a research question or questions that are logically related to the problem statement. The research question(s) are usually related to the purpose or objectives of the study. The research questions also imply what research methods will be used to answer them. For instance, if the research question begins with 'What ...' as in 'What is the main reason students are not learning?', the research method could be a survey that lists a number of potential reasons and then allows the instructor to examine the distribution of students' answers. However, if the research question starts with 'Why ...' as in 'Why are students not learning?', then the research method could be interviews that allow the instructor to discover why from students through in-depth interviews. Whatever research methods are used, they should always answer the specific research question(s). Sometimes, if a teacher-researcher asks a number of research questions, he or she will need to use a number of methods. We call such an endeavour 'mixed methods' as the nature of the research calls for multiple methods. Whether a novice researcher conducts qualitative or quantitative research, or a combination of both, he or she needs to be aware that it is the nature of the research questions that dictates the most appropriate research methods.

4. Collect data thoroughly

We cannot do research without data, but different kinds of research use different sets of data. In qualitative research, we rely on 'thick' data or 'fat' data, as we need rich context and descriptions to piece together whatever we have in order to make sense. In quantitative research, we rely on more precise data in an experimentally controlled setting in order to make sense of the differences between independent and dependent variables. Research questions call for certain types of data collected via appropriate research methods. In some cases, researchers collect a lot of data, only to realize that most of the data is useless after the fact. The problem with this discrepancy is largely due to the mismatch between research questions and research methods on the one hand, and inadequate or inappropriate data collection on the other. For instance, if the purpose of a survey is to understand high school students' difficulties in learning English in Brazil, and the data collected are only from a few classes in Grade 10, the data set is obviously skewed and there is a lack of representation. Collecting the correct data and appropriate amount of data driven by the research question is as important as finding the right research questions to address the identified problem.

5. Analyse data objectively

Collecting the right data is important, but sorting through and analysing the data to answer the research question(s) is even more important. While researchers usually try to use data to answer their specific research questions, sometimes the data collected will offer insights beyond the answers to the predetermined research questions if the analytical framework is used to its best potential. Making sense out of the data is what a researcher needs. In qualitative research, for instance, using coding and themes to delineate data from interview transcripts or documents allows a researcher to understand the data. In quantitative research, usually we rely on statistics packages or analytical schemes to highlight the results. In one way or another, a researcher should build data analysis into the research design and know exactly how he or she plans to make sense out of the data collected. Data can be overwhelming. Inexperienced researchers sometimes find that they spend a lot of time analysing their data and may even get 'lost' in the amount of data they've collected.

6. Interpret data subjectively

Interpreting data is a step beyond analysing data. While the purpose of data analysis is to come up with research findings, the purpose of interpreting data is to recommend what we can do with the findings of the research. In other words, data interpretation answers the 'So what?' question. Since the ultimate purpose of TESOL research is to help improve language learning and teaching, the pedagogical implications derived from research findings make TESOL research unique. However, in interpreting the findings of research, a researcher should not only seek the answers to the original research questions, but also look for answers to solve problems based on the findings of the research. Moreover, by interpreting the data, the researcher should also acknowledge the limitations of the current research and point out directions for future research.

7. Write up the research carefully

Once the research is done, it is important to write it up for presentation and then publication. It is always a good idea to share the study with colleagues via conference presentation as the feedback you get from presentations will help shape the presentation materials into a publishable paper. Understandably, preparing for presentation is different from writing for publication with regard to the structure, the style, and the audience. The latter requires much more effort and scrutiny. Depending on the editorial requirement and the readership of the journal, it is not a bad idea to first have a journal in mind and to read a few issues to get a feel for the published articles as well as the editorial policies of that journal before you start writing up your research. Regardless of the journal, TESOL research papers usually follow a particular format. It begins with an introduction to provide context, background, and to state the problem(s) addressed, followed by a literature review that captures the latest research on the topic and the salient findings and implications. Research design is another necessary part of the paper that includes the research purpose and objectives, research questions, research methods in data collection, and analysis. The essence of the paper will be the sections on Findings, Interpretations, and Recommendations. For help with writing up research, we recommend Swales and Feak's (2004) *Academic Writing for Graduate Students.*

8. Choose a journal appropriately

There are many journals in language learning and teaching in the field, and many serve as outlets for TESOL research.[1] But choosing an appropriate journal for submission sometimes can be daunting, as different journals have different readership and expectations. Before you write up your research, you should spend time familiarizing yourself with various journals and determine which journal/s you might want to submit your papers to so that the research write-up will be more purposeful and focused. An excellent source for this stage of the publication process is a list that TIRF (The International Research Foundation on English Language Education) has assembled of the most relevant professional journals in the field. It is available online at the following address: http://www.tirfonline.org/resources/journals/.

Due to the fierce competition in academic publication and the relative lack of professional journals for TESOL research, TESOLers often face a lot of challenges and are discouraged from writing for publication, not to mention from doing TESOL research in the first place. However, there are always strategies that TESOLers can employ to better meet such challenges. In addition to having a realistic assessment of their own strengths and weaknesses as potential authors of research output, here are some tips for novice TESOL researchers to follow when aiming for publication:

- Identify journals that could be potential venues for your research.

- Study their submission guidelines.

- Study articles in the prospective journals to get a good feel for the type of research they prefer.

- Prepare and/or revise your paper accordingly.
- Share with a colleague or experienced peer to review your paper and give you some feedback.
- Revise your paper based on peer feedback before you send it out.
- Expect and anticipate rejection.
- Revise according to reviewers' comments.
- Shop around, find another similar journal, and tailor your revision accordingly.
- Submit again, and repeat the same cycle if rejected.
- Wait until three rejections before you put the manuscript aside.
- Never throw away editors'/reviewers' comments.

9. Revise the article based on editors' and reviewers' comments accordingly

Once a paper is submitted to a journal, it is normal to wait for a few months before hearing back from the editor. There are usually three scenarios reflected in the editor's feedback: (1) Accept 'as is' with minor revision; (2) Revise and resubmit with concrete suggestions for revision; and (3) Reject. The first case is rare but possible, while the second case is common and expected, although many journals have an unusually high amount of submissions and the acceptance rate is very low for such journals. Some journals will go through in-house review as well as peer (external) review to protect the time of external reviewers. Others will only have peer review.

There are many reasons for rejection. The most common reasons are as follows:

- lack of theoretical framework;
- unanswerable research questions;
- insufficient data and irrelevant topics;
- wrong sampling and flawed methodology;
- mere surface analysis of data;
- nothing new and nothing beyond the current knowledge base;
- mismatch between your data and your analysis/interpretation;
- mismatch between your article and the nature of the journal;

- inappropriate length, unwanted style, and incomplete paper;
- not in line with current literature and jargon/theory;
- cannot convey ideas and express opinions;
- reviewers (taking offence, dislike the research, bad mood);
- the novice factor (i.e. lack of confidence, vague statements, or any inexperience that makes the writing seem weak or less professional).

Since rejection is normal, part of the process of academic publication involves learning how to conduct better research and how to write research through the helpful comments received from reviewers and editors. In order to have better luck with publishing, sometimes writers need to develop strategies to avoid rejection. For instance, writers should understand who reads their paper (the background of the editorial board and reviewers). Equally important is their understanding of who and how many people submit their articles to a particular journal, as well as its acceptance rate. Finally, writers should make sure that in their study they have sufficient data and that the methodology used for their study is sound and directly related to their research question/s.

Novice researchers should remember that editors are looking for particular things in a paper, such as topic of interest, sound methods and research design, clarity in writing, sufficient information and explanation, proper formatting, and ethics, among others.

10. Resubmit the revised article confidently

The acceptance of a paper after resubmission is not guaranteed. It really depends on individual cases. But there are some strategies in negotiating with editors. For instance, a writer needs to establish professionalism by following preferred communication protocol. He or she needs to study the reviewers' and editors' comments thoroughly. While not all the comments are acceptable, writers who are revising should justify why they accept and do not accept certain comments with thoughtful but to-the-point arguments.

In sum, it is both challenging and rewarding to conduct research and get published. Here are ten strategies we recommend to become a published TESOL researcher:

1 Keep abreast of the current and relevant literature and pay close attention to both the content and the rhetoric of the published journal articles in your areas of interest.

2 Have a realistic assessment of yourself as a writer in selecting your topics and in choosing research methodologies.

3 Think about a paper for a period of time before you start, and make sure that the topic you are interested in is worth pursuing.

4 Pay attention to how frequently published writers write in English, and ask yourself how your usual style compares to theirs.

5 Familiarize yourself with journal guidelines and conventions (e.g. issues such as originality, discourse structure, rhetorical styles, plagiarism, and illustration) before you submit a paper.

6 Enlist help from both native and non-native English-speaking professionals, get their feedback before the manuscript is submitted, and allow time to revise in between drafts.

7 View the editors' and reviewers' negative comments and decisions positively as constructive criticism, and always keep trying and revising.

8 Collaborate with experienced researchers and writers in your field to learn from their procedures in doing research and writing for publication.

9 Keep focused on one topic area before you move on to other areas of interest.

10 Maintain a strong sense of ownership and compose your own identity and voice through publication.

What is the TESOL Research Agenda?[2]

In 2000, the TESOL Association made a commitment to periodically publish a research agenda that would reflect the changing nature of the discipline and its research priorities while remaining open, inclusive, and representative of the best interests of the field at large. The first TESOL Research Agenda was published in June 2000, to help TESOL professionals and colleagues in related fields to 'organize and coordinate inquiry in the field, and to promote a broader awareness of what constitutes research in TESOL' (TESOL, 2004, p. 1). Because of rapid changes and many emerging hot topics in the field of TESOL, TESOL International Association has again formed a research task force to devise the third TESOL Research Agenda, based on a membership survey, with the goal of better understanding the status of research in TESOL and identifying existing gaps between research and practice in current research, as well as important issues that need to be addressed in the TESOL profession.

TESOL Research Agenda serves as a blueprint for the types of research needed in the field, as well as areas of research called for to tackle the most relevant and pertinent issues in the field given a specific period of time. Therefore, it is not static, but it indicates the direction of TESOL research within a numbers of years forward. Constant review of the research agenda is needed as the field is changing. The TESOL Research Agenda benefits teacher-researchers or novice researchers in particular as it points out the direction where research is needed. It also sets the tone for research topics or themes as they emerge. Moreover, it suggests the future direction of the field and calls for reconsideration of what has been done and what needs to change for the field to move forward.

Just like a strategic plan, the TESOL Research Agenda serves its purpose for only a few years, and it needs to be revised every five to seven years (the most recent was published in 2014). It is not meant to be prescriptive, but descriptive and suggestive. For TESOL researchers, it can be a good resource to refer to and to reflect upon. For TESOL as a field of study to move forward, we do need to make a concerted effort to tackle a number of pertinent issues consistently, strategically, and alternatively in order to bring new understanding and changes, and ultimately to be in synch with the development of the society, technology, and the social function of English. What has been done previously will no longer be useful for now and the future. What has been researched predominantly as a topic of interest in one discipline will no longer shed light if other disciplinary boundaries are not broken or mingled. As learning English becomes more complex, so does teaching English, especially as the role of English continues to expand.

Eventually, we believe that the TESOL Research Agenda will need to be co-constructed by all TESOL researchers. With all of our input and research practice, we can make the TESOL Research Agenda our own.

TESOL research methodology

TESOL methodological considerations

The past few decades have witnessed a blurring of disciplinary boundaries, as well as of research methodologies. Just as multiple research paradigms other than positivism have increasingly gained ground in the social sciences and humanities, so have alternative paradigms greatly influenced the field of language learning and teaching in general, and the field of TESOL in particular.

Where only statistics, experimental designs, and survey research once stood, researchers have begun to employ critical ethnography, the wide-open interview, document analysis, participant observation, and action research. Where the divide between qualitative and quantitative research methods is still visible, TESOL has embraced mixed methods to tackle complex issues in the process of learning and teaching.

The multiplicity of emergent methodologies in TESOL has produced a new generation of teacher-researchers, or action researchers, who are making connections between theories and practice in many innovative ways. In the field of TESOL, more attention is being paid to classroom-oriented or classroom-based research. Studies which have looked at issues of clear relevance to language classroom practice and which have investigated learners inside actual classrooms are in fact receiving as much attention as studies conducted outside the classroom.

TESOL researchers are encouraged to see single events on different levels simultaneously. In language classrooms there are always many things happening at the same time, and there are always multiple issues that TESOLers are concerned with in their classrooms. Being able to choose the most appropriate option to examine an identified problem is what makes us competent as TESOL researchers.

TESOL research methodological options

As we discussed earlier in this chapter, TESOL researchers must identify problems for research, formulate their research questions, modify their research objectives, and find compatible research methods and techniques. In the first part of a triadic conceptual framework for research in the field of TESOL, there is the belief system one has about the nature of reality. The second part of the framework is the relationship between the knower and the known, and the third part is the goal of the research.

For instance, one methodological option is to view reality as objective, to believe that inquiry can be objective and free of values, and that the researcher can remain unbiased and detached from what is being researched. The goal of the research is to discover cause and effect relationships, accomplished by manipulating the natural environment. A different methodological option is to question that 'truth' exists and to believe that reality is socially constructed and multiple. All knowledge is therefore subjective and the researcher cannot be detached from the researched. For example, such a perspective might argue that TESOL researchers bring subjectivity into the research via the theories they choose, the questions they ask, and the methods they use to carry out the research. The goal of research within this methodological option, therefore, is to make sense of a case and to understand a situation. A third methodological option enables TESOL researchers to understand social constructions via symbolic representation; its goal is to raise questions in order to heighten awareness of injustices and to begin the process of change. As seen, methodological options reflect the goals of research driven by one's beliefs and epistemological stances.

Methodological options are therefore crucial in identifying problems as well as in formulating research questions. The more methodological options one has, the better research decisions one can make, given contexts and problems in terms of when and where to focus on what, how, and why (Markee, 1998).

Once a research goal is identified by assessing methodological options, one needs to determine the methods and techniques that best match the chosen methodological option(s). Methodological options affiliated with certain research paradigms tend to imply research methods. For instance, if *to explore and to describe* is the methodological option, then a survey could be one of the matching methods. Likewise, if the methodological option is *to establish a cause and effect relationship*, then experimental or quasi-experimental research would be the choice of method. But it is important to keep in mind that research techniques can be boundary-free. For instance, data from the techniques of observation can be quantified for statistical analysis or studied for emerging patterns from a qualitative perspective. Similarly, interviews as a research technique can be used for both discourse analysis and frequency counts of occurrence for their salient patterns and themes.

The boundaries between methods and techniques are not rigid, and researchers often combine different methods and techniques in order to gain different perspectives and a deeper understanding of the phenomenon under study, thus leading to hybrid research methods. Few studies are located entirely within one method, and researchers typically employ multiple techniques in their research. In fact, Lier (1988) calls classroom research a hybrid activity, due to the use of multiple techniques, while others advocate viewing the various research methods on a continuum, from more controlled and structured (experimental) to less structured and less controlled (case studies) (Allwright and Bailey, 1991; see also Lier, 1988).

Research methods as ways to do research are determined by methodological options, while techniques as tools for research methods are employed in the process of conducting the research. If *establishing a cause and effect relationship* is a methodological option, an experiment becomes a method, and statistical analysis can be used as a technique. Likewise, if *to interpret* is the methodological option, ethnography becomes a method, and participant observation and journal writing are probably more appropriate techniques. Moreover, if *to change* is the defined methodological option, then critical ethnography is a possible method, and fieldwork, interviews, observations, discourse analyses, and self-report measures all become useful techniques.

Action research as a TESOL research methodological option

Where does action research belong? Is action research a method or a TESOL research methodological option? If we view action research as a method, which is actually what is commonly believed, then its meaning, scope, agent, and image in scholarship are not of the same calibre as all other research methods, whether experimental, survey, ethnographic or case study.

Defining *action research* is no simple task. The term itself was coined by social psychologist Kurt Lewin (1890–1947) in the 1940s to describe a type of research that addressed social problems with programmes of social action (Burns, 1999). Kemmis and Henry (1989) define action research as:

> A form of self-reflective inquiry undertaken by participants in social situations in order to improve the rationality and justice of their own social and educational practices, as well as their understanding of these practices and the situations in which these practices are carried out. (p. 2)

Others have gone on to define *action research* in a variety of ways. For example, Brown (2007) refers to action research simply as classroom research, which is 'carried out not so much to fulfill a thesis requirement or to publish a journal article as to improve our own understanding of the teaching-learning process in the classroom' (p. 437). Allwright and Bailey (1991) refer to action research as classroom research that can be directed towards trying to understand and deal with the immediate practical problems facing teachers and learners (p. 39), while Wallace (1998) posits that action research is 'the systematic collection and analysis of data relating to the improvement of some aspect of professional practice' (p. 1). Nunan (1992) further defines action research as a form of self-reflective inquiry carried out by practitioners, aimed at solving problems, improving practice, or enhancing understanding.

Strickland (1988) suggests that action research is a series of repeated steps which should (a) identify an issue, interest or problem, (b) seek knowledge, (c) plan an action, (d) implement the action, (e) observe the action, (f) reflect on your observations, and (g) revise the plan. This cycle then begins once more, with the revisions incorporated in a new action. This process allows teachers who wish to investigate events in their own classrooms to take constructive steps towards solving immediate problems, systematically reflecting on the outcome. Thus the goal of action research is achieving local understanding and developing variable solutions to problems. In his book *Doing Teacher Research: From Inquiry to Understanding*, Freeman (1998) succinctly explains how teachers can become more involved in doing action research and making it public for the benefit of all second language teaching professionals.

Ultimately, these definitions and explanations reflect the diverse perspectives and expectations researchers hold towards what is called *action research* rather than how action researchers themselves describe their rationale in doing what they do in language classrooms. *Action research* as a term given to practitioners by researchers is political in itself. What we are repeatedly reminded of from the existing definitions about action research is that it is supposedly local, inside classrooms, small-scale, practitioner-oriented, and comprising trial and error. Such messages imposed by researchers set boundaries for practitioners that confine their practice to their local level, and limit methodological options from entering into these practitioners' research repertoire. Unlike experimental research or naturalistic inquiry, action research is seen not only as the only available research method for teachers but as a method only for teachers. The results of action research are shared, if at all, at local conferences, and the publication of action research reports is usually limited to a few pages in less research-oriented journals. As Markee (1998) points out, there are three common objections to action research. First, action research is wasteful because it perennially reinvents the wheel. Second, action research is rarely of high enough quality to be published. Third, a teacher's job is to teach, not to do research.

The fact that action research is seen as a marginalized type of inquiry and is undervalued by the research community is a sad reality. Indeed, our second language acquisition theories would be much better constructed if they took into consideration the realities of language learning, contributed to by classroom research at different levels across various contexts. Furthermore, our second language acquisition research methods would find greater potential in classrooms if we promoted the status of action research to a higher level by equipping teacher-researchers with multiple methodological options. The word *action* does not define the nature of research. Instead, it implies that all other research methods are *actionless*. This has two possible implications. First of all, if only action research has action, then no other research methods can change pedagogical practice. Second, by labelling this type of classroom research as action rather than research in itself, it implies that the nature of the research is pedagogical only, and does not contribute to the theoretical knowledge base. Both of these implications are misleading and do a disservice to research as a whole, for just as experimental research can improve pedagogical practice and therefore inspire action, so-called action research can generate knowledge to strengthen the social constructions of theories. Therefore, we believe that the field should not treat action research as a research *method*, such as experimental research, survey research, or case study; instead, action research should be viewed as a *methodological option*, such as interpretive/naturalistic inquiry or critical/emancipatory option. The goal of action research as a methodological option in language classrooms is therefore to improve pedagogical praxis and enhance language learning.

Three cases

In this section, we will use three studies that one of the authors conducted as a classroom teacher in both EFL and ESL contexts (Liu, 1988, 1998, 2000) to illustrate how action research can be considered as a methodological option rather than a research method in conducting language classroom research. Each case will be described in terms of (a) the teaching context, (b) the problems encountered, (c) the methodological option chosen, (d) the research methods and techniques used, and (e) the main results of the study.

Case 1

1   *Context:* This study was conducted in a Chinese middle school in a large city from September 1984 to July 1985, when the teacher-researcher taught beginning English to a junior class (n = 45). Prior to 2000, students in China usually began formal English instruction at the age of 14 when they entered middle school. As a required school subject, English is taught five hours a week, with one hour each day. Textbooks are centralized with pattern drills and are gradually replaced by selected classic literature pieces with word studies. There are 40 to 50 students in a class. As a daily routine the teacher uses the audiolingual method combined with grammar translation – a typical scenario of English teaching in China in the late 1970s and early 1980s.

2   *Problem:* Large class size, centralized textbooks and college exam system, lack of teacher training, and the prevalence of traditional teaching methods produce learners who are good at grammar and reading and yet incompetent in communication. No matter how enthusiastic many students appear to be in English classes taught through mechanical repetition and word-for-word translations, problems such as the lack of motivation and the absence of meaningful communication and creative classroom activities exist. To

many Chinese middle school students, learning English becomes a tedious task rather than an enjoyment.

3 *Methodological options:* The goal as a classroom teacher was to enhance students' motivation in learning English by using the non-traditional teaching method, Suggestopedia (Lozanov, 1978), the then-fashionable language teaching method, and to improve the overall quality of language learning by providing opportunities for students to use English while learning English usage. This twofold goal prompted the researcher to choose action research as the methodological option since it allowed the researcher to change his teaching praxis to improve students' English learning by addressing a series of related research questions: how does Suggestopedia as an innovative method motivate students, improve their vocabulary learning and retention, and help their communication skills in English? What are the differential effects of Chinese music versus baroque music on students' vocabulary acquisition and retention? Is there a correlation between students' personalities and types of music on their vocabulary learning and retention?

4 *Research methods/techniques:* To address these questions within an action research methodological option, the researcher used a series of quasi-experimental research designs at the method level as he could not randomly select subjects, a constraint all classroom teachers face. But he could manipulate variables within the classroom setting and verify treatments among small groups within the class to see the differential effects of variables/treatments on students in the course of their study to determine better ways of teaching in the subsequent classes. Three major suggestopedic factors (background music, environmental suggestion, and physical relaxation) were built into the daily lesson plans. Emphasis was laid on students' vocabulary learning and retention, and daily communication under different musical treatments (types, styles, steps, and volumes) coupled with the adjustment of light and relaxation exercises. In conducting this year-long study, he used observation, descriptive statistics, journal writing, and interviews as the main research techniques.

5 *Main results:* Students in this class demonstrated high motivation and interest in learning English, as evidenced in seven students' choosing English as their college major upon graduation from high school. Their retention of new vocabulary was about 20 per cent higher than that of students in three other classes serving as comparison groups, which in turn demonstrates the collaborative effort needed in action

research as a methodological option (Burns, 1999). Results indicate that students' memory and retention of new words was affected by different musical treatments, especially the types of music. The use of ancient Chinese music had a similar effect on the learning of vocabulary as did baroque music, and it was thus asserted that baroque and other types of Western classical music are not the only types effective in a Suggestopedia class. The study also revealed that students with different temperaments reacted differently to various musical treatments.

Case 2

1   *Context:* This study was conducted in the autumn of 1994 in an intermediate graduate ESL composition course. International graduate students at a large research university in the Midwest of the United States were required to take a one-hour placement exam upon enrolment. Based on their writing, which was holistically evaluated by the trained ESL composition staff, these students were placed at three levels: low-intermediate, intermediate, and advanced. Only a small percentage of these students were exempted from taking any of these courses. Twelve students representing seven countries were required to write three papers (an extended definition paper, a problem-solution paper, and a data analysis paper) over the 10-week quarter.

2   *Problem:* Based on the researcher's prior teaching experience in the same course, he found that students at this level in general liked both peer review and one-on-one tutorial activities. However, in doing peer review activities, students often felt uncertain as to whether the comments made by their peers were accurate, and their insecurity led to a lack of enthusiasm towards this activity. Meanwhile, without the presence of the instructor, some students came to peer review sessions underprepared, thus seriously hindering the mutual exchange of comments. One-on-one tutorials, on the other hand, were very time-consuming, and many students would revise their papers based on their teachers' comments in the tutorial without questioning. Although their revised papers were much improved, the same mistakes occurred in their later papers.

3   *Methodological options:* The goal as classroom teacher-researcher was to find an efficient way to maximize students' benefits from peer review activities. Such a goal was in agreement with action research as a methodological option. The change he made in

teaching was to combine peer review activities with one-on-one tutorials, and the focus of the research was to see the effects of the teacher's presence on students' peer review activities with the following research questions: what effect does peer review with the instructor have on students' revisions of their papers? Does peer review with the instructor help students' revisions better than two activities conducted separately? Does the presence of the instructor in peer review activities enhance or inhibit students' participation and engagement in the peer review activity? What are the students' perceptions towards peer review before and after their experience with the peer review activity?

4   *Research methods/techniques:* The research method he chose to address the above questions was a multiple-group case study, and he used participant observation, interviews, textual analysis, and questionnaires as the main techniques for this study. To integrate tutorials with peer reviews, he divided the 12 students in this class into four groups. Each group had a chance to do peer review activities with his presence between their first and second drafts of each of the three major assignments for the course. When he participated in the peer review activities, the teacher-researcher assumed the role of a peer by completing the written comments prior to the peer review activities, by asking questions and raising issues for discussion, and by offering his opinion whenever appropriate. Instead of dominating their discussion, he had each group select a leader to facilitate the discussion of each other's papers. However, the teacher-researcher's role as the teacher was also available when there was a need for confirmation, clarification, or explanation.

5   *Main results:* Both follow-up interviews and surveys revealed that there were three major reasons why students liked peer review with the instructors: first, students could get rich and diverse feedback from both peers and the instructor at the same time; second, they felt secure and confident in assessing their peers' comments with the teacher's presence and/or confirmation; and third, they felt more efficient in time management in their revision. As a participant observer, the teacher-researcher noticed that the combination of the two activities not only held students accountable for the entire process of peer review (e.g. pre-reading of peers' papers, competing the written comments, exchanging opinions and negotiating meanings, and raising consciousness about their own writing through critiquing others' papers), but also improved the overall quality of their writing.

Case 3

1   *Context:* This study was conducted in an intermediate-level
undergraduate ESL composition class at a large research university in
the Midwest, USA. The majority of undergraduate students whose L1
was not English were required to take one of the three ESL writing
courses (low-intermediate, intermediate, and advanced) based on
their writing performance on a placement test upon enrolment at the
university. In the winter quarter of 1997, the teacher-researcher taught
14 ESL students at the aforementioned university in an intermediate-
level class designed to improve writing skills through literature.
The materials chosen for reading, which served as the primary
sources for students' writing, were mainly short stories, personal
anecdotes, familiar essays, and the like. The rationale was to enhance
the students' abilities to reflect upon, evaluate, revise, and value
their own writing and gain deeper insight into their reading while
completing a wide range of reading/writing tasks.

2   *Problems:* As the main purpose of this course was to improve
students' writing through reading literature, the students had a heavy
reading load. While reading journals and portfolios were required to
help them keep track of their reading, they could still get by without
being fully engaged in reading and in class discussion. Many students
were not motivated in reading literature as they did not see the
immediate connection between literature and their intended majors.
It was thus a challenge for teachers to bring the literature alive to
stimulate the students' enthusiasm for and response to the selected
pieces for the course through writing.

3   *Methodological options:* The goal of this study as a classroom
researcher was to design a classroom task that would help students
improve their writing through engagement in reading literature.
This, again, positioned the researcher to use action research as his
methodological option as he was trying to justify and implement
a task for the class, to observe the effects of such a task, and to
adjust this task to maximize its effects on learning. The researcher
incorporated Readers' Theater (RT), a dramatic activity to enhance
reading comprehension and writing productivity (Liu, 2000), as the
task, and addressed the following research questions: Does the use
of RT as a pedagogical practice increase student interest in literature?
How do RT activities help student writing? What is the effect of RT on
learner motivation as well as on reading and writing? Does the use of

RT help students produce qualitatively and quantitatively better texts and increase their level of engagement and motivation in L2 reading and writing?

4 *Research methods and techniques:* The research method the researcher used to address these questions was a classroom case study. The techniques he used in this case study included participant observations, reflective journals, portfolios, and discourse analysis. He explored three phases of RT activities with his students for each assignment. In Phase 1, students read aloud their chosen sentences from the source text to generate discussion of the main idea of the text. Phase 2 used student-chosen salient passages to extrapolate individual responses and meaning from the source text. In Phase 3, students created their own conclusions to the text or wrote their reflections on the reading. All these tasks were then acted out in an improvisational setting.

5 *Main results:* RT appeared to be cognitively challenging, socioculturally rewarding, and affectively appealing to students. According to the survey results and student journals, the students saw three key benefits: (a) RT improved language skills; (b) RT encouraged peer collaboration; and (c) RT enlivened the classroom atmosphere. The majority of the students confessed that they wished they had read the assigned readings more carefully, an indication of increased motivation in completing the learning tasks as a result of the RT activities. Textual analysis of student essays revealed not only the increased length of their writing, but also the complexity of their sentence structures and the improved organization of their papers.

What the three cases described above have in common is action research as a methodological option. This is clear from the shared goal in each of the three studies: to change educational practice via a method as in Case 1, or via an activity or task as in Case 2 and Case 3. The classroom teacher acted as the agent for change, and the motivation for change in classroom teaching was usually triggered by careful observation, self-reflection, and the desire for change. By considering action research as a methodological option, the language teacher was free to use whatever research methods (quasi-experiment in Case 1, multiple-group case study in Case 2, and classroom case study in Case 3) to address the research questions driven by the methodological option. In the actual conducting of the study, the teacher-researcher had to rely on the techniques most appropriate for the particular research, such as observation, descriptive statistics, journal writing, and interviews in Case 1, participant observation, interviews, textual analysis, questionnaires in Case 2, and participant observations, reflective journals, portfolios, and discourse analysis in Case 3.

As can be seen from the three case studies above, various techniques can be used across different research methods, while multiple research methods can be used within the same methodological option. When action research is considered as a methodological option, teacher-researchers are liberated to do what they feel more strongly about in their daily practices.

The uniqueness of TESOL research as a methodological option

As seen above, multiple methodological options coexist simultaneously. Some TESOL researchers would argue that a methodological option is chosen based on what kinds of questions are being asked. Others might say that each TESOL researcher has a particular view of the nature of knowledge, and that they choose their questions depending on this methodological stance. We would argue that whether research questions determine the choice of a methodological option, or methodological options dictate the questions one asks, all TESOL researchers should first of all familiarize ourselves with and be aware of multiple methodological options to make informed decisions in the course of doing research while teaching. As TESOL researchers, we should also strive to be reasonably comfortable with such ambiguities, since it is not true that we can do completely unbiased research: the notion that we can examine human behaviour in measureable variables is in itself a bias. Furthermore, the very methodological option we are choosing to operate within is filled with politics and bias.

TESOL researchers need to be equipped with multiple methodological options to assess research possibilities and to formulate appropriate research questions, and to determine research actions given the context, the problem, and the time commitment. We need to be clear about our methodological options, as these are ultimately the tools with which we ask research questions. We also need to identify appropriate research methods to address our research questions and utilize research techniques that match research methods driven by research questions. It is this cyclical process of searching, mapping, matching, doing, and reflexive thinking that makes TESOL research unique.

Pertinent issues in TESOL

Of course, not all TESOL practitioners will become or wish to become researchers. As we explained in Chapter 1, the term *TESOL practitioner* in this book is intended to apply to a range of roles and areas of expertise within the field of TESOL. However, regardless of whether a practitioner is an applied linguistics researcher or an administrator, teacher educator, materials designer, language policy planner, or English language instructor, he or she still needs to be well-versed in the key issues relevant to the field, many of which are articulated and challenged through the discourse of academic research.

An important component of becoming a TESOL practitioner is developing familiarity with the shared discourse of the wider TESOL community of practice (Lave and Wenger, 1991). For example, even though novice teachers may have no intention of becoming researchers per se, it is still extremely important for them to become 'well-informed, critical users of the principles, empirical results, and collective knowledge embodied' in the field (Hedgcock, 2009, p. 146). We also believe that teachers can benefit from being socialized into the discourse of TESOL and applied linguistics scholarship so that they are better able to recognize, utilize, reproduce, and ultimately, to challenge said scholarship. For any TESOL practitioner, 'a vital means of participation involves reading and acting on the field's literature with awareness' (Hedgcock, 2009, p. 147).

With this in mind, the remainder of Chapter 3 will be devoted to pertinent issues in the field of TESOL comprising a body of knowledge shared by many TESOL practitioners. The topics chosen are not exhaustive. Nor is the annotated literature sampled below each topic by any means intended to serve as a complete review of a particular issue. Rather, the following ten topics have been selected because we believe they represent an overview of knowledge that is especially relevant to the global TESOL community today. In other words, we believe that English language teaching professionals in the twenty-first century, regardless of their teaching context, should be aware of certain issues, concerns, controversies, etc., that comprise the ever-evolving knowledge base of the TESOL profession. In order to determine these key issues, we used our findings from a previous study investigating current and future trends in the field of TESOL (see Chapter 1 for a complete description of this study).

For each issue, seven to ten journal articles and/or book chapters have been selected and annotated. Selection criteria for these readings vary according to their respective topics. In most cases, we selected readings that offered a comprehensive, accessible, and/or current treatment of the research topic in question. By *comprehensive*, we mean that a selected reading provides a coherent overview of a particular research area and situates itself within the larger conversation about a particular topic. Texts with complete and articulate literature reviews, especially state-of-the-art articles and book chapters, were particularly helpful towards meeting this criterion. In seeking out readings that were *accessible*, we looked for articles that were comprehensible and less jargon-loaded. Finally, *current* was interpreted depending on the evolution of the topic at hand. In many cases, classic texts are listed but were not reviewed in detail, as we ultimately felt that more recent articles and chapters provided greater scope in tracing the development of an issue under study and also offered a state-of-the-art overview of a topic under discussion. Wherever possible, we have included references to some classic texts as suggestions for further reading on a given topic. At other times, we chose to annotate certain texts that, although somewhat dated, offer a theoretical foundation for readers who may be new to a particular topic, or who lack a thorough and/or historical understanding of its genesis and subsequent development. Regardless, suggestions for further reading are included (both classic texts and more recent ones) for readers who would like to explore a particular issue further.

Ultimately, this section of Chapter 3 has the potential to serve a variety of purposes. Newcomers to the field of TESOL, for example, may use this section to develop their knowledge of the field's key research areas and to seek out literature on said topics in a principled manner. At the same time, a teacher educator may find the annotations helpful in selecting readings for undergraduate or MA TESOL students. More specifically, a programme director who hires non-native English speakers may wish to better educate herself or himself on the NNEST movement and thus find the relevant section below enlightening, while a practitioner recently charged with developing a placement test for his or her language programme may wish to review the literature on testing and assessment.

Communicative competence

The notion of communicative competence originated with Hymes (1972) and was developed further by SLA researchers in the 1980s (see Breen and Candlin, 1980; Canale and Swain, 1980). Defined by Lyons (1996) as 'the ability to produce situationally acceptable, and more especially socially acceptable, utterances, which … would normally be held to be part of a native speaker's competence' (p. 24), communicative competence has often resulted in pedagogical approaches which value speaking and inter-action with native speakers over the established focus on reading and writing, the latter of which traditionally involved a great deal of translation and memorization. Larsen-Freeman and Anderson (2011) suggest that the development of communicative competence occurred when '... being able to communicate required more than linguistic competence ... The shift in focus towards the "real-world" use of language required considering the dimensions of context, topic, and roles of the people involved. In methodology and materials such a new paradigm led to revisiting our view of language and how it is used, how a language may be learned and how it can be taught' (p. 115).

Annotated readings in this section were selected based on their ability to provide a broad but up-to-date overview of communicative competence, particularly its evolution and (critical) evaluation since it was first introduced in the field. Selected readings are intended to offer TESOL practitioners a thorough introduction to communicative competence (its genesis, revisions, and reconceptualizations) as well as a useful collection of resources from which to pursue further investigation into communicative competence. Particularly formative works that are now somewhat outdated have been listed below under 'Classic texts'. Most of these are also referenced in the more contemporary selections below.

Thompson, G. (1996), Some misconceptions about communicative language teaching. *ELT Journal*, 50(1), 9–15

In this article, Thompson lays out four key misconceptions about Communicative Language Teaching (CLT). He suggests that teachers' persistent confusion about CLT is owing to its relatively rapid development and to discrepancies regarding how best to apply the theory underpinning CLT to classroom practice. In defence of CLT, Thompson addresses the following misunderstandings: (1) CLT prohibits the teaching of grammar; (2) CLT involves teaching speaking only; (3) CLT activities are restricted to pair work and role plays; and (4) CLT requires too much of the speaker. This brief and accessible pedagogic article would be suitable for pre-service and in-service teachers who are somewhat dubious about CLT's applications in the classroom. Teacher educators who help to better train their teacher-learners in CLT-oriented classroom practices may be find this article useful as well.

Alptekin, C. (2002), Towards intercultural communicative competence in ELT. *ELT Journal*, 56(1), 5–64

In this article, Alptekin critically examines the notion of communicative competence and argues that in its traditional sense, communicative competence fails to acknowledge English as an international language (EIL) and relies too heavily on unrealistic native-speaker norms within a monolingual target culture. In its place, Alptekin calls for a more intercultural pedagogic model of communicative competence that recognizes learners' need to use EIL in a variety of diverse settings. Such a model would incorporate both local and global contexts into pedagogy and materials, posit bilingualism as the ultimate pedagogic goal, and expose learners to interactions involving non-native speakers (rather than solely native speakers of English). This brief, accessible article is a good start for any TESOL practitioner (teachers in training, pre-service teachers, teacher trainers, material designers, administrators, etc.) seeking a more critical and globally informed perspective of communicative competence.

Leung, C. (2005), Convivial communication: Re-contextualizing communicative competence. *International Journal of Applied Linguistics*, 15 (2), 119–44

This article offers yet another (arguably more thorough than Alptekin's) critical examination of the concept of communicative competence, 'a central doctrine for ELT' (p. 124) which the author considers to be 'the intellectual anchor' (p. 120) for the versions of CLT that are still prevalent today in TESOL pedagogy, materials, and teacher training. Leung offers a history of communicative competence's original formulation by Hymes (1972), followed by an overview of its recontextualizaion into language pedagogy (initially by Canale and Swain, 1980) as an 'idealized pedagogic doctrine' (p. 124). Such a re-contextualization, Leung explains, was accompanied by a shift away from Hymes's original investigation of how meaning-making occurs in local contexts towards a concern for fixed curricula and pedagogic principles. Language content, then, was not derived from ethnographic research of how language is used in specific cultural contexts, but based on imagined native-speaker norms. In his call for a reorientation/reconceptualization of the notion of communicative competence, Leung draws on insights from World Englishes, English as a lingua franca (used among non-native speakers), and more critical approaches to SLA that acknowledge the complex role of 'social'. This article is recommended for its accessible history of the evolution of the notion of communicative competence, as well as its coverage of contemporary insights derived from World Englishes and ELF.

Kramsch, C. (2006a). From communicative competence to symbolic competence. *The Modern Language Journal*, 90(2), 249–52

In her brief contribution to *Modern Language Journal*'s annual column *Perspectives*, Kramsch argues that previously held conceptions of communicative competence are ultimately too narrow for a world in which 'power, status, and speaking rights are unequally distributed and where pride, honor, and face are as important as information' (p. 250). While CLT – as influenced by communicative competence – has historically focused on verbal communicative strategies, Kramsch suggests that 'human communication is more complex than just saying the right word to the right person in the right manner' (p. 251). In order for language learners to participate in an increasingly globalized and multilingual world, they will need to develop *symbolic competence*, a term Kramsch uses to capture the 'subtle semiotic practices that draw on a multiplicity of perceptual clues to make and convey meaning' (p. 251). Thus, the very 'practice of meaning making itself' (p. 251) – beyond mere communication – enters the realm of language pedagogy. TESOL practitioners and researchers who find this article compelling are recommended to read the entire *Perspectives* column from this issue of *Modern Language Journal*. While the column itself is entitled 'Interrogating Communicative Competence as a Framework for Collegiate Foreign Language Study', implications apply to TESOL teaching and learning contexts as well.

Savignon, S. J. (2007), Beyond communicative language teaching: What's ahead? *Journal of Pragmatics*, 39(1), 207–20

In this journal article, Savignon, one of the early promoters of the notion of *communicative competence* in second language scholarship, traces the historical development of CLT in language pedagogy and its relationship to various interpretations of *competence* since the 1970s. Savignon discusses implications for CLT in the light of these developments and in acknowledgement of ongoing changes in technology, the role of English, and an emphasis on localized language learning. She concludes with a sampling of studies that illustrate contemporary manifestations of CLT and suggest the 'dynamic and contexualized nature of language teaching in the world today' (p. 217). This article offers a thorough overview of the significance of *communicative competence* on second language pedagogy today. It also highlights the contextualized nature of CLT and the evolving interpretations of communicative competence today. Savignon's article is recommended for graduate TESOL students, in-service teachers, researchers, and any other TESOL practitioner who wishes to better understand the needs of learners today and the role that teachers play as 'professional decision-makers and theory builders' (p. 218).

Celce-Murcia, M. (2007), Rethinking the Role of Communicative Competence in Language Teaching. In E. A. Soler and M. Pilar Safont Jordà (eds), *Intercultural Language Use and Language Learning* (pp. 41–57). Dordrecht: Springer

In this book chapter, Celce-Murcia presents a revised and updated model of communicative competence that is especially relevant to language teachers (as opposed to researchers in language acquisition or assessment). Celce-Murcia gives a brief overview of the notion of communicative competence since Hymes (1967, 1972) initially proposed the construct as a response to Chomskyan (1957, 1965) linguistic competence, before drawing on previous models by Celce-Murcia et al. (1995) and Celce-Murcia (1995) to propose her revised model of communicative competence, which emphasizes social contextual factors, stylistic appropriateness, and cultural factors (p. 46). The full model proposed by Celce-Murcia includes sociocultural competence, linguistic and formulaic competence, and interactional competence, all four of which are centred around discourse competence (i.e. 'the selection, sequencing, and arrangement of words, structures, and utterances to achieve a unified spoken message', p. 46) and interlocked by strategic competence, which includes strategies related to both learning (e.g. memory-related strategies) and use (e.g. stalling). At the end of the chapter, Celce-Murcia suggests implications for language pedagogy that arise from her proposed model. This chapter provides a coherent overview of previous models of communicative competence, including a helpful figure (Figure 3.1, p. 43) that visually illustrates the chronology of past models, as well as a digestible explanation of the proposed model and the ways in which it revises and elaborates those that came before it. Importantly, Celce-Murcia presents communicative competence in a manner that is relevant to language teachers. This chapter would be appropriate for teachers in training, in-service teachers, and teacher trainers who hope to gain a better grasp of the evolution of communicative competence and its implications for language pedagogy.

Kern, R. and Kramsch, C. (2014), Communicative Grammar and Communicative Competence. In C. A. Chapelle (ed.), *The Encyclopedia of Applied Linguistics* (1–6). Malden, MA: Wiley

In this brief entry in *The Encyclopedia of Applied Linguistics*, Kern and Kramsch suggest that our notion of pedagogical communicative competence is directly dependent on how we conceive of and define grammar. If language is conceived as rule-governed, then grammar will drive communication; however, if language emerges through interaction, then grammar is 'at the periphery rather than at the center of communication' (p. 1). A third relationship the authors pose is non-hierarchical; i.e., grammar and communication interact. Kern and Kramsch discuss the implications of these perspectives on language teaching and suggest a 'broader, multidisciplinary and multilingual perspective on the training of language teachers' (p. 5). Because this article is an encyclopedia entry, it also offers a concise history of the development of communicative competence from an anthropological concept in the 1970s to one that involves intercultural, socio-pragmatic, and/or discourse competence in more recent scholarship. This text is recommended for any TESOL practitioner who would like a more nuanced perspective on communicative competence, including its more contemporary manifestations and reinterpretations.

Classic texts

Byram, M. (1997), *Teaching and Assessing Intercultural Communicative Competence*. Bristol: Multilingual Matters.

Canale, M. (1987), The measurement of communicative competence. *Annual Review of Applied Linguistics*, 8(1), 67–84.

Canale, M. and Swain, M. (1980), Theoretical bases of communicative approaches to second language teaching and testing. *Applied Linguistics* 1(1), 1–47.

Hymes, D. (1972), On Communicative Competence. In J. Pride and J. Holmes (eds), *Sociolinguistics* (pp. 269–83). Harmondsworth: Penguin Books.

Kramsch, C. (1986), From language proficiency to interactional competence. *The Modern Language Journal*, 70(4), 366–72.

—(1993), *Context and Culture in Language Teaching*. Oxford: Oxford University Press.

Paulston, C. B. (1974), Linguistic and communicative competence. *TESOL Quarterly*, 347–62.

Savignon, S. J. (1983), *Communicative Competence: Theory and Classroom Practice*. Reading, MA: Addison-Wesley.

Swain, M. (1985), Communicative competence: Some roles of comprehensible input and comprehensible output in its development. *Input in Second Language Acquisition*, 15, 165–79.

Young, R. (1996), *Intercultural Communication: Pragmatics, Genealogy, Deconstruction*. Bristol: Multilingual Matters.

Further reading

Chun, D. M. (2011), Developing intercultural communicative competence through online exchanges. *CALICO Journal*, 28(2), 392–419.

Gilmore, A. (2011), 'I prefer not text': Developing Japanese learners' communicative competence with authentic materials. *Language Learning*, 61(3), 786–819.

Hall, J. K., Cheng, A. and Carlson, M. T. (2006), Reconceptualizing multicompetence as a theory of language knowledge. *Applied Linguistics*, 27(2), 220–40.

Louhiala-Salminen, L. and Kankaanranta, A. (2011), Professional communication in a global business context: The notion of global communicative competence. *Professional Communication*, 54(3), 244–62.

Jessner, U. (2007), Multicompetence Approaches to the Development of Language Proficiency in Multilingual Education. *Bilingual Education*. New York: Springer.

Royce, T. D. (2007), Multimodal Communicative Competence in Second Language Contexts. In T. D. Royce and W. L. Bowcher (eds), *New Directions in the Analysis of Multimodal Discourse* (pp. 361–89). Mahwah, NJ: Lawrence Erlbaum.

Affective variables

Any experienced language teacher knows that learners' cognitive ability is not the sole factor in determining whether that learner will achieve success in the language classroom, and even less so as a language user outside of the classroom. Similarly, most teachers recognize that learners have diverse experiences in the classroom and learn differently from one another.

The term individual differences (IDs) is used in applied linguistics research to refer to the idea that 'each individual person comprises a unique combination of aspects that might determine learning outcomes' (Murphey and Falout, 2013). While early SLA research of IDs focused primarily on learners' innate cognitive abilities (e.g. Carroll and Sapon, 1959) and (presumably) fixed personality traits (e.g. Taylor et al., 1969), Gardner and Lambert (1972) were among the first to acknowledge the role of emotional and affective variables in successful language learning. Since then, SLA researchers have continued to view IDs as more dynamic and interdependent, at the same time that they have begun to explore the role of sociocultural factors in language learning (Murphey and Falout, 2013).

In this section, we discuss affective variables rather than individual differences, because we believe that the former better capture the degree to which learner experience is variable and dependent on a variety of non-fixed, non-cognitive environmental or situational factors. The texts below were selected for their overview of affective variables that have been demonstrated to influence language learning; these include motivation, identity, investment, anxiety, preferred learning style, and learning strategies, among others. For the sake of prioritizing the most current scholarship for annotation, some classic texts have been included as suggestions for further reading.

Norton, B. (1995), Social identity, investment, and language learning. *TESOL Quarterly*, 29 (1), 9–31

In this article, Norton suggests that SLA replace the notion of *motivation* with *investment*, as the latter better 'capture[s] the complex relationship of language learners to the target language and their sometimes ambivalent desire to speak it' (p. 9). Writing from a critical social theory and poststructuralist perspective, Norton argues that the field of SLA needs to better acknowledge the degree to which power relations have an effect on both language learning and the nature of interaction between L2 speakers and native speakers of the target language. Furthermore, Norton advocates for a reconceptualization of the individual in SLA research, recommending instead the notion of *social identity*, which encompasses both the language learner and his or her learning context. This article provides a valuable critical perspective for graduate TESOL students, practitioners, and researchers who are interested in affective variables and wish to better understand the complex social, historical, and cultural dimensions that contribute to language learning, learner identity, and a learner's relationship to the target language.

Cohen, M. and Dörnyei, Z. (2002), Focus on the Language Learner: Motivation, Styles and Strategies. In N. Schmidt (ed.), *An Introduction To Applied Linguistics* (pp. 170–90). London: Edward Arnold

This book chapter provides a comprehensive summary and literature review of learner style preferences, learning strategies, and motivation. The three individual differences are presented as interrelated variables that intersect to influence learning in unique ways. The authors discuss their pedagogical implications and suggest steps for both style- and strategies-based instruction. A self-assessment activity is also provided to aid readers in determining their own learning style. This book chapter would offer pre-service teachers and novice graduate students a thorough introduction to the notion of individual differences in the language classroom. It may also be illuminating for in-service instructors who wish to better understand the role of affective variables in language learning.

Dörnyei, Z. (2003), Attitudes, orientations, and motivations in language learning: Advances in theory, research, and applications. *Language Learning*, 53 (Supplement 1), 3–32

This article provides a 'big picture' of research into the influence of motivation in L2 learning. Dörnyei discusses the social dimension of L2 learning and offers an overview of Gardner's motivation theory, as well numerous alternative theories to motivation, including self-determination theory, attribution theory, goal theories, and investigations into the neurobiology of L2 motivation. Dörnyei also recognizes more situated approaches to classroom L2 motivation and explains how the dynamic nature of L2 motivation has led to more process-oriented approaches to the study of L2 motivation. In addition to suggesting several educational implications of research into L2 classroom motivation, Dörnyei expresses a need for greater integration between L2 motivation research and SLA. Because of its broad coverage, this article offers an accessible overview of the various approaches to the study of L2 motivation for graduate TESOL students, in-service teachers, and/or researchers interested in motivation.

Rivera-Mills, S. V. and Plonsky, L. (2007), Empowering students with language learning strategies: A critical review of current issues. *Foreign Language Annals*, 40, 535–48

This journal article critically reviews a range of research literature that has investigated language learning strategies in second language acquisition. The authors separate their analysis into three categories of research that have addressed this topic: research about types of learning strategies, strategies training and learner autonomy, and other factors related to strategies (e.g. gender, proficiency level, etc.). In their conclusion, Rivera-Mills and Plonsky offer implications for second language pedagogy and offer specific suggestions for instructors who wish to better reflect the field's knowledge about learning strategies in their own practice. This article is recommended for graduate TESOL students, in-service teachers, and researchers who wish to gain a more complete understanding of learner strategies and the breadth of research that has explored this topic in the field of SLA and TESOL.

Dörnyei, Z. (2007), Creating a Motivating Classroom Environment. In J. Cummins and C. Davison (eds), *International Handbook of English Language Teaching* (vol. 2) (pp. 719–31). New York: Springer

This chapter draws on interdisciplinary research to investigate what creates a motivating language classroom. As Dörnyei explains, the basic assumption of his chapter is that 'long-term, sustained learning ... cannot take place unless the educational context provides ... sufficient inspiration and enjoyment to build up continuing motivation in the learners' (p. 719). Dörnyei offers a review of research to suggest how cultivating such inspiration in the classroom is possible when language teachers consciously intervene to enhance learner *motivation*. This chapter is appropriate for in-service teachers, teachers in training, and other TESOL practitioners concerned with the role of motivation in L2 learning. Teacher educators may also find it instructive.

Horwitz, E. K., M. Tallon and H. Luo (2009), Foreign Language Anxiety. In J. C. Cassady (ed.), *Anxiety in Schools: The Causes, Consequences, and Solutions for Academic Anxieties*. New York: Peter Lang

Though this book chapter is specific to foreign language anxiety (FLA), it provides a comprehensive introduction to the reality that anxiety has the potential to inhibit the learning and/or use of a foreign (or second) language. After explaining what FLA is, the authors proceed to discuss the various causes of FLA and ways that language educators and administrators might go about reducing learners' anxiety. This chapter is accessible enough to be appropriate for graduate TESOL students, in-service teachers, and programme administrators who are interested in learning more about the role of anxiety as an affective variable in language learning; however, the authors' thorough inclusion of literature throughout would make this chapter useful to researchers new to this topic as well.

Block, D. (2009), *Second Language Identities*. London: Continuum

This book examines learner identity as a key variable in second language learning. Block provides an overview of research in L2 identity from the latter half of the twentieth century until 2009, ultimately arguing that identity, like learning, is context-dependent and socially constructed. Drawing on theory from the social sciences, Block also re-examines and evaluates research focusing on the L2 identity of adult migrants, foreign language learners, and study abroad learners, specifically. The topic of this book would be of interest to any TESOL practitioner or researcher who wishes to better understand the dynamic nature of identity in language learning and how language learners' experiences can influence their learning. *Second Language Identities* would be particularly appropriate for graduate students of TESOL, in-service teachers, programme administrators, and teacher educators.

Benson, P. (2013), *Teaching and researching autonomy* (2nd edn). Abingdon: Routledge

This accessible and easily navigable resource defines, explores, and problematizes the construct of learner autonomy, loosely defined by Benson as learners' capacity to take charge of their own learning (p. 2). In addition to examining the effectiveness of practices frequently used to foster learner autonomy, *Teaching and researching autonomy* investigates the origins of learner autonomy, discusses directions for future research, and offers several case studies of action research conducted with the aim of better understanding learner autonomy. A final section provides resources for teachers and researchers. This book is recommended for TESOL graduate students, researchers, and other practitioners interested in learner autonomy as a necessary condition for successful language learning. In-service teachers especially will find the author's emphasis on the importance of action research for understanding learner autonomy to be refreshing.

Classic texts

Brown, H. D. (1973), Affective variables in second language acquisition. *Language Learning*, 23(2), 231–44.
Crookes, G. and Schmidt, R. W. (1991), Motivation: Reopening the research agenda. *Language Learning*, 41, 469–512.
Gardner, R. (1985), *Social Psychology and Second Language Learning: The Role of Attitude and Motivation*. London: Edward Arnold.
Gardner, R. C. and Lambert, W. E. (1959), Motivational variables in second language acquisition. *Canadian Journal of Psychology*, 13, 266–72.
—(1972), *Attitudes and Motivation in Second Language Learning*. Rowley, MA: Newbury House.
Melvin, B. S. and Stout, D. S. (1987), Motivating Language Learners Through Authentic Materials. In W. Rivers (ed.), *Interactive Language Teaching* (pp. 44–56). New York: Cambridge University Press.
Peirce, B. N. (1995), Social identity, investment, and language learning. *TESOL Quarterly*, 29(1), 9–31.
Ramage, K. (1991), Motivational factors and persistence in second language learning. *Language Learning*, 40(2), 189–219.

Rubin, J. (1975), What the 'good language learner' can teach us. *TESOL Quarterly*, 41–51.

Scovel, T. (1978), The effect of affect on foreign language learning: A review of the anxiety research. *Language Learning*, 28(1), 129–42.

Further reading

Brophy, J. (1998), *Motivating Students to Learn*. New York: McGraw-Hill.

Brown, S., Armstrong, S. and Thompson, G. (1998), *Motivating Students*. London: Kogan Page.

Chambers, G. (1999), *Motivating Language Learners*. Bristol: Multilingual Matters.

Dörnyei, Z. (2001a). *Motivational Strategies in the Language Classroom*. Cambridge: Cambridge University Press.

—(2001b). *Teaching and Researching Motivation*. Harlow: Longman.

Dörnyei, Z. and Csizér, K. (1998), Ten commandments for motivating language learners: Results of an empirical study. *Language Teaching Research*, 2, 203–29.

—(2002), Some dynamics of language attitudes and motivation: Results of a longitudinal nationwide survey. *Applied Linguistics*, 23, 421–62.

Dörnyei, Z. and Skehan, P. (2003), Individual Differences in Second Language Learning. In C. J. Doughty and M. H. Long (eds), *The Handbook of Second Language Acquisition* (pp. 589–630). Malden, MA: Blackwell.

Ehrman, M. (1996), An Exploration of Adult Language Learner Motivation, Self-efficacy, and Anxiety. In R. Oxford (ed.), *Language Learning Motivation: Pathways to the New Century* (pp. 81–103). Honolulu, HI: University of Hawai'i Press.

Gardner, R. C. (2001), Integrative Motivation and Second Language Acquisition. In Z. Dörnyei and R. Schmidt (eds), *Motivation and Language Acquisition* (pp. 1–19). Honolulu, HI: University of Hawai'i Press.

—(2010), *Motivation and Second Language Acquisition: The Socio-Educational Model*. New York: Peter Lang.

Gardner, R. C. and Tremblay, P. F. (1994), On motivation, research agendas, and theoretical frameworks. *The Modern Language Journal*, 78, 359–68.

Grabe, W. (2009), Motivation and reading. In W. Grabe (ed.), *Reading in a Second Language: Moving from Theory to Practice* (pp. 175–93). New York: Cambridge University Press.

Hadfield, J. (2013), A Second Self: Translating Motivation Theory into Practice. In T. Pattison (ed.), *IATEFL 2012: Glasgow Conference Selections* (pp. 44–7). Canterbury: IATEFL.

Koromilas, K. (2011), Obligation and motivation. *Cambridge ESOL Research Notes*, 44, 12–20.

Lamb, M. (2004), Integrative motivation in a globalizing world. *System*, 32, 3–19.

Lamb, T. (2009), Controlling Learning: Learners' Voices and Relationships Between Motivation and Learner Autonomy. In R. Pemberton, S. Toogood and A. Barfield (eds), *Maintaining Control: Autonomy and Language Learning* (pp. 67–86). Hong Kong: Hong Kong University Press.

MacIntyre, P. D. (2002), Motivation, Anxiety and Emotion in Second Language Acquisition. In P. Robinson (ed.), *Individual Differences and Instructed Language Learning* (pp. 45–68). Amsterdam: John Benjamins.

MacIntyre, P. D., MacMaster, K. and Baker, S. C. (2001), The Convergence of Multiple Models of Motivation for Second Language Learning: Gardner, Pintrich, Kuhl, and McCroskey. In Z. Dörnyei and R. Schmidt (eds), *Motivation and Language Acquisition* (pp. 461–92). Honolulu, HI: University of Hawai'i Press.

Noels, K., Pelletier, L., Clement, R., et al. (2000), Why are you learning a second language? Motivational orientations and self-determination theory. *Language Learning,* 50(1), 57–85.

Peacock, M. (1997), The effect of authentic materials on the motivation of EFL learners. *ELT Journal,* 51(2), 144–56.

Ushioda, E. (2008), Motivation and Good Language Learners. In C. Griffiths (ed.), *Lessons from Good Language Learners* (pp. 19–34). Cambridge: Cambridge University Press.

Wachob, P. (2006), Methods and materials for motivation and learner autonomy. *Reflections on English Language Teaching,* 5(1), 93–122.

Wu, X. (2003), Intrinsic motivation and young language learners: The impact of the classroom environment. *System,* 31, 501–17.

Xu, H. and Jiang, X. (2004), Achievement motivation, attributional beliefs, and EFL learning strategy use in China. *Asian Journal of English Language Teaching,* 14, 65–87.

Yung, K. W. H. (2103), Bridging the gap: Motivation in year one EAP classrooms. *Hong Kong Journal of Applied Linguistics,* 14(2), 83–95.

The role of grammar

Many novice TESOL instructors in teacher training courses balk at the first mention of grammar. This is because many non-experts still conceive of grammar as a memorized list of rules for piecing together a language, in part due to the nearly 200-year dominance of the grammar-translation method (which prioritized learning the explicit grammar rules of the target language). Beginning in the latter half of the twentieth century, however, pedagogical approaches to the teaching of grammar began to take more inductive approaches, under the assumption that learners discovering patterns for themselves would ultimately be more meaningful than having pattern-based rules handed down to them by a teacher. Communicative language teaching especially emphasized a move away from grammar towards authentic language use both inside and outside the classroom. That said, the realization that some grammatical errors made by learners need to be explicitly addressed in order to avoid fossilization has led to a renewal of interest in grammar pedagogy, one that still prioritizes meaningful, communicative approaches to language teaching.

Each annotated text below was chosen for its specific relevance to TESOL instructors. Though some contain original research, or comprehensive reviews of research, the central criterion for selecting a journal or book chapter was its potential for pedagogical application. Still, we were careful to select article, books, and book chapters that reflect the most current research regarding grammar in TESOL, aspects of which include a focus on description (over prescription) and an acknowledgement of the integration of vocabulary and grammar.

Celce-Murcia, M. and Larsen-Freeman, D. (1999), *The Grammar Book: An ESL/EFL Teacher's Course* (2nd edn). Boston, MA: Heinle and Heinle

A well-known textbook and/or reference of the English language for teachers of English, *The Grammar Book: An ESL/EFL Teacher's Course* divides grammatical description and pedagogical suggestions into three sections pertaining to the dimensions of Form, Meaning, and Use. Celce-Murcia and Larsen-Freeman address grammatical phenomena at the morphological, syntactic, and discourse level, while offering a variety of examples and explanations to illustrate and clarify the linguistic descriptions throughout. The end of each chapter includes a bibliography, as well as exercises for users to practise the concepts they learn in the book. A chapter devoted to introducing the metalinguistic terminology used when discussing grammar makes this book especially useful for English language teachers in training; however, *The Grammar Book* would also be beneficial to current language teachers and may even serve as a helpful reference for advanced English language learners.

Biber, D., Johansson, S., Leech, G., et al. (1999), *Longman Grammar of Spoken and Written English*. Harlow: Longman

This corpus-based, descriptive reference grammar serves as a thorough reference of the English language for teachers, researchers, textbook creators, and language testing specialists. Based on an extensive corpus-investigation of the Longman Spoken and Written English Corpus, the *Longman Grammar of Spoken and Written English* reports the distribution of grammatical structures, tenses, and lexical choices across four text types – conversation, fiction, news, and academic prose – thus helping readers to better understand how certain syntactic and lexical choices are dependent on discourse factors. Authentic examples from actual corpora are provided throughout to illustrate linguistic descriptions. Because this reference grammar would be overwhelming to language students, we suggest the much smaller student handbook, *Longman Student Grammar of Spoken and Written English*, as an appropriate choice for advanced language learners.

Thornbury, S. (2000), *How to Teach Grammar*. Harlow: Pearson Education

This book offers novice language teachers a concise and accessible summary of the arguments for and against grammar teaching, followed by practical advice on three different approaches to teaching grammar: teaching from examples, from texts, and from rules. In addition to illustrative examples and sample lessons, Thornbury incorporates suggestions for how best to integrate grammar into common pedagogical methods, including task-based language teaching. While this book does not present original research, it does offer introductory, practical hands-on training to language teachers in training. We recommend *How to Teach Grammar* for undergraduate TESOL students, in-service teachers, and teacher educators.

Hunston, S. and Francis, G. (2000), *Pattern Grammar: A Corpus-Driven Approach to the Lexical Grammar of English*. Amsterdam: John Benjamins

Pattern Grammar describes the corpus-investigation that led to the publication of Collins's *Cobuild English Dictionary* (1995) and to the *Cobuild Grammar Patterns* series (1996; 1998). Rooted in the concept of phraseology, *Pattern Grammar* explores the linguistic patterns that emerge from research of large corpora and emphasizes the correlations between patterns and meaning, as well as the significance of individual lexical items in controlling the patterns with which they co-occur. Significantly, Hunston and Francis draw no clear distinction between grammar and the lexicon. Both theoretical and pedagogical implications of such a corpus-driven lexico-grammatical description are discussed. *Pattern Grammar* is recommended reading for TESOL practitioners and researchers interested in grammar, corpus linguistics, discourse, and the lexicon. In particular, *Pattern Grammar* is a good example of the ways in which corpus data can reveal insights about language not readily available via introspection or native-speaker intuition. It may also be a useful reference for English language teachers interested in using the *Cobuild English Dictionary* or *Cobuild Grammar Patterns* series with their students.

Willis, D. (2003), *Rules, Patterns, and Words: Grammar and Lexis in English Language Teaching*. Cambridge: Cambridge University Press

This book presents task-based learning as a framework for addressing the link between vocabulary and grammar in language teaching. Examples of the type of language phenomena discussed that suggest a linkage between vocabulary and grammar include lexical phrases, polywords, and collocations. *Rules, Patterns, and Words* also features a separate chapter devoted to the unique distinction between spoken and written grammar, as well as sections on implications for teaching and syllabus design. Pre-service and in-service language teachers will appreciate the various teaching exercises included, as these offer immediate, practical applications of techniques discussed in the book. We also recommend this book for graduate TESOL students, language teacher educators, and programme administrators.

Thompson, G. (2004), *Introducing Functional Grammar* (2nd edn). London: Edward Arnold

This book offers an introductory, novice-friendly approach to Michael Halliday's systemic functional grammar (SFG) model of language, which focuses on the meaning of language in social contexts and treats the lexicon (vocabulary) and grammar as constituting two ends of the same continuum ('lexicogrammar'). Such a functional – versus formal – approach to grammar provides language teachers with an awareness of the broader sociocultural contexts for language use, while emphasizing the meaningfulness of grammar over mere form. Due in part to the helpful exercises at the end of this chapter, *Introducing Functional Grammar* would be especially appropriate as a textbook for graduate TESOL students, though selected chapters would be instructive for undergraduate students as well. In-service teachers and teacher educators new to SFG will also find it enlightening. Individuals interested in reading original Halliday (the most recent edition is Halliday and Matthiessen, 2004) might consider *Introducing Functional Grammar* as a 'primer' of sorts to scaffold Halliday's more challenging work.

Ellis, R. (2006), Current issues in the teaching of grammar: An SLA perspective. *TESOL Quarterly*, 40, 83–107

This article uses an SLA framework to problematize eight key issues pertaining to grammar pedagogy. In attempting to address the issues, Ellis draws on insights from current SLA theory and research and suggests a number of alternative solutions. Ellis concludes his article with a statement of his own beliefs about grammar teaching, including the recommendation that grammar instruction should be taught explicitly while simultaneously being integrated into meaningful, communicative activities that entail attention to form. This article will be of interest to L2 teachers and researchers who question what it means to 'teach grammar', when and how grammar should be taught, and how the distinction between explicit and implicit grammatical knowledge influences pedagogical decision-making. Teacher educators may also find this article to be useful reading in teacher training courses.

Folse, K. (2009), *Keys to Teaching Grammar to English Language Learners: A Practical Handbook*. Ann Arbor, MI: University of Michigan Press

More practical than theoretical, *Keys to Teaching Grammar* is designed for English language teachers who wish to better anticipate, identify, and address the grammar problems of their students. Folse uses actual instances of English language learners' 'errors' to illustrate his intended grammar points and suggested pedagogical strategies. Learners' first-language and proficiency level are explored as potential factors that may allow teachers to predict certain grammatical 'errors' from their students. Folse also includes a contrastive analysis chart identifying common 'errors' that learners of seven different L1 backgrounds might make. A supplementary workbook, *Workbook for Keys to Teaching Grammar to English Language Learners*, which allows readers to practise the concepts presented in the handbook, makes this resource a potential textbook for English language teachers in training.

Liu, D. (2014), *Describing and Explaining Grammar and Vocabulary in ELT: Key Theories and Effective Practices*. New York: Routledge

This book, written primarily for English language educators and material designers, emphasizes the role of language description in the teaching of grammar. In doing so, the author takes a more lexico-grammatical approach to his topic, i.e. he acknowledges the integration of grammar and vocabulary as existing at opposite ends of the same continuum. The first section of the book focuses on specific linguistic theories which impact pedagogical practice (e.g. Systemic Functional Linguistics, Cognitive Linguistics), while the second section addresses how best to put theory into practice and highlights particularly challenging issues in the teaching of grammar and vocabulary (e.g. articles, tense, and aspect). Because of its scope and focus on pedagogy, this book would be appropriate for graduate TESOL students and teacher educators, as well as for researchers who wish to broaden and update their understanding of pedagogical grammar, especially as it relates to vocabulary and to more descriptive approaches to grammar and vocabulary in general.

Classic texts

Canale, M. and Swain, M. (1980), Theoretical bases of communicative approaches to second language teaching and testing. *Applied Linguistics*, 1(1), 1–47.
Chomsky, N. (1965), *Aspects of the Theory of Syntax*. Cambridge, MA: MIT Press.
Ferris, D. R. (1999), The case for grammar correction in L2 writing classes: A response to Truscott (1996), *Journal of Second Language Writing*, 8(1), 1–11.
Halliday, M. A. and Matthiessen, C. M. (2004), *An Introduction to Functional Grammar* (3rd edn). London: Edward Arnold.

Further reading

Carter, R. and McCarthy, M. (2006), *Cambridge Grammar of English: A Comprehensive Guide to Spoken and Written Grammar and Usage*. Cambridge: Cambridge University Press.
Fotos, S. and Ellis, R. (1991), Communicating about grammar: A task-based approach. *TESOL Quarterly*, 25(4), 605–28.
Godwin-Jones, R. (2009), Emerging technologies focusing on form: Tools and strategies. *Language Learning and Technology*, 13(1), 5–12.
Goldberg, A. E. (1995), *Constructions: A Construction Grammar Approach to Argument Structure*. Chicago, IL: Chicago University Press.
Harmer, J. (1999), *How to Teach Grammar*. White Plains, NY: Pearson/Longman.
Hinkel, E. and Fotos, S. (eds) (2001), *New Perspectives on Grammar Teaching in Second Language Classrooms*. Mahwah, NJ: Lawrence Erlbaum.
Keck, C. and Kim, Y. (2014). *Pedagogical Grammar*. Amsterdam: John Benjamins Publishing Company.
Larsen-Freeman, D. (2003), *Teaching Language: From Grammar to Grammaring*. Boston, MA: Heinle & Heinle.
Spada, N. and Tomita, Y. (2010), Interactions between type of instruction and type of language feature: A meta-analysis. *Language Learning*, 60(2), 263–308.

The role of technology and online learning

The term technology, when used in reference to its applications in the field of TESOL, can be used to refer to a broad range of technological tools, applications, and innovations. For example, technology in the language classroom may refer to hardware (tablets, electronic dictionaries, cell phones, PCs, interwrite pads, clickers, LCD projectors, etc.), software (Rosetta Stone, Skype, Facebook, PowerPoint, etc.), interactive audio/video tools (podcasting, iTunes U, video blogging, eLuminate, WIMBA, etc.), corpus-based software and corpora (MICUSP, COCA, the AWL, etc.), distance/online learning, and/or CALL-based assessment (E-raters, TOEFL, etc.).

Due to the constraints of time and space, we have selected a handful of texts that we believe constitutes a brief yet broad overview of the following aspects of technology in TESOL. These include Computer Assisted Language Learning (CALL), online language learning, corpus linguistics, digital literacy, second language education, and theoretical perspectives on the role of technology in TESOL. Because of the rapid pace of technological advancement, only relatively recent articles, chapters, etc., have been annotated. For this same reason, we firmly reiterate that these annotations are in no way comprehensive. Readers particularly interested in this topic are encouraged to stay abreast of the most up-to-date technological advances relevant to TESOL by joining special interest groups, attending conferences, and reading scholarly journals that focus specifically on technology and language pedagogy.

Chapelle, C. (2003), *English Language Learning and Technology: Lectures on Applied Linguistics in the Age of Information and Communication Technology* (vol. 7). Amsterdam: John Benjamins

In this collection of lectures, Chapelle explores the intersection of technology and applied linguistics, and, specifically, the ways in which technology is changing the nature and scope of English language teaching. Chapelle reflects on the ways in which data derived from technology-facilitated learning might be analysed from a theoretical perspective, as well as how technology can be used as a tool for research in applied linguistic. Other sections of the book are devoted to potential applications of technology to language learning and language assessment. This comprehensive, book-length collection is suggested for TESOL graduate students, educators, and researchers with a particular interest in the potential for technology in L2 learning from a theoretical perspective. In-service teachers will find the first chapter, 'The changing world of English language teaching', particularly instructive.

Kern, R. (2006), Perspectives on technology in learning and teaching languages. *TESOL Quarterly*, 40(1), 183–210

This article from *TESOL Quarterly* addresses several key issues pertaining to Computer Assisted Language Learning (CALL), in addition to reviewing the literature on computer-mediated communication (CMC), electronic literacy, and telecollaboration (i.e. long-distance collaborations between multiple class-rooms). Kern also discusses the implications of CALL for language teaching and research, suggests directions for future research into technology and second language learning, and encourages readers to reflect on critical issues concerning technology and culture. This article would be beneficial to pre-service and in-service TESOL educators, as well as to TESOL researchers, for its comprehensive and accessible synthesis of the trends and scholarship regarding technology in second language learning.

Warschauer, M. (2007), The paradoxical future of digital learning. *Learning Inquiry*, 1(1), 41–9

In this article, Warschauer suggests that the interaction of social, economic, and cultural factors will influence learning and literacy as much as digital technology. Through his critical examination of popular assumptions about the future of the digital era, Warschauer reveals three paradoxes related to digital learning and (1) *what* is learned, (2) *how* it is learned, and (3) *where* it is learned. This article is recommended for TESOL teachers, language educators, administrators, or material designers who seek a critical perspective on technology and learning which acknowledges the impact of cultural and socio-economic forces.

Reindeers, H. (2009), Technology and Second Language Teacher Education. In A. Burns and J. C. Richards (eds), *The Cambridge Guide to Second Language Teacher Education* (pp. 230–7). Cambridge: Cambridge University Press

In this book chapter, Reindeers takes on the challenge of how best to incor-porate technology education into second language teacher education. In addition to explaining what exactly technology education for language teachers constitutes, Reindeers discusses the various ways that the teaching of technology to language teachers can be implemented and draws on a range of sources to present six key factors that are likely to determine the success of technology education in SLTD. Before concluding, Reindeers acknowl-edges a number of controversies regarding technology in SLTD, and changes that the field will see in the future as the result of advances in technology. The chapter will primarily be of interest to language teacher educators and SLTD researchers, as well to curriculum designers and administrators of teacher training programmes. Graduate students interested in the above roles will also find this chapter enlightening.

Blake, R. (2011), Current trends in online language learning. *Annual Review of Applied Linguistics*, 31, 19–35

This article reviews current trends in OLL (online language learning), an acronym which refers to learning that takes place entirely via the internet, as well as to Web-facilitated and/or hybrid courses that combine Web-based learning with traditional bricks-and-mortar classroom learning. The following three applications of OLL to L2 learning are discussed: computer assisted language learning (CALL) tutorials (i.e. exercises for grammar, vocabulary, etc., including those that provide individualized feedback); social computing (both synchronous and asynchronous communication); and language learning games. This article is suggested for language educators interested in online applications for second language learning, particularly those instructors in teaching contexts where student access to technology is readily available.

Lotherington, H. and Jenson, J. (2011), Teaching multimodal and digital literacy in second language settings: New literacies, new basics, new pedagogies. *Annual Review of Applied Linguistics*, 31, 226–46

In this article, published in the same volume of *Annual Review of Applied Linguistics* as Blake (2011, see above), Lotherington and Jenson provide an overview of the concept of multimodal literacy, which expands the notion of linear, paper-based literacy to include dynamic, multidimensional, and multi-modal (i.e. visual, physical, social, audio, etc.) interaction between diverse participants. The authors also discuss several pedagogical approaches to cultivate digital literacy in second language learning contexts, while acknowl-edging critical concerns currently hindering the successful implementation of multimodal literacy education in L2 learning. This article is recommended for TESOL practitioners with some background in TESOL/applied linguistics research pertaining to literacy and/or technology in second language learning.

Römer, U. (2011), Corpus research applications in second language teaching. *Annual Review of Applied Linguistics*, 31(1), 205–25

In this third article from the 31st volume of the *Annual Review of Applied Linguistics*, Römer reviews the range of both direct and indirect pedagogical corpus applications available to language educators. The former – *direct corpus application* – refers to the actual use of corpora and/or corpus-based tools by students and teachers in the classroom, while the latter – *indirect application* – refers to the results of corpus-based research influencing syllabus and material design (i.e. *what* is taught and *when* it is taught). Römer describes several general and specialized language corpora, as well as a variety of corpus tools and methods (i.e. techniques used to analyse corpus data) currently available. Any TESOL practitioner who is unfamiliar with emerging trends in corpus linguistics and/or the potential for corpus-based tools and methods in the language classroom will benefit from reading this article.

Classic texts

Chapelle, C. A. (1994), CALL activities: Are they all the same? *System,* 22(1), 33–45.

Egbert, J. and Hanson-Smith, E. (eds) (1999), *Computer-Enhanced Langauge Learning.* Alexandria, VA: TESOL.

Jamieson, J. and Chapelle, C. A. (1987), Working styles on computers as evidence of second language learning strategies. *Language Learning,* 37, 523–44.

Nagata, N. (1993), Intelligent computer feedback for second language instruction. *Modern Language Journal,* 77(3), 330–9.

Stansfield, C. (ed.) (1986), *Technology and Language Testing.* Washington, DC: TESOL.

Taylor, C., Jamieson, J. and Eignor, D. (2000), Trends in computer use among international students. *TESOL Quarterly,* 34(3), 575–85.

Warschauer, M. (1998), Researching technology in TESOL: Determinist, instrumental, and critical approaches. *TESOL Quarterly,* 32(4), 757–61.

Further reading

Chamberlin-Quinlisk, C. (2012), TESOL and Media Education: Navigating Our Screen-Saturated Worlds. *TESOL Quarterly,* 46(1), 152–64.

Chapelle, C. A. (2001), *Computer Applications in Second Language Acquisition.* Cambridge: Cambridge University Press.

Crossley, S. A. (2013), Advancing research in second language writing through computational tools and machine learning techniques: A research agenda. *Language Teaching,* 46(02), 256–71.

Ducate, L. and Arnold, N. (eds) (2006), *Calling on CALL: From Theory and Research to New Directions in Foreign Language Teaching.* Computer Assisted Language Instruction Consortium.

Kramsch, C., A'Ness, F. and Lam, W. (2000), Authenticity and authorship in the computer-mediated acquisition of L2 literacy. *Language Learning and Technology,* 4(2), 78–104.

Levy, M. (2009), Technologies in use for second language learning. *The Modern Language Journal,* 93, 769–82

Meskill, C. and Anthony, N. (2010), *Teaching Languages Online,* vol. 6. Bristol: Multilingual Matters.

Prensky, M. (2001), Digital natives, digital immigrants. *On the Horizon,* 9(5), 1–5.

Reppen, R. (2010), *Using Corpora in the Language Classroom.* Cambridge: Cambridge University Press.

Salaberry, M. R. (2001), The use of technology for second language learning and teaching: A retrospective. *The Modern Language Journal,* 85(1), 39–56.

Thorne, S. L., Black, R. W. and Sykes, J. M. (2009), Second language use, socialization, and learning in internet interest communities and online gaming. *Modern Language Journal,* 93, 802–21.

Warschauer, M. (2004), *Technology and Social Inclusion: Rethinking the Digital Divide.* Cambridge, MA: MIT Press.

English as a lingua franca (ELF), English as an international language (EIL), and World Englishes (WE)

Due to the interdependency of a number of social, historical, and cultural developments, of which colonization, globalization, and the internet are key, the role of English in the world has expanded to become the primary language for international communication. In this regard, English serves as an unofficial 'lingua franca': it is frequently used to communicate between non-native speakers of the language, who may never need (or desire!) to use English, and so-called 'native speakers'. In fact, it is universally acknowledged today that the majority of English speakers worldwide are non-native speakers of English. An appreciation of such a reality has surely influenced TESOL in myriad ways, including far-reaching implications in areas such as pedagogy, language policy, syllabus and curricula design, development of assessment measures, standards, definitions of competence, materials development, etc.

Since the 1970s, three overlapping, yet distinct, approaches to acknowledging and addressing the above phenomenon have developed in the fields of TESOL and applied linguistics: English as a lingua franca (ELF), English as an international language (EIL), and World Englishes (WE). For a thorough definition of each, we encourage readers to consult the glossary. Additionally, we have selected and annotated the following texts to help readers new to ELF, EIL, and/or WE develop a better grasp of each at the same time that they better familiarize themselves with the consequent pedagogical applications, common critiques, and implications for language learning and teaching. As before, classic texts and suggestions for further reading are listed as well.

McArthur, T. (2002), *Oxford Guide to World English*. Oxford: Oxford University Press

This reference volume organizes its comprehensive descriptions of English dialects and varieties according to continent and/or region, from Pennsylvania Dutch and Rasta Talk in the Americas to Nepalese English and *gairaigo* in Asia. Throughout, McArthur provides helpful maps and chronologies to explain the spread of English worldwide, both as a universalizing lingua franca and as a potential endangerment to other languages. *Oxford Guide to World English* concludes with a section devoted to exploring current issues in World English, such as political correctness, the status of so-called 'broken' English, English language teaching, and standards. This book would serve as a useful reference to TESOL practitioners interested in better grasping the diversity of English varieties spoken worldwide, as well as to researchers who are particularly interested in one specific World English variety or region of speech. TESOL instructors will be particularly interested in a section in the final chapter entitled 'English teaching: Profession, social service, or global industry?'.

Jenkins, J. (2002), A sociolinguistically based, empirically researched pronunciation syllabus for English as an International Language. *Applied Linguistics*, 23 (1), 83–103

In this article, Jenkins addresses the pedagogical implications of the reality that there are now more non-native speakers of English in the world than native speakers. She sees a need for an established model of English as an international language (EIL) that includes phonological norms, classroom pronunciation models, and a focus on intelligibility for non-native speakers (rather than for native speakers). Jenkins draws on empirical data from interaction between non-native speakers of English to propose the *Lingua Franca Core* (LFC), a pronunciation syllabus based on the notion of achieving mutual intelligibility between non-native speakers while promoting 'regional appropriateness'. In additional to being pedagogically feasible, Jenkins claims that LFC more accurately represents the evolving sociolinguistic landscape of EIL. She concludes her article by suggesting that learners will also need to develop EIL accommodation skills in order to interact with speakers from a variety of L1 backgrounds.

McKay, S. L. (2002), *Teaching English as an International Language: Rethinking Goals and Approaches*. Oxford: Oxford University Press

This book attempts to challenge many of the assumptions traditionally held by language teachers regarding the notion of native-like competence, the goals of English language learners worldwide, and the role of English outside English-dominant countries. McKay provides a thorough overview of EIL and its historical development before problematizing the use of the term 'native speaker' as a standard for competence, and demonstrates that there are clearly more bilingual users of English in the world than so-called native speakers. She continues by devoting separate chapters to issues central to EIL that are likely to be the most important to teachers, including standards, the relationship between culture and EIL, and methodological approaches appropriate to EIL. Because of its emphasis on teaching, we recommend this book for graduate and undergraduate TESOL students, as well as for in-service teachers, teacher educators, and programme administrators.

Seidlhofer, B. (2002), Closing a conceptual gap: The case for a description of English as a lingua franca. *International Journal of Applied Linguistics*, 11 (2), 133–58

In this article, Seidlhofer advocates for the legitimization of English as a lingua franca through description and codification, the latter of which, she argues, depends upon the former. Seidlhofer suggests that, while discussion of English as a lingua franca (ELF), or at least a more informed perspective on the varieties of English spoken globally, has become fairly widespread, neither empirical research nor classroom practice seem to be following suit. Thus, Seidlhofer proposes a research agenda that would include a reorientation in linguistic research to include ELF as a legitimate target for language pedagogy and linguistic research. Both English as a native language (ENL) and EFL could then serve as alternate target languages, depending on contextual appropriateness. Such a research agenda is directly tied to codification of ELF, 'with a conceivable ultimate objective of making it a feasible, respectable, and accepted alternative to ENL in respected contexts of use' (p. 150). Seidlhofer argues that corpus linguistics has the potential to better describe, and thus potentially codify, EFL. She describes an ELF corpus compilation project in progress at the time of her article's publication, the Vienna–Oxford International Corpus of English (VOICE, http://www.univie.ac.at/voice/page/corpus_information). Seidlhofer concludes that the codification that can occur as the result of such projects has the potential to reframe the competence and legitimacy of ELF speakers.

Jenkins, J. (2005a), Implementing an international approach to English pronunciation: The role of teacher attitudes and identity. *TESOL Quarterly*, 39 (3), 535–43

In this brief forum article, Jenkins describes a sampling of findings from a larger research project that investigated the feasibility of English as a lingua franca (ELF) approaches in language pedagogy. As part of her project, Jenkins conducted interviews with highly proficient English language teachers, asking them various questions related to their language background, their identity as non-native speakers of English (NNESs), and language pedagogy. In the current article, Jenkins shares data regarding participants' accent attitudes, the effects of experience on accent attitudes, and the teaching of ELF/EIL. Results indicate some ambivalence on the part of NNES teachers towards their desire to identify as members of an international ELF community, suggesting that earlier assumptions made by Jenkins (2000, 2002) may have been inaccurate. For its accessibility and brevity, this article is especially recommended for both pre-service and in-service teachers who wish to reflect on their own attitudes towards L1/L2 identity, accent, ELF/EIL, and ELF/EIL pedagogy. Readers who would like a more thorough description of this research project are encouraged to read Jenkins (2005b) in *TESOL Quarterly* (see 'Suggestions for further reading' below).

Canagarajah, A. S. (2006c), Negotiating the local in English as a lingua franca. *Annual Review of Applied Linguistics*, 26, 197–218

In this article, Canagarajah highlights the heterogeneity of the English language use worldwide and argues that effective communication is achieved through 'sociolinguistic, pragmatic, and discourse strategies of negotiation' (p. 211), not 'systematized' varieties or norms of uniformity. Canagarajah suggests that the field of applied linguistics should challenge any research construct predicated on homogeneous conceptions of language or of competence. He also argues that English as a lingua franca (ELF) initiatives should do more to acknowledge and accommodate local identities and values. This article is recommended for graduate TESOL students, in-service teachers, and administrators in EIL contexts, and/or researchers who wish to develop or further explore a critical perspective towards English as a lingua franca.

Kachru, B., Kachru, Y. and Nelson, C. (eds) (2009), *The Handbook of World Englishes*, (vol. 48). Oxford: Wiley-Blackwell

This edited book comprises contributions from writers who examine the spread of English worldwide from a critical perspective. Chapters are written by scholars who represent a diverse sampling of the many varieties of English spoken around the world. Importantly, *The Handbook of World Englishes* includes references to English as a lingua franca, global English, English as an international language, etc., thus serving to illuminate and complement the occasionally divergent terminologies and concepts that constitute each inherently limited perspective on the global use of English. This comprehensive and interdisciplinary handbook collection would serve as a valuable resource for graduate TESOL students, in-service teachers, and/or researchers interested in investigating World Englishes and their political, social, economic, and pedagogical implications. Selected chapters may be appropriate for use in undergraduate TESOL courses as well.

Seidlhofer, B. (2009), Common ground and different realities: World Englishes and English as a lingua franca. *World Englishes*, 8 (2), 236–45

In this symposium paper, Seidlhofer suggests that there is less of a contradiction between the World Englishes (WE) paradigm and English as a lingua franca (ELF) than other scholars have previously suggested. While it is true that the two frameworks have emerged out of divergent socio-historical contexts, Seidlhofer argues that they share common ground to the degree that both challenge prior research about non-native Englishes while confronting orthodox assumptions about the 'ownership' of English in a rapidly globalizing world. In this regard, most of the issues central to ELF are ultimately compatible with the WE paradigm. As such, the author recommends that the body of ELF research and its potential contributions to World Englishes research be taken more seriously. This article is recommended for TESOL graduate students, researchers, and other practitioners interested in the congruence of World Englishes and ELF.

Mauranen, A., Hynninena, N. and Ranta, E. (2010), English as an academic lingua franca: The ELFA project. *English for Specific Purposes*, 29 (3), 183–90

This article acknowledges the role that English plays as an academic lingua franca and explains the collection of a corpus dedicated to exploring the use of English in this role, the one-million-word ELFA (*English as a Lingua Franca in Academic Settings*) corpus of spoken academic discourse. ELFA consists of over 131 hours of spoken English academic discourse taken from ELF interactions in which not all participants shared the same L1; in the case of recorded lectures, the dominant speaker (i.e. the lecturer) was never a native speaker of English. A related project, SELF (*Studying in English as a Lingua Franca*), which takes a more qualitative approach in exploring ELF participants' experience of university discourse, is also described. Initial findings from these two projects (ELFA and SELF) are summarized, with reference to the specific articles and edited volumes in which readers can find more detailed information. This article would be a good initial source for TESOL researchers interested in investigating and/or describing the use of English as a lingua franca in academic discourse. TESOL instructors or material developers who work in the field of EAP may also like to read this article in order to better understand the needs of learners who will use English as the unofficial language of academia.

Classic texts

Kachru, B. B. (1976), Models of English for the third world: White man's linguistic burden or language pragmatics? *TESOL Quarterly*, 10(2), 221–39.
—(1986), *The Alchemy of English: The Spread, Functions and Models of Non-Native Englishes*. Oxford: Pergamon.
Pennycook, A. (1994), *The Cultural Politics of English as an International Language*. London: Longman.
Phillipson, R. (1992), *Linguistic Imperialism*. Oxford: Oxford University Press.
Quirk, R. (1969), English today: A world view. *TESOL Quarterly*, 3(1), 23–9.
Wardbaugh, R. (1972), TESOL: Our common cause. *TESOL Quarterly*, 6(4), 291–303.

Further reading

Canagarajah, A. S. (ed.) (2005), *Reclaiming the Local in Language Policy and Practice*. Mahwah, NJ: Erlbaum.
Jenkins, J. (2005a), Implementing an international approach to English pronunciation: The role of teacher attitudes and identity. *TESOL Quarterly*, 39(3), 535–43.
—(2006a). Current perspectives on teaching World Englishes and English as a Lingua Franca. *TESOL Quarterly*, 40(1), 157–81.
Kachru, B., Kachru, Y. and Nelson, C. (eds) (2009), *The Handbook of World Englishes* (vol. 48). Oxford: Wiley-Blackwell.
Matsuda, A. (2003), Incorporating World Englishes in teaching English as an international language. *TESOL Quarterly*, 37, 719–29.
Pennycook, A. (2001), *Critical Applied Linguistics: A Critical Introduction*. London: Lawrence Erlbaum.

Teachers of English to Speakers of Other Languages (2008a), *Position statement on English as a global language*. Retrieved July 8, 2010 from http://www. tesol.org/s_tesol/bin.asp?CID=32andDID=10884andDOC=FILE.PDF

Non-native English speakers in TESOL

Since a pioneer article on this topic in *TESOL Quarterly* (Liu, 1999), numerous articles have been contributed to this growing body of research and topic of interest in the fields of TESOL and applied linguistics. Admittedly, there are more non-native than native English-speaking teachers around the world (Braine, 2010) and it is natural that research has focused on the very teachers who have the most contact with English language learners. On the other hand, after the publication of Medgyes's (1994) original work focusing on NNES professionals, and the establishment of the NNEST Caucus (now an interest section) in TESOL International Association in 1998, NNEST professionals have become more visible in TESOL. Over the last 15 years, there has been a wealth of publications, including a variety of books, journal articles, dissertations, and theses focusing on issues of NNEST professionals.

In the selected annotations, we try to include more syntheses on the issues to capture the broad spectrum of research in this fast-growing area (e.g. Braine, 1999, 2010; Moussu and Liurda, 2008; Mahboob, 2010), and also the impact of NNEST research on teacher development (e.g, Kamhi-Stein, 2009; Liu, 2007). A number of classic research papers on this topic appear in the recommended list.

Braine, G. (ed.) (1999), *Non-Native Educators in English Language Teaching*. Mahwah, NJ: Lawrence Erlbaum

An early response to the issue of non-native English-speaking teachers in TESOL, each of the 13 chapters in this volume is written by a non-native English-speaking scholar in the field of TESOL. Chapters contain autobiographical narratives as well as contributors' discussions of various sociopolitical concerns and their implications for teacher education. Key chapters include 'From their own perspectives: The impact of non-native ESL professionals on their students', by Jun Liu; 'To be a native or a non-native speaker: Perceptions of 'non-native' students in a graduate TESOL program', by K. K. Samimy and J. Brutt-Griffler; and 'Interrogating the "native speaker fallacy": Non-linguistic roots, non-pedagogical results', by A. S. Canagarajah. Edited by the founder of TESOL International Association's first ever caucus for NNESTs, this book was intended to give voice to non-native English-speaking TESOL professionals and served as the impetus for a great deal more scholarship in the field of non-native English teachers. It is thus recommended for non-native English speakers wishing to enter the field of TESOL, as well as for undergraduate and graduate students of TESOL, teacher educators, and anyone else interested in issues pertaining to NNESTs.

Mahboob, A. (2005), Beyond the native speaker in TESOL. *Culture, Context, and Communication*, 30, 60–93

In this article, Mahboob explains how the privileging and mythologizing of the 'native' speaker in TESOL and applied linguistics is a consequence of the Chomskyan paradigm's legacy, which persists even in 'ideological and attitudinal loading' of terms such as 'interlanguage' and 'fossilization' (p. 68). Mahboob examines the assumptions underlying the often cited beliefs that (1) native speakers make better teachers of a language and (2) language students necessarily prefer native-speaking teachers, citing considerable research from the last 20 years that suggests otherwise. Ultimately, this article serves to de-mythologize the native speaker and re-evaluate the historically centralized role of the native speaker in TESOL and applied linguistics, at the same time that it stresses the need for 'professional credentials over linguistic inheritance' (p. 88) in L2 teaching. Mahboob's article is recommended for upper-level undergraduate and graduate TESOL students, as well as for teacher educators, policy developers, and language programme administrators. Researchers in SLA, SLTD, or critical discourse analysis may find the first half of the chapter particularly compelling.

Snow, Don (2006), *More than a Native Speaker: An Introduction to Teaching English Abroad* (2nd edn). Alexandria, VA: TESOL

This teacher guide is premised on the acknowledgement that being a native speaker of a language does not necessarily qualify a person to teach that language. Written from this perspective, Snow's book serves as a practical and accessible guide for native speakers of English who plan to teach EFL abroad. In addition to covering basic issues pertaining to classroom teaching and language skills, *More than a Native Speaker* also addresses cultural considerations in language teaching, common problems that arise in the language classroom, and the potential for culture shock upon moving to a new country. True to an earlier edition's focus on volunteerism, a final chapter discusses the various ways for volunteers to become involved in language teaching. This book would be appropriate for any novice teacher – volunteer or otherwise – who is teaching EFL abroad. Teacher educators who prepare EFL instructors may also be interested in the practical advice that this non-technical guide offers.

Liu, J. (2007b), Empowering Non-native English-speaking Teachers Through Collaboration with their Native English-speaking Colleagues in EFL Settings. In J. Liu (ed.), *English Language Teaching in China: New Approaches, Perspectives and Standards* (pp. 107–23). London: Continuum

In this book chapter, readers are reminded that the majority of English teachers in the world today are non-native English speakers. Liu argues that treating NESs and NNESs as if they exist separately at opposite ends of a spectrum is a false dichotomy that (1) is no longer supported by the academic or professional community and (2) oversimplifies the complexity of language use. Rather, Liu suggests that both NESTs and NNESTS should be considered to have competencies that complement one another. Liu reviews the emerging field of non-native English-speaking teachers (NNESTs), and outlines the unique skills, qualities, and contributions that NNESTs bring to the field of TESOL. He describes three different models for greater cooperation and collaboration between NESTs and NNESTs, and offers teacher development initiatives at the English Language Center at Shantou University as an example. This chapter is recommended for both NES and NNES TESOL instructors worldwide, as well as for teacher educators and TESOL practitioners who work in programme development or administration.

Moussu, L. and Llurda, E. (2008), Non-native English-speaking English language teachers: History and research. *Language Teaching*, 41 (3), 315–48

In this state-of-the-art article in *Language Learning*, Moussu and Llurda make clear that the NNES teacher movement has become a rapidly evolving research agenda in its own right. Through their chronological examination of two decades of literature on this topic, the authors conclude that the so-called NS-NNS dichotomy is a theoretically unsound and intuitive construct based on perceived differences that do not reflect the complexity of conditions or the diversity of language use and expertise by English speakers worldwide. Yet, despite the fact that some native speakers of English may actually be less intelligible in global contexts than well-educated speakers of English as a second language, Moussu and Llurda cite evidence suggesting that some non-native speakers still are not taken into consideration for English teaching positions. The authors conclude by suggesting that more research from a World Englishes framework may be able to further delegitimize the NS-NNS dichotomy. As a thorough state-of-the-art on the top of NNESTs, this article is recommended reading for all TESOL graduate students, researchers, and administrators. In-service teachers who work with NNESTs or who are NNESTs themselves will also find this article valuable.

Kamhi-Stein, L. D. (2009), Teacher Preparation and Nonnative English-Speaking Educators. In A. Burns and J. C. Richards (eds), *The Cambridge Guide to Second Language Teacher Education* (pp. 91–101). Cambridge: Cambridge University Press

In this chapter, Kamhi-Stein discusses the issue of non-native English-speaking teachers from the perspective of second language teacher preparation. Kamhi-Stein offers a brief overview of the research that has emerged regarding NNESTs both in EFL settings and in so-called Inner Circle countries (Canada, United States, United Kingdom, Australia, New Zealand). While research in the former context typically focuses on issues related to the English proficiency of instructors, research in English-dominant countries has more recently addressed issues related to NNES teacher preparation with regard to pre-service teachers' self-perception, identity development, and socialization processes. Kamhi-Stein also discusses various responses to the above research questions within current teacher preparation practices and suggests recent trends that are likely to influence SLTD in general and NNES teacher preparation specifically. This chapter would provide a helpful introduction to the issue of NNESTs in SLTD for undergraduate and graduate TESOL students. Teacher educators and TESOL researchers who are interested in pursuing this research area further will also find its literature review and 'suggestions for further reading' useful.

Mahboob, A. (ed.) (2010), *The NNEST Lens: Non Native English Speakers in TESOL*. Newcastle upon Tyne: Cambridge Scholars Press

In this edited collection, 16 different contributors reflect on issues related to multilingualism, multiculturalism, and multinationalism in TESOL. While the latter are key themes of the book, NNESTs serve as a 'lens' through which both native and non-native English-speaking authors explore theoretical and pedagogical aspects related to diversity in TESOL; these include negotiation of identity, attitudes towards NNESTs, language policy, pedagogical considerations, strategies for NNESTs and NESTs partnership, etc. Throughout, contributors challenge the native-speaker bias prevalent in the field's history and emphasize the need for more contextually relevant, culturally situated practice in the TESOL profession as a whole. This collection – either selected articles or the volume in its entirety – is recommended for undergraduate and graduate TESOL students, in-service teachers, teacher educators, administrators, and any other TESOL professional who values diversity in TESOL and wishes to better grasp the role that NNESTs have to play in enhancing the profession.

Braine, G. (2010), *Non-native Speaker English Teachers: Research, Pedagogy, and Professional Growth.* New York: Routledge

This state-of-the-art book offers a thorough introduction to the NNEST movement and its development as a field of research. Written by George Braine, founder of TESOL International's first ever Non-native Speaker Caucus (now an Interest Section), *Non-native Speaker English Teachers* describes the history of the NNEST movement, offers a summary of the development of NNEST research, discusses the challenges frequently faced by NNESTs, and makes suggestions for the future of the movement, including recommended strategies for NNESTs' professional growth. While *Non-native Speaker English Teachers* would be appropriate course reading in a graduate-level TESOL course, we also recommend this book to any TESOL practitioner who would like a brief, yet thorough, overview of the birth of the NNEST movement and its current status as a significant area of research within TESOL. NNESTs themselves will be particularly interested in Chapter 10, which offers specific strategies for NNESTs' professional development, including academic publication.

Classic texts

Amin, N. (1997), Race and the identity of the nonnative ESL teacher. *TESOL Quarterly*, 31(3), 580–3.

Cook, V. J. (1999), Going beyond the native speaker in language teaching. *TESOL Quarterly*, 33(2), 185–209.

Higgins, C. (2003), 'Ownership' of English in the outer circle: An alternative to the NS-NNS dichotomy. *TESOL Quarterly*, 34(3), 618–44.

Kamhi-Stein, L. D. (2006), *Learning and Teaching from Experience: Perspectives on Nonnative English-Speaking Professionals.* Ann Arbor, MI: University of Michigan Press.

Liu, J. (1999), Nonnative-English-speaking-professionals. *TESOL Quarterly*, 33(1), 85–102.

Llurda, E. (ed.) (2005a), *Non-Native Language Teachers: Perceptions, Challenges and Contributions to the Profession.* New York: Springer.

Medgyes, P. (1992), Native or nonnative: Who's worth more? *ELT Journal,* 46(4), 340–9.

—(1994), *The Non-Native Teacher.* London: Macmillan.

Phillipson, R. (1996), ELT: The Native Speaker's Burden. In T. Hedge and N. Whitney (eds), *Power, Pedagogy and Practice* (pp. 23–30). Oxford: Oxford University Press.

Widdowson, H. G. (1994), The ownership of English. *TESOL Quarterly,* 28(2), 377–89.

Further reading

Braine, G. (2005), A Critical Review of the Research on Non-native Speaker English Teachers. In C. Gnutzman and F. Intemann (eds), *The Globalization of English and the English Language Classroom* (pp. 275–84). Tübingen: Gunther Narr.

Butler, Y. G. (2007), How are nonnative English speaking teachers perceived by young learners? *TESOL Quarterly,* 41(4), 731–55.

Canagarajah, A. S. (1999), Interrogating the 'Native Speaker Fallacy': Non-linguistic roots, Non-pedagogical Results. In G. Braine (ed.), *Non-Native Educators in English Language Teaching* (pp. 77–92). Mahwah, NJ: Lawrence Erlbaum.

Carless, D. and Walker, E. (2006), Effective team teaching between local and native-speaking English teachers. *Language and Education,* 20, 463–77.

Cook, V. J. (1999), Going beyond the native speaker in language teaching. *TESOL Quarterly,* 33(2), 185–210.

Davies, A. (2003), *The Native Speaker: Myth and Reality.* Bristol: Multilingual Matters.

Frazier, S. and Phillabaum, S. (2011/2012). How TESOL educators teach nonnative English-speaking teachers. *CATESOL Journal,* 23(1), 155–81.

Holliday, A. (2013), 'Native Speaker' Teachers and Cultural Belief. In S. A. Houghton and D. J. Rivers (eds), *Native Speakerism in Japan: Intergroup Dynamics in Foreign Language Education* (pp. 17–26). Bristol: Multilingual Matters.

Ilieva, R. (2010), Non-native English-speaking teachers' negotiations of program discourses in their construction of professional identities within a TESOL program. *The Canadian Modern Language Review/La Revue Canadienne des langues vivantes,* 66(3), 343–69.

Kamhi-Stein, L. D. (2009). Teacher Preparation and Nonnative English-Speaking Educators. In A. Burns and J. Richards (eds), *The Cambridge Guide to Language Teacher Education* (pp. 91–100). Cambridge: Cambridge University Press.

—(2014). Non-native English-speaking Teachers in the Profession. In M. Celce-Murcia, D. Brinton and M. A. Snow (eds), *Teaching English as a Second or Foreign Language* (4th edn). Boston, MA: Heinle Cengage Learning.

Kang, O. (2010), Relative salience of suprasegmental features on judgments of L2 comprehensibility and accentedness. *System,* 38, 301–15.

Kubota, R. and Lin, A. (2009), Race, Culture, and Identities in Second Language
    education: Introduction to Research and Practice. In R. Kubota and A. Lin
    (eds), *Race, Culture, and Identities in Second Language Education: Exploring
    Critically Engaged Practice* (pp. 1–23). New York: Routledge.
McKay, S. L. and Bokhorst-Heng, W. D. (2008), *International English in its
    Sociolinguistic Contexts: Toward a Socially Sensitive EIL Pedagogy.* New York:
    Routledge.
Medgyes, P. (1994), *The Non-Native Teacher.* London: Macmillan.
Moussu, L. and Llurda, E. (2008), Non-native English-speaking English language
    teachers: History and research. *Language Teaching*, 41(3), 315–48.
Phillabaum, S. and Frazier, S. (2012), Student perceptions of how TESOL
    educators teach nonnative English-speaking teachers. *CATESOL Journal*,
    24(1), 245–71.
Pickering, L. (2006), Current research on intelligibility in English as a lingua
    franca. *Annual Review of Applied Linguistics*, 26, 219–33.
Soheili-Mehr, A. H. (2008), Native and non-native speakers of English: Recent
    perspectives on theory, research, and practice. *Language Teaching*, 41,
    445–57.
Tsui, A. B. M. (2007), The complexities of identity formation: A narrative inquiry
    of an EFL teacher. *TESOL Quarterly*, 41(4), 657–80.

Teacher education

Teacher education in TESOL has been and continues to be subsumed by the
field of second language teacher education (SLTE), which itself has been
heavily influenced for the last 25 years by the reflective teaching movement,
a movement which, among other things, rejected the false dichotomy of
theory and practice (Lockhart and Richards, 1994; Schon, 1983) (for a more
thorough discussion of reflective teaching, see Chapter 2). On the whole,
the 1990s served as a turning point for SLTE, as the field began to inquire
more about how L2 instructors learn to teach, rather than merely what they
should teach (Freeman, 1998). Thus, rather than reducing teacher education
to the transmission of predetermined skills, SLTE has come to be seen as
an activity, one situated in specific social and cultural contexts, that involves
an individual's gradual socialization into the profession of L2 teaching over
time (see Johnson, 2006, below). Readers will undoubtedly see the trends
described above reflected in the readings below.

    In selecting texts to annotate for this section, we chose not to focus
exclusively on teacher training or preparation – terms frequently used to
refer to what a pre-service instructor initially experiences during structured
coursework and practicum, prior to entering the profession – or on teacher
development, i.e. the ongoing professional development that in-service
teachers participate in over the course of their career. Rather, in this section,
we intend for teacher education to include the manner in which TESOL

instructors are initially trained, as well as the variety of ways in which instructors who have completed pre-service training continue to participate in ongoing education and development. As usual, these annotations are not comprehensive. We encourage readers interested in this topic to explore the classic texts and suggestions for further reading below.

Casanave, C. P. and Schecter, S. R. (eds) (1997), *On Becoming a Language Educator: Personal Essays on Professional Development.* Mahwah, NJ: Lawrence Erlbaum

This collection of personal essays written by language teachers and scholars recounts each writer's personal journey in the process of becoming a language professional. Written as first-person narratives, each of the chapters relates the challenges faced and insights gained by the various authors during their development as language educators. In addition, several chapters offer reflection on critical issues concerning identity and ideology (i.e. power) in language education. Particularly compelling chapters include: 'My professional transformation', by S. R. Schecter; 'Strength from weakness, insight from failure', by T. Scovel; and 'Working on the margins', by C. Edelsky. This book would be of interest to teachers in training, in-service teachers, and teacher educators, as well as to researchers particularly interested in critical pedagogy.

Murphy, J. M. and Byrd, P. (eds) (2001), *Understanding the Courses We Teach: Local Perspectives on English Language Teaching.* Ann Arbor, MI: University of Michigan Press

This collection of edited essays written by in-service language educators includes a description of each instructor's locally situated teaching context, as well as his or her reflection on theory, practice, and pedagogical decision-making within that context. Each chapter is structured around description of a seasoned practitioner's specific teaching setting and the conceptual underpinnings, goals, and objectives of a particular course within that setting, as well as the course syllabus design, activity types, learner and teacher roles, instructional materials produced/utilized, and lesson particulars. Chapters are arranged thematically by course type (rather than by theory or pedagogical technique) into the following four sections: general instruction courses, English as a foreign language courses, credit bearing university-level EAP courses, and non-credit bearing Intensive English Programs (IEPs). In this regard, the focus of the book is on the local particulars of teachers' situated experiences in specific settings, rather than on generic, decontextualized pedagogical strategies or theory. *Understanding the Courses We Teach* would be a valuable resource to both in-training and in-service language teachers, as well as for language teaching educators who hope to better understand the diversity of teaching contexts their students are likely to experience.

Richards, J. C. and Farrell, T. S. C. (eds) (2005), *Professional Development for Language Teachers: Strategies for Teacher Learning.* Cambridge: Cambridge University Press

This book offers a practical focus on 11 different professional development practices for second and foreign language teachers: workshops, self-monitoring, support groups, teaching journals, peer observation, teaching portfolios, analysis of critical incidents, case analyses, peer coaching, team teaching, and action research. Each brief chapter focuses on a different professional development procedure, offering a survey of each, followed by suggested procedures, reflection, and summary. All chapters are interspersed with vignettes from past teachers who have utilized the various professional development strategies. This book is recommended for novice teachers, teachers in training, in-service teachers, and teacher educators, as well as any language education administrator interested in fostering professional development among his or her employees.

Tedick, D. J. (ed.) (2005), *Second Language Teacher Education: International Perspectives.* Mahwah, NJ: Lawrence Erlbaum

Second Language Teacher Education: International Perspective is an edited volume comprising articles written by well-known scholars in the field of SLTE, each of whom combine theory and practice to explore complex issues in SLTE from a variety of language teaching contexts around the world. Chapters are organized thematically into the following sections: the knowledge base of SLTE, contexts of SLTE, collaboration in SLTE, and SLTE in practice. Particularly compelling chapters include: 'Second language teacher learning and student second language learning: Shaping the knowledge base', by E. Tarone and D. Allwright; 'Key themes in TESOL MA teacher education', by M. A. Snow; and 'Preparing preservice teacher for English language learners: A content-based approach', by C. L. Walker, S. Ranney and T. W. Fortune. This book is written primarily for second language educators and/or researchers interested in SLTE.

Johnson, K. E. (2006), The sociocultural turn and its challenges for second language teacher education. *TESOL Quarterly*, 40, 235–57

In *TESOL Quarterly*'s 40th anniversary issue, Karen Johnson explains how a more sociocultural stance in the human sciences has impacted second language teacher education. Rather than viewing learning as an internal psychological process, sociocultural theory 'define[s] human learning as a dynamic social activity that is situated in physical and social contexts, and distributed across persons, tools, and activities' (Johnson, 2006, p. 3). Humans develop as they engage in social and cultural activities; thus, both cognitive and social elements are involved in learning. Johnson's article explores this 'sociocultural turn' in the social sciences and lays out several challenges that the epistemological shift poses for second language teacher education. As a seminal article in SLTD research, we recommend this article to teachers in training, teacher educators, and in-service teachers alike. Researchers interested in SLTD are recommended to read Johnson's book-length treatment of the subject, *Second Language Teacher Education: A Sociocultural Perspective* (2009), which uses the perspective of sociocultural theory as its conceptual basis.

Burns, A. and Richards, J. C. (eds) (2009), *The Cambridge Guide to Second Language Teacher Education*. Cambridge: Cambridge University Press

This book offers a comprehensive overview of core topics, both theoretical and practical, in the preparation and ongoing education of second language teachers. Each of the collection's 30 chapters is written by a different scholar in the field of second language teacher development (SLTD), with contributions from well-known researchers such as Karen Johnson, Donald Freeman, Rod Ellis, Simon Borg, and Kathleen Bailey. Topics covered include language teacher professionalism, pedagogical knowledge, teacher identity and cognition, context, collaboration, and research and practice. The brevity and accessibility of each chapter make this collection useful reading material for teachers in training, in-service teachers and teacher educators alike, while the scope of issues it explores and the suggestions for further reading at the end of each chapter make *The Cambridge Guide to Second Language Teacher Education* a valuable reference for SLTD researchers.

Wright, T. (2010), Second language teacher education: Review of recent research on practice. *Language Teaching*, 43(3), 259–96

In this state-of-the-art journal article, Wright examines how many of the changes in the field of SLTE scholarship that have occurred over the past 25 years (some of which are discussed in the introduction to this section above) are actually influencing current practices. In addition to discussing what constitutes SLTE and reviewing its early manifestations, Wright outlines key trends that have shaped the evolution of SLTE over the last several decades. Focusing exclusively on teacher training, Wright reviews the accounts of several SLTE programmes to determine the degree to which the above trends have guided current practices. This article is recommended for teacher educators, SLTE researchers, and for graduate TESOL students interested in becoming teacher educators and/or SLTE researchers themselves. Administrators who oversee teacher training programmes may also find this article instructive.

Farrell, T. S. C. (ed.) (2012), Special Issue: Novice Professionals in TESOL. *TESOL Quarterly*, 46(3), 435–604

In his introduction to this special issue of *TESOL Quarterly*, guest editor Thomas S. C. Farrell is particularly concerned with the factors that influence L2 teacher retention and attrition, noting that the field could do more to support novice professionals as they move from pre-service training to in-service teaching. As a result, Farrell has selected five research articles, two reports, and a forum paper, all of which are devoted to the experiences of novice TESOL instructors and how they negotiate their first three years of teaching across a diversity of settings. We recommend that graduate TESOL students particularly interested in teacher training and/or second language teacher development choose selected articles from this issue or the full issue in its entirely. Teacher educators and researchers in the field of SLTD will also find this special issue informative, including a provocative forum piece by Chappell and Moore on the need for more linguistic training for pre-service TESOL professionals.

Classic texts

Brown, K. (1993), Second Language Teacher Education. *TESOL Quarterly*, 27(4), 753–6.
Day, R. R. (1990), Teacher observation in second language teacher education. In J. C. Richards & D. Nunan (eds), *Second Language Teacher Education* (pp. 43–61). Cambridge, UK: Cambridge University Press.

Freeman, D. (1989), Teacher training, development, and decision making: A model of teaching and related strategies for language teacher education. *TESOL Quarterly*, 23(1), 27–45.

Freeman, D. and Johnson, K. E. (1998), Reconceptualizing the knowledge-base of language teacher education. *TESOL Quarterly*, 32(3), 397–417.

Richards, J. C. (1987), The dilemma of teacher education in TESOL. *TESOL Quarterly*, 21(2), 209–26.

Richards, J. C. and Crookes, G. (1988), The practicum in TESOL. *TESOL Quarterly*, 22(1), 9–27.

Richards, J. C. and Nunan, D. (eds) (1990), *Second Language Teacher Education*. Cambridge: Cambridge University Press.

Roberts, J. (1998), *Language Teacher Education*. London: Edward Arnold.

Tedick, D. J. and Walker, C. L. (1994), Second language teacher education: The problems that plague us. *The Modern Language Journal*, 78(3), 300–12.

Further reading

Beck, C. and Kosnik, C. (2006), *Innovations in Teacher Education: A Social Constructivist approach*. Albany, NY: State University of New York Press.

Brandt, C. (2006a). Allowing for practice: a critical issue in TESOL teacher preparation. *ELT Journal*, 60(4), 355–64.

Carrier, K. A. (2003), NNS teacher trainees in Western-based TESOL programs. *ELT Journal*, 57(3), 242–50.

Crandall, J. (2000), Language teacher education. *Annual Review of Applied Linguistics*, 20, 34–5.

Freeman, D. (2002), The hidden side of the work: Teacher knowledge and learning. *Language Teaching*, 35, 1–13.

Hedgcock, J. S. (2002), Toward a socioliterate approach to second language teacher education. *The Modern Language Journal*, 86(3), 299–317.

Korthagen, F. A. J., Kessels, J., Koster, B., et al. (2001), *Linking Practice and Theory: The Pedagogy of Realistic Teacher Education*. Mahwah, NJ: Lawrence Erlbaum.

Llurda, E. (2005b). Non-native TESOL students as seen by practicum supervisors. In E. Llurda (ed.), *Non-Native Language Teachers: Perceptions, Challenges and Contributions to the Profession* (pp. 131–54). New York: Springer.

Nemtchinova, E., Mahboob, A., Eslami, Z., et al. (2010), Training Non-native English Speaking TESOL Professionals. In A. Mahboob (ed.), *The NNEST Lens: Non Native English Speakers in TESOL* (pp. 222–38). Newcastle upon Tyne: Cambridge Scholars.

Schwartz, A. M. (2001), Preparing Teachers to Work with Heritage Language Learners. In J. K. Peyton, D. Ranard and S. McGinnis (eds), *Heritage Languages in America: Preserving a National Resource* (pp. 229–52). McHenry, IL: Center for Applied Linguistics.

Snow, M. A., Kamhi-Stein, L. D. and Brinton, D. M. (2006), Teacher training for English as a lingua franca. *Annual Review of Applied Linguistics*, 26, 261–81.

Multilingualism

Today, the increasing interconnectedness of the world due to phenomena such as globalization, transnational migration, and commerce, and advances in technology has led to an increased appreciation of the ability of both individuals and societies to use more than one language in a variety of ways and for a multiplicity of purposes, perhaps even on a daily basis. This reality has resulted in a greater emphasis on multilingualism in education, language policy, and applied linguistics research. Thus, rather than including a section specifically devoted to second language acquisition (SLA) here (which is arguably its own field somewhat tangential to, though certainly overlapping with, TESOL), we have chosen to embrace the notion of multilingualism instead. In doing so, we hope to further a relatively new movement in TESOL, one that reconsiders ways of thinking about language, language learners, pedagogy, and research, based on a traditional monolingual bias (see May, 2013, below).

At its heart, multilingualism is a complex, interdisciplinary phenomenon that can be examined from a variety of perspectives (Cenoz, 2013, below). The texts we have included in this section are in no way representative of the breadth of approaches to multilingual scholarship. Instead, we offer a handful of annotated journals, book chapters, and edited collections that provide a general overview of multilingualism as it is most relevant to the TESOL profession and to relatively recent interdisciplinary trends in multilingualism research.

On a final note for readers new to multilingualism, we feel it is helpful to point out that researchers use the terms bilingual and multilingual differently depending on the perspective of analysis and area of specialization. We encourage readers to consult Cenoz (2013, below) for guidance in teasing apart these terms as they are encountered in the literature.

Cenoz, J., Hufeisen, B. and Jessner, U. (eds) (2001), *Cross-Linguistic Influence in Third Language Acquisition: Psycholinguistic Perspectives.* Bristol: Multilingual Matters

This volume comprises original research that investigates cross-linguistic influence in third language acquisition. The first of its kind, Cenoz, Hufeisen and Jessner's collection explores the interaction between the multiple languages a learner knows or is learning, thus serving to bridge the fields of SLA and bi-/multilingualism. This book will be of interest to TESOL graduate students and researchers interested in SLA, third language acquisition (TLA), psycholinguistics, bilingualism, and multilingualism. It will also prove valuable to TESOL practitioners and administrators who would like for TLA to better inform language policy and curricula development.

Kramsch, C. (2006b). Preview Article: The multilingual subject. *International Journal of Applied Linguistics*, 16 (1), 97–110

In this preview article to her book-length *The Multilingual Subject: What Language Learners Say about Their Experience and Why it Matters*, Kramsch explains her examination of the 'third place' – a space in which linguistic, social, and cultural aspects of a language learner's identity interact. Her notion of the third place highlights the subjective aspects of SLA in the experience of multilingual individuals, with a focus on young people around the world who learn foreign languages as part of their general education. This article, which would be appropriate for graduate TESOL students, offers a preview of the themes Kramsch explores in her body of work, including the mythical and symbolic dimensions of language learning. Readers who find Kramsch's approach to multilingualism compelling are encouraged to read her 2009 book *The Multilingual Subject: What Language Learners Say about Their Experience and Why it Matters* (see 'Suggestions for further reading' below).

Cummins, J. (2009), Multilingualism in the English-language classroom: Pedagogical considerations. *TESOL Quarterly*, 43 (2). 317–21

In this *TESOL Quarterly* article, Cummins challenges the monolingual principle, i.e. a directive to use the target language only in the classroom, and its influence on pedagogical practices in language teaching for the last century. In addition to providing empirical and theoretical justification for eschewing the 'common-sense knowledge' of the monolingual principle, Cummins calls on TESOL International Association to explicitly reject the monolingual practice and to embrace certain bilingual strategies in its stead. This brief article is recommended both for teachers in training and for in-service instructors who may have been operating within the constraints of the monolingual principle for a number of years. Any other TESOL practitioner interested in teacher education, language policy, or multi-/bilingualism will also find this article of interest.

Alptekin, C. (2010), Redefining multicompetence for bilingualism. *International Journal of Applied Linguistics*, 20 (1), 95–110

In Alptekin's article, he advocates for a more usage-based reconceptualization of multicompetence (see Cook, 1991), one that acknowledges the developing linguistic and cultural knowledge of a bilingual speaker and the degree to which both bilingualism *and* biculturalism are involved. Alptekin notes that in English as a lingua franca (ELF) language contexts, there may be no 'native-speaker culture' for the language variety spoken, in which case speakers are more likely to develop a form of multicompetence that essentially synthesizes a 'variety of cultural features interacting with bilingualism' (p. 107). Thus, Alptekin suggests that ELF-situated multicompetence entails bilingualism and multiculturalism; as a result, its implications for norms and appropriateness are necessarily different from those of bicultural (ESL/EFL) multicompetence. This article is recommended for TESOL graduate students, practitioners, and researchers with an interest in multiculturalism, multi-/ bilingualism, and/or ELF.

Aronin, L. and Singleton, D. (2012), *Multilingualism*. Amsterdam: John Benjamins

This book addresses the complexity of multilingualism with significant breadth, focusing not only on linguistic aspects of multilingualism, but also on its social, political, cultural, educational, and psychological dimensions, including the field's historical background and relevant controversies and debates. *Multilingualism* would be appropriate for undergraduate or graduate TESOL students, as well as for researchers new to the burgeoning field of multilingualism. TESOL practitioners and administrators interested in multilingualism as it relates to language policy or teaching English to young learners (TEYL) will also find Chapter 6, 'Language development in multilingual conditions,' of interest.

Bhatia, T. K. and Ritchi, W. C. (eds) (2012), *The Handbook of Bilingualism and Multilingualism (2nd edn)*. Chichester: Wiley-Blackwell

This comprehensive collection contains state-of-the-art research pertaining to bilingualism and multilingualism (or 'plurilingualism,' as the editors suggest for the sake of convenience). Its 36 chapters, written by contributors from an array of scholarly disciplines, are organized into four main sections dedicated to: a general introduction of plurilingualism; the neurological and psycholinguistic aspects of plurilingualism; its social manifestations and effects; and several global case studies that reveal the challenges posed by bilingualism and multilingualism. Undergraduate and graduate students of TESOL are likely to find this last section particularly compelling, as each of the nine case studies provides a contextual framework for observing and describing plurilingual phenomena. As a general reference volume, this book would also serve as a valuable resource for TESOL researchers.

Martin-Jones, M., Blackledge, A. and Creese, A. (eds) (2012), *The Routledge Handbook of Multilingualism.* London: Routledge

This edited collection takes a sociolinguistic – as opposed to a cognitive – approach to multilingualism. Its 32 chapters each investigate multilingualism from a social, cultural, and/or political perspective. In addition to offering an overview of the key themes, controversies, and research developments in multi-lingualism, this handbook critically examines discourses about multilingualism and reports on a range of actual multilingual practices (e.g. code-switching). While most appropriate for researchers and graduate students of TESOL, in-service language teachers, teacher educators, and programme administrators will likely find Section II, 'Multilingual and education', relevant to their profession, particularly Gardner's chapter on 'Global English and bilingual education'.

Cenoz, J. (2013), Defining multilingualism. *Annual Review of Applied Linguistics*, 33, 3–18

This brief article introduces a volume of the *Annual Review of Applied Linguistics* dedicated entirely to topics in multilingualism. Cenoz presents multilingualism as both a phenomenon and an emerging area of interdisci-plinary research. He suggests that discussions of multilingualism should take into account the following three key dimensions: the individual vs. the social, proficiency vs. use, and bilingualism vs. multilingualism. Cenoz goes on to outline various research agendas pertaining to multilingualism (e.g. cross-linguistic interaction, multilingualism as a social construct, etc.), in addition to identifying a trend in approaches to multilingualism that take a more holistic (as opposed to an atomistic) perspective. This article is recommended for TESOL undergraduate and graduate students who are new to the study of multilingualism, as well as for TESOL researchers who may be considering this topic for the first time. Readers are also encouraged to explore other articles in the 33rd volume of *Annual Review of Applied Linguistics* in which this article was published (editor Charlene Polio).

May, S. (2013), *The Multilingual Turn: Implications for SLA, TESOL, and Bilingual Education*. New York: Routledge

This book is written in response to what the editor sees as a monolingual bias in SLA and TESOL to view language learning as a process isolated from the other language(s) a speaker already knows. Furthermore, while so-called 'critical applied linguistics' has already made the multilingual turn, SLA and TESOL (the latter term May uses to refer to the ELT 'industry' as a whole) have not. Thus, the chapters in this book focus on multilingualism in applied linguistics in general, and on the potential interaction of the sub-disciplines of SLA, TESOL, and bilingualism from within a multilingual framework specifically. Chapters feature contributions from scholars including Lourdes Ortega, Suresh Canagarajah, and Bonnie Norton. *The Multilingual Turn* would be appropriate for upper-level undergraduate and graduate TESOL students, as well as for researchers in the fields of SLA, psycholinguistics, or bilingualism. TESOL practitioners and administrators who specialize in bi-multilingual education will also find this collection illuminating.

Classic texts

Cook, V. J. (1992), Evidence for multicompetence. *Language Learning*, 42 (557–91).
Grosjean, F. (1985), The bilingual as a competent but specific speaker-hearer. *Journal of Multilingual Multicultural Development*, 6, 467–77.
Rampton, B. (1995), *Crossing: Language and Ethnicity among Adolescents*. London: Longman.

Further reading

Blackledge, A. and Creese, A. (2010), *Multilingualism: A Critical Perspective*. London: Continuum.
Brinton, D. M., Kagan, O. and Bauckus, S. (eds) (2008), *Heritage Language Education: A New Field Emerging*. New York: Routledge.
Cabrelli Amaro, J., Flynn, S. and Rothman, J. (eds) (2012), *Third Language Acquisition in Adulthood*. Amsterdam: John Benjamins.
Clark, J. B. (2012), Introduction: Journeys of integration between multiple worlds: Reconceptualising multilingualism through complex transnational spaces. *International Journal of Multilingualism*, 9(2), 132–7.
Cook, V. J. and Bassetti, B. (eds) (2011), *Language and Bilingual Cognition*. Oxford: Psychology Press.
De Groot, A. M. B. (2011), *Language and Cognition in Bilinguals and Multilinguals: An Introduction*. New York: Psychology Press.
Ellis, E. (2004), The invisible multilingual teacher: The contribution of language background to Australian ESL teachers' professional knowledge and beliefs. *The International Journal of Multilingualism*, 1, 90–108.

Franceschini, R. (2011), Multilingualism and multicompetence: A conceptual view. *The Modern Language Journal*, 95(3), 344–55.

House, J. (2003), English as a lingua franca: A threat to multilingualism? *Journal of Sociolinguistics*, 7(4), 556–78.

Kramsch, C. (2009), *The Multilingual Subject: What Language Learners Say about Their Experience and Why it Matters*. Oxford: Oxford University Press.

Kroll, J. F., Gullifer, J. W. and Rossi, E. (2013), The multilingual lexicon: The cognitive and neural basis of lexical comprehension and production in two or more languages. *Annual Review of Applied Linguistics*, 33, 102–27.

Li, W. and Moyer, M. (eds) (2008), *The Blackwell Handbook of Research Methods on Bilingualism and Multilingualism*. Oxford: Blackwell.

Ortega, L. (2013), SLA for the 21st century: Disciplinary progress, transdisciplinary relevance, and the bi/multilingual turn. *Currents in Language Learning*, 63, Supplement 1, 1–24.

Pavlenko, A. (2005), *Emotions and Multilingualism*. New York: Cambridge University Press.

—(ed.) (2011), *Thinking and Speaking in Two Languages*. Bristol: Multilingual Matters.

Polio, C. (ed.) (2013), *Annual Review of Applied Linguistics: Topics in multilingualism, 33*.

Schmidt, T. and Worner, K. (eds) (2012), *Multilingual Corpora and Multilingual Corpus Analysis*. Amsterdam: John Benjamins.

Shohamy, E. (2004), Assessment in Multicultural Societies: Applying Democratic Principles and Practices to Language Testing. In B. Norton and K. Toohey (eds), *Critical Pedagogies and Language Learning* (pp. 72–92). Cambridge: Cambridge University Press (annotated in 'Assessment and Testing, below').

Todeva, E. and Cenoz, J. (eds) (2009), *The Multiple Realities of Multilingualism: Personal Narratives and Researchers' Perspectives*. Berlin: Mouton de Gruyter.

Teaching English to Young Learners (TEYL)

While the field of Teaching English to Young Learners (TEYL) certainly isn't new, it has expanded rapidly in the last 15–20 years, both in English-dominant countries, as a result of increased immigration, and in EFL settings (i.e. so-called expanding and outer circle countries), as English for young learners has grown in popularity, and, in some cases, become compulsory (see Liu, 2007, below). As a result, many teachers who have little background in working with children find themselves teaching younger and younger learners. While some principles of TESOL apply to both adults and children, there are unique differences between child and adult learners, cognitively, linguistically, emotionally, and socially.

The sampling of literature offered below is meant to serve as a starting point for novice TEYL instructors, experienced teachers working with young learners for the first time, teacher educators who wish to better prepare their students for TEYL, and for policymakers making decisions about how and when to initiate TEYL. Because the expansion of TESOL to include young learners is not without controversy, particularly in EFL contexts, critical perspectives are included below as well. As always, we encourage readers who are interested in TEYL to investigate further by making use of the 'Suggestions for Further Reading' below.

Marinova-Todd, S., Marshall, D. and Snow, C. (2000), Three misconceptions about age and L2 learning. *TESOL Quarterly*, 34 (1), 9–34

Among other things, this article argues that common conceptions about age and language learning are inaccurate. Marinova-Todd, Marshall and Snow suggest that the varying outcomes between adult and child language learning are more likely attributable to differences in learning situation rather than learning ability or age-imposed cognitive constraints. In addition to examining the missteps committed by researchers and laypersons alike with regard to age and language learning, the authors discuss the implications of their claim for bilingual education and the early teaching of foreign languages, as well as for teachers of adult ESL. This article is recommended for graduate TESOL students, in-service teachers, researchers, and any other TESOL practitioner interested in TEYL, the so-called 'critical period', and the impact of age on language learning.

Moon, J. (2005), *Children Learning English*. Oxford: Macmillan

This practical guide for teachers includes teaching techniques and ready-to-use activities that are both creative and contextually aware. Moon also offers reflective commentary after each activity she proposes, so that readers have the opportunity to consider the affordances and constraints of what they've read in light of their own teaching context. Individual chapters focus on topics such as child language learning, classroom management and interaction, cross-curricular approaches, and assessment, among others. Throughout, Moon includes examples that draw on real-life teaching situations in order to allow readers to relate their own experience to teaching contexts around the world. This book is recommended for pre-service and in-service teachers who are planning to work with children or are currently doing so. In particular, *Children Learning English* would be helpful to teachers who may not have access to SLTD courses and would like an accessible book that allows them to independently further their knowledge of TEYL and repertoire of best practices in the TEYL classroom.

Cameron, L. (2003), Challenges for ELT from the expansion in teaching children. *ELT Journal*, 57 (2), 105–12

This article describes several challenges posed by the expansion of ELT to include teaching English to young children. Cameron cautions against the assumption that more successful learning will occur merely because a child begins learning English at a younger age, particularly in certain EFL contexts in which children rarely encounter the L2 outside the classroom. The implications of two key aspects of child foreign language learning are discussed: the tendency for children to prioritize communicative meaning when they encounter a new language (rather than focusing on its structure); and the fact that young learners rarely begin studying English with fully developed literacy skills in their L1. These aspects of child foreign language learning will impact the way that language is described in TEYL, as well as the assessment measures used to evaluate children's developing oral skills, which will necessarily vary across individuals. Cameron also explains how a move towards TEYL will have an impact upon secondary level teaching and second language teacher education. This article is recommended for teachers in training and for in-service teachers who work with young learners. Any TESOL practitioner who is directly or indirectly involved in teaching EFL to young children is recommended to read this article as well.

Pinter, A. (2006), *Teaching Young Language Learners*. Oxford: Oxford University Press

More than a 'recipe book' of suggested activities, *Teaching Young Language Learners* offers a comprehensive but accessible overview of TEYL theory with the end goal of more effective and informed classroom practice. Chapters cover a range of topics in TEYL, including first-language development, language policy, learning strategies, and textbook evaluation, to name a few. Each chapter also features a recommended reading section organized into resources that either expand on the background theory of the chapter theme or serve as practical resources for teachers. *Teaching Young Language Learners* is recommended for undergraduate and graduate TESOL students, as well as for teacher educators who work with pre-service TEYL instructors. It would also serve as a valuable reference to TESOL instructors and administrators currently working in TEYL contexts.

Liu, J. (2007a), Critical Period Hypothesis Retested: The Effects of Earlier English Education in China. In J. Liu (ed.), *English Language Teaching in China: New Approaches, Perspectives and Standards.* London: Continuum

This book chapter responds to the global trend of compulsory early English learning and to advocates of such policies who cite a critical period for L2 learning as justification. Liu believes that justification for early English education based on belief in the critical period is problematic for the following two reasons: 1) the critical period is still controversial in the field of SLA; and 2) most research on the critical period has been conducted in ESL, rather than EFL, settings – in the former, learners are immersed in the target language, while in the latter, learners have very little exposure to the target language outside of the classroom. Liu reports on his study of two junior high schools in China, in which he discovered that any advantage early English learners had over late learners only lasted for a short period of time (a year or two). His findings also suggested that early L1 literacy training can help aid later L2 literacy development. In his conclusion, Liu suggests a number of factors that policymakers should take into consideration before instituting compulsory English learning at an early age. This article is recommended for TESOL instructors and practitioners worldwide, particularly those involved with language policy planning and TEYL.

García, O. (2009), Emergent Bilinguals and TESOL: What's in a Name?. *TESOL Quarterly*, 43(2), 322–6

In this brief and accessible *TESOL Quarterly* article, García suggests that referring to young English learners in the United States as *emergent bilinguals*, rather than as English language learners (ELLs) or Limited English proficient students (LEPs), is more beneficial to the learners themselves, as well as to teachers, parents, policymakers, the field of TESOL, and to society as a whole. Importantly, García argues that the term *emergent bilingual* highlights the potential advantages of bilingualism, rather than framing it as a deficit or a limitation. In this manner, García calls on TESOL to embrace multilingualism as a valuable resource and to rethink English monolingualism as a framework for constructing learners' identities. This article is recommended for both pre-service and in-service TESOL instructors who teach young children in the United States, as well as for any other TEYL practitioner operating in an English-dominant teaching context.

Nunan, D. (2011), *Teaching English to Young Learners*. Anaheim, CA: Anaheim University Press

Nunan's concise book offers an overview of the key principles, skills, and challenges involved in TEYL in either an ESL or an EFL setting. Each of this book's 16 chapters addresses a different aspect of TEYL, including first-language acquisition, teaching the various language skills (e.g. listening, writing, vocabulary, etc.), addressing the learning styles of younger learners, working with parents, technological considerations, and assessment of TEYL. Throughout, young learners' tendency to approach language learning holistically (vs. analytically) is addressed. This book is recommended for any pre-service or in-service teachers who are either currently working with young language learners or intend to do so in the future. TESOL teacher educators who wish to expand their knowledge of TEYL would find this book useful as well.

Shin, J. K. and Crandall, J. (2014), *Teaching Young Learners English*. Boston, MA: National Geographic Learning / Cengage Learning

This book outlines key concepts relevant to teaching EFL to young learners, with a focus on teaching children at the primary school level. Each chapter focuses on relevant theory and practical application, contains sample lesson plans, and includes a 'teacher to teacher' section which allows readers to encounter the practices and perspectives of committed TEYL teachers around the world. The final two chapters in *Teaching Young Learners English* discuss potential assessment measures for young learners and make suggestions for further professional development. This book is appropriate for both pre-service and in-service TEYL teachers. While its format and coverage make it a suitable textbook for TESOL students, it could also be valuable to more experienced TESOL practitioners who are just beginning to work with young English learners.

Classic texts

Brewster, J., Ellis, G. and Girard, D. (1992), *The Primary English Teacher's Guide*. Harmondsworth: Penguin.

Brumfit, C., Moon, J. and Tongue, R. (eds) (1991), *Teaching English to Children: From Practice to Principle*. London: Collins ELT.

Dulay, H. C. and Burt, M. K. (1973), Should we teach children syntax? *Language Learning*, 23(2), 245–58.

Garvie, E. (1990), *Story as Vehicle: Teaching English to Young Children*. Bristol: Multilingual Matters.

Krashen, S. D., Long, M. A. and Scarcella, R. C. (1979), Age, rate and eventual attainment in second language acquisition. *TESOL Quarterly*, 13(4), 573–82.

Scott, W. and Ytreberg, L. (1990), *Teaching English to Children*. London: Longman.

Williams, M. (1991), A Framework for Teaching English to Young Learners. In C. Brumfit, J. Moon and R. Tongue (eds), *Teaching English to Children: From Practice to Principle* (pp. 203–12). London: Collins ELT.

Further reading

Bourke, J. M. (2006), Designing a topic-based syllabus for young learners. *ELT Journal*, 60(3), 279–86.

Cameron, L. (2001), *Teaching English to Young Learners*. Cambridge: Cambridge University Press.

Cummins, J. (2000), *Language, Power, and Pedagogy: Bilingual Children in the Crossfire*. Bristol: Multilingual Matters.

Dantas-Whitney, M. and Rilling, S. (2010), *Authenticity in the Language Classroom and Beyond: Children and Adolescent Learners. TESOL Classroom Practice Series*. Alexandria, VA: TESOL.

Davies, P. (2000), *Success in English Teaching: A Complete Introduction to Teaching English at Secondary School Level and Above*. Oxford: Oxford University Press.

Hasselgreen, A. (2005), Assessing the language of young learners. *Language Testing*, 22(3), 337–54.

Huang, K. M. (2011), Motivating lessons: A classroom-oriented investigation of the effects of content-based instruction on EFL young learners' motivated behaviours and classroom verbal interaction. *System*, 39(2), 186–201.

Janzen, J. (2008), Teaching English language learners in the content areas. *Review of Educational Research*, 78(4), 1010–38.

Liao, P. (2007), Teachers' beliefs about teaching English to elementary school children. *English Teaching and Learning*, 31(1), 43–76.

Nunan, D. (2013), Innovation in the Young Learner Classroom. In K. Hyland and L. L. C. Wong (eds), *Innovation and Change in English Language Education* (pp. 233–47). New York: Routledge.

Paul, D. and Chan, M. (2010), *Teaching English to children in Asia*. Hong Kong: Pearson Longman.

Shaaban, K. (2001). Assessment of young learners. *English Teaching Forum*, 39(4), 16–23.

Shin, J. K. (2006), Ten helpful ideas for teaching English to young learners. *English Teaching Forum*, 44(2), 2–13.

Wu, X. (2003), Intrinsic motivation and young language learners: The impact of the classroom environment. *System*, 31, 501–17.

Assessment and testing

Language assessment is not confined to the realm of psychometricians and large-scale standardized testing. Nearly all TESOL practitioners, regardless of whether or not they are actual classroom teachers, will likely find themselves involved in a position where they need to participate in at least one, if not several, of the following activities: evaluate learners' knowledge and abilities; choose a tool for measuring learner performance or develop one's own tool; interpret the results of an assessment procedure; make decisions about learners, course curricula, or future teacher training as a result of assessment outcomes; prepare learners for a future test; use students' test results to refine an existing syllabus; develop materials that allow learners to practise what they might encounter on a test; determine which learners might need extra help; etc. Furthermore, because assessment itself refers to a rather broad practice, of which testing is merely one 'genre' of techniques (Brown and Abeywickrama, 2010, p. 3), all good language teachers are constantly assessing their students, regardless of whether or not the students' performance is quantified or recorded in any way.

Because assessment is somewhat unavoidable in the TESOL profession, we offer below a sampling of readings that provide a broad overview of assessment research, practices, and controversies in the field. As teachers comprise the majority of TESOL professionals, we have chosen topics about TESOL assessment and testing that we believe are the most relevant to instructors (although any TESOL professional will find these readings instructive). Even with such a criterion in place, choosing selections for this topic was challenging. The majority of annotations in the sample below reference full books. Bachman and Palmer (2010) is one exception: while the authors' book-length treatment of language assessment is certainly recommended, Chapter 3 is highlighted as a thorough introduction to the construct of language ability, something we believe any TESOL practitioner should be familiar with, not just specialists. Weigle's (2002) volume, with its focus on writing, was highlighted due to what we perceive as a form of assessment that intimidates many novice language teachers; Purpura's (2004) book on assessing grammar was included for similar reasons. Furthermore, while space restrictions haven't allowed us to list all of the books in the Cambridge Language Assessment Series, they are all highly recommended.

Douglas, D. (2000), *Assessing Languages for Specific Purposes*. Cambridge: Cambridge University Press

In this book, Douglas offers a framework for developing and using tests that assess language for specific purposes. Written for both test developers and classroom teachers, *Assessing Language for Specific Purposes* takes as its foundation the various ways in which conceiving of contextualized language in use should influence principles of test design. In addition to several chapters focusing on context, strategic competence, the design of test tasks, and technology, two chapters address reading/writing assessment and speaking/listening assessment separately. Throughout, Douglas provides examples from a variety of different assessment situations to illustrate his claims. TESOL graduate students, teacher educators, and assessment and/ or ESP researchers will appreciate the way in which this book acts as a bridge between the fields of language assessment and English for Specific Purposes (ESP).

Weigle, S. C. (2002), *Assessing Writing*. Cambridge: Cambridge University Press

This book offers a 'one-stop shop' for both theory and practice related to second language writing assessment. *Assessing Writing* explains *what* writing assessment attempts to measure (i.e. the construct of writing ability), *why* language learners should be tested on writing, *how* they should be tested, and *what tasks* best elicit writing performance conducive to assessment. The book begins by examining the construct of writing itself, thus offering a conceptual framework that forms the basis of subsequent chapters which address the design, development, scoring, and use of both large-scale and classroom writing assessment. A key chapter also empha- sizes the potential uses of portfolio assessment. This book is recommended for MA TESOL students, in-practice teachers, and teacher educators, as well as for any TESOL researcher or practitioner who is interested in developing or using large-scale and/or classroom-based writing assessment.

Shohamy, E. (2004), Assessment in Multicultural Societies: Applying Democratic Principles and Practices to Language Testing. In B. Norton and K. Toohey (eds), *Critical Pedagogies and Language Learning* (pp. 72–92). Cambridge: Cambridge University Press

In this chapter, Shohamy introduces critical language testing (CLT), an area of scholarly interest in applied linguistics that has emerged in acknowl- edgement of the degree to which assessment practices may create and/ or reinforce asymmetrical relationships of power. Shohamy investigates the testing practices in a number of settings, all of them multicultural, in order to 'examine, question, and monitor' the ways in which assessment measures may force examinees to participate in assimilative behaviour. She then recommends more egalitarian assessment practices and argues that test developers should hold themselves accountable for the tools they create. This chapter is recommended for TESOL graduate students, as well as for TESOL researchers who are directly or indirectly involved in language assessment.

Purpura, J. E. (2004), *Assessing Grammar*. Cambridge: Cambridge University Press

Written for readers interested in the assessment of grammar specifically, this book reflects on what is meant by the term 'grammar', offers a thorough review of the existing research in grammar assessment, and explores the construct of grammatical ability at length. The author also offers a framework for the reliable assessment of grammatical knowledge/ability in L2 learners. Pre-service and in-service teachers will find sections on designing tests and test tasks for measuring grammatical ability to be particularly instructive, as well as the chapter that explores grammatical ability as a construct. While the specialized language and expert knowledge upon which this book draws might make it challenging for beginners in the field, *Assessing Grammar* is suggested reading for any TESOL practitioner or researcher seriously interested in grammar assessment.

Canagarajah, S. (2006a). Changing communicative needs, revised assessment objectives: Testing English as an international language. *Language Assessment Quarterly*, 3, 229–42

In this article, Canagarajah suggests that postmodern globalization has rendered the ongoing debate between Standard English and World Englishes irrelevant, thus heralding a new orientation to language norms and language proficiency, one that should affect change in traditional assessment practices. Canagarajah re-examines Kachru's (1986) World Englishes model in light of postmodern globalization and calls for a new egalitarian model of English that acknowledges a multitude of norms. In order to be deemed proficient in this less hierarchical model of Englishes, one requires multidialecticalism. However, multidialecticalism does't imply proficiency in every single variety of English; rather, it suggests the ability to negotiate meaning across varieties in order to communicate. This means that assessment practices need to shift from a focus on what test-takers *know* (local standards or inner-circle standards) to what they can *do*. Negotiation skills and 'proficiency in pragmatics' (p. 233) thus become the focus of attention in language assessment. Canagarajah suggests that the following features should be assessed in determining a test-taker's readiness for negotiating diverse varieties of English: language awareness, sociolinguistic sensitivity, and negotiating skills. He goes on to explain how a modification of the First Certificate of English would allow (multiple) raters to assess test-takers' social negotiation skills and pragmatic competence.

Coombe, C. A., Folse, K. S. and Hubley, N. J. (2007), *A Practical Guide to Assessing English Language Learners.* Ann Arbor, MI: University of Michigan Press / ESL

This book is intended for novice teachers and newcomers to the field of language assessment. *A Practical Guide to Assessing English Language Learners* not only introduces readers to the most frequent concepts and terminology encountered in the field of language assessment (e.g. washback, reliability, validity, etc.), it also familiarizes them with the various types of language tests that exist in TESOL, as well as the most common large-scale language assessment tests (e.g. TOEFL, MELAB, etc.). Helpful features include the end-of-chapter 'Ten Things to Remember' lists, as well as the authors' inclusion of case studies which highlight the decision-making of two language instructors. *A Practical Guide to Assessing English Language Learners* is recommended for undergraduate or graduate TESOL students or for teachers in practice who feel that their knowledge of language assessment within the field of TESOL is lacking.

Bachman, L. F. and Palmer, A. S. (2010), Describing Language Use and Language Ability. In L. F. Bachman and A. S. Palmer (eds), *Language Assessment in Practice* (pp. 33–58). Oxford: Oxford University Press

In chapter 3 of their book *Language Assessment in Practice*, Bachman and Palmer offer a straightforward and accessible overview of their framework for describing language use and language ability, as well as a description of individual attributes that may interact with language use and thus influence test-takers' assessment performance, positively or negatively. The authors offer uncomplicated explanations of the terminology they introduce and include illustrative examples throughout. The tables and figures provided are intuitively explanatory and helpful in reinforcing concepts discussed in the authors' prose. This chapter (and the book in which it appears) is recommended for test developers and researchers in assessment, as well as for TESOL graduate students who wish to better understand the nature of language assessment and the construct of language ability.

Brown, H. D. and Abeywickrama, P. (2010), *Language Assessment: Principles and Classroom Practices* (2nd edn). White Plains, NY: Longman

Language Assessment: Principles and Classroom Practices offers a comprehensive and accessible survey of principles and practices related to various forms of second language assessment. Similar in format to Brown's popular (2007) *Teaching by Principles: An Interactive Approach to Language Pedagogy*, this book begins by outlining the fundamental concepts and principles in language assessment, before focusing on specific types of assessment (e.g. classroom, standardized, alternative, etc.) and the ways in which discrete language skills (e.g. speaking, reading, etc.) can be assessed. A final chapter addresses issues related to student grading and evaluation. Throughout, Brown and Abeywickrama offer helpful syntheses of key findings from research in the field of assessment and provide illustrative examples to clarify otherwise difficult concepts. For its coverage, accessibility, and emphasis on classroom practice, *Language Assessment* would be an appropriate textbook for undergraduate and graduate TESOL students, as well for in-practice instructors and teacher educators who wish to broaden their knowledge of second language assessment.

Fulcher, G. (2010), *Practical Language Testing*. Oxford: Oxford University Press

This practical introduction to language testing acknowledges both the locally situated context of the language classroom, and the broader social, political, and historical contexts in which language assessment is embedded. In this regard, *Practical Language Testing* takes a principled approach to language assessment with a focus on test developers' and test users' dedication to social responsibility and professionalism. Throughout, Fulcher maintains a purposeful balance between attention to standardized testing and to classroom assessment, offering examples of actual language transcripts, test tasks, test items, scoring data, etc., to scaffold technical concepts related to scoring and testing procedures. The author's website, http://languagetesting.info/, acts as a companion site to the book, offering explanatory videos, additional articles, and links to further resources. *Practical Language Testing* would be useful to graduate TESOL students, as well as to practising teachers and/or TESOL researchers new to the sub-discipline of assessment.

Classic texts

Alderson, J. C. and Clapham, C. (1995), Assessing student performance in the
    ESL classroom. *TESOL Quarterly*, 29(1), 184–7.
Brown, J. D. (1998), *New Ways of Classroom Assessment. New Ways in TESOL
    Series II. Innovative Classroom Techniques*. Alexandria, VA: TESOL.
Burt, M. and Dulay, H. (1978), Some guidelines for the assessment of oral
    language proficiency and dominance. *TESOL Quarterly*, 12(2), 177–92.
Cohen, A. D. (1994), *Assessing Language Ability in the Classroom*. Boston:
    Heinle & Heinle.
LeBlanc, R. and Painchaud, G. (1985), Self-Assessment as a second language
    placement instrument. *TESOL Quarterly*, 19(4), 673–87.

Further reading

Bailey, K. M. (ed.) (1998), *Learning about Language Assessment: Dilemmas,
    Decisions, and Directions*. Boston, MA: Heinle & Heinle.
Brown, J. D. and Hudson, T. (1998), The alternatives in language assessment.
    TESOL Quarterly, 32(4), 653–75.
Buck, G. (2001), *Assessing Listening*. Cambridge: Cambridge University Press.
Davison, C. and Leung, C. (2009), Current issues in English language teacher-
    based assessment. *TESOL Quarterly*, 43(3), 393–415.
Douglas, D. and Hegelheimer, V. (2007), Assessing language using computer
    technology. *Annual Review of Applied Linguistics*, 27, 115.
Fulcher, G. (2003), *Testing Second Language Speaking*. Harlow: Pearson
    Education.
Fulcher, G. and Davidson, F. (2007), *Language Testing and Assessment: An
    Advanced Resource Book*. London: Routledge.
Jamieson, J. (2005), Trends in computer-based second language assessment.
    Annual Review of Applied Linguistics, 25(1), 228–42.
Oscarson, M. (2004), Alternative forms of assessment and student participation.
    Language Testing Update, 36, 114–15.
Read, J. (2000), *Assessing Vocabulary*. Cambridge: Cambridge University Press.
Ross, S. J. (2008), Language testing in Asia: Evolution, innovation, and policy
    challenges. *Language Testing*, 25(1), 5–13.
Shaaban, K. (2001). Assessment of young learners. *English Teaching Forum*,
    39(4), 16–23.
Tsagari, C. (2004), Alternative assessment: some considerations. *Language
    Testing Update*, 36, 116–24.
Weigle, S. C. (2007), Teaching writing teachers about assessment. *Journal of
    Second Language Writing*, 16(3), 194–209.
Wilhelm, K. H. (2005), Developmental and alternative assessment: Knowing
    what they know (and don't know!). *Crosslinks in English Language Teaching*,
    2, 63–93.

4

TESOL as a Professional Association

The evolution of TESOL as an International Association

The history of TESOL as an association: An interview with James Alatis

TESOL Inc. (now TESOL International Association) was founded in 1966. Dr James Alatis was the first Executive Secretary (now referred to as the 'Executive Director') of TESOL Inc., while the founding President of TESOL was Professor Harold B. Allen. Both James and Harold were instrumental in implementing the policies set forth by the membership through the Executive Committee in the earlier years of TESOL Inc.

Because James Alatis, in particular, has been involved with TESOL Inc. for nearly five decades, we felt that no one in TESOL would be a better historian of the association than James. In February of 2009, one of the authors of this book, Jun Liu (TESOL President 2006–7), interviewed James Alatis about the history and evolution of TESOL. We reproduce excerpts from this interview here with the intention of offering readers the most nuanced and in-depth history of the association possible.

Liu: James, many people in the field of TESOL refer to you as the 'father of TESOL' because of your longevity in the position as Executive Secretary-Treasurer for 21 years starting from the first TESOL President, Professor Harold B. Allen from University of Minnesota, in 1966 to President Joan Morley of the University of Michigan in 1986. How would you reflect on this experience?

Alatis: It was a true privilege not only to play a part in the birth of an essential and prestigious professional organization, but, in fact, also the development of the field of TESOL. It is no coincidence that the organization and the field share the same name. It was through the dynamic efforts of the founders and the very active membership that the field gained the definition and respect we take for granted today.

Liu: What prompted the founding of TESOL as an association?

Alatis: It was President Allen who produced the document, *A Survey of the Teaching of English to Non-English Speakers in the United States*, or the TENES survey[1] as it was known. This report was commissioned by the Office of Education in 1964 and was ground-breaking in describing the social and cultural environment in which the teaching of English took place in post-World War II America. By the end of the 1940s, large numbers of foreign students had arrived to matriculate in US universities. These students were adult learners at college level who came to the US to embark on studies in fields from public administration to air traffic control in order to return to their home countries with their expertise. It soon became clear that special English classes were needed for this group for which instructors were drawn from English and foreign language departments. Eventually, special materials were developed for TEFL, or Teaching English as a Foreign Language. By 1953, 150 institutions had English programs for foreign students. Instruction for this group of learners became more specialized and eventually the idea of TEFL deserving attention as a separate discipline took hold. At this time, there also emerged another significant group of English language learners: children in US elementary and secondary schools whose native tongue was not English and who were studying together with native English speakers. While the foreign college students were in the US temporarily, these children were non-native speakers who were born in the US. They needed TESL, or Teaching English as a Second Language.

Liu: What were the findings of the TENES survey and what impact did the survey results have in the field of TESOL?

Alatis: Until Professor Allen's TENES survey, teaching ESL was not considered a separate area of professional competence. There was not even a list of teachers of ESL. These are some of the facts revealed by the TENES survey (Allen, 1966) about the elementary and secondary school teachers sampled:

- 91 per cent had no practice teaching in ESL.

- 85 per cent had no formal study in methods of teaching ESL.

- 75 per cent had no formal training in English phonetics, morphemics, or syntax.

- 61.8 per cent had no training in general linguistics.

The powerful data from the TENES survey brought to light the full scope of the challenges faced by EFL and ESL teachers in the US and gave weight to calls for more professional training that included facts, theory and practice. Also needed were teaching materials that addressed the special needs of culturally distinct groups of learners as diverse as Native American children in the Southwest and illiterate non-English speaking adults. The issues were complex and required overt study. The time had come for full recognition of the teaching of ESL and EFL as a distinct professional discipline. To adequately include both groups in this discipline, the organization was named Teachers of English to Speakers of Other Languages (TESOL), with the subtitle, A Professional Organization for Those Concerned with the Teaching of English as a Second or Foreign Language.

Liu: What efforts did TESOL Inc. make after its inception in 1966?

Alatis: From its very beginning, TESOL, the organization, saw rapid growth and dynamic development. While we had no formal speaking and consulting program in operation, the President, Executive Secretary and other officers of TESOL constantly made themselves available for meetings, institutes and workshops to the membership and public at large. These efforts served to promote the new discipline and support research.

The first TESOL Central Office was established in August 1966 with a part-time Executive Secretary-Treasurer in a small shoe-box of an office at the School for Languages and Linguistics of Georgetown University. The next year, the organization was incorporated as a non-profit professional association in the District of Columbia. TESOL thus started as a small operation but the environment was ripe for us to make an impact almost immediately. In 1967, Harold Allen identified the need for national guidelines for the preparation and certification of ESOL teachers. It took several years of brisk discussion within TESOL before the final version was ratified by the Executive Committee in 1975. Those guidelines paved the way for accreditation and certification in ESOL and Bilingual Education in various states, thus giving the profession greater authority and credibility.

Liu: What external support did TESOL Inc. have in the earlier years of the association that furthered TESOL's mission?

Alatis: It was also Professor Allen who began TESOL's cooperation with bodies outside the field of education. Under his tenure, TESOL entered into contracts with government offices such as the Defense Language Institute's Lackland Air Force Base, and the Bureau of Indian Affairs, which wanted an evaluation of English teaching on the Navajo reservation. TESOL also began fruitful links with private foundations. The Asia Foundation, for example, awarded TESOL five successive grants beginning in 1972 to encourage professional relationships between ESOL teachers in Asia and the US and other countries. The grants funded TESOL memberships for Asian teachers, ESOL materials for libraries in their universities and language centres, and travel assistance for teachers attending the annual TESOL conventions.

Liu: You mention the annual TESOL Convention, which has become the biggest annual event in the field with a record high of attendees (more than 10,000) in New York in 1999. What was the original thinking about the purpose, the venue, and scope of TESOL annual conventions?

Alatis: From the beginning, holding annual conventions was a priority for TESOL. It was decided that the conventions would be held in large metropolitan areas with a great demand for teaching English to non-native speakers, with a different location every year so that everyone would have the opportunity to attend. We chose Miami Beach for the first convention in 1967, and optimistically continued to select cities with tempting distractions, such as San Francisco, San Juan, and Honolulu. There was never a doubt that the session rooms would not be filled with ESOL professionals eager to learn methods and techniques from each other. In fact, the TESOL conventions quickly became known as 'mini universities' that offered impressive rosters of invited speakers.

Liu: TESOL is a membership association. Many TESOLers are busy with their teaching and research. What was your vision about TESOL Central Office and what functions did you envision this office would play?

Alatis: TESOL's Central Office also took on an important role as a clearinghouse for the profession, supplying information to legislative and other government offices and in this way contributing to subsequent consideration of legislation in ESL, bilingual education and language education in general. For example, in 1967, the TESOL office submitted testimony to the hearings before the General Subcommittee on Education on bills to amend the Elementary and Secondary Education Act of 1965 in order to assist Bilingual Education programs. Other early achievements of the Central Office were the establishment of the *TESOL Quarterly* as the profession's own scholarly journal focusing on ESOL, Bilingual Education and Applied Linguistics; as well as the long-awaited assembling of a national register of ESOL personnel. This was not only a major step towards identifying TESOL members but was also the beginning of a job bank for teachers. The TESOL office maintained a candidate file with résumés of job seekers and also operated a modest placement service.

Liu: In retrospect, what would you say has been the biggest accomplishments TESOL founders like yourself have made to the TESOL profession?

Alatis: Without a doubt, TESOL founders accomplished a great deal to set in motion the creation of an ESOL community, which through all these years has never failed to impress me with its sense of youthful idealism and social mission. While its creation was influenced by social forces in the US, the focus of TESOL has always been on the role of English as it is used internationally. TESOL founders deliberately chose not to identify the organization as 'American' or 'national'; rather, it was always understood that memberships would come from around the world. In fact, its first organizational meeting in May 1964 saw attendance from colleagues from Canada, Japan, Mexico, the Netherlands, and the Philippines. TESOL has maintained this tradition of emphasizing open discussion and collective wisdom as the means to address the needs of its diverse membership. TESOL was never the kind of organization that sought to restrict access to the profession. As language teachers, I believe we all understood the power of language to foster peace and progress, and to this end only a policy of inclusion and free exchange would work for our professional organization.

Liu: TESOL Inc. has now evolved as TESOL International Association over almost five decades of changes and development. Any final thoughts on the association and its members today?

Alatis: Now, in TESOL's fifth decade, members [should] continue their efforts to document and understand the process of learning English in today's world with its new communication options and social networks. I was among the fortunate few to start the ball rolling, and I am ever grateful for the privilege of witnessing first-hand what the energies of language teachers can achieve.

Liu: Thank you very much, James. You are the inspiration of TESOL and, on behalf of TESOL members, I would like to thank you for your decades of dedication to create a TESOL community where we all work hard to achieve the excellence of English language education worldwide.

Reflections of leaders of TESOL

In preparation for writing the following section of this chapter we collected the written reflections of 12 past presidents of TESOL Association International. These reflections span from John Fanselow's presidential tenure beginning in 1981 to Suzanne Panferov's recent 2012–13 presidency. All past presidents were asked to consider a number of issues during their tenure, including the challenges they faced and the contributions they made both to the association and to the field as whole during their time as president. All contributors were also asked to reflect on the nature of TESOL as an association – particularly its leadership – and their concerns and predictions for TESOL in the future.

The results of our request resulted in a rich assortment of expository, narrative, and creative writing. Unfortunately, due to space limitations, we are unable to reprint this complete collection of past TESOL presidents' reflections. However, we are pleased to offer readers a brief synthesis of the input we received, structured as responses to key lines of inquiry that emerged from respondents' reflections. The section below is intended to summarize many of the most salient comments and insights shared by past presidents of TESOL International Association. When possible, we have included excerpts in their entirety so as to preserve the original author's eloquence. While our goal in the following section is to offer a representative account of the substance of respondents' reflections, any mistakes or inaccuracies are of course our own.

What's so special about TESOL International Association?

In reflecting back on their years with the association, a number of past presidents discussed the various ways in which they have found TESOL International Association to be unique from other professional associations. Across responses, the following key qualities of the TESOL Association and its membership emerged:

● creativity and problem-solving

● volunteering

● egalitarianism and diversity

● breadth of coverage.

It was the creativity of TESOL members and volunteers that first attracted past president Amy Schlessman (2003–4) to the association. In the following passage, Schlessman explains the term 'TESOLvers', a word she coined to refer to the innovative manner with which professionals she encountered early on in her dealings with the association approached problems:

> TESOLvers are interested in identifying patterns or frameworks used in ways of knowing; transferring skills, pattern, and frameworks from one area to another; and in using abstraction abilities such as similarities, differences, analogy, metaphor, sequences. Because we are language teachers, we most often focus on language as our symbols; yet, we do not exclude other ways to intelligently approach the world.

For past president John Fanselow (1981–2), egalitarianism has always stood out as a particularly unique feature of the organization. Unlike other academic professional organizations, in which the majority of the leadership consists primarily of university-level professors accustomed to an institutional hierarchical paradigm, Fanselow explains that the TESOL Board is consistently composed of professionals from a variety of backgrounds, including 'public and private schools, boards of education, developers of textbooks, intensive language institutes, adult education, college prep and literacy programs, authors of curriculum guides and program coordinators'. Throughout his reflection, Fanselow frequently used the term 'vibrant' to describe TESOL, noting the very large number of volunteers, from all over the world, that have worked to make TESOL what it is today.

Similarly, Sandy Briggs (2007–8) argues that TESOL International Association is 'the leading association in the field because its members and its work encompass a very wide spectrum of the field'. Past president Neil Anderson (2001–2) also appreciates the degree to which TESOL has always welcomed and encouraged diverse leadership styles, including those who may not have arrived at leadership naturally:

> Some leaders seem to be born to lead. These leaders have a natural ability to set goals and organize others in accomplishing those goals. Other leaders need to cultivate and prepare themselves to lead. Sometimes it is difficult to tell the difference between these two types of leaders. TESOL is a place where both can thrive and help build others.

Several other past presidents also commented on the diversity of TESOL and the degree to which the association brings together a diverse mix of individuals. Interestingly, in its past attempts 'to be all things to all people', past president David Nunan (1999–2000) suggests that TESOL Association may have left some members of the TESOL community, especially researchers, dissatisfied. In fact, it was this dissatisfaction that was influential in the formation of the American Association of Applied Linguistics (AAAL) in 1977. Originally intended to complement the activities of TESOL, AAAL has historically been considered more research-oriented than TESOL in the field of applied linguistics and TESOL.

While other professional associations in the field certainly exist (like AAAL, for example), Sandy Briggs (2007–8) argues that such associations 'focus exclusively on research in the field or testing or one particular type of teaching, such as intensive English programs. These are very good associations, but they do not represent the field as a whole'. It would seem that while its sheer size and breadth of ambition have occasionally resulted in less focus, TESOL International Association's diversity and comprehensiveness ensure that it remains the leading professional association in the field today.

What issues were most important to TESOL Association in the past?

When asked about issues that were the most salient during their various tenures as presidents of TESOL International Association, many respondents discussed concerns that seem to have emerged from the field's evolving acknowledgement of the role of English in the world and of the highly situated nature of language teaching. Such issues included the following:

- standards
- TESOL's international profile
- ESL vs. EFL dichotomy

- professional development

- advocacy (for both learners and teachers)

- the influence of technology

- World Englishes (or English as a world language)

- language minority rights.

Interestingly, many of these issues were mentioned by past presidents who served in completely different decades, suggesting that the above concerns have been relevant to the association for a significant span of time. It would also appear that the evolution of a global perspective towards English and acknowledgement of its various teaching contexts worldwide was an ongoing effort in the association that required more than a few short years to achieve.

Many past presidents felt that language-related issues on an international level resulted in greater attention to both advocacy initiatives and standards during their tenure. For example, past president Denise Murray (1996–7) noted the degree to which TESOL-related events occurring in the US in 1996–7 – immigration, language varieties, and standards – mirrored global issues that affected the world at large. During MaryAnn Christison's (1997–8) presidency, she worked to ensure that proper standards might prevent discrimination and unfair hiring practices against non-native English speaking teachers. This issue led to the creation of the TESOL interest section called Non-native English Speakers in TESOL (NNEST), a group that continues to be active in preventing discrimination and supporting NNESTs today. For Denise Murray as well, it was important that the association be active in the development of standards, ultimately a job for 'professionals, not politicians'.

Past president Christine Coombe (2011–12) commented on the attempt to 'internationalize' TESOL as a primary concern during her tenure. Recall that it wasn't until 2011 that TESOL changed its name (and logo) to TESOL International Association in the hope of rebranding the association as one that is principally global (as opposed to North American). Still, John Fanselow (1981–2) lamented the fact that even today TESOL is still perceived by many as primarily a North American (as opposed to an international) organization. Many other past presidents listed concern for TESOL's international profile as a pressing issue during their tenure.

Past president David Nunan (1999–2000) noted the breakdown of the ESL vs. EFL dichotomy as a significant topic during his presidency. Interestingly, past president Sandy Briggs (2007–8) also reported that the expansion of TESOL beyond the ESL vs. EFL distinction was particularly salient during her time as president, seven years after David Nunan's tenure (Briggs adds that she preferred *English Language Teaching (ELT)* for its all-encompassing perspective on the traditional ESL vs. EFL distinction). Again, we see that a more nuanced perspective of English's role in the world and of the situated nature of language teaching was more than a decade in the making.

Several other past presidents discussed the influence of technology on the field during their time as president. For example, David Nunan commented on the degree to which advances in technology 'provided a tool for the development of global communication networks' during his tenure, 'thus accelerating the pace of globalization'. His discussion of the problematic impact of globalization on TESOL is excerpted further below:

> Globalization created an unprecedented demand for English language teachers and related educational services. In some sectors of the educational industry, this led to increased professionalism. In other areas, it led to deprofessionalisation and deskilling. Simply being a native speaker of English, or a competent user of the language was sufficient to enable one to hang up one's shingle and begin practicing as a language teacher. In some parts of the world we saw the commodification of English. It was a resource, not to enable communication, but to make money.

Due in part to the same trends that Nunan describes above, Christison (1997–8) explained how the notion of World Englishes (indeed, the very term itself) was a particularly relevant issue during her time as presidency, as 'TESOL professionals could no longer assume that learner goals would include communication with L1 speakers of English'. Christison saw the emergence of several different movements as a result of the growing worldwide dominance of English during her tenure. Among them were an increased need for professional development opportunities and teaching English to younger learners. Amy Schlessman's (2003–4) time as president saw language policies emerging worldwide that mandated English for young learners as well. In reference to the above issues, Christison observed that each was 'tied closely to issues of economic power and stability'. Not surprisingly, concerns regarding power and the growing dominance of English resulted in a concern for language minority rights during Christison's tenure as well. She explained that while outsiders might find it surprising to see such an advocacy movement within TESOL, 'if you know anything at all about the TESOL profession, it is not. TESOL professionals have always been concerned about diversity'.

What issues matter to TESOL Association today?

When asked about which issues matter the most to TESOL International Association today, the majority of responses centred on the following three key concerns:

- second language teacher education/development

- advocacy and outreach

- technology.

In her response, Denise Murray (1996–7) indicated that she continues to see teacher preparation as a pressing issue, noting that '[i]f anything, more untrained teachers are working as ESOL instructors [today], not because of lack of advocacy or clarity by TESOL, but because of the tremendous growth in English language learners worldwide'. David Nunan (1999–2000) is another past president who believes that TESOL struggles to meet the demand for professional, qualified teachers worldwide, largely due to the rise of global English.

John Fanselow (1981–2) wrote about his anxiety regarding today's focus on 'knowing' vs. 'doing' in teacher preparation, especially in MA TESOL programmes. In addition, he believes that the professional jargon used in TESOL should be less exclusive and more accessible for newcomers and non-specialists in the field. To the above, Fanselow added the following:

> Issues that cry out for a range of views include these: dual language programs versus bilingual programs, external exams alone versus external exams used to verify local tests, student centered learning versus teacher centered learning, integration of ESOL and content classes versus their separation, providing time for teachers to analyze their own teaching by transcribing and analyzing audio and video excerpts of their teacher as well as providing time for supervisions to discuss teachers' classes, the balance between reading articles and writing essays and analyzing how applying suggestions in articles influence teaching practices and student engagement and learning.

With regard to the most pressing concerns for TESOL International Association today, past president Kathleen Bailey (1998–9) believes that the association is shaped by issues related to technology, professional development, and advocacy and outreach. With regard to advocacy, past president John Fanselow expressed concern with the negative effects of standardized testing, noting that TESOL International Association has the potential to affect positive change in this arena.

Of course, many of the issues that matter to TESOL are interrelated and cannot easily be isolated into discrete categories. Past president MaryAnn Christison (1997–8) referred to this interrelatedness as the 'all roads lead to Rome phenomenon'. For example, it's clear that technological advances and globalization have led to a rise in English use worldwide, which has led to more demand for well-trained teachers, many of whom are NNESTs who may benefit from TESOL-initiated advocacy efforts and/or professional development, etc.

What now? The future of TESOL Association, its challenges, and advice for members

Nearly all past presidents who responded to our request for reflections acknowledged the future challenges that TESOL will inevitably face. From these responses, four broad themes emerged:

- membership concerns
- advocacy and volunteering
- commercialization of the field
- innovation.

Concerns related to TESOL Association membership ranged from ageing members, to the need for greater member outreach, to potential competition from other associations. Christine Coombe (2011–12) was one past president who indicated that membership will be an important issue for TESOL International Association in the future. She believes that TESOL should do more to attract younger members, a generation of language professionals who may not initially value membership in professional associations the way older generations have. Coombe also argued that the association should attempt to attract and retain more non-US-based practitioners and members. Past president Neil Anderson (2001–2) is concerned that there are still more English teachers worldwide than members of TESOL. He wonders how TESOL International Association might best reach and support these teachers.

David Nunan (1999–2000) warned that competition from other professional associations may pose challenges to TESOL International Association. He explained that the local and regional associations that are flourishing around the world 'are often seen as more relevant to the needs of teachers in geographic locations outside of North America than the global association'. Similarly, Amy Schlessman (2003–4) predicted that '[o]ther language education associations will make contributions [to the field] as they fill a specific niche within a context'.

When asked how TESOL might continue to be the leading association in the field, past president Sandy Briggs (2007–8) argued that the association should '[listen] to its members and [work] to adjust to the technological changes and the educational changes in the field'. Briggs added that she is particularly pleased to see the association becoming better at articulating just what the TESOL profession is to those outside the field.

With regard to advocacy and volunteering, past president John Fanselow (1981–2) believes that TESOL has the 'potential ... to influence government policies [and] encourage the raising of expectations for ESOL students and the standards for TESOL teacher preparation programs'. Similarly, Christine Coombe (2011–12) suggested that TESOL should continue to lead the field in standards while carefully considering its role in accreditation.

Fanselow also called for newcomers to the profession to maintain the vibrancy of TESOL through volunteering, adding that TESOL is able 'to stay vibrant, grow and become stronger only to the extent that graduates of TESOL programs commit themselves to volunteer service in the professional organizations'. Past president Mark Algren (2009–10) feels similarly regarding the value of volunteering. He offered the following advice to professionals who may be seeking associational and/or leadership involvement in the field of TESOL:

> Be involved in your professional association at ANY level – local, regional, national, international. You meet people, you learn so much, you get a bigger picture of your profession and all that it has to offer. Take the opportunities as they present themselves if and when you can. It's never too late.

Past president Joy Reid (1995–6) offered interesting advice on the topic of volunteering specifically: she encouraged future volunteers to be 'choosy' as they seek out opportunities that are mutually beneficially and meet the needs of all parties involved.

Other past presidents commented on the impact of globalization on TESOL, which includes the potential commodification of the field. For example, past president Suzanne Panferov (2012–13) is concerned with what she perceives as the mass commercialization of ELT, resulting in a potential 'watering down of the profession'. As a result, Panferov called for more credentialing and professional development initiatives on behalf of the association, so as to prevent commercialization 'without qualification' in the field. She advised that TESOL professionals and future leaders as individuals continually pursue professional development.

Mark Algren (2009–10) argued that as 'English language learning continues to grow globally ... TESOL needs to ... continue to embrace professionals globally and build up locale-specific knowledge bases'. Sharing others' concern regarding the commodification of English as a result of globalization,

Algren also foresees a future in which TESOL may have to 'work with varying modalities of institutions including corporate (LARGE corporate) entities that have a very different view of language education (a commodity and business) to be traded and built upon promises of success'. Despite the uncertainty caused by advances in technology, commodification, and the changing role of English in a rapidly globalized role, past president Denise Murray (1996–97) is confident that the TESOL profession will endure:

> So what of the future? Where will this era of globalization lead? Will the world embrace it and power be more equitably distributed? Will social justice prevail or will nations become more nationalistic and isolationist? What will be the new advances in technology? I don't know. But, the teaching of languages will no doubt continue, even if computer translation becomes more accurate. This is because many people want to use another language not just for transactional purposes, but for experiential ones – to get to know and understand another community.

Returning to her notion of TESOL professionals as problem solvers (or TESOLvers), Amy Schlessman (2003–4) argues that TESOL Association will continue to lead the field to the degree that it continues to innovate:

> By always taking that next step, and being prepared to take that step, TESOL will continue to lead education. TESOL's commitment to a 5th part of language learning, whether we label it 'thinking,' 'creativity,' 'innovation,' or more generically 'intelligence,' keeps our categories from hardening ... TESOL will flourish as it offers paths to desirable qualities for any decade of the 21st century ... As TESOL continues to take steps beyond competence, there will be giant leaps for learners, professionals, and education worldwide.

Lastly, past president MaryAnn Christison (1997–8) predicted that if TESOL International Association continues to change and innovate at the rate that it has in the last 30 years, the association may eventually be unrecognizable from its current state: 'What I hope, though, is that no matter what TESOL looks like, it will continue to serve the profession in ways that are central to the work that we do'.

The scope of TESOL International Association today

In the following section, we lay out the scope of TESOL International Association today. As MaryAnn Christison observed in the preceding section of this chapter, the dynamic and innovative nature of the TESOL International Association precludes any static description of the association that will remain accurate over time. Still, our attempt here is to offer a brief snapshot of the association as it stands today, in the hope that readers who are unfamiliar with the association, or with a particular aspect of the association, will gain a better understanding of the breadth of its mission, activities, offerings, opportunities, etc.

The information below was gleaned from the TESOL International Association website; its various published brochures, documents, and briefs; personal communication from current and past TESOL leaders; and extensive interviews conducted with the helpful and enthusiastic staff at TESOL International Association's Central Office in Alexandra, Virginia. As with other sections of this book, we follow a question-and-answer format to structure the presentation of material. Readers who wish to know more about the various facets of TESOL International Association or to verify the currency of the information given below are encouraged to consult the TESOL website (http://www.tesol.org/) and/or to inquire from the association directly. General inquiries can be submitted via email to info@tesol.org, while the following webpage contains more detailed contact information: http://www.tesol.org/about-tesol/staff-office-and-directory/.

TESOL membership

How many members does TESOL International Association have?

As of May 2014, TESOL International Association had over 13,000 members worldwide (TESOL, 2014). This number was higher prior to the 2008 recession (approximately 14,000), after which membership of professional associations worldwide plummeted. TESOL staff noted, however, that the association's membership numbers have been gradually increasing again for the last several years. Furthermore, TESOL staff reminded us that membership is dynamic and not only socioeconomically dependent but also convention-dependent. For example, prior to the TESOL Convention in Portland, Oregon, in 2014, TESOL International Association saw its membership numbers rise on the west coast and in Asian countries.

What does a TESOL member 'look like'?

Because a TESOL member is difficult to describe in general terms, we offer some statistics that will help readers better understand the nature of TESOL membership. In Table 4.1 below, which lists the ten countries with the most TESOL International Association members in descending order, one notices immediately that the majority of TESOL members are from the United States.

As of April 2014, of the members who choose to report their area of work (Table 4.2), the majority (27.9 per cent) were employed in postsecondary education. The second largest work area reported by TESOL members was adult education (17.8 per cent). Perhaps not surprisingly, mainstream practitioners make up the smallest portion of TESOL membership (0.8 per cent). TESOL staff estimated offhand that roughly 75 per cent of their members have master's degrees, while about 15–20 per cent have PhDs. From these numbers,

Table 4.1 TESOL membership by country. Based on 2014 membership statistics (TESOL, 13 May 2014)

Country	Percentage of total TESOL membership
USA	72.0%
China	4.2%
Japan	3.2%
Canada	2.7%
Brazil	1.7%
Cameroon	1.6%
Mexico	1.1%
Peru	0.7%
India	0.6%
Thailand	0.5%
Others	11.7%

Table 4.2 Area of membership work (self-reported) (adapted from TESOL, 13 May 2014)

Area of work	Members paid through April 2014	
	Raw count	Percentage
Elementary education	828	6.6%
Secondary education	1,023	8.1%
Community / 2 year college	824	6.5%
Postsecondary education	3,517	27.9%
Adult education	2,252	17.8%
Mainstream	101	0.8%
Other	1,212	9.6%
Unreported	2,871	22.7%

Table 4.3 Statistics on membership areas of interest and areas of expertise (adapted from TESOL, 13 May 2014)

Area of interest	Total	Area of expertise	Total
Teacher education	2,025	English as a foreign language	1,274
Materials development / curriculum	2,013	Materials development / curriculum	1,093
English as a foreign language	1,994	Adult education	1,062
Second language acquisition	1,911	Writing/composition	1,040
Applied linguistics	1,806	Intensive English programme	992

we can conclude that TESOL International Association membership body is well educated and that many of them work in contexts with adult learners.

When new members initially join TESOL International Association, they are encouraged to declare both areas of interest and areas of expertise.

The former is intended to reflect areas that members are interested in; it is separate from joining a TESOL Interest Section (which is discussed further below). The latter, areas of expertise, allows members to denote areas in which they have experience. Table 4.3 indicates the top five areas of interest and of expertise for TESOL members as of May 2014.

These numbers offer an even more nuanced impression of the TESOL membership body. Surprisingly, although the vast majority of TESOL members are located in the United States, the most widely declared area of expertise is EFL. This may suggest that many members in the United States have spent time teaching English in other contexts. Of further note is the fact that while teacher education is reported as the top area of interest, it is not in the top five areas of expertise. This may indicate a need for greater expertise in second language teacher education within the body of membership as a whole.

During conversations with TESOL staff, three different profiles of TESOL members began to emerge. The first consists of members who believe it is both vital and necessary to be a member of the leading association in their field. These members are typically the most active, contributing the most to the association and taking the most advantage of its resources. The second profile is an individual who joined TESOL several years ago out of obligation and feels some amount of loyalty to the association. These members renew every year, though their participation may have waned since their initial membership, and they are less likely to utilize the resources available to them. Such members may also simply want to maintain membership with a professional organization on their résumé. Finally, a third type of member tends to rotate in and out of the association. They may join for a year or two to join a conference in their region or to take advantage of a specific resource. As TESOL has attempted to offer an even wider range of resources to members, the office has seen this third group maintain their memberships for longer. The office is hopeful that this trend will continue. That said, a potential problem with TESOL membership is that the average age of a TESOL member continues to increase. Staff indicated that a challenge for TESOL will be attracting younger individuals in the field who are at an early stage in their career and may not see joining a professional association as a priority.

What does membership cost?

TESOL International Association offers different types of membership, with varying rates for students, professionals, retirees, etc. (we recommend consulting the TESOL International Association website for the most updated rates: http://www.tesol.org/about-tesol/membership). TESOL also offers reduced membership rates for new professionals, professionals earning less than US$25,000 per year, and for global members living in countries with less than US$15,000 gross national income per capita. All members who join TESOL have the option of adding a subscription to *TESOL Quarterly* for an additional fee (again, the fee is reduced for global members). Additionally, TESOL International Association has begun to offer an institutional membership plan, referred to as 'Institutional Professional Development Bundles'. These cater to a variety of different institutions with different member sizes and budgets and include a variety of bulk membership benefits that include association memberships, waived fees for online courses, convention registration, and a set amount of free online books.

It may be surprising to readers to learn that the contribution of membership fees to TESOL International Association's annual revenue is actually rather modest (less than 20 per cent). It is other forms of revenue generation, especially from the association's annual convention, that allow the association to offer a high value for membership at a relatively low cost. In fact, TESOL staff indicated that a constant concern for the association is how to ensure that access to TESOL membership is easier and less expensive, especially for students and global members.

TESOL governance

How is TESOL governed?

TESOL International Association is governed by an elected 12-member board of directors, plus the TESOL executive director, who is also considered a member of the board. The board of directors meets in person twice a year (once during convention plus one other time) and is responsible for approving and implementing TESOL International Association's strategic plan, i.e. a document delineating the association's goals and objectives for the following three years (e.g. the current strategic plan was approved by the board of directors in March 2011 and will expire in 2014). Current strategic plans are available on TESOL's website (http://www.tesol.org/about-tesol/association-governance/strategic-plan), along with the association's byelaws and standing rules.

In addition to the board, 17 standing committees (more about these below) help the board of directors manage association business and carry out the strategic plans: seven are staffed by board members and ten are volunteers. A separate executive committee consists of the current TESOL president, president-elect, and previous president.

TESOL standing committees

What are standing committees?

TESOL International Association's 17 standing committees support the board of directors' goal of implementing the current TESOL strategic plan and any other association-related business (see 'TESOL Governance', above). TESOL member volunteers comprise ten of the committees, while the remaining seven are staffed by the board of directors. Every standing committee has both a staff liaison and a board liaison. The former handles administrative duties, while the latter liaises with the board of directors. Each standing committee also has a group page in *TESOL Community*. A list of current standing committees, organized by staffing, has been provided below (TESOL International Association, 2014f).

What does each standing committee do?

Awards Committee. The Awards Committee selects the various awards and grants offered by TESOL each year, with the exception of three (Presidents' Award, the TESOL Award for Distinguished Research, and the James E. Alatis Award for Service to TESOL). Committee members also fundraise for TESOL General Awards Fund and help to publicize the awards and grants offered. Awards committee membership is open to any current member of TESOL International Association.

Table 4.4 TESOL standing committees

Member standing committees	Board standing committees
Awards Committee	Board Operations Committee
Book Publications Committee	Convention Committee
Diversity Committee	Development Committee
Employment Issues Committee	Executive Committee
Global Professional Issues Committee	Finance Committee
Membership Committee	Membership Committee
Nominating Committee	
Professional Development Committee	
Research Committee	
Rules and Resolutions Committee	
Serial Publications Committee	
Standards Standing Committee	
Board Standing Committees	

Books Publication Committee. As its name suggests, the Book Publication Committee selects books and book series for publication by TESOL International Association. The seven-member committee works together to identify areas of interest and topics appropriate to TESOL's overall mission, especially the association's current strategic plan. All manuscripts chosen are intended to be representative and beneficial to TESOL as a professional community. However, TESOL International Association does not, nor have they ever, publish textbooks. Staff indicated that doing so would constitute more of a commercial enterprise. Books Publication Committee members ideally have some experience with publication and are familiar with publication in the field of TESOL specifically.

Diversity Committee. According to the TESOL International Association website, the Diversity Committee 'focuses attention on inclusiveness throughout the association; identifies internal and external strategies, concerns, and recommendations to integrate inclusiveness within TESOL; aligns inclusiveness with TESOL's strategic plan; monitors and evaluates diversity efforts; and brings any issues or concerns to the board' (TESOL International Association, n.d.1). Diversity Committee membership is open to any current member of TESOL International Association; however, the demographics of the committee itself are intended to represented TESOL's membership body worldwide.

Employment Issues Committee. The Employment Issues Committee serves as a forum for issues related to employment in the field of TESOL and makes recommendations directly to the TESOL Board of Directors regarding members' concerns. Employment Issues Committee membership is open to any current member of TESOL International Association; however, committee membership as a whole should represent the diversity of employment types that exist within the field of TESOL itself.

Global Professional Issues Committee (GPIC). The Global Professional Issues Committee serves as a forum for English language educators living outside the United States. Like the Employment Issues Committee, the GPIC makes recommendations to the TESOL Board of Directors concerning the unique needs and challenges of global TESOL professionals.

Nominating Committees. The Nominating Committee, as its name suggests, seeks nominations for the following: president of TESOL, TESOL Board of Directors, and the subsequent year's Nominating Committee. The majority of the work that the Nominating Committee does is conducted in June and July. Qualifications for serving on the Nominating Committee are more specific and include at least four years of TESOL membership and significant service to TESOL within the previous six years; the latter might consist of membership in a standing committee, service on the Board of

Directors, and/or strong evidence of leadership within certain areas of TESOL that compel professional involvement.

Professional Development Committee. The Professional Development Committee (PDC) seeks to identify the unique needs of TESOL educators and recommend specific programmes and professional development opportunities designed to address those needs. The PDC is also charged with overseeing the implementation of such programmes and evaluating their effectiveness. Five portfolios, representing five distinct types of professional development opportunities, are actively maintained by the PDC. These include preconvention institutes, academies, online professional development and distance education, leadership development, and symposia. PDC members should have a background in providing professional development, as well as familiarity with a specific type of language instruction.

Research Committee. The Research Committee coordinates with the Serial Publications, Books Publication, Professional Development, and Conference Committees, as well as with various members of research-oriented interest sections, to foster, assess, and promote the development of activities related to TESOL research. A significant objective of the Research Committee is to develop and implement the TESOL Research Agenda (see Chapter 3) while also encouraging endeavours that foster TESOL-related research in the future.

Rules and Resolutions Committee. The Rules and Resolutions Committee reviews any resolutions before they are put before voting members at the TESOL Convention's annual business meeting. The Rules and Resolutions Committee may also supervise the execution of approved resolutions and/or evaluate or recommend editorial corrections to TESOL governance documents. Other than strong editorial skills, members of the Rules and Resolutions Committee should be familiar with TESOL as an organization and with the structure of TESOL resolutions specifically.

Serial Publications Committee. The Serial Publications Committee oversees and ensures the relevance and quality of TESOL's serial publications. The committee also develops and communicates the mission of each serial publication to its respective editors. Members of the Serial Publications Committee may have prior editorial experience; however, all members should be familiar with TESOL Serial Publications specifically and with scholarly publications in the field of TESOL as a whole.

Standards Standing Committee. As its name suggests, the Standards Standing Committee oversees all projects and initiatives concerning TESOL standards. In addition to proposing future standards, the Standards Standing Committee also monitors the implementation and development of TESOL standards. Standards Standing Committee membership is open to TESOL members with both experience and knowledge pertaining to standards in language education.

Boards Operations Committee. The Boards Operations Committee reviews TESOL's Standing Rules and Operational Procedures and evaluates any revisions to the standing rules submitted by entities outside the Boards Operations Committee itself. Boards Operations Committee members are composed of members of the TESOL Board of Directors.

Convention Committee. The Convention Committee is concerned with all policy and decisions related to the annual TESOL Convention, including development of the convention theme and supervision of its academic programme. The Convention Committee is composed of the incoming convention programme chair, the current convention programme chair, and the immediate past convention programme chair.

Development Committee. The Development Committee oversees and recommends policy concerning the diversification of TESOL International Association's revenue-generating activities. In addition to making recommendations directly to the Board of Directors regarding revenue diversification, the Development Committee is charged with educating TESOL members about TESOL's revenue diversification objectives and undertakings. Development Committee members are composed of TESOL Board of Directors members with knowledge or experience in development and fundraising. Development Committee members should also represent a balance of socioeconomic and demographic backgrounds.

Executive Committee. The Executive Committee decides policy and handles any TESOL-related business that occurs between meetings of the Board of Directors. The Executive Committee is composed of just three members: the previous TESOL president, the president-elect, and the current president.

Finance Committee. The Finance Committee evaluates and presents TESOL International Association's proposed budget to the Board of Directors. Additionally, the Finance Committee reviews TESOL's investment portfolio, quarterly financial reports, and annual audit report, as well as drafting and submitting financial policy to the board. The Finance Committee is composed of current members of the TESOL Board of Directors.

Membership Committee. The Membership Committee is concerned with membership development activities, as well as with the various levels/types of membership and the benefits that apply to each. The Membership Committee is composed of members of the Board of Directors, as well as two non-board TESOL members.

How do I join a standing committee?

Each year, TESOL International Association releases an official call for committee members for its various standing committees. Available slots within the committees depend upon which previous members happen to be completing their term of service. Current TESOL members who are interested in joining a committee are encouraged to visit the TESOL Standing Committee website (http://www.tesol.org/about-tesol/association-governance/standing-committees) and look for the most recent 'Call for Volunteers'. We should point out that committee applicants must be able to attend TESOL's annual convention at their own expense, in addition to several other responsibilities and commitments.

TESOL Interest Sections

What are TESOL Interest Sections?

There are currently 21 TESOL Interest Sections (ISs) available to members of the association (see list below). While members may join and follow any number of ISs, new members are asked to declare a *primary* IS through which they can connect with other TESOL professionals worldwide who share their specific interest and expertise. As of May 2014, the three ISs with the highest number of members were *English as a Foreign Language*, *Teacher Education*, and *Intensive English Programs* (TESOL International Association, n.d.). However, the top three ISs chosen as members' *primary* interest were *English as a Foreign Language*, *Intensive English Programs*, and *Adult Education*. From these numbers, as well as the membership statistics above, we can see a trend in TESOL interest toward EFL, IEPs, teacher education, and adult education.

- Adult Education
- Applied Linguistics
- Bilingual Education
- Computer-Assisted Language Learning
- Elementary Education
- English as a Foreign Language
- English for Specific Purposes
- Higher Education
- Intercultural Communication

- Intensive English Programs
- International Teaching Assistants
- Materials Writers
- Non-native English Speakers in TESOL
- Program Administration
- Refugee Concerns
- Second Language Writing
- Secondary Schools
- Social Responsibility
- Speech, Pronunciation, and Listening
- Teacher Education
- Video and Digital Media.

What do TESOL Interest Sections do?

Perhaps the most significant contribution of TESOL ISs to the association as a whole is their reviewing of proposals for the Annual TESOL International Convention and English Language Expo (for more about the convention, see below). Furthermore, the Interest Section Leadership Council helps facilitate and maintain the relationship between interest sections and the board of directors, standing committees, affiliates, and other bodies within TESOL.

For IS members, however, having the opportunity to connect with other members with similar interests is probably one of the greatest advantages of joining such a group. Without a doubt, ISs are an excellent way for practitioners to join a community of experts in the field and to develop a network of peers within the profession worldwide. In particular, ISs serve as venues through which practitioners can ask important questions of colleagues and experts in a low-stakes environment without needing to conduct research or contact the TESOL Association directly. One example of such a question referenced by TESOL staff was a threaded discussion in an IS stemming from a question regarding whether or not to excuse absences for non-US recognized holidays in IEP programmes.

Many interest sections also publish their own online newsletters. We highly recommend that readers new to the field become involved with a TESOL International Association interest section (or several sections!) right away.

TESOL affiliates

What is a TESOL affiliate?

Ideally, a TESOL affiliate represents a distinct membership, whether it be regional or professional in nature. State, national, or regional associations who have at least 50 members and are committed to the teaching and learning of English may apply to become TESOL affiliates. Benefits available to affiliates include keynote speaker requests, a limited number of complementary memberships and annual conference registrations, special accommodations and marketing opportunities at TESOL's annual conference (including an affiliate booth, colloquium, and leadership workshop), an online newsletter (*The Affiliate News*) specifically published for affiliates worldwide, access to event promotion via TESOL's online Worldwide Calendar of Events, and opportunities to network and exchange information online via the affiliate leaders online community.

Importantly, all TESOL affiliates remain independent, autonomous organizations, despite their status as TESOL affiliates. They are represented by the Affiliate Leadership Council, which works to address any affiliate concerns and issues. The Affiliate Leadership Council consists of the four members elected by the affiliate leaders to serve as affiliate representatives, as well as one board liaison and one staff liaison who serve as non-voting members.

Currently, TESOL is affiliated with over 100 independent associations representing more than 47,000 language professionals. (For a list of current TESOL affiliates, see the following website: http://www.tesol.org/connect/affiliates-regional-organizations/worldwide-affiliate-directory). Readers who may be interested in helping their regional association become a TESOL affiliate are encouraged to consult the guidelines for prospective affiliates at the following address: http://www.tesol.org/connect/affiliates-regional-organizations/become-a-tesol-affiliate/.

TESOL advocacy

What is the role of advocacy in TESOL International Association?

TESOL International Association seeks to support both the field and the profession of TESOL, as well as the learners that it serves. Such advocacy support may take different forms, ranging from the development of standards, to the publication of position papers, and to more grassroots advocacy. TESOL staff indicated that most advocacy efforts within the association come down to education and networking. In this regard, advocacy can mean outreach to members and/or legislators on a particular issue or policy, while at the same time it can refer to the creation of relationships with existing agencies and the fostering of supportive networks between members.

What type of specific advocacy efforts is TESOL International Association engaged in?

As a non-profit organization in the United States, TESOL International Association may engage in *advocacy*, but not *political activity*. The former is considered issue-based, while the latter is defined as support for (or opposition to) a particular candidate or political party. While many of the advocacy activities that the association engages in are specific to the United States (e.g. articulating positions on issues and/or legislation that influence the profession, making statements on US Department of Education initiatives, etc.), others are not. For example, TESOL staff indicated that policy issues such as teacher evaluation and teacher preparation are relevant internationally.

Furthermore, TESOL staff indicated that coalitions with like-minded organizations are an important part of advocacy for TESOL International Association. For example, at the time of publication, the Association was a member of the National Coalition for Literacy (NCL), which is focused on adult education policies in the United States.

How can I become more involved with TESOL advocacy?

One way to begin becoming involved with TESOL advocacy is to be fully aware of the issues, controversies, legislation, etc., that most influence the field and its learners. A good place to start is TESOL International Association's membership newsletter, *TESOL Connection* (see below), which features a regular column on policy issues. Readers are encouraged to use this resource as a way to stay abreast of the most pressing issues that influence English language teaching and learning. For more in-depth coverage of the issues that most matter to TESOL, readers can consult TESOL professional papers and/ or policy briefs (more about these below).

The association also hosts its annual *TESOL Advocacy and Policy Summit* (formerly Advocacy Day) during which attendees can receive training on how best to serve as advocates within their communities while also learning about federal education policy and political trends that influence the field of TESOL as a whole. For more on *TESOL Advocacy and Policy Summit*, which is usually held in Arlington, Virginia, see http://www.tesol.org/advance-the-field/advocacy-resources/tesol-advocacy-policy-summit/. Finally, readers are encouraged to inquire about specific advocacy initiatives within the TESOL Interest Sections to which they belong.

TESOL Central Office

What is the Central Office?

In addition to the many member volunteers who help run the organization, TESOL International Association has a central staff office located in Alexandria, Virginia, USA. The Central Office holds regular business hours and at the time of publication employed 19 members. Essentially, the role of TESOL staff is to support the efforts of members and leaders of the association and to ensure that the vision of the volunteer membership is operationalized.

What does the Central Office do?

Staff members assume a multitude of responsibilities for the association, including the management of advocacy issues, grant writing, handling government relations, directing educational programmes, management of digital content (both the website and social media), membership development, media and marketing, convention planning, publications, and many, many other tasks and duties too numerous to name. Clearly, the importance of the Central Office to TESOL International Association's continued success cannot be overestimated. Still, TESOL staff themselves reminded us that they are not the experts in the field; rather, their role is to support the volunteer effort of association members and leadership.

Resources of TESOL International Association

TESOL conventions

What is the TESOL Convention?

The annual International Convention and English Language Expo is the largest convention for English language teaching professionals in the world. It hosts over 6,500 international attendees, 700 education sessions, and 150 exhibits. To date, the TESOL Convention has always been hosted within a relatively large city in North America (the United States or Canada). For readers interested in the history of TESOL conventions since the origins of the association, the list below contains past TESOL annual convention themes, dates, and locations, beginning with the first annual convention in Miami, Florida, in 1967:

- 2015: 25–28 March, TESOL Convention and English Language Expo, Toronto, Canada

  Crossing Borders, Building Bridges

- 2014: 26–29 March, TESOL Convention and English Language Expo, Portland, Oregon

  Explore, Sustain, Renew ELT for the Next Generation

- 2013: 20–23 March, TESOL Convention and English Language Expo, Dallas, Texas

  Harmonizing Language, Heritage and Cultures

- 2012: 28–31 March, Annual TESOL Convention and English Language Expo, Philadelphia, Pennsylvania

  A Declaration of Excellence

- 2011: 16–19 March, 45th Annual Convention, New Orleans, Louisiana

  Examining the 'E' in TESOL

- 2010: 24–27 March, 44th Annual Convention, Boston, Massachusetts

  Re-imagining TESOL

- 2009: 26–28 March, 43rd Annual Convention, Denver, Colorado

  Uncharted Mountains – Forging New Pathways

- 2008: 2–5 April, 42nd Annual Convention, New York

  Worlds of TESOL – Building Communities of Practice, Inquiry and Creativity

- 2007: 21–24 March, 41st Annual Convention, Seattle, Washington

  Spanning the Globe – Tides of Change

- 2006: 15–19 March, 40th Annual Convention, Tampa Bay, Florida

  Daring to Lead

- 2005: 29 March–2 April, 39th Annual Convention, San Antonio, Texas

  Teaching Learning, Learning Teaching: A Nexus in Texas

- 2004: 29 March–3 April, 38th Annual Convention, Long Beach, California

  Soaring Far – Catching Dreams

- 2003: 25–29 March, 37th Annual Convention, Baltimore, Maryland

  Hearing Every Voice

- 2002: 9–13 April, 36th Annual Convention, Salt Lake City, Utah

  Language of the Human Spirit

- 2001: 27 February–3 March, 35th Annual Convention, St Louis, Missouri

  Gateway to the Future

- 2000: 14–18 March, 34th Annual Convention, Vancouver, British Columbia, Canada

  Navigating the New Millennium

- 1999: 9–13 March, 33rd Annual Convention, New York

  Avenues to Success

- 1998: 17–21 March, 32nd Annual Convention, Seattle, Washington

  Connecting Our Global Community

- 1997: 11–15 March, 31st Annual Convention, Orlando, Florida

  Creating Magic with TESOL '97

- 1996: 26–30 March, 30th Annual Convention, Chicago, Illinois

  The Art of TESOL

- 1995: 28 March–1 April, 29th Annual Convention, Long Beach, California

  Building Futures Together

- 1994: 8–12 March, 28th Annual Convention, Baltimore, Maryland

  Sharing Our Stories

- 1993: 13–17 April, 27th Annual Convention, Atlanta, Georgia

  Designing Our World

- 1992: 3–8 March, 26th Annual Convention, Vancouver, British Columbia, Canada

  Explore and Discover

- 1991: 24–28 March, 25th Annual Convention, New York

  25 Years as an International Family

- 1990: 6–10 March, 24th Annual Convention, San Francisco, California

  'On Track' in San Francisco

- 1989: 7–11 March, 23rd Annual Convention, San Antonio, Texas

  Festival '89

- 1988: 8–13 March, 22nd Annual Convention, Chicago, Illinois

  Connecting in Chicago … Our Kind of Town

- 1987: 21–25 April, 21st Annual Convention, Miami Beach, Florida

  Coming of Age – TESOL '87

- 1986: 3–8 March, 20th Annual Convention, Anaheim, California

  TESOL '86 – California

- 1985: 5–14 April, 19th Annual Convention, New York

  New Ideas, New Faces, New York

- 1984: 6–11 March, 18th Annual Convention, Houston, Texas

- 1983: 15–20 March, 17th Annual Convention, Toronto, Ontario, Canada

- 1982: 1–6 May, 16th Annual Convention, Honolulu, Hawai'i

- 1981: 3–8 March, 15th Annual Convention, Detroit, Michigan

- 1980: 4–9 March, 14th Annual Convention, San Francisco, California

- 1979: 27 February–4 March, 13th Annual Convention, Boston, Massachusetts

- 1978: 4–9 April, 12th Annual Convention, Mexico City

- 1977: 26 April–1 May, 11th Annual Convention, Miami Beach, Florida

  Hub of the Americas

- 1976: 2–7 March, 10th Annual Convention, New York

- 1975: 4–9 March, Ninth Annual Convention, Los Angeles, California

- 1974: 5–10 March, Eighth Annual Convention, Denver, Colorado
- 1973: 9–13 May, Seventh Annual Convention, San Juan, Puerto Rico

  In Puerto Rico English is a Second Language
- 1972: 26 February-1 March, Sixth Annual Convention, Washington, DC
- 1971: 3–7 March, Fifth Annual Convention, New Orleans, Louisiana
- 1970: 18–21 March, Fourth Annual Convention, San Francisco, California
- 1969: 5–8 March, Third Annual Convention, Chicago, Illinois
- 1968: 6–9 March, Second Annual Convention, San Antonio, Texas

  The Second Convention of the Association of Teachers of English to Speakers of Other Languages
- 1967: 20–22 April, First Annual Convention, Miami Beach, Florida

  First Convention of the Association of Teachers of English to Speakers of Other Languages
- 1966: 17–19 March, New York

  Third National Conference on Teaching English to Speakers of Other Languages

What is the purpose of the TESOL Convention?

The primary purpose of the TESOL Convention is to offer high quality education to TESOL professionals. In doing so, the convention also serves as a venue for disseminating the most updated information on issues that influence the field, including the most recent scholarship, technology, resources, techniques, etc. Beyond the information gained from time spent in sessions, workshops, key note addresses, etc., it may be that the greatest benefit to members who attend TESOL Convention is the opportunity to meet peers and network with others in the field. For TESOL International Association itself, the annual TESOL Convention is by far its largest source of revenue.

How can I become more involved in the annual convention?

Members who wish to become involved in the convention beyond attendance are encouraged to pursue any of the following:

1 Apply to become a reviewer of proposals.

2 Submit a proposal.

3 Volunteer at the convention.

4 Participate in online discussions before the convention.

5 Comment on the blogs written by plenarists that are published prior
   to the convention.

TESOL symposia

TESOL symposia are one-day programmes collaboratively hosted by TESOL
International Association and one of its affiliates worldwide (see our
discussion of TESOL affiliates above). Each symposium is centred on
a key topic chosen by the affiliate. Recent TESOL symposia have been
held in Egypt, China, Cameroon, and Puerto Rico. For a complete list of
past symposia, including the topics chosen for each, see the following
website: http://www.tesol.org/attend-and-learn/symposiums-academies/
past-symposiums-academies/.

What is the purpose of TESOL symposia?

TESOL staff suggested in interviews that the symposia are an important way
that the association achieves international visibility while acknowledging the
contribution of global constituents on a much smaller scale than the annual
convention allows. The association is also able to be somewhat strategic in its
choice of symposia locations and to carefully craft the message that will be
articulated through a particular symposium in a particular region of the world.

TESOL Academies

What are TESOL Academies?

TESOL Academies are intensive workshops for a relatively small number
of TESOL practitioners (approximately 35). Each academy takes place at
a university and includes 10 hours of both traditional conference-style
format and in-depth workshops, led by an expert in the field. Recent TESOL
academies have been held throughout the United States and in Brazil, while an
upcoming TESOL Academy at the time of publication was to be held in Seoul,
Korea. For a complete list of past academies, including the topics chosen

for each, see the following website: http://www.tesol.org/attend-and-learn/
symposiums-academies/past-symposiums-academies/.

What is the purpose of TESOL Academies?

TESOL Academies are designed to provide participants with concentrated
study in a key area of practice or issue in the field of English language teaching.
Additionally, the Academies offer networking opportunities, hands-on practice,
and potential continuing education credit for some practitioners.

TESOL position statements, professional papers, and briefs

What are TESOL position statements?

TESOL International Association has developed 59 various position statements over the years, the earliest going back to the 1970s. These are
intended to serve as official positions taken by the association as a whole
on a particular issue or policy. Some developed in response to legislation in
the United States, while others are responses to a broad range of controversies and trends in the field. All position papers are ultimately approved
by the TESOL Board before release. Depending on the nature of the paper,
dissemination channels may include other organizations, legislators, and/or
key decision-makers (e.g. federal agencies). Regardless, all position papers
are published on the TESOL website. Interested readers are encouraged to
visit the following website for links to TESOL position statements grouped
thematically according whether they are most relevant to adult education;
higher education; social issues and diversity; teacher education; US education
policies and legislation; or young learners (http://www.tesol.org/advance-the-
field/position-statements). For the sake of better understanding the trajectory
of TESOL position statements, they are listed chronologically below:

- Position Statement on Academic and Degree-Granting Credit for
  ESOL Courses in Postsecondary Education, June 2012.

- Increasing Academic Achievement and Enhancing Capacity for
  English Language Learners: Principles and Recommendations for
  the Reauthorization of the Elementary and Secondary Education Act,
  March 2011.

- Position Statement on the Acquisition of Academic Proficiency in
  English at the Postsecondary Level, November 2010.

- TESOL and AZ-TESOL Joint Statement on the Arizona Teacher English Fluency Initiative, May 2010.

- Position Statement on Adult English as a Second or Additional Language Programs, March 2010.

- Position Paper on Language and Literacy Development for Young English Language Learners, March 2010.

- TESOL Issues Joint Statement with AAIEP, UCIEP on IEP Governance, January 2010.

- Position Statement on Teaching English as a Foreign or Additional Language to Young Learners, October 2009.

- Position Statement on Independent Short-Term TESL/TEFL Certificate Programs, July 2009.

- Position Statement on the Rights of Deaf Learners to Acquire Full Proficiency in a Native Signed Language, July 2009.

- Position Statement Opposing Bullying, Harassment, and Hate Crimes, March 2009.

- Position Statement on English Entrance Exams for Non-native English Speakers at Schools and Universities, March 2009.

- Position Statement on Fairness and Equity in ESL Program Reduction, March 2009.

- Position Statement on Academic and Degree-Granting Credit for ESOL Courses, October 2008.

- Position Statement on the Status of, and Professional Equity for, the Field of Teaching English to Speakers of Other Languages, June 2008.

- Position Statement on Teacher Preparation for Content-Based Instruction, March 2008.

- Position Statement on Professionalization and Credentialing for Adult ESOL Educators, April 2008.

- Position Statement on English as a Global Language, April 2008.

- Statement of Principles and Preliminary Recommendations for the Reauthorization of the Elementary and Secondary Education Act, October 2006; amended October 2007.

- Position Statement on Terminal Degree for Teaching English as a Second, Foreign, or Additional Language, October 2007.

- Position Statement on the Role of Teachers' Associations in Education Policy and Planning, October 2007.

- Position Statement on Teacher Credentialing for Teachers of English to Speakers of Other Languages in Primary and Secondary Schools, June 2007.

- Position Statement on the Status and Rights of Teachers, March 2007.

- Position Statement on the Identification of English Language Learners with Special Educational Needs, March 2007.

- Position Statement on the Diversity of English Language Learners in the United States, October 2006.

- Position Statement on Immigration Reform in the United States, June 2006.

- Position Statement Against Discrimination of Non-native Speakers of English in the Field of TESOL, March 2006.

- Position Statement on Adolescent English Language Learners in Adult ESL Programs in the United States, March 2006.

- Position Paper on Assessment and Accountability under NCLB, October 2005.

- Position Statement on US Visa Policy, October 2005.

- Position Paper on English-Only Legislation in the United States, June 2005.

- Position Statement on US Visa Issues for International Students and Educators, June 2005.

- Position Statement on Research and Policy, February 2005.

- Position Statement on Highly Qualified Teachers Under No Child Left Behind, February 2005.

- Position Statement on the Redesign of the US Citizenship Exam, October 2004.

- Position Statement on Multilingualism, October 2004.

- Position Statement on the Use of B-Visas for Short-Term Language Study, June 2004.

- Position Statement on the Value of Intensive English Programs in the United States, June 2004.

- Position Statement on Accreditation for Intensive English Programs in the United States, March 2004.

- Position Statement on Professional Equity for the Field of Teaching English to Speakers of Other Languages, October 2003.

- Position Statement on the Preparation of Pre-K-12 Educators for Cultural and Linguisitic Diversity in the United States, October 2003.

- Position Statement on Teaching English as a Foreign Language to Young Learners, October 2003.

- Position Statement on Local Flexibility in the Education of English Language Learners, June 2003.

- Position Statement on Teacher Quality in the Field of Teaching English to Speakers of Other Languages, June 2003.

- Position Statement on Independent TESL/TEFL Certificate Programs, June 2003.

- Position Paper on High-Stakes Testing for K-12 English Language Learners in the United States of America, March 2003.

- Position Statement on International Education, March 2003.

- Position Paper on Equitable Treatment for Part-time, Adjunct, and Contingent Faculty, March 2003.

- Position Statement Opposing Discrimination, October 2001.

- Adult ESL Language and Literacy Instruction: A Vision and Action Agenda for the Twenty-first Century, October 2001.

- Position Statement on Language Right, October 2000.

- Assessment and Accountability for English for Speakers of Other Languages (ESOL) Students, June 2000.

- Position Statement on Degree-Granting Credit for ESL Courses, June 2000.

- Position Paper on Family Involvement in the Education of English for Speakers of Other Languages (ESOL) Students, June 2000.

- Position Statement on Native Language Support in the Acquisition of English as a Second Language (ESL), December 1999.

- Position Statement on the Acquisition of Academic Proficiency in English, August 1999.

- Position Statement of the TESOL Board on African American Vernacular English, March 1997.

- Position Statement of the TESOL Board on Language Varieties, October 1996.

What are TESOL professional papers?

While position papers were begun because TESOL leadership felt that they ought to take explicit positions with regard to certain issues and policies, professional papers (also referred to as 'White Papers') are intended to go a step further. Professional papers offer an in-depth discussion of an issue, without necessarily advocating a specific position in the same manner that position papers do. They are typically longer than position statements or briefs (approximately 10–20 pages) and include thoughtful dialogue and support from literature, research, etc. The audience for these papers is both the field at large and the general, non-academic public. While position statements are written by the association, authors of these longer professional papers are usually commissioned. Thus far, TESOL International Association has issued two professional papers. These can be accessed at the following website: http://www.tesol.org/read-and-publish/newsletters-other-publications/tesol-professional-papers-and-briefs/.

What are TESOL Policy Briefs?

These are intended to be explanatory pieces, with less elaboration than professional papers (or 'White Papers'). They essentially offer more concise versions of what is offered by professional papers. At the time of publication, TESOL International Association had published one policy brief, which was prompted by the Obama administration's initiation of the Deferred Action for Childhood Arrivals policy. This policy brief can be viewed here: http://www.tesol.org/docs/advocacy/tesol-daca-policy-brief-sept-2012-final.pdf?sfvrsn=8/.

What are TESOL Issue Briefs?

Similar to policy briefs, TESOL issue briefs offer concise explanations of issues (as opposed to explicit policies) relevant to English language teaching and learning, both within the United States and abroad. At the time of publication, the two TESOL Issue Briefs published thus far by TESOL have been related to the Common Core State Standards in the United States and how they affect English language learners and teachers. To read these briefs, visit TESOL's 'Professional Papers and Briefs' website: http://www.tesol.org/read-and-publish/newsletters-other-publications/ tesol-professional-papers-and-briefs/.

Where do I begin?

The above publications may seem overwhelming to readers who are interested in gaining a better understanding of the issues and policies that most influence TESOL but don't quite know where to start. We recommend the following strategies for newcomers to the field attempting to navigate TESOL position statements, professional papers, and briefs:

- Don't try to read everything at once. Begin with your particular area(s) of interest. For example, the position statements are organized by category so that a practitioner who works with younger learners can access all of these statements in the same place (http://www.tesol.org/read-and-publish/newsletters-other-publications/tesol-professional-papers-and-briefs).

- Read two key position statements that we believe are especially relevant to the field as a whole: 'Position Statement on Language Rights' (http://www.tesol.org/docs/pdf/2115.pdf?sfvrsn=2), released in October of 2000, and 'Position Statement on English as a Global Language' (http://www.tesol.org/docs/pdf/10884.pdf?sfvrsn=2), released in April of 2008.

- Scan briefs and position statements for policies and issues relevant to your own teaching context.

- Read the first TESOL Professional Paper, 'A Principles-Based Approach for English Language Teaching Policies and Practices' (Mahboob and Tilakaratna, 2012), which outlines six key principles for implementing language policy, standards, and practices across a variety of contexts.

TESOL publications

What sorts of things does TESOL publish?

In addition to the professional papers and policy briefs described above, TESOL International Association publishes books, two refereed journals (*TESOL Quarterly* and *TESOL Journal*), newsletters (*TESOL Connections*, in addition to Interest Section newsletters), *English Language Bulletin*, *TESOL Blog*, and a range of standards (see our discussion of standards in Chapter

2). While we describe each briefly below, we also recommend exploring TESOL International Association's 'Read and Publish' page on the association website: http://www.tesol.org/read-and-publish/.

The books that TESOL International Association publishes are primarily targeted at teachers. They are written by authors who have significant experience in the English language classroom themselves. They are practical and offer excellent professional development to English language teachers, especially novice instructors. For a complete catalogue of TESOL International Association's published books, visit the association's virtual bookstore, where members receive a significant discount on purchases: http://www.tesol. org/read-and-publish/bookstore/. Anecdotally, TESOL staff indicated that the association's bestsellers include Don Snow's (2006) *More than a Native Speaker* and the *New Ways* series, which is a collection of small volumes that each contain collections of activities on a given topic.

TESOL Quarterly is widely considered the flagship journal for the field of TESOL as a whole (see our chronological study of *TESOL Quarterly* articles in Chapter 1). Its audience is primarily researchers and practitioners in higher education who study English teaching and learning. *TESOL Journal*, which is solely published electronically, is slightly more practice-oriented, although its perspectives on practice are rooted in research and theory. *TESOL Journal* addresses graduate programmes, classroom teachers, and classroom practice, while its mission emphasizes a range of research relevant to language teaching at all levels and across a variety of contexts.

TESOL Connections is published as an electronic newsletter for members of TESOL International Association. It contains highly practical articles specifically written for classroom teaching, i.e. practical teaching tips, strategies, and resources relevant to classroom teaching. While subscriptions to the newsletter itself are only available to current members, past issues are now freely accessible and searchable online via the *TESOL Connections* website: http://www.tesol.org/read-and-publish/newsletters-other-publications/ tesol-connections/.

English Language Teaching Bulletin is a bi-weekly digest that compiles news from around the world relevant to ELT, as well as a small section devoted to association news. At the time of publication, *English Language Teaching Bulletin* reached over 37,000 subscribers. Email subscriptions are free to anyone, and archives of past and current issues are available online. *English Language Teaching Bulletin* is somewhat unique in that it features news articles rather than scholarly articles. Because it also serves as a form of revenue generation for TESOL International Association, *English Language Teaching Bulletin* does contain advertisements.

TESOL Blog (http://blog.tesol.org/) is a slightly more informal venue for association news, teaching tips, teaching and learning resources, etc., relevant to TESOL. Because it is a blog, *TESOL Blog* is likely to contain more current and/or time-dependent topics than some other sources. For example, in the summer of 2014, *TESOL Blog* included an entry entitled '4 World Cup Writing Activities' (Shvidko, 2014).

TESOL Community

What is TESOL Community?

TESOL Community refers to a peer-to-peer online network that allows TESOL members to connect with other members worldwide regarding shared interests, resources, etc. In accordance with the conventions of online social networking, *TESOL Community* participants are encouraged to upload profile pictures, include a profile bio that introduces themselves to other community members, and to join online groups aligned with various interests within the field of TESOL. Participants may join existing discussions or begin new ones relevant to their interests and expertise. Additionally, *TESOL Community* connects member participants with resources, opportunities for professional development, and a calendar of events that includes regional happenings as well as national.

To date, *TESOL Community* is arguably the most interactive resource currently offered by the association. It is especially beneficial to members in that it provides a venue for members of the same interest section to connect. Every TESOL International Association interest section (see our discussion of interest sections above) has its own 'group' within *TESOL Community* with access to a variety of tools, including a group email list, a space for threaded discussions (within the specific interest section or with the entire *TESOL Community*), a blog, and a virtual library for posting resources.

How do I join TESOL Community?

At the time of publication, participation in *TESOL Community* requires a TESOL International Association membership login and password. See the *TESOL Community* webpage at the following address for further details: http://community.tesol.org/welcome.htm/.

TESOL Resource Center

What is the TESOL Resource Center?

TESOL Resource Center (TRC) is a component of the TESOL International Association website which compiles user-generated materials and resources uploaded by other TRC users. The TRC is searchable according to the type of resource (e.g. lesson plan, assessment, teaching tip), its audience (e.g. university, teacher training), the audience language proficiency, and by TESOL Interest Section. Recorded plenaries, virtual seminars, sessions from TESOL Convention, symposia, etc., as well as some live face-to-face events are also offered via TRC, though some of these are for TESOL members only. At the time of TESOL staff interviews, the TRF featured 354 resources, with an average of one new resource added per week.

Who has access?

At the time of publication, the TRC is divided into member-only and all-access resources. Members and non-members alike are encouraged to visit the website for further details, as availability of certain resources is likely to change: http://www.tesol.org/connect/tesol-resource-center/.

TESOL webinars and online courses

Currently, TESOL International Association offers six online courses, four certificate programmes, and 12–16 virtual seminars per year. The prices for each vary according to the resource offered and the membership status of the participant (e.g. virtual seminars are often free to members but approximately US$45 for non-members). As these prices are likely to change, we encourage readers interested in taking advantage of these offerings to consult the TESOL 'Online Courses & Virtual Seminars' website (http://www.tesol.org/attend-and-learn/online-courses-seminars), the 'Online Certificate and Leadership Training' website (http://www.tesol.org/attend-and-learn/certificate-leadership-programmes), or contact TESOL Education Programs directly (edprograms@tesol.org).

TESOL awards and grants

TESOL International Association offers a variety of grants and scholarships, both to encourage research and service in the field, and to enable more

TESOL members to attend the Annual TESOL Convention and English Language Expo. The TESOL Awards and Grants website (http://www.tesol.org/about-tesol/tesol-awards-grants) contains links to convention grants and scholarships; awards for excellence and service; and need-based grants especially for adult ESL education programmes. Again, because programmes of this nature are likely to change, we encourage readers to consult the website directly for details.

5

TESOL Resources

Common TESOL acronyms and initialisms

In the space below, we've compiled a list of common acronyms and initialisms which readers are likely to encounter in TESOL-related discourse. While some refer to professional organizations and popular assessment measures, others pertain to well-known concepts within the field (i.e. interlanguage). For the latter, we recommend consulting 'TESOL-related terminology' (below) for further explanation.

AAAL American Association of Applied Linguistics

ACTFL American Council on the Teaching of Foreign Languages

AILA International Association of Applied Linguistics

BC British Council

CAELA Center for Adult English Language Acquisition

CAL Center for Applied Linguistics

CALL Computer-Assisted Language Learning

CBI Content based instruction; also Computer-Based Instruction

CEELT Cambridge Examination in English for Language Teachers

CELTA Certificate in English Language Teaching for Adults

CLL Community language learning

CLT Communicative language teaching; also Critical Language Teaching

CMC Computer-Mediated Communication

CPE Cambridge Proficiency Examination

DELTA Diploma in Teaching English to Speakers of other Languages

EAP	English for Academic Purposes
EFL	English as a Foreign Language (English study in a non-English-dominant context)
EIL	English as an International Language
ELF	English as a Lingua Franca
ELL	English Language Learner
ELT	English Language Teaching
ESL	English as a Second Language (English study in an English-dominant country)
ESOL	English to Speakers of Other Languages
ESP	English for Specific Purposes
ETS	Educational Testing Service
FL	Foreign language
GRE	Graduate Record Examinations
IATEFL	International Association of Teachers of English as a Foreign Language (organization)
IELTS	International English Language Testing System
IEP	Intensive English programme (for non-matriculated university students who wish to improve their academic English for study at an English-dominated university)
IL	Interlanguage
IPA	International Phonetic Alphabet
JET	Japan Exchange and Teaching Program
L1	First Language (the first language a child hears and speaks, sometimes referred to as 'native language' or 'mother tongue')
L2	Second Language (any language learned after the L1 is acquired)
LEP	Limited/low English proficient/proficiency (used less frequently today; may have negative connotations)
MMOG	Massively Multiplayer Online Game (e.g., World of Warcraft)
NES	Native English Speaker
NEST	Native English-Speaking Teacher

NNES   Non-native English Speaker

NNEST   Non-native English Speaking Teacher

NNS   Non-native speaker

NS   Native speaker

PDP   Professional development plan

SCT   Sociocultural Theory

SLA   Second Language Acquisition

SLL   Second language learning/Second language learner

SLTD   Second language teacher development

SLTE   Second language teacher education

TBL   Task-Based Learning

TBLT   Task-Based Language Teaching

TEFL   Teaching English as a Foreign Language (English study in a non-English dominant context)

TESL   Teaching English as a Second Language (English study in an English dominant country)

TESOL   Teaching English to Speakers of Other Languages (refers to the term in general and to the organization)

TL   Target language

TLL   Technology Enhanced Language Learning (more from dept. of education)

TOEFL   Test of English as a Foreign Language

TOEIC   Test of English for International Communication

TPR   Total Physical Response

TSE   Test of Spoken English

TWE   Test of Written English

UG   Universal Grammar

WE   World Englishes

ZPD   Zone of Proximal Development

TESOL-related professional associations

While TESOL International Association is arguably the largest and most well-known professional association in the field, other local, regional, national, and/or specialist organizations also contribute to the vitality and diversity of TESOL as a research field and as a profession. Due to space limitations, we have not been able to include them all. However, in the space below we briefly describe six organizations that we believe continue to make unique contributions to TESOL.

IATEFL

The International Association of Teachers as a Foreign Language (IATEFL) is an organization based in the UK that is dedicated to supporting English language professionals worldwide through fostering professional development and offering opportunities for teachers to network with one another. IATEFL hosts an annual four-day conference that attracts over 2,500 attendees. Membership in the organization includes its magazine, *IATEFL Voices*, access to special interest groups, eligibility for scholarships, and participation in networks of teachers from around the world, among other benefits. The IATEFL website also features a page devoted to the English language teaching job market and offers monthly webinars free of charge to members and non-members alike. For more information on IATEFL, visit http://www.iatefl.org/.

TIRF

The International Research Foundation for English Language Education (TIRF) is a foundation that seeks to generate new knowledge about language learning and teaching, ensure that research is applied to actual language practices, organize and disseminate existing language research, and influence relevant language education policies. The TIRF website provides access to a variety of resources, including commissioned reports on key issues in English language education; links to other organizations and associations relevant to TIRF; free online slideshows and training; and thorough reference lists on a variety of key topics in the field of English language teaching and learning. In addition, TIRF sponsors research by offering doctoral dissertation and research grants and compiles information related to outside grants and upcoming conferences. All TIRF resources are free to the general public. While the association does not have paid memberships, it does accept donations. For more information, visit the TIRF website at http://www.tirfonline.org/.

Asia TEFL

Asia TEFL (Teachers of English as a Foreign Language) is a regional English language teacher association founded in 2002 to empower TESOL professionals in Asia to tackle pertinent issues in English language learning and teaching, both in Asia and beyond. Asia TEFL aims at promoting scholarship, disseminating information, and facilitating intercultural and transcultural understanding among people concerned with teaching and learning English in EFL contexts. In particular, this association enables TESOL professionals to do research on issues and concerns rooted in an Asian context. In addition to publishing its own professional journal (*AsiaTESOL*) as an outlet for research in teaching and learning English in Asia, Asia TEFL hosts an annual conference that rotates among countries in the region and is sometimes held jointly with conferences hosted by national associations such as JALT (Japanese Association for Language Teaching), ThaiTESOL, KOTESL (Korea TESOL), and MELTA (Malaysian English Language Teaching Association), among others. For more information, please visit the association's website directly: http://www/asiatefl.org/.

AAAL

AAAL (American Association for Applied Linguistics) was founded in 1977 to promote and disseminate knowledge pertaining to language-related issues that influence individuals and society. The organization hosts an annual conference that attracts applied linguists from all over the world. Membership in AAAL includes complementary membership in AILA (see below), In addition to consideration for distinguished scholar awards and travel grants for attending the conference, AAAL members receive a twice yearly newsletter (*AAAL Letter*) and subscriptions to the *Annual Review of Applied Linguistics* (*ARAL*), *AILA Review*, and *Encyclopedia of Applied Linguistics*. The AAAL website also features a members-only job resources page.

A relatively new feature of the AAAL website of interest to graduate students is the Graduate Student Corner (http://www.aaal.org/content.asp?contentid=154). This section of the website includes a forum, blog, and a collection of resources specific to graduate students. It is hosted by AAAL's Graduate Student Committee, which serves to promote the professional development of graduate students within the committee and to better prepare them for joining the community of applied linguistics as they begin their future careers.

For more information about AAAL, visit http://www.aaal.org/.

AILA

AILA is an abbreviation for *Association Internationale de Linguistique Appliquée*, or *International Association of Applied Linguistics*. This organization, begun in 1964, serves to amalgamate regional and national applied linguistics associations. It boasts over 8,000 members worldwide. In addition to its triennial world congresses, which typically attract approximately 2,000 attendees, AILA helps to connect international researchers, collaborates with a variety of other regional associations, and offers scholarship for attendance to the world congress. The organization also publishes a scholarly review, *AILA Review*, and a book series, *AILA Applied Linguistics Series (ALLS)*, both with publisher John Benjamins. For more information about AILA, see http://www.aila.info/.

SLRF

The Second Language Research Forum (SLRF) is an annual conference held within North America devoted to a range of research interests and practices within the field of SLA. SLRF is unique in that it is more of a travelling conference than a professional association. In other words, there are no memberships for SLRF. It is also entirely student-run. Each year, graduate students from universities across North America compete to host SLRF at their home institution. Student committees are also charged with choosing the theme for SLRF each year and managing abstract reviews. Because each host institution creates its own website each year, there is no central website for SLRF. However, readers who are interested in exploring SLRF further can easily locate past institutions' SLRF websites by using their preferred search engine. In October of 2015, SLRF will be held at Georgia State University in Atlanta, Georgia, USA.

TESOL job market and job placement resources

In the space below, we offer a variety of online resources helpful to readers interested in exploring the myriad opportunities in TESOL-related employment. Because it proved difficult to organize these according to the type of employment advertised (for example, while the HERC website only features positions in higher education, others are more eclectic), we have simply listed the sources in alphabetical order. Readers are encouraged to visit the websites themselves to gain a better understanding of the type of jobs available through each.

- AAAL's Job Search Website (for members only): http://www.aaal.org/jobs_search.asp/
- ACTFL's Career Resources Jobs Page: http://jobcentral.actfl.org/jobs/
- Canadian Linguistic Association (for jobs in Canada): http://cla-acl.ca/
- Center for Applied Linguistics: http://www.cal.org/about/jobs.html
- The Chronicle of Higher Education: http://chronicle.com/section/jobs/61
- Dave's ESL Cafe Job Center: http://www.eslcafe.com/jobs/
- Embassy.org's Business Directory for Educators and Students: http://www.embassy.org/ibc/educators/
- ESL Employment: http://www.eslemployment.com/
- ESL Job's World: http://www.esljobsworld.com/
- Higher Education Recruitment Consortium (HERC): http://www.hercjobs.org/
- IATEFL Job Market: http://www.iatefl.org/jobs/jobs-market/jobs-market-overview/
- Institute of International Education: http://www.iie.org/
- International School Services (ISS): http://educatorcareers.iss.edu/
- The Linguist List's Job Area Index: http://linguistlist.org/jobs/
- Linguistic Society of America Job Center: http://www.linguisticsociety.org/jobs-center/
- Mark's ESL World job page: http://marksesl.com/JobBoard/index.pl/
- The Modern Language Association: http://www.mla.org/jil/
- OverseasJobs.com: http://www.overseasjobs.com/
- TESOL International Association's Career Center (some features are only available to members): http://careers.tesol.org/
- The International Educator (TIE): http://www.tieonline.com/
- U.S. Department of Education Job Postings: http://www.ed.gov/jobs/

- U.S. Department of State: http://careers.state.gov/work/opportunities
- Bureau of Educational and Cultural Affairs Exchange Programs: http://exchanges.state.gov/
- English Language Programs: http://elprograms.org/
- Office of Overseas Schools: http://www.state.gov/m/a/os/
- World Learning: http://www.worldlearning.org/employment/

TESOL research outlets

The following journals serve as outlets for TESOL research publication and scholarly participation (reading current research, learning about new publications in the field, engaging with other subscribers' responses to articles, etc.). Readers are encouraged to visit a journal's website and familiarize themselves with the quality and content of a journal before submitting a manuscript. For more guidance on the process of publication, see our discussions on this topic in Chapter 2 and Chapter 3.

Advances in Language and Literary Studies

http://www.journals.aiac.org.au/index.php/alls/

AILA Review

http://www.aila.info/en/publications/aila-review.html/

Annual Review of Applied Lingusitics

http://journals.cambridge.org/action/displayJournal?jid=APL/

Argentinian Journal of Applied Linguistics

http://www.faapi.org.ar/ajal/home.html/

Asian EFL Journal

http://www.asian-efl-journal.com/

The Asian Journal of English Language and Pedagogy

http://ajelp.upsi.edu.my/

Asian Journal of English Language Teaching

http://www.cuhk.edu.hk/ajelt/

Applied Language Learning

http://www.dliflc.edu/publications.aspx/

Applied Linguistics

http://www.oxfordjournals.org/our_journals/applij/about.html/

Applied Psycholinguistics

http://journals.cambridge.org/action/displayJournal?jid=APS/

Applied Research in English

http://uijs.ui.ac.ir/are/index.php?slc_lang=enandslc_sid=1

Australian Review of Applied Linguistics

http://www.nla.gov.au/openpublish/index.php/aral/

Bilingual Research Journal

http://www.tandf.co.uk/journals/ubrj/

CALICO Journal

https://calico.org/page.php?id=515/

Canadian Journal of Applied Linguistics

http://journals.hil.unb.ca/index.php/CJAL/

Canadian Modern Language Review

http://www.utpjournals.com/Canadian-Modern-Language-Review.html/

Chinese Journal of Applied Linguistics

http://www.degruyter.de/journals/cjal/detailEn.cfm/

Computer Assisted Language Learning – Electronic Journal

http://callej.org/index.html/

Computer Assisted Language Learning

http://www.tandfonline.com/action/aboutThisJournal?show=aimsScopean
  djournalCode=ncal20/

Discourse and Society

http://www.sagepub.in/journals/Journal200873?productType=Journalsand
  subject=L00andsortBy=sortTitle%20ascandfs=1/

E-JournALL (EuroAmerican Journal of Applied Linguistics and Languages)

http://www.e-journall.org/

ELT Journal

http://eltj.oxfordjournals.org/

Engaging Cultures and Voices: The Journal of English Learning through Media

http://ecv.missouri.edu/index.html/

English for Specific Purposes

http://www.journals.elsevier.com/english-for-specific-purposes/

English Language Teacher Education and Development

http://www.elted.net/

English Language Teaching World Online: Voices from the Classroom (ELTWO)

http://blog.nus.edu.sg/eltwo/

English Teaching Forum

http://americanenglish.state.gov/english-teaching-forum/

English Today

http://journals.cambridge.org/action/displayJournal?jid=ENG/

The European Journal of Applied Linguistics and TEFL/

http://www.theeuropeanjournal.eu/

Foreign Language Annals

http://www.actfl.org/i4a/pages/index.cfm?pageid=3320/

GIST: Education and Learning Research Journal

http://gisteducation.weebly.com/

Indian Journal of Applied Linguistics

http://bahripublications.in/volumes.php?j_id=27andtyp=cur/

International Journal of Applied Linguistics and English Literature

http://www.ijalel.org/

International Journal of Innovation in English Language Teaching and Research

https://www.novapublishers.com/catalog/product_info.
php?products_id=14903/

The International Journal of Language Learning and Applied Linguistics World (IJLLALW)

http://www.languagelearningworld.org/

International Journal of Multilingualism

http://www.tandf.co.uk/journals/rmjm/

International Journal of Society, Culture, and Language

http://www.ijscl.net/

The internet TESL Journal (no longer accepting submissions but still serves as online resource)

http://iteslj.org/

Issues in Applied Linguistics

http://www.escholarship.org/uc/appling_ial/

Hong Kong Journal of Applied Linguistics

http://www2.caes.hku.hk/hkjal/

Iranian Journal of Language Teaching Research

http://www.urmia.ac.ir/ijltr/default.aspx/

JALT Journal

http://jalt-publications.org/jj/

Journal for Language Teaching

http://www.ajol.info/index.php/jlt/index/

Journal of Education and Training Studies

http://redfame.com/journal/index.php/jets/index/

Journal of English for Academic Purposes

http://www.journals.elsevier.com/journal-of-english-for-academic-purposes/

Journal of Immersion and Content-based Language Education

http://benjamins.com/#catalog/journals/jicb/

Journal of Language, Identity and Education

http://www.tandfonline.com/action/aboutThisJournal?journalCode=hlie20/

Journal of Multilingual Discourses

http://www.tandf.co.uk/journals/rmmd/

Journal of Multilingual and Multicultural Development

http://www.tandf.co.uk/journals/rmmm/

Journal of Language and Learning

http://www.jllonline.co.uk/journal/jllearn_home.htm/

Journal of Language and Linguistics

http://www.jllonline.co.uk/journal/jlling_home.html/

Journal of Latinos and Education

http://www.tandfonline.com/toc/hjle20/10/2/

Journal of Linguistics

http://journals.cambridge.org/action/displayJournal?jid=LIN/

*Journal of Research Design and Statistics in Linguistics and
    Communication Science*

https://www.equinoxpub.com/journals/index.php/JRDS/index/

Journal of Response to Writing

http://journalrw.org/index.php/jrw/index/

Journal of Second Language Pronunciation

https://benjamins.com/#catalog/journals/jslp/main/

Journal of Second Language Writing

http://www.elsevier.com/wps/find/journaldescription.cws_home/620372/
    description#description/

Korea TESOL Journal

http://www.koreatesol.org/content/korea-tesol-journal-0/

Language Acquisition

http://languageacquisition.org/

Language and Dialogue

http://benjamins.com/cgi-bin/t_seriesview.cgi?series=LD/

Language and Intercultural Communication

http://www.tandf.co.uk/journals/rmli/

Language Assessment Quarterly

http://www.tandfonline.com/action/aboutThisJournal?show=aimsScopean
  djournalCode=hlaq20/

Language at Work – Bridging Theory and Practice

http://www.languageatwork.eu/

Language in Society

http://journals.cambridge.org/action/displayJournal?jid=LSY/

Language, Interaction, and Acquisition

http://benjamins.com/cgi-bin/t_seriesview.cgi?series=LIA/

Language Learning (LL)

http://onlinelibrary.wiley.com/journal/10.1111/%28ISSN%291467-9922/

Language Learning and Technology

http://llt.msu.edu/

The Language Learning Journal

http://www.tandfonline.com/action/aboutThisJournal?show=aimsScopean
  djournalCode=rllj20/

Language Magazine

http://languagemagazine.com/

Language Teaching

http://journals.cambridge.org/action/displayJournal?jid=LTA/

Language Teaching Research

http://www.uk.sagepub.com/journalsProdDesc.
  nav?prodId=Journal201815/

Language Testing

http://ltj.sagepub.com/

Latin American Journal of Content and Language Integrated Learning

http://journals.sfu.ca/laclil/index.php/LACLIL/index/

The Mental Lexicon

http://benjamins.com/cgi-bin/t_seriesview.cgi?series=ML/

Metaphor and the Social World

http://benjamins.com/cgi-bin/t_seriesview.cgi?series=MSW/

Modern English Teacher

http://www.modernenglishteacher.com/

Modern Journal of Language Teaching Methods

http://www.mjltm.com/

Modern Language Journal

http://onlinelibrary.wiley.com/journal/10.1111/(ISSN)1540-4781/

Narrative Inquiry

http://benjamins.com/cgi-bin/t_seriesview.cgi?series=NI/

NYS (New York State) TESOL Journal

http://www.journal.nystesol.org/

Papers in Language Testing and Assessment (PLTA) (Formerly, Melbourne Papers in Language Testing)

http://www.altaanz.org/papers-in-language-testing-and-assessment-plta. html/

Pragmatics and Cognition

http://www.benjamins.com/cgi-bin/t_seriesview.cgi?series=p%26c

Prospect: An Australian Journal of TESOL

http://www.ameprc.mq.edu.au/resources/prospect/

ReCALL

http://www.eurocall-languages.org/recall/

Reading in a Foreign Language

http://nflrc.hawaii.edu/rfl/

The Reading Matrix: An International Online Journal

http://www.readingmatrix.com/journal.html/

The RELC Journal

http://rel.sagepub.com/

Research on Language and Social Interaction

http://rolsi.lboro.ac.uk/

Review of Cognitive Linguistics

http://benjamins.com/cgi-bin/t_seriesview.cgi?series=RCL/

Southern African Linguistics and Applied Language Studies

http://www.nisc.co.za/journals?id=9/

Second Language Research (SLR)

http://intl-slr.sagepub.com/

Studies in Second Language Acquisition (SSLA)

http://journals.cambridge.org/action/displayJournal?jid=SLA/

System

http://www.elsevier.com/wps/find/journaldescription.cws_home/335/
description#description/

*Teachers College Columbia University Working Papers in TESOL and
Applied Linguistics*

http://journals.tc-library.org/index.php/tesol/index/

Tennessee Foreign Language Teaching Association

http://www.tflta.org/

TESL Canada Journal

http://www.teslcanadajournal.ca/index.php/tesl/

TESL-EJ

http://www.tesl-ej.org/wordpress/

TESL Reporter

https://ojs.lib.byu.edu/spc/index.php/TESL/index/

TESOL Journal

http://www.tesol.org/read-and-publish/journals/tesol-journal/

TESOL Quarterly

http://www.tesol.org/s_tesol/seccss.asp?CID=632andDID=2461/

Translation Spaces

http://benjamins.com/cgi-bin/t_seriesview.cgi?series=TS/

World Englishes

http://onlinelibrary.wiley.com/journal/10.1111/(ISSN)1467-971X/

Web resources for TESOL

In the space below, we offer a sampling of recommended web tools and interactive websites, most of which are free or offer some free features. What is unique about these two lists of resources is that they are not designed specifically for TESOL. Rather, we have chosen them because we see the potential for TESOL instructors and their students to utilize these web tools and interactive websites in new and innovative ways. We encourage readers to explore these resources and to share their usefulness with others.

Web tools

- Blogger: http://www.blogger.com/
- Lino: http://en.linoit.com/
- Murally: https://mural.ly/
- OneWord: http://www.oneword.com/
- Podcast Garden: http://www.podcastgarden.com/h/en/
- PodBean: http://www.podbean.com/
- Quill: Writing Worksheets Made Interactive: http://www.quill.org/

- Skype in the Classroom: https://education.skype.com/
- SuperLame!: http://www.superlame.com/
- ThinkBinder: http://thinkbinder.com/
- Wordle: http://www.wordle.net/

Interactive websites

- ePals: Global Community: https://www.epals.com/
- NASA Kids Club:http://www.nasa.gov/audience/forkids/kidsclub/flash/index.html#.U5yL8Y1dWBk/
- Pop Tropica: http://www.poptropica.com/
- Smithsonian Folkways: Tools for Teaching: http://www.folkways.si.edu/tools_for_teaching/introduction.aspx/
- TedEd: http://ed.ted.com/
- Voice of America (VOA): Learning English: http://learningenglish.voanews.com/
- Web Rangers (U.S. National Park Service): http://www.nps.gov/webrangers/
- The World in Words: http://www.pri.org/collections/world-words/

TESOL-related terminology

We conclude this chapter by providing readers with brief yet thorough explanations of TESOL-related terminology they are likely to encounter in both their scholarly reading and their professional participation in the TESOL community of practice. While some of the terms below have appeared elsewhere in this book, others have not: our intention is for this compendium of terminology to serve as a reference resource, not necessarily as a glossary of *TESOL: A Guide* per se. Term descriptions are also accompanied by key reading(s) so as to comprise a general encyclopaedic glossary that will be valuable for novice and experienced TESOL practitioners alike.

Additive/subtractive bilingualism

A term referring to a bilingual (one who speaks more than one language) whose first language is not negatively impacted by learning the second. This can lead to development of a balanced bilingual, meaning that a similar degree of fluency is achieved in both languages. It also applies to adult learners who do not necessarily gain high levels of proficiency in the second language, but who do not lose ability in their native language because of their second language learning. This also involves the cultures of linguistic communities, such that additive bilingualism involves adhering to certain cultural norms of the foreign language community without having to rescind those from the native language group. Subtractive bilingualism, on the other hand, is when the learning of the second language leads to attrition in the first. In extreme cases, the learner may lose all ability to communicate in the first language. In others, the learner may lack lexical or grammatical richness, or the pragmatics needed for a variety of encounters. Others may keep their receptive abilities but respond to first language interlocutors in the second language.

Lambert, W. (1974), Culture and Language as Factors in Learning and Education. In F. E. Aboud and R. D. Meade (eds), *Cultural Factors in Learning and Education* (pp. 91–122). Bellingham, WA: Fifth Western Symposium on Learning.

Affective filter

A concept from Krashen's Monitor Model, the affective filter is part of a system that allows input to be received for learning (when the filter is 'low', not inhibited by anxiety or too much conscious attention) or that prevents input from being received (when the filter is 'high', because of learner anxiety or too much conscious attention). This idea is part of what drove more use of the target language in foreign language teaching, along with a de-emphasis on learning and practice of grammatical rules (as compared to older teaching methods, like grammar-translation). Although widely cited, Krashen's formulation is also widely criticized for its vague nature (will all 'anxious' students be bad language learners because their affective filter would naturally be high?) and the impossibility to test it empirically due to circularity of the theory (how to identify learners with a low affective filter for research other than by their good language learning?).

Krashen, S. (1982), *Principles and Practice in Second Language Acquisition.* Oxford: Pergamon.
Mitchell, R. and Myles, F. (1998), *Second Language Learning Theories.* London: Edward Arnold.

Affective strategies

With the advent of approaching foreign language learning from not only a cognitive perspective, but also an affective one, a variety of correlational studies began to associate particular affective personality traits and behaviours with success in language acquisition. Part of a typology of language learning strategies set out in Chamot (1987), social/affective strategies are meant to help students with motivation and the willingness to engage in certain types of learning behaviours. For example, risk-taking correlates with language learning success, so strategies to encourage risk-taking might be to praise students' efforts even when they don't immediately arrive at a perfect response, work in smaller groups to minimize the number of people who would notice them being wrong, or just operating outside their comfort zone, etc. (Brown, 2006). Other affective strategies include interacting with members of the target language group, and staying engaged and active in the learning process by asking for clarifications, repetitions, etc.

Brown, H. D. (2006), *Principles of Language Learning and Teaching* (5th edn). White Plains, NY: Pearson-Longman ESL.
Chamot, A. (1987), The Learning Strategies of ESL Students. In A. Wenden and J. Rubin (eds), *Learner Strategies in Language Learning* (pp. 71–83). Englewood Cliffs, NJ: Prentice Hall.

Aptitude

Drawn from psychology, aptitude is a natural ability that helps the learning process in some area. Aptitude for language learning in particular speaks to a natural ability for language learning, irrespective of other factors such as intelligence or personal interest in the subject. However, there are particular skill sets that correlate with language aptitude. These skill sets are included in Language Aptitude Tests (i.e. the *Modern Language Aptitude Test*, and the *Pimsleur Aptitude Battery*), which are used to predict a language learner's likelihood of success in second language learning by testing their general ability in certain skill areas. For example, the ability to recognize and remember sounds of language, or to identify the grammatical roles of words and phrases in sentences, are seen as vital to the strong language learner. In addition, the ability to memorize (sounds, words, grammatical endings, etc.) and the ability to infer meaning and recognize patterns in language input without explicit explanations are also common to those with language aptitude.

Carroll, J. B. and Sapon, S. M. (1959), *Modern Language Aptitude Test (MLAT)*. San Antonio, TX: Psychological Corporation.

Mitchell, R. and Myles, F. (1998), *Second Language Learning Theories*. London: Edward Arnold.

Pimsleur, P. (1966), *Pimsleur Language Aptitude Battery*. New York: Harcourt-Brace-Jovanovich.

Richards, J. C. and Schmidt, R. (2010), *Longman Dictionary of Language Teaching and Applied Linguistics*. London: Longman.

Asynchronous

Asynchronous internet tools (often those from the first generation internet) are classified as such because they allow for online communication between multiple parties, but in a time-deferred state, rather than in real time. These communicative tools have been applied in various ways to language learning. For example, email has been used for online exchanges between language learners, such as American English speakers learning German who then communicate with Austrian German speakers learning English. Here it is useful to avoid real-time communication, as the time difference between North America and Europe might not allow for real-time chat. Other asynchronous tools, such as bulletin boards, blogs and wikis, are also components of hybrid and distance-learning courses, which are often populated by students with work or family commitments that make real-time online or in-class meetings difficult.

Blake, R. J. (2007), New trends in using technology in the language curriculum. *Annual Review of Applied Linguistics*, 27, 76–97.

Godwin-Jones, R. (2003), Blogs and wikis: Environments for online collaboration. *Language Learning and Technology*, 7(2), 12–16.

Attitude

In general, attitude is a fixed set of feelings about someone or something. Gardner and Lambert (1972) pioneered research in attitude and foreign language learning, tied closely with research on motivation. Gardner and colleagues sought to find out if a student's attitude (positive or negative) towards the cultural group represented by the foreign language being studied would influence the interest in the language, motivation to study, and degree of proficiency attained. They do find correlations between positive attitudes and foreign language learning success, and vice versa, but Gardner himself concedes that it is impossible to know if the positive attitudes cause the success in learning, or if the success in learning helps foster such attitudes. In any case, such correlations are found in specific behaviours, whereby students with positive attitudes towards foreign language learning are more likely to continue their foreign language study, and more likely to really participate/engage in the activities of their language classes.

Gardner, R. C. and Lambert, W. E. (1972), *Attitudes and Motivation in Second Language Learning*. Rowley, MA: Newbury House.
Gardner, R. C. (1991), Attitudes and Motivation in Second Language Learning. In Allan G. Reynolds (ed.), *Bilingualism, Multiculturalism, and Second Language Learning: The McGill Conference in Honour of Wallace E. Lambert* (pp. 43–54). Hillsdale, NJ: Lawrence Erlbaum.

Automatic processing

Drawn from the Information Processing approach to learning processes, *automatic processing* is the point in learning where knowledge can be accessed and used but requires less focused attention from the learner than its predecessor in the central processing stage, *controlled processing*. This is because repeated access of particular structures (also-called *automatization*) secures them in long-term memory, making them readily available more quickly. *Automatic processing* precedes restructuring, a phase of reorganization and integration of information, which can also be seen as learners going back and forth between controlled and automatic processing. The Information Processing framework explains the phenomenon of *fossilization* in language learning as the problem of incorrect patterns being repeated often enough in controlled processing that they become automatic and stabilize, and it explains the variability in learner language from the movement of the restructuring phase.

McLaughlin, B. (1987), *Theories of Second Language Learning*. London: Edward Arnold.
Schmidt, R. (1990), The role of consciousness in second language learning. *Applied Linguistics*, 11, 129–88.

Automatization

See Automatic processing.

Anxiety (state and trait)

From psychology, anxiety is broken down into two types: that which is experienced for particular out-of-the-ordinary situations (state) and that which is experienced as a response to most events and circumstances because of personality type (trait). Scovel (1978) applied psychology's definitions of anxiety to difficulties in foreign language learning to realize that *facilitating anxiety* and *debilitating anxiety* cause different reactions to foreign language learning but had been lumped together in previous studies. Horwitz (1986) discussed a scale to determine students' levels of anxiety specific to foreign language learning and concluded that such anxiety is at the root of approximately 25 per cent of grade inconsistencies for foreign language learners. Gardner and MacIntyre (1993) consider trait anxiety and its negative effect on second language learning, noting that it results in general feelings of nervousness, physical responses (such as increased heartbeat) and less willingness or desire to speak in the second language.

Gardner, R. C. and MacIntyre, P. D. (1993), A student's contributions to second language learning. Part II: Affective Variables. *Language Teaching*, 26, 1–11.
Horwitz, E. (1986), Preliminary evidence for the reliability and validity of a foreign language anxiety scale. *TESOL Quarterly*, 20(3), 559–61.
Scovel, T. (1978), The effect of affect on foreign language learning: A review of the anxiety research. *Language Learning*, 28(1), 129–42.

Behaviourism

A general psychological theory that views learning as a process of habit formation, behaviourism was also applied to language acquisition and learning (Skinner, 1957). With the main ideas of *stimulus* (language exposure/given communicative situations), *response* (what a language learner says/doesn't say in the given situation) and *reinforcement* (interlocutors' responses), behaviourists assumed that learners realize when their responses are appropriate (because they get the expected reinforcement from interlocutors) and learn language. Behaviourism influenced pedagogical practice in foreign language learning, as well, with grammar-translation and audiolingual methods both focusing on repetition, practice and error correction (to avoid repeating and thus learning the 'wrong' answers). In 1959, Chomsky published a review of Skinner's 1957 work that criticized the behaviourist viewpoint, citing the fact that children produce utterances they have never heard before, and that children master complex grammar without it being 'taught' to them, both impossible feats in the framework of *stimulus, response, reinforcement*.

Chomsky, N. (1959), Review of B. F. Skinner, *Verbal Behavior*. *Language*, 35, 26–58.
Skinner, B. F. (1957), *Verbal Behavior*. New York: Appleton-Century-Crofts.

Bilingual/multilingual

One who speaks two or more languages. From a chronological perspective, bilingualism/multilingualism can be *simultaneous*, where multiple languages are acquired together, or *consecutive*, where one language is acquired after another is already established. From a psychosocial perspective, multilingualism can be *additive*, allowing for maintenance of the first language while other languages are being acquired, or *subtractive*, where one language deteriorates (loss of fluidity, grammatical accuracy, or vocabulary, for example) due to more use or higher priority of other languages (Lambert, 1974). From a psycholinguistic perspective, it has been viewed as *coordinate*, meaning separate semantic systems are at play in the multiple languages, or *compound*, meaning that one semantic system overlaps in the use of all languages (Weinrich, 1953). For varying social, political and economic reasons, the majority of people in the world are multilingual to some degree (Saville-Troike, 2006).

Lambert, W. (1974), Culture and Language as Factors in Learning and Education. In F. E. Aboud and R. D. Meade (eds), *Cultural Factors in Learning and Education* (pp. 91–122). Bellingham, WA: Fifth Western Symposium on Learning.
Saville-Troike, M. (2006), *Introducing Second Language Acquisition.* Cambridge: Cambridge University Press.
Weinrich, U. (1953), *Languages in Contact.* New York: Linguistic Circle of New York.

Blended/hybrid learning

Blended learning, or hybrid learning, is the term used for classes that are a combination of traditional classroom time and online learning. Not simply 'web-enhanced' courses (which meet the traditional amount of time face-to-face but may include some web-based activities), they see a significant amount of face-to-face class time reduced (which frees up space for scheduling more classes) and replaced with online activities. The online activities are usually created specifically to address the course content that would have traditionally been treated by lecture in the classroom, and include such projects as reviews of case studies, self-assessments, simulations, and online group work with peers. The reduced classroom time can be accomplished with a variety of schedules: shorten each class meeting, omit one or two class meetings, or even meet for several weeks and then take several weeks for more independent work. The goal of blended learning is to combine traditional and online learning in an optimal way to improve upon both.

Garnham, C. and Kaleta, R. (2002), Introduction to hybrid courses. *Teaching with Technology Today*, 8(6). [online publication; no pagination]
Thorne, K. (2003), *Blended Learning: How to Integrate Online and Traditional Learning*. London and Sterling, VA: Kogan Page.

Blog

A blog ('web log') is a webpage that a writer usually posts to regularly with links to other websites, text, pictures or video and commentary. As its name suggests, it is a log or online diary of sorts, with each post stamped according to its time and date, and usually displayed chronologically. While asynchronous, it is still interactive (and thus a Web 2.0 tool): readers may comment on any post, or on other comments about posts. In foreign language classes, blogs can be used as online journals or portfolios, and peers as well as teachers can join the conversation by reviewing class blogs and sharing thoughts or questions through the commenting features. Ducate and Lomicka (2008) found that reading blogs and writing their own blogs increased language students' creativity and ownership in the use of their foreign language, allowed them a way to express themselves in a low-anxiety environment, and gave cultural insights not found in textbooks.

Ducate, L. C. and Lomicka, L. L. (2008), Adventures in the blogosphere: From blog readers to blog writers. *Computer Assisted Language Learning,* 21(1), 9–28.
Godwin-Jones, R. (2003), Blogs and wikis: Environments for online collaboration. *Language Learning and Technology,* 7(2), 12–16.

Bottom-up/top-down processing

From psychology and the literature on learning styles, bottom-up and top-down processing represent ways of learning with regard to previous knowledge and analysis. Bottom-up processing sees learners making more use of the object to be studied (i.e. language learners might look up words in a dictionary or look up grammatical inflections to piece together the meaning of a text) and may correspond to a more detail-oriented learning style. Top-down processing, on the other hand, sees learners using already-held knowledge in combination with the object to be studied (i.e. language learners might use their knowledge of texts' structures to look for important information in headings and subheadings or use accompanying graphics to gain a general understanding of a text) and may correspond to a more global or holistic learning style. While classically presented as opposites, in fact one learner may use both approaches even in the same task, such as the above example of reading a text.

Saville-Troike, M. (2006), *Introducing Second Language Acquisition*. Cambridge: Cambridge University Press.

Central processing

In the Information Processing framework, *central processing* is the middle stage of the language learning process, preceded by reception of input and followed by production of output. Subdivided into phases, central processing consists first of *controlled processing*, where learners must specifically attend to language information to begin learning it (contrary to the notion that foreign language learning may be a matter of natural acquisition). After a period of practice in *controlled processing*, material can move to the phase of *automatic processing*, where less conscious attention is required (and can be used to focus on learning more new material). Finally, the information of automatic processing undergoes *restructuring*, where reorganization occurs and allows the learner to produce output.

McLaughlin, B. (1987), *Theories of Second Language Learning*. London: Edward Arnold.

Cognitive strategies

Understanding that language learning will be influenced by individual differences in learners (age, aptitude, motivation, personality, etc.), it is useful to recognize a variety of learning strategies. In Chamot (1987), a classification of different types of learning strategies was put out, with cognitive strategies focusing on analysing different aspects of language and language use. Many cognitive learning strategies will be recognized as those used in older teaching methods such as grammar-translation and the audiolingual method. For example, students might listen and repeat samples from the target language, or translate from one language to another. They also might use cognates over non-cognates in remembering new vocabulary items (for example, a French student might choose to use the English word 'ameliorate', like French 'améliorer', instead of 'improve'). Students also might use reasoning to deduce patterns in language, such as noticing that English 3rd person singular present tense verbs take an -s ending.

Chamot, A. (1987), The Learning Strategies of ESL Students. In A. Wenden and J. Rubin (eds), *Learner Strategies in Language Learning* (pp. 71–83). Englewood Cliffs, NJ: Prentice Hall.

Cognitive style

A dimension of learning style, cognitive style is the optimal way that individuals process information when they learn, and is often viewed as pairs of opposing traits on two sides of a continuum. One very common such pair in foreign language learning research is field-dependent (usually related in the end to a more holistic learner) and field-independent (generally viewed as a more analytic learner). Deductive and inductive reasoning are also often applied to foreign language learning. Deductive reasoning is more of a top-down approach (for example, using an already formulated language rule to understand a reading passage), whereas inductive reasoning is more bottom-up (reading a passage and noticing the regularities to figure out the 'rules'). Cognitive style can also include learner preferences with regard to sense, such as visual, auditory, and kinaesthetic.

Saville-Troike, M. (2006), *Introducing Second Language Acquisition*. Cambridge: Cambridge University Press.

Communicative competence

The notion of communicative competence originated with Hymes (1972) and was developed further by SLA researchers in the 1980s. Defined as 'the ability to produce situationally acceptable, and more especially socially acceptable, utterances, which ... would normally be held to be part of a native speaker's competence' (Lyons, 1996, p. 24), communicative competence has often resulted in pedagogical approaches which value speaking and interaction with native speakers over the established focus on reading and writing, the latter of which traditionally involved a great deal of translation and memorization. In place of communicative competence, a view of language competence is emerging which is arguably more appropriate for a global world in which challenges such as social mobility, diverse speech communities, unpredictability, and a global 'communication culture' require a high level of contextual awareness and the ability to adapt language use (Kramsch, 2007).

Hymes, D. (1972), On Communicative Competence. In J. Pride and J. Holmes (eds), *Sociolinguistics* (pp. 269–83). Harmondsworth: Penguin Books.
Lyons, J. (1996), On Competence and Performance and Related Notions. In G. Brown, K. Malmkjaer and J. Williams (eds), *Performance and Competence in Second Language Acquisition* (pp. 11–32). Cambridge: Cambridge University Press.

Compound bilingualism/coordinate bilingualism

A series of psycholinguistic studies in the 1960s and 1970s (see Albert and Obler, 1978) sought to discover if bilinguals had a single cognitive system that was used for both their languages (compound bilingualism), or if there were two separate systems at work for the first language and the second language (coordinate bilingualism). Code-switching could provide evidence for the notion of compound bilingualism, as it seems to involve using two languages at the same time, which would be easier if both were operational out of the same system. On the other hand, having different associations for translation pairs based on the language and context of each individual word would lend support to the idea of coordinate bilingualism, where two separate systems treat each language. For example, for an English–French bilingual, 'bread' might conjure an image of evenly sized slices of manufactured bread from a supermarket, whereas 'pain' in French would produce images of a baguette, fresh and unsliced, from a corner bakery.

Albert, M. and Obler, L. K. (1978), *The Bilingual Brain: Neuropsychological and Neurolinguistic Aspects of Bilingualism*. New York: Academic Press.

Computer-assisted language learning (CALL)

Computer-assisted language learning (CALL) is a subgroup of foreign language teaching (sometimes conflated with the more general 'technology and language learning') that works to integrate computers to facilitate the processes of learning and teaching language. For example, a traditional language classroom could benefit from *computer-mediated communication* (i.e. email, text or voice chat), with other students of the target language, or with native speakers of the target language, or even just between the students and the instructor. Students may also use computing to create multimedia learning portfolios or cultural research projects, where they may at times use online dictionaries or translators. Distance-learning (classes offered via the internet) and blended learning (classes combining traditional and distance-learning), as well as course management websites and software are also part of CALL. iCALL (Intelligent CALL), CALL applications that can effectively interact with language learners, is an area of CALL currently under development.

Blake, R. J. (2007), New trends in using technology in the language curriculum. *Annual Review of Applied Linguistics, 27*, 76–97.
Chappelle, C., Compton, L., Kon, E. et al. (2004), Theory, Research and Practice in CALL: Making the links. In L. Lomicka and J. Cooke-Plagwitz (eds), *Teaching with Technology* (pp. 189–208). Boston, MA: Heinle & Heinle.

Computer-based instruction (CBI)

Computer-based instruction (pedagogical instruction that relies on use of computer software) began in the 1960s and has been applied to many areas of learning and testing for students of all levels. By the early 1990s, most research suggested that computer-based instruction had positive effects on learning outcomes (Kulik and Kulik, 1991) and by the mid-1990s it became understood in the field of second language teaching that optimizing computer-based instruction was an important goal (Chapelle, 2001). Computer-based instruction can take many forms. As an auxiliary to traditional classroom learning, students can use software for practice drills, self-tests, recording and listening to their own speech and more. Commercial programmes also exist for independent language learning, but are often met with scepticism by language teachers, who question their ability to ingrain students with the necessary pragmatics to function effectively in their second language, even if they are successful in basic linguistic skills. The interactivity of Web 2.0, with Second Life and other online simulated environments specific to language learning, may answer those doubts, however.

Chapelle, C. (2001), *Computer Applications in Second Language Acquisition: Foundations for Teaching, Testing and Research*. Cambridge: Cambridge University Press.

Kulik, C. L. C. and Kulik, J. A. (1991), Effectiveness of computer-based instruction: An updated analysis. *Computers in Human Behavior, 7*, 75–94.

Computer-mediated communication (CMC)

Computer-mediated communication (CMC) is, generally speaking, communication using the computer and internet instead of face-to-face interaction. In the field of second language teaching, CMC is used for a variety of interactions (and particularly by those who favour an Interactionist approach). For example, it is used for peer-to-peer interactions among students in the same class, either to confer about homework outside class, or to perform specific communicative activities. It is also used for non-native speaker to native speaker communication in 'exchange' programmes of sorts, where German learners of English communication with English learners of German, for example. CMC can be *synchronous* (meaning the communication occurs in 'real time', such as in video, voice or text chat, thus requiring all parties to be present at the same time) or *asynchronous* (meaning turn-taking in the 'conversation' can occur at different times, such as in message boards and email).

Chapelle, C. (2007), Technology and second language acquisition. *Annual Review of Applied Linguistics, 27*, 98–114.

Comprehensible input

A term coined by Krashen in the formulation of his Input Hypothesis, which states that natural language development occurs as a result of being exposed to *comprehensible input*. The simple definition of *comprehensible input* is input that is just one level beyond the ability of the L2 learner (also commonly referred to as *i + 1*). If input is too simple (at the learner's level, with forms they have already acquired) or too complex (*i + 2*, for example) then it will not lead to acquisition. Like other theories of his Monitor Model, this one is criticized for vagueness (there is no operational definition of *i* or the levels above it) and circularity (language develops from comprehensible input; the input was comprehensible if language has developed). Despite these criticisms, this hypothesis is one of the driving forces of the Communicative Approach to language teaching.

Krashen, S. (1985), *The Input Hypothesis: Issues and Implications*. Harlow: Longman.
Mitchell, R. and Myles, F. (1998), *Second Language Learning Theories*. London: Edward Arnold.

Connectionism

A general theory applied to language learning, Connectionism uses the metaphor of the brain as a computer network. Rather than creating or possessing abstract rules to learn language, the brain instead keeps track of associated events and creates links between them. When particular events are repeated, existing links are 'activated' and strengthened. At the same time, links that are not being associated are weakened by their lack of activation. Computer modelling to test the idea for first language acquisition seemed successful (Rumelhart and McClelland, 1986), and second language studies followed. Ellis and Schmidt (1997) compared a computer model to second language learners' productions of regular and irregular plurals in an artificial language and found similar patterns of acquisition in the two as well. If such theories of learning proved correct, then second language learning may require much less discussion and practice of rules and much more input and use.

Ellis, N. and Schmidt, R. (1997), Morphology and longer distance dependencies: Laboratory research illuminating the A in SLA. *Studies in Second Language Acquisition*, 18, 145–71.
Rumelhart, D. and McClelland, J. (1986), On Learning the Past Tense of English Verbs. In J. McClelland and D. Rumelhart (eds), *Parallel Distributed Processing: Explorations in the Microstructure of Cognition, Volume 2:*

Psychological and Biological Models (pp. 216–71). Cambridge, MA: MIT Press.

Controlled processing

Controlled processing is the first phase of learning within the central processing stage of language learning in the Information Processing framework. For controlled processing to take place, two conditions must be met. First, the learner must receive input (the first stage of learning); second, the learner must attend to or notice the input. Noticed input, called intake, is what makes up the material of the controlled processing stage of learning. Practice within this stage leads to automatic processing, and then restructuring, which allows learners to produce output (the final stage of the learning process). Schmidt (1990) reports on a variety of ways in which foreign language pedagogy can attempt to help learners turn input into intake for the controlled processing stage, such as by increasing the frequency of certain types of input, trying to make particular material more salient, and generally raising students' awareness of their learning processes.

McLaughlin, B. (1987), *Theories of Second Language Learning*. London: Edward Arnold.
Schmidt, R. (1990), The role of consciousness in second language learning. *Applied Linguistics*, 11, 129–88.

Coordinate bilingualism

See Compound bilingualism.

Corpus linguistics

The term *corpus* refers to a large body of texts, written or spoken, that are collected for quantitative and/or qualitative analysis (the former typically involves a computer). In addition to the text itself, a corpus may be annotated with additional linguistic information. Analyses of language corpora make possible data-driven descriptions of domain-specific language use far more accurate than native-speaker intuition can offer researchers, teachers, or learners. In the sub-field of ESP, language corpora and corpus-based tools allow researchers to more accurately describe a particular genre or register, while precluding the need for instructors to be experts in the particular genre in which their students may need guidance. More recently, learner corpora (i.e. texts produced by non-native speakers of a particular language) have also begun to receive attention for their insights into learner language and SLA. Corpora and corpus-based tools are also becoming increasingly prevalent in language classrooms due to their ability to enhance data driven learning.

McEnery, T., Xiao, R. and Tono, Y. (2006), *Corpus-Based Language Studies*. London: Routledge.
O'Keeffe, A., McCarthy, M. and Carter, R. (2007), *From Corpus to Classroom: Language Use and Language Teaching*. Cambridge: Cambridge University Press.
Römer, U. (2011), Corpus research applications in second language teaching. *Annual Review of Applied Linguistics*, 31(1), 205–25.

Course management software

Course management software is a computer application, usually teacher-directed but used by the whole class, which facilitates learning in a variety of areas and serves as the information point for the whole class. Its uses can be as basic as being a website with course syllabus and materials posted for easy student and instructor access. Course management software also often contains tools for discussion (usually asynchronous, like bulletin boards, but sometimes live chat as well) and can host grades and progress reports for students as well. In addition, some course management systems support entire online classes, the online portion of hybrid classes, or independent learning environments. Commercial software such as WebCT and Blackboard are popular systems, as is Moodle, an open-source system supported by a team of programmers and its community of users. Course management systems also often include a monitoring function, allowing teachers to see when students access and submit assignments, and how much they spend on them.

Brandl, K. (2005), Are you ready to Moodle? *Language Learning and Technology*, 9(2), 16–23.
Godwin-Jones, R. (2003), Blogs and wikis: Environments for online collaboration. *Language Learning and Technology*, 7(2), 12–16.

Critical period hypothesis

A general biological theory, the Critical Period Hypothesis states that certain skills must be acquired before a given stage in development, or else they can no longer be acquired normally. With regard to human language, Lenneberg (1967) posited that language acquisition must occur before puberty for normal linguistic development. However, this is difficult to prove, as the few cases known where children were not exposed to language regularly before puberty also involved abuse and neglect (i.e. Genie, documented in Curtiss, 1977). There is much debate about whether there is a critical period for second language learning, but many of the studies focus on different time periods (short-term learning vs. more longitudinal studies), and different subparts of language learning as criteria (children are better at native-like pronunciation; adults are better at grammaticality judgements), making it problematic to come to a conclusion. Still, non-native patterns in adult second language are often attributed to learners having begun after the critical period.

Curtiss, S. (1977), *Genie*. New York: Academic Press.
Lenneberg, E. (1967), *Biological Foundations of Language*. New York: Wiley and Sons.
Saville-Troike, M. (2006), *Introducing Second Language Acquisition*. Cambridge: Cambridge University Press.

Dynamic systems theory

Born out of chaos and complexity theory from the natural sciences, dynamic systems theory has been applied to understanding language learning by Diane Larsen-Freeman, Nick Ellis, Kees deBot and others. In essence, language learning is seen as a complex, changing system, which in turn is actually made up of many other complex, changing systems. For example, a speech community is a complex system, always changing because its members are also dynamic. From there, it must also be recognized that each member's brain is a complex, dynamic system, as are all the levels of language being learned, which are also interconnected and always changing (pragmatics can influence lexical choice, which influences syntax, for example). Implied in this theory is that language learning is psychological, but also social, with interactions with peer learners, teachers and/or members of speech communities part of the dynamic nature of learning and language acquisition.

deBot, K. (2008), Introduction: Second language development as a dynamic process. *Modern Language Journal*, 92(2), 166–78.
deBot, K., Lowie, W. and Verspoor, M. (2007), A dynamic systems theory approach to second language acquisition. *Bilingualism: Language and Cognition*, 10(1), 7–21.
Ellis, N. C. (2008), The dynamics of second language emergence: Cycles of language use, language change, and language acquisition. *Modern Language Journal*, 92(2), 232–49.
Larsen-Freeman, D. and Cameron, L. (2008), Research methodology on language development from a complex systems perspective. *Modern Language Journal*, 92(2), 200–13.

English for academic purposes (EAP)

This field of English language learning stems from English for Special Purposes (which was historically considered more occupational in nature, such as English for Hotel Management), and refers to the learning of English specifically to function in an English language academic environment. EAP differs from learning English for general communicative purposes, in that it must address specific skills (e.g. research, note-taking) and also address the communicative needs of students in various academic settings (reading and writing solo, participating in classes, etc.). In the last decades, the increase in the need for EAP has led to an increase in the number of non-native-speaking EAP instructors, which in turn has led to a change in the focus of materials and teacher training. At its inception, EAP referred to university-level education; however, with time EAP has grown to meet the needs of high-school students whose first language is not English and who may not have academic skills in their first language.

Hyland, K. and Hamp-Lyons, L. (2002), EAP: Issues and directions. *Journal of English for Academic Purposes,* 1(1), 1–12.

English as an international language (EIL)

Less commonly used than English as a lingua franca, English as an international language is a term used to describe the use of English as a contact language between non-native English speakers of diverse backgrounds. For example, Brazilians and Germans working together in business or research may communicate together in English if the Germans do not speak Portuguese and the Brazilians do not speak German. Similarly to ELF, EIL research seeks to describe the English spoken in such situations with the goal of understanding it as a language variety in its own right, but does not seek to eradicate norms of Teaching English as a Foreign Language, which may be needed for those who spend time in an English-dominant area and communicate mostly with native English speakers.

Jenkins, J. (2009), *World Englishes: A Resource Book for Students.* Oxford and New York: Routledge.

English as a Lingua Franca (ELF)

English as it is spoken by non-native speakers to other non-native speakers. For example, Brazilians' and Germans' working together in business or research might have only one shared language to use in communication with each other: English. This field of study prioritizes data collection and description of Englishes spoken only by non-native English speakers (as opposed to world Englishes, which treats English as spoken by non-native and native speakers similarly). ELF researchers seek to discover which forms (phonological, lexical and grammatical) are most commonly used among non-native English speakers of different language backgrounds. The goal is not to put forth a single form of English as standard, but rather to inform English teaching and communication practices. ELF descriptions are not intended to replace the norms of traditional TEFL, especially if learners will need to communicate primarily with native speakers rather than with a diverse group of speakers.

Jenkins, J. (2009), *World Englishes: A Resource Book for Students*. Oxford and New York: Routledge.

English for specific purposes (ESP)

Contrary to a model of language teaching which assumes all students' interest in general communicative ability, English for specific purposes recognizes that students have diverse needs and goals with regard to learning English, whether they be occupational, vocational, or academic. ESP began to develop in concert with more communicative language teaching approaches which sought to expose students to more natural language input, thus aligning well with the realization that learners' needs would vary given their communicative situations. ESP instruction should ideally have the learners' goals in mind, use the content and materials of the field in question, and target language use appropriate to its field at all levels of language (lexicon, discourse, etc.) (Dudley-Evans and St. John, 1999). Typically ESP students are intermediate or advanced language learners who have already attained basic language skills.

Dudley-Evans, T. and St. John, M. J. (1999), *Developments in English for Specific Purposes: A multi-Disciplinary Approach*. Cambridge: Cambridge University Press.

Field-dependent/field-independent

Originating from a psychological study of how individuals' perceptions are linked to their cognitive processes (Witkin et al., 1954), field dependence is one of the primary ideas discussed with regard to learners' cognitive styles in foreign language learning (for a review see Chappelle and Green, 1992). A common measure of field dependence comes from embedded figures tests, where some shapes or images lie within greater and distinct ones. Those who readily see the 'image within the image' are termed field-independent (which correlates with a more analytic learning style), whereas those who have difficulty finding the image within are termed field-dependent (which correlates with a more global approach to learning). Later re-evaluation of the studies on field dependence/independence considers embedded figures tests to measure ability rather than cognitive style, and sees no relevance to foreign language learning (Griffiths and Sheen, 1992).

Chappelle, C. and Green, P. (1992), Field independence/dependence in second language acquisition research. *Language Learning*, 42, 47–83.
Griffiths, R. and Sheen, R. (1992), Disembedded figures in the landscape: A reappraisal of L2 research on field dependence/independence. *Applied Linguistics*, 13(2), 133–48.
Witkin, H. A., Lewis, H., Hertzman, M., et al. (1954), *Personality through Perception*. New York: Harper & Brothers.

Field-Independent

See Field-dependent.

Fossilization

Fossilization was originally intended to describe the state of foreign language learning where some or many interlanguage forms did not correspond to target language forms; thus, fossilization could be seen as the 'final state' of foreign language learning that still contained consistent errors (Selinker, 1972). Those errors could be at any level of language (phonological, lexical, morphological, syntactic, etc.), thus making it possible for fossilization to occur in any part of the interlanguage system. However, some underlying assumptions within the concept of fossilization are seen as problematic. First, simply assuming that a second language learner's goal should be 'native-like' competence in the target language is unfounded, as many want to use the language for specific purposes and do not need to be native-like. Second, deciding what the 'target' language should be is difficult for a language like English, with many prominent varieties worldwide, such as Australian, American, British or Indian English.

Saville-Troike, M. (2006), *Introducing Second Language Acquisition*. Cambridge: Cambridge University Press.
Selinker, L. (1972), Interlanguage. *International Review of Applied Linguistics*, 10, 209–31.

Hybrid learning

See Blended/hybrid learning.

Immersion

A language learning setting that involves content learning in a second or foreign language, with the second language being the language of instruction for all students. Some programmes are entirely carried out in the target language (full immersion), whereas others provide some instructional time in the students' first language as well (partial immersion). Immersion programmes are appealing because students learn both language and content simultaneously, which is seen as a more efficient and meaningful approach to language learning. However, students of immersion programmes have been shown to lack in grammar and pragmatic ability in the target language (Harley and Swain, 1984) or in content knowledge. This can be due to systemic problems, such as students having too little exposure to the target language before immersion education begins (Spada and Lightbown, 2002) or teachers having insufficient proficiency in the target language (Johnson, 1997). Researchers now emphasize the importance of content and language instruction in immersion settings (Echevarria et al., 1997).

Echevarria, J., Vogt, M., and Short, D. J. (2004), *Making Content Comprehensible for English Language Learners: The SIOP Model*. Boston, MA: Pearson.
Harley, B. and Swain, M. (1984), The Interlanguage of Immersion Students and its Implications for Second Language Teaching. In A. Davies, C. Criper and A. Howatt (eds), *Interlanguage* (pp. 291–311). Edinburgh: Edinburgh University Press.
Johnson, R. K. (1997), The Hong Kong Education System: Late Immersion Under Stress. In R. K. Johnson and M. Swain (eds), *Immersion Education: International Perspectives*. Cambridge: Cambridge University Press.
Spada, N. and Lightbown, P. (2002), L1 and L2 in the education of Inuit children in northern Quebec: Abilities and perceptions. *Language and Education*, 16(3), 212–40.

Independent learning

Part of a movement to allow for more autonomous and individualized language learning, independent learning is usually undertaken at a self-access centre. Known by a variety of terms (i.e. independent learning, self-access learning, learner self-management), independent learning has been applied to diverse settings and language learning goals, such as language teacher refreshers at Hong Kong's Institute of Education, language for job skills in the Australian Migrant Education Program, and investigation into learning styles and strategies throughout North America. Independent learning can occur in a variety of physical settings and has been categorized based on the degree of autonomy necessary for success in a given programme. Some programmes are designed to include initial diagnostics of learning styles and regular consultation of teachers/advisers, librarians and technicians, whereas others assume that students have a certain degree of self-knowledge and language proficiency already in place, thus making them capable of choosing their own materials and plans.

Gardner, D. and Miller, L. (1999), *Establishing Self-Access: From Theory to Practice*. Cambridge: Cambridge University Press.

Information processing

Information processing is a psychological theory that considers foreign language learning to happen in three stages: input, central processing, and output. In general, the theory sees learning a foreign language as similar to learning other complex skills, rather than being something innate like acquiring a first language. It is assumed that the actual learning occurs during *central processing*: first *controlled processing* of *input* (explicitly focusing on the material and skills to be learned) is necessary, but with more exposure and practice, what has already been learned can move to *automatic processing*. After this point, then *restructuring* occurs, where learners more fully integrate what has been learned. *Output* is possible after some learning in *central processing* has occurred. Also, while *input* can be any type of language exposure, learners must notice it explicitly for it to become *intake*, or information that will definitely be processed in the learning cycle.

McLaughlin, B. (1987), *Theories of Second Language Learning*. London: Edward Arnold.

Inhibition

In general, inhibition is a feeling that prevents one from acting in a relaxed way, usually involving self-consciousness and self-esteem. In 1972, H. D. Brown declared the need to focus on egocentric and social factors, in addition to purely cognitive factors, in second language learning, among which ranked inhibition. Brown postulated that being too inhibited would be detrimental to foreign language learning, because engagement with other speakers and practice of all skills are vital to improvement. Later work by Brown proclaimed that inhibition in language learning is due to fear of being unable to respond to or interpret different language situations correctly. This inability to respond appropriately gives rise to losing face and threatening the individual's self-esteem. Brown recommends practical ways to reduce students' inhibition in the language learning process, such as working in small groups instead of always as a whole class.

Brown, H .D. (1973), Affective variables in second language acquisition. *Language Learning,* 23(2), 231–44.
—(2006), *Principles of Language Learning and Teaching* (5th edn). White Plains, NY: Pearson-Longman ESL.

Input

In general, input is the exposure to language, whether written, oral or signed, in the language learning process. Within the Information Processing approach, which sees language learning as analogous to other complex learning, input is specifically only that exposure. Intake, on the other hand, is input that has been noticed or attended to explicitly, and is what leads to actual learning. However, input in Krashen's Monitor Model should specifically not be brought to conscious attention for explicit learning, or the affective filter will be too high and prevent the actual goal, which is acquisition. Krashen deems the ideal kind of input to be comprehensible input. Also known as *i + 1*, comprehensible input is defined as being just one level higher than that of the learner, so as to challenge the learner and give exposure to new material, but not overwhelm with too many unknowns.

McLaughlin, B. (1987), *Theories of Second Language Learning.* London: Edward Arnold.
Krashen, S. (1978), The Monitor Model for Second Language Acquisition. In R. C. Gingras (ed.), *Second Language Acquisition and Foreign Language Teaching* (pp. 1–26). Arlington, VA: Center for Applied Linguistics.

Intake

Intake can be defined as language that is in the process of being learned. Within the Information Processing framework, language exposure is not enough for learning. Rather, because language learning is viewed as similar to any other kind of complex learning, learners must notice, or consciously attend to, their language exposure, or input. Once input has been noticed, it then becomes intake, which can be exploited by the central processing stage of the learning process. At first it will be subject to controlled processing, where attention and awareness are still necessary. Gradually, with more practice and exposure, the knowledge in question will become more ingrained, less reliant on conscious awareness, and will have moved into automatic processing, thus freeing up conscious attention for learning other new things (McLaughlin, 1987). Instructional strategies to heighten awareness of particular structures and the learning process have been used in an effort to facilitate input becoming intake (see Schmidt 1990).

McLaughlin, B. (1987), *Theories of Second Language Learning.* London: Edward Arnold.
Schmidt, R. (1990), The role of consciousness in second language learning. *Applied Linguistics,* 11, 129–88.

Interference

See Transfer.

Interlanguage

When talking of foreign language learning, there are multiple languages involved: a learner's native language (L1) and the target language (the language being learned). Selinker (1972) pointed out, however, that learners' foreign language production contains elements of the first language (transfer of accent, lexicon, grammar, etc.) and elements of the target language (new vocabulary and syntax, new sounds, etc.). He considers this amalgamation of the learners' native and target languages to be the actual language they speak, termed *interlanguage* to represent the 'between languages' nature. Like all language, interlanguage is not static, but ever-changing with development and learning of the target language, and changed usage patterns of all languages. The term 'fossilization' was coined to describe the final state of L2 learners, as it was assumed that most of them would not achieve native-like language use, but would instead stop their development, or fossilize, short of target-like norms.

Selinker, L. (1972), Interlanguage. *International Review of Applied Linguistics,* 10, 209–31.

Instrumental motivation

See Motivation.

Integrative motivation

See Motivation.

Investment

Coined by Norton (1995), the concept of investment is inspired by Bourdieu's work on identity and meant to improve upon Gardner and Lambert's classification of integrative and instrumental motivation, which Norton saw as inadequate. Norton's own characterization of investment seeks to 'capture the relationship of the language learner [and his/her identity] to the changing social world' (Norton Peirce, 1995, p. 10). Therefore, rather than these motivation types being static, personality-based traits relevant only to the learner, Norton's conceptualization sees the learner as part of the social world, considering identity, power and the relationships involved in each interaction. For example, research on immigrant women learning English in Canada showed that despite extremely high motivation, certain women had great difficulty in practising outside of the classroom because of their reluctance to speak in situations of power imbalance.

Norton, B. (2000), *Identity and Language Learning: Gender, Ethnicity, and Educational Change*. London: Longman/Pearson Education.
Norton Peirce, B. (1995), Social identity, investment, and language learning. *TESOL Quarterly*, 29(1), 9–31.

Learnability hypothesis

See Teachability hypothesis.

Learner autonomy

Learner autonomy is the idea of the learner being in charge of his/her learning process and outcomes, rather than the teacher. Benson and Voller (1997) postulated four dimensions of autonomy in language learning: technical (language learning without a traditional classroom or teacher), psychological (the innate ability of learners to be more autonomous), political (conditions of society and educational institutions that allow learners to be autonomous) and social (the capability of interacting with others to further autonomous learning). Oxford (2003) followed with a similar model, which she introduces within the framework of learning strategies. Her model also contains a technical and psychological perspective, as well as a sociocultural perspective (which focuses on the mediated learning of Sociocultural Theory) and a political-critical perspective (which focuses on power and access to learning, much in line with Critical Pedagogy). Strategies to develop learner autonomy include: teachers taking on the role of facilitator more than authority; learners having a voice in curriculum design; and chronicling their learning process.

Benson, P. (2001), *Teaching and Researching Autonomy in Language Learning.* Harlow: Pearson Education.
Benson, P. and Voller, P. (eds) (1997), *Autonomy and Independence in Language Learning.* London: Longman.
Oxford, R. L. (2003), Toward a more Systematic Model of Second Language Learner Autonomy. In D. Palfreyman (ed.), *Culture and Learner Autonomy.* London: Palgrave Macmillan.

Learning strategies

In Oxford (1990), foreign language learning strategies are seen as actions and behaviours by students that facilitate the language learning process. Different types of language skills may benefit more or less from particular strategies. For example, improvement in speaking in a foreign language may come from risk-taking and circumlocution, whereas foreign language writing may require more planning and organizational strategies. In general, social and affective strategies have received less attention than cognitive and metacognitive strategies in foreign language learning research, and students often do not have an awareness of their feelings in relation to foreign language learning. O'Malley and Chamot (1990), who classify foreign language learning strategies as affective, cognitive and metacognitive, have noted that learners with successful strategies are usually aware of them and can articulate what they are and how they work together. Oxford (1990) also recognizes that different strategies will be useful to individual students depending on factors like learning style and cultural background.

O'Malley, J. M. and Chamot, A. U. (1990), *Learning Strategies in Second Language Acquisition.* Cambridge: Cambridge University Press.
Oxford, R. L. (1990), *Language Learning Strategies: What Every Teacher Should Know.* Boston, MA: Heinle & Heinle.

Metacognitive strategies

Understanding that language learning will be influenced by individual differences in learners (age, aptitude, motivation, personality, etc.), it is useful to recognize a variety of learning strategies. In Chamot (1987), a classification of different types of learning strategies was put out, with metacognitive strategies focusing on bringing learners' attention to their own learning processes. Such strategies can include previewing material before it is introduced in class, or practising particular language structures to be used in later activities. Other possible strategies include focusing on particular language structures or pragmatic situations (i.e. watch this film and notice the greeting practices of the characters), and paying attention to one's own learning progress (i.e. self-ratings for class participation, proofreading of one's own writings, listening back to recordings of one's own speech).

Chamot, A. (1987), The Learning Strategies of ESL Students. In A. Wenden and J. Rubin (eds), *Learner Strategies in Language Learning* (pp. 71–83). Englewood Cliffs, NJ: Prentice Hall.

Morpheme order studies

Brown (1973) discovered that native English-speaking children learned particular morphemes (markers of grammatical meaning, such as the 'plural -s') in a predictable order. Dulay and Burt investigated this first with native Spanish-speaking children learning English, and later with both native Spanish and Chinese speakers (of various proficiency levels) learning English. In their studies, they found, as Brown had, that there was a predictable order of acquisition of particular English morphemes. For example, it was seen that children first acquire the progressive -ing ('The child is playing.'), and next the plural -s ('Those cats are nice.'). The fact that this order was similar for native speakers of Chinese and Spanish lent support to the notion that language acquisition involved innate mechanisms, and to the idea that first and second language acquisition could be similar processes.

Brown, R. (1973), *A First Language: The Early Stages*. Cambridge, MA: Harvard University Press.
Dulay, H. and Burt, M. (1974), A new perspective on the creative construction process in child second language acquisition. *Working Papers on Bilingualism*, 4, 71–98.

Motivation

In foreign language learning, two types of motivation are most often cited: instrumental and integrative. Terms coined by Gardner and Lambert, these motivation types refer to the situation of the learners and the reason they need to learn a foreign language. *Instrumental motivation* is at issue when the language will be a tool, or instrument, to learners for some purpose. For example, they might need to know English for a retail job that sees many tourists, or to read scientific journals in their career field. Contrary to *instrumental motivation*, *integrative motivation* is seen as internal to the individual learners, meaning they learn the language because they want to, for some reason or another. They may want to emulate someone they admire ('I remember as a child that my uncle could read English; I was so impressed.') or they may be interested in the cultures related to English and want to learn it for that reason. See also Investment.

Gardner, R .C. and Lambert, W. E. (1972), *Attitudes and Motivation in Second Language Learning*. Rowley, MA: Newbury House.

Linguistic imperialism

An extension of the general concept of imperialism (extending a country's power through diplomacy or military force), linguistic imperialism is the idea of extending a language's power (and therefore its cultural attachments as well) through official governmental policy or through economic practices (e.g. the capitalist economies of the USA and the UK). Proponents of the idea, such as Phillipson (1992) and Pennycook (1994), assert that the spread of English is a result of British colonial policy and American capitalism. Phillipson and Pennycook view linguistic imperialism as a force that is detrimental to the preservation of linguistic and cultural diversity and representative of continued oppression in a post-colonial world. Others disagree. Crystal (2003) calls the notion of linguistic imperialism overly simplistic, since countries who were not previously subject to English colonial power (i.e. France, Germany, many Latin American countries) are under similar global pressure to use English in certain domains (science, business).

Crystal, D. (2003), *English as a Global Language*. Cambridge: Cambridge University Press.
Pennycook, A. (1994), *The Cultural Politics of English as an International Language*. Harlow: Longman.
Phillipson, R. (1992), *Linguistic Imperialism*. Oxford: Oxford University Press.

Massively multiplayer online gaming spaces (MMOGs)

MMOGs are internet games that allow for multiple players across the world to play the same game together. The games, such as World of Warcraft, involve a fictional world with social rules to navigate. Each player creates an identity (involving race, class, and profession) within the fictional world and must behave 'appropriately' to advance in the game. Social experimentation is common, with players often creating multiple identities to experience the game from different perspectives. Such experimentation applies well to second language learning, with inherent awareness raising for appropriate language usage and pragmatic behaviours depending on one's role, status and relationship to interlocutors. Thorne (2008) noted the positive potential for language learning after studying interaction between an English speaker and a Russian speaker, where there was natural communication and negotiation of meaning, and a range of communicative functions (greeting, leave-taking, apologizing, etc.). The ideas behind MMOGs have been combined with those of sites like Second Life to create synthetic immersion environments for educational purposes (see Second Life).

Sykes, J. M., Oskoz, A. and Thorne, S. L. (2008), Web 2.0, Synthetic immersive environments, and mobile resources for language education. *CALICO Journal,* 25(3), 528–46.
Thorne, S. L. (2008). Transcultural Communication in Open Internet Environments and Massively Multiplayer Online Games. In S. Magnan (ed.), *Mediating Discourse Online* (pp. 305–27). Amsterdam: John Benjamins.

Multilingual

See Bilingual/multilingual.

Non-native speaker inferiority complex

See Non-native English-speaking teachers.

Native English-speaking teachers (NEST)

With regard to the long-held notion that the authorities of EFL are native speakers of English, Widdowson (1994) points out that being a native English speaker and being a foreign language teacher are two separate enterprises, and that native English speakers, in and of themselves, may be useful informants for EFL learners, but the best EFL teachers will be those who have expertise in FL teaching. Others argue that simply being a native speaker does not mean you cannot also gain teaching expertise and explicit linguistic knowledge (Kershaw, 1996; Parrot, 1998). However, a majority of native-speaking English teachers are still monolinguals with training only from short certification programmes, but may still project and be conceded more authority in the profession than those with strong linguistic and pedagogic backgrounds who are non-native speakers (Jenkins, 2000).

Jenkins, J. (2000), *The Phonology of English as an International Language.* Oxford: Oxford University Press.

Kershaw, G. (1996), The developing roles of native-speaker and non-native speaker teachers. *Modern English Teacher,* 5(3), 7–11.

Parrot, M. (1998), A personal response from Martin Parrot. *The IH Journal,* 5, 20–1.

Widdowson, H. G. (1994), Pragmatics and the Pedagogic Competence of Language Teachers. In T. Sebbage and S. Sebbage (eds), *Proceedings of the 4th International NELLE Conference.* Hamburg: NELLE.

Non-native English-speaking teachers (NNEST)

In the past, non-native English speaking teachers in the field of TESOL were seen as disadvantaged, compared to native English speakers, because the canonical goal of language learning had been attainment of native-like language use. However, the reality is that few language learners attain native-like use, and the field has come realize that such a goal can be undesirable, as it does not allow for self-expression and maintenance of identity of learners. Still, the non-native speaker inferiority complex can persist, where non-native teachers feel inadequate as language instructors. However, while native and non-native teachers differ in some practices and styles, non-native speakers can often give more specific explanations, directions and learning strategies as they too were learners of the language. NNEST is also the acronym for a special interest group in TESOL that was originally created to address issues specific to those of non-native teachers, such as gaining/maintaining confidence and a sense of authority or expertise in the domain.

Jenkins, J. (2000), *The Phonology of English as an International Language.* Oxford: Oxford University Press.

Medgyes, P. (1994). *The Non-Native Teacher.* London: Macmillan.

Online translator

Online translators are websites that, through use of concordancing and machine translation, purport to instantaneously translate words, phrases and even pages of text from one language to another (e.g. Babel Fish or Google Translate). The line between online dictionaries and online translators can be blurred, as well, given that translators still offer word translation, and many dictionaries translate phrases or collocations. Teachers may feel uncomfortable encouraging students to use online translators, either due to a notion of other-translation as cheating, or the inability of many translation tools to effectively master large chunks of text (because they literally translate phrases instead of recognizing collocations). However, given their widespread availability and potential usefulness as learning tools, others suggest engaging students in learning activities to demonstrate their strengths and weaknesses.

Godwin-Jones, R. (2010), Literacies and technologies revisited. *Language Learning and Technology,* 14(3), 2–9.

Output

In the Information Processing framework of language learning, output is the final stage in a three-part process of learning: reception of input, central processing, and output. After exposure to language input which has been noticed, and is therefore able to go through initial controlled processing, later automatic processing and then restructuring, learners may produce output in the form of written or spoken language (McLaughlin, 1987). Swain (1985) formulated the Output Hypothesis, claiming that producing spoken/signed or written language is a part of the language learning process, rather than a mere product of it. Output has three functions: triggering noticing (raising awareness for students of what they do and do not know), hypothesis testing (showing learners if their intended message is transmitted with the forms they've chosen), and metalinguistic awareness/reflection (inspired by Vygotsky's ideas of social, symbolically mediated learning, which results from the co-construction of meaning in dialogue).

McLaughlin, B. (1987), *Theories of Second Language Learning.* London: Edward Arnold.
Swain, M. (2005), The Output Hypothesis: Theory and Research. In E. Hinkel (ed.), *Handbook of Research in Second Language Teaching and Learning* (pp. 471–84). New York: Routledge.

Pushed output

A term coined by Swain (1985) in his formulation of the Output Hypothesis, pushed output is that which learners produce under some pressure to clarify their productions in actual communication. Later research confirmed more uptake (appropriately corrected errors by the learner) in situations where learners were 'pushed' by the communicative situation (or the teacher, in the classroom) to work to express their meaning in multiple ways until arriving at one that properly conveys the message. Loewen (2002), for example, found that 'elicitative strategies' that encourage pushed output led to much more uptake than recasts, which simply supplied the correct answer to language students. Also important to note is that the goal of output or pushed output is not simply getting the message across, but rather to convey the message precisely and appropriately, in linguistic and pragmatic terms.

Loewen, S. (2002), The occurrence and effectiveness of incidental focus on form in meaning-focused ESL lessons. Unpublished doctoral dissertation, University of Auckland, New Zealand.
Swain, M. (2005), The Output Hypothesis: Theory and Research. In E. Hinkel (ed.), *Handbook of Research in Second Language Teaching and Learning* (pp. 471–84). New York: Routledge.

Risk-taking

Related to other affective factors in foreign language learning, such as inhibition, risk-taking behaviour has been shown to correlate with more successful language learning outcomes. Brown sees risk-taking as essential to effective language learning, as students must regularly take the risk of not interpreting or responding to a situation correctly in the practice associated with foreign language learning. Really engaging in communication and classroom activities allows for the maximum amount of practice and feedback to facilitate improvement and learning, whereas fearing to engage in risk-taking behaviour leaves fewer opportunities for both. For this reason, Brown recommends that teachers encourage risk-taking behaviour in their students in a variety of ways. For example, teachers must be risk-takers themselves, and also must praise students' efforts at engaging in the learning process even when the result is not an immediately correct or appropriate response.

Brown, H. D. (2006), *Principles of Language Learning and Teaching* (5th edn). White Plains, NY: Pearson-Longman ESL.

Scaffolding

From Vygotsky's theories of learning as a social, symbolically mediated process (Sociocultural Theory), scaffolding refers to the process of guiding a learner with cooperative talk towards a given skill or knowledge based on other knowledge they have, rather than just giving the answer or letting them struggle alone (Wood et al., 1976). Using knowledge that learners already have is part of staying within Vygotsky's *Zone of Proximal Development*, allowing learners to make their own connections and learn more. Scaffolding can be done by teachers or other learners, who may be engaged together in small-group interactions. In language teaching, scaffolding may be realized through repetition, recasting, and/or discussion of a particular point or linguistic structure. For example, Donato and McCormick (1994) share a dialogue where French students work together to get from 'tu as souvenu' (an incorrect production of 'you remembered') to the correct production (requiring a reflexive and a change of helping verb) 'tu t'es souvenu'.

Donato, R. and McCormick, D. (1994), A sociocultural perspective on language learning strategies: The role of mediation. *Modern Language Journal*, 78(4), 3–64.
Wood, D., Bruner, J. and Ross, G. (1976), The role of tutoring in problem solving. *Journal of Child Psychology and Psychiatry*, 17, 89–100.
Vygotsky, L. S. (1962), *Thought and Language*. Cambridge, MA: MIT Press.

Second Life

Part of the collaborative environment of Web 2.0, Second Life is a virtual open space where users create identities (avatars), choosing gender and clothing for their self-representations, and then modify their behaviour based on the context and the other avatars present. Users can also take on multiple identities, thus experiencing the environment from multiple perspectives. Given the opportunities for natural communication and sensitization to pragmatics in such virtual open spaces and in massively multiplayer online gaming spaces, the two have been combined into synthetic immersion experiences for language learning, where students create identities within the target language community or from their L1 community and must success-fully navigate their new world linguistically and pragmatically. Not only does this offer learners 'immersion' experiences, it also may increase motivation, tapping into the emotional investment common to gaming. One drawback of these environments is the potential resistance from the academic community to engage in 'playing', seeing it as antithetical to learning.

Sykes, J. M., Oskoz, A. and Thorne, S. L. (2008), Web 2.0, synthetic immersive environments, and mobile resources for language education. *CALICO Journal*, 25(3), 528–46.

Social networking

Social networking is the umbrella term for Web 2.0's social environments, such as Facebook and MySpace, where users create self-profiles (including photos, identifying information like name/pseudonym, age, gender, profession, religion, hobbies, relationship status and goals on the networking site). Each user has an individualized online community, depending on whom they link to and share information with (or whom they 'friend', in Facebook terms). Users may post updates about their thoughts or activities on their own profile pages, which are posted into a larger feed which people in their online community read and comment on. Such networking sites allow for communication between individuals and groups (with internal messaging systems akin to email), or within the user's entire online community (through posting and commenting). Used worldwide, social networking sites can also offer opportunities for L2 reading and writing practice, but teachers may be uncomfortable with the reality that such communication is typically short, informal and personal, thus 'non-academic' by many standards.

Godwin-Jones, R. (2010), Literacies and technologies revisited. *Language Learning and Technology*, 14(3), 2–9.

Sociocultural theory

Stemming from Lev Vygotsky's work *Thought and Language*, Sociocultural Theory applies to language learning first in that it sees any mental activity as symbolically mediated, with language as the primary set of symbols to express our thoughts (Lantolf, 1994). The theory further sees learning as a social process involving mediation with language, where those with certain skills or knowledge (termed capable of 'self-regulation') help those still learning them (who are still 'other-regulated') through collaboration. This cooperative talk, edging learners closer to their goals without just revealing answers, is scaffolding (Wood et al., 1976). The Zone of Proximal Development, a metaphorical space in the learning process, is the place where the student can learn the most, because of appropriate materials, tasks, levels of difficulty and scaffolding. Private speech, where children 'talk themselves through' tasks and processes, is part of learning self-regulation.

Lantolf, J. P. (1994), Introduction to the special issue (Sociocultural theory and second language learning). *Modern Language Journal*, 78, 418–20.
Wood, D., Bruner, J. and Ross, G. (1976), The role of tutoring in problem solving. *Journal of Child Psychology and Psychiatry*, 17, 89–100.
Vygotsky, L. S. (1962), *Thought and Language*. Cambridge, MA: MIT Press.

Stabilization

Stabilization, sometimes treated as synonymous with fossilization, is said rather to share a place on the same continuum as fossilization (Han, 2004). Stabilization can involve at least three different situations in the learning process. First, it may involve simply 'getting stuck' on a structure for an indeterminate period of time. Second, it may be the result of interlanguage restructuring. Both instances can give the appearance of a stabilized form that is actually not yet fixed. Finally, stabilization can also be the precursor to fossil-ization, in which case one may see one of at least four situations: invariant uses of a form over a long period of time; 'backsliding', or a reappearance of some forms that were thought to have passed out of the interlanguage grammar; a reappearance of some forms based on context (target-like in some circumstances but non-target-like in others); or a reappearance of some old forms in the same context, but sometimes target-like and sometimes non-target-like.

Han, Z. (2004), *Fossilization in Adult Second Language Acquisition*. Bristol: Multilingual Matters.

Standard English

According to Jenkins (2009), 'standard language is the term used for that variety of a language which is considered to be the norm' (p. 33). However, from the perspective of world Englishes research, it is difficult to decide what the 'norm' should be for English, given its use worldwide as a first language, a second language, and a foreign language, and given the histories (colonial, economic, etc.) that afforded English its particular status (common language, official language, language of business or education, etc.) in given areas. Trudgill (1999) instead defines it for what it is *not*, explaining that it is not a whole language, but only one variety of a language; it is not associated with any particular accent or style, and it is not just a set of rules from grammarians. Instead, Standard English is a social dialect, more prestigious than other non-standard varieties. Standard English is also commonly believed to be the English used in the formal education, government and commerce of English-speaking countries.

Jenkins, J. (2009), *World Englishes: A Resource Book for Students*. Oxford and New York: Routledge.
Trudgill, P. (1999), Standard English: What it isn't. In T. Bex and R. Watts (eds), *Standard English: The Widening Debate*. London: Routledge.

Subtractive bilingualism

See Additive/subtractive bilingualism.

Synchronous

Synchronous internet tools, so named because they allow for communication between multiple parties in real time, are popular in language teaching to facilitate communication among students, between students and teachers, or among native and non-native speakers of the target language. Earlier computer-mediated communication focused on text chat, which, although in written format, was said to approximate spoken language because of its shorter utterances, frequent turn-taking and real-time format. Now voice chat and video chat are common and used for group work focused on content or speaking practice, also appreciated for real-time conversation, now approximating to face-to-face interaction. Social networking sites like Facebook also have chat functions which are commonly used in conjunction with asynchronous tools on those same sites. Newer virtual social spaces like Second Life and massively multiplayer player gaming spaces like World of Warcraft also allow for synchronous communication between users around the world as their avatars navigate the sites' social spaces.

Blake, R. J. (2007), New trends in using technology in the language curriculum. *Annual Review of Applied Linguistics,* 27, 76–97.
Godwin-Jones, R. (2003), Blogs and wikis: Environments for online collaboration. *Language Learning and Technology,* 7(2), 12–16.
Sykes, J. M., Oskoz, A. and Thorne, S. L. (2008), Web 2.0, synthetic immersive environments, and mobile resources for language education. *CALICO Journal,* 25(3), 528–46.

Teachability Hypothesis

The Teachability Hypothesis (Pienemann, 1984) (also referred to as the Learnability Hypothesis) states that formal language teaching can improve natural second language acquisition, but only if it targets structures when learners are ready for them. Readiness for a structure is psycholinguistic, based on a hierarchy of processability, where findings already indicate a natural, systematic order of second language acquisition based on the difficulty of processing given structures (Clahsen, Meisel and Pienemann, 1983). The Teachability Hypothesis states that this order of acquisition should be taken into account in syllabus design, because formal instruction of structures from near the learners' level on the interlanguage continuum will result in a more advanced use of the structures than would be seen in natural second language acquisition. However, targeting structures that learners are not ready for (whose acquisition would presuppose previous acquisition of other, more easily processed structures), will not lead to increased learning and may even disrupt the natural developmental sequences at play.

Clahsen, H., Meisel, J. and Pienemann, M. (1983), Deutsch als Zweitspraches der Spracherwerb ausländischer Arbeiter. Tübingen: Gunter Narr.
Pienemann, M. (1989), Is language teachable? Psycholinguistic experiments and hypotheses. *Applied Linguistics,* 10(1), 52–79.

Teaching English as a Foreign Language (TEFL)

The field of teaching English to those living in their native land (which is not English-dominant) and studying English in foreign language classes. As a foreign language, English may not be regularly used or applicable in daily life, but is either being learned to fulfil an institutional requirement, or for use later in a business or educational context at home or abroad. More recently, the broader term English as a lingua franca or English as an international language is applied to the English language as used by many TEFL learners, where they may be communicating in English with other non-native speakers, again for business or educational purposes, rather than only going abroad to English-speaking countries to communicate primarily with native English speakers.

Jenkins, J. (2009), *World Englishes: A Resource Book for Students.* Oxford and New York: Routledge.
Saville-Troike, M. (2006), *Introducing Second Language Acquisition.* Cambridge: Cambridge University Press.

Teaching English as a Second Language (TESL)

The field of teaching English to those who live in an English-dominant environment while learning English. Often the learners of TESL are immigrants in a new country, and may be using their first language at home and within social communities, but learning to use English for work, education and other official purposes. TESL is also sometimes used more generally to simply mean the teaching of English to anyone whose native language is not English, such that it could encompass the field of Teaching English as a Foreign Language as well.

Richards, J. C. and Schmidt, R. (2010), *Longman Dictionary of Language Teaching and Applied Linguistics.* London: Longman.
Saville-Troike, M. (2006), *Introducing Second Language Acquisition.* Cambridge: Cambridge University Press.

Teaching English to Speakers of Other Languages (TESOL)

The field of teaching English to anyone who is not a native speaker of the language, this term can encompass Teaching English as a Foreign Language (where learners are in their home country that does not use English for social or official purposes) and Teaching English as a Second Language (where learners are in an English-dominant society and likely learning the language for education, work or other official purposes). TESOL is also the name of the worldwide professional organization focused on providing resources for optimum English teaching and learning for speakers of other languages. The organization hosts myriad workshops and symposia, a yearly convention, and publishes a variety of journals (such as the research-based *TESOL Quarterly*).

Richards, J. C. and Schmidt, R. (2010), *Longman Dictionary of Language Teaching and Applied Linguistics*. London: Longman.
www.tesol.org.

Top-down processing

See Bottom-up/top-down processing.

Transfer (positive or negative)

Transfer is the process by which foreign language learners use properties or rules of the first language in expressing themselves in the foreign language. Transfer can occur at all linguistic levels (i.e. phonology, morphology, syntax, lexicon, pragmatics, etc.), and can be positive (when structures in both languages are similar, and it is helpful to replicate L1) or negative (when structures in each language are different, and replicating L1 leads to errors in L2; this is also-called interference).

> *Positive Transfer:* a native Spanish speaker learning French will unwittingly produce the correct structure of adjective phrases, first putting an article, then a noun, then an adjective:

Spanish: el libro rojo (the book red)

French: le livre rouge (the book red)

Negative Transfer/Interference: a native English speaker learning French, on the other hand, will unwittingly produce the adjective phrase structure incorrectly when using English rules:

English: the red book

French: le rouge livre (the red book)

Lado, R. (1957), *Linguistics across Cultures*. Ann Arbor, MI: University of Michigan Press.
Saville-Troike, M. (2006), *Introducing Second Language Acquisition*. Cambridge: Cambridge University Press.

Universal grammar

Noam Chomsky presents the idea that there is a *universal grammar* of all human languages (part and parcel of his belief in the innate capacity of humans to learn language), and that this is why humans can learn their first language so quickly (contrary to the previous structuralist/behaviourist view that language is learned like other skills or behaviours, through trial, error and practice). This grammar contains *principles* (i.e. any language will have a specified word order) and *parameters* (the possible word orders are 'subject-verb-object', 'subject-object-verb' and 'verb-subject-object'). In language acquisition, humans just need a few examples from the language to determine which parameters apply to their first language. There is still debate in the field about to what degree second language learners have access to universal grammar in the acquisition of their second language. Some postulate no access at all (meaning that second language learning is inherently different from native language acquisition), others complete access (meaning that first and second language acquisition are similar processes), and still others postulate partial access, with some but not all principles and parameters available to the second language learner.

Chomsky, N. (1981), *Lectures on Government and Binding*. Dordrecht: Foris.
—(1986), *Knowledge of Language: Its Nature, Origin and Use*. New York: Praeger.
Mitchell, R. and Myles, F. (1998), *Second Language Learning Theories*. London: Edward Arnold.

Uptake

Uptake is the term given when a student recognizes feedback on an error and uses it to modify subsequent utterances. Originally uptake was studied only on reactive feedback like error correction, such as in Chaudron (1977), which found that repetition of a correct form with added emphasis was the most likely repetitive form of error feedback to lead to uptake. However, the majority of corrections, regardless of type, did not lead to any form of uptake in that study, a phenomenon seen in other studies as well. On the other hand, later studies by Rod Ellis and colleagues working within the 'focus on form' framework see uptake as facilitative of language learning, and thus worthy of continued study. One such study showed a large amount of uptake, but showed that the degree of uptake was dependent on the nature of the negotiation (meaning- or form-based) and classroom context (teacher- or peer-initiated negotiation) (Ellis et al., 2001).

Chaudron, G. (1977), A descriptive model of discourse in the corrective treatment of learners' errors. *Language Learning*, 27, 29–46.
Ellis, R., Basturkmen, H. and Loewen, S. (2001), Learner uptake in communicative ESL lessons. *Language Learning*, 51(2), 281–318.

Web 2.0

Web 2.0 (also 'second-generation web') is so-called because its tools represent a paradigm shift in internet usage: one-sided, writer/website focused presentation of content became a two-way conversation, as readers of the web could now more easily create web content, or comment on others' creations. Much of the computer technology used in foreign language teaching today is part of Web 2.0, such as blogs, wikis (i.e. Wikipedia: spaces for collaborative creation of content) and social bookmarking (i.e. del.icio.us: use of one webpage to list, describe and categorize a variety of webpages). Virtual open spaces (i.e. Second Life) and massively multiplayer online gaming (e.g. World of Warcraft) offer opportunities to choose your role in 'society' and require you to interact appropriately with others to meet goals. Synthetic immersive environments (i.e. Croquelandia, a learning site for Spanish language and pragmatics) combine the attributes of virtual open spaces and massively multiplayer online gaming for educational contexts.

Sykes, J. M., Oskoz, A. and Thorne, S. L. (2008), Web 2.0, synthetic immersive environments, and mobile resources for language education. *CALICO Journal*, 25(3), 528–46.

Working memory

Stemming from general studies of cognition, the concept of working memory has been developed with relation to language learning. In Anderson's *Adaptive Control of Thought* (1983) model, working memory is a short-term memory with limited power that is used when first learning something, when much attention is required, analogous to the short-term memory used in controlled processing in McLaughlin's (1987) Information Processing approach. Ellis (2001) explains that the Working Memory Model is necessarily basic, positing limited attention possible during learning, and specialized systems for perception and representation of auditory (speech) and visual (writing) information. Like Anderson (1983, 1985) and McLaughlin (1987), more recent research on working memory has distinctions between short-term and long-term memory, assuming that perception of language input (speech or writing) is organized by information held in long-term memory (what we have already learned), and treats the process of learning as using controlled attention before moving towards development of automaticity.

Anderson, J. (1983), *The Architecture of Cognition.* Cambridge, MA: Harvard University Press.
Ellis, N. (2001), Memory for Language. In P. Robinson (ed.), *Cognition and Second Language Instruction* (pp. 33–68). Cambridge: Cambridge University Press.
McLaughlin, B. (1987), *Theories of Second Language Learning.* London: Edward Arnold.

World Englishes (WE)

A field which recognizes the multiple varieties of English that are spoken by English users worldwide, including those spoken in countries where English is not an official language, and by speakers who may traditionally be classified as non-native. Kachru (1992) classifies these speakers as belonging to the Inner, Outer, and Expanding Circles.

Inner Circle: Largely monolingual countries where English is an official or socially dominant language (e.g. Great Britain, Canada, the USA and Australia).

Outer Circle: Areas formerly colonized by English-speaking powers (e.g. India and Singapore), where English is now widely spoken and used in conjunction with other languages in multilingual societies.

Expanding Circle: Countries not formerly colonized by English-speaking powers who recognize the importance of knowing and using English as a Foreign Language (EFL) for global communication (e.g. Japan).

Some consider EIL (English as an International Language) and ELF (English as a Lingua Franca) as part of the WE framework; see EIL and ELF entries.

Kachru, B. B. (1992), Teaching World Englishes. In B. B. Kachru (ed.), *The Other Tongue: English across Cultures* (2nd edn) (pp. 355–65). Urbana, IL: University of Illinois Press.

World Standard Spoken English

Crystal (1997) hypothesized that with the increasingly global role of English, there would be an increase in regional varieties of English which would be spoken in their given communities (e.g. Singlish, for English in Singapore), but because of the regional influences, such varieties of English would become increasingly different from each other. Thus, he also postulated a World Standard Spoken English, a variety of English that would be used by speakers of most varieties when they communicate outside their regional communities. This hypothesis did not include a detailed account of how change would occur in given varieties, or how they would converge for the WSSE, but Crystal did assert that American English's influence would likely be more strongly felt than other varieties. However, American English itself would not simply become the standard; other varieties (including those of non-native speakers of English) would also influence WSSE, making it a hybrid of the world's varieties of English.

Crystal, D. (1997), *English as a Global Language*. Cambridge: Cambridge University Press.

Zone of proximal development (ZPD)

In Sociocultural Theory, which stems from Lev Vygotsky's theories of social, symbolically mediated learning, the ZPD is a metaphorical space in the learning process which has the optimal conditions for a student's learning. This space would include activities/tasks/goals at an appropriate level for the student (not too easy or too difficult). Equally, with language as the primary symbol of thought and mental processes, the ZPD involves scaffolding, or cooperative talk with the student to help him/her use existing knowledge to arrive at the learning goal (a skill or some knowledge). This scaffolding can come from a teacher or another learner. In essence, the ZPD is the space where the learner can reach a higher level of understanding with scaffolding than what would be reached if the learner pursued the learning goal alone.

Mitchell, R. and Myles, F. (1998), *Second Language Learning Theories*. London: Edward Arnold.
Vygotsky, L. S. (1962), *Thought and Language*. Cambridge, MA: MIT Press.

Notes

Chapter 1

1 In this chapter, *TESOL Quarterly* will be referred to as *TQ*.

2 See our annotated section in Chapter 3 for a more thorough treatment of English as a Lingua Franca (ELF), English as an International Language (EIL), and World Englishes (WE). For the sake of brevity, we only refer to ELF in this chapter.

3 TESOL Inc. has been changed to TESOL International Association because of the demand for, as well as the reality that, TESOL is going global.

4 It could also be argued that some of the highest compensated jobs for ELT professionals are currently in Asia/Asia-Pacific, resulting in a greater demand and opportunity for research from this region of the world.

5 While acknowledging the convincing nature of current research on the importance of integrated teaching (see Hinkel, 2010), for the purposes of this *TQ* analysis, which spanned multiple decades of TESOL research, we maintained the discrete language skills components of reading, writing, listening, and speaking for the sake of examination.

6 For a more thorough treatment of communicative competence, see our annotated section on the topic in Chapter 3.

7 TESOL International Association has developed various position statements over the years. Some are developed in response to US legislation, while others are responses to developments and trends in the field. The position papers analysed for this study were released between the years 1996 and 2011.

8 This short email survey was sent to various TESOL leaders, practitioners, and researchers both in the United States and abroad.

9 We do not intend to suggest that the predominance of English should be accepted uncritically, nor that it be considered inevitable, for that matter. Rather, the present role of English in the globalized world is a lens through which this book will examine critical issues surrounding this phenomenon.

10 Proponents of initiatives such as the English-only movement in the United States (see TESOL International Association's 'Position Paper on English-only Legislation in the United States') have arguably interpreted this latter entitlement as an obligation.

11 Interestingly, Cook (2007) concedes that young learners in certain EFL contexts may be considered language 'learners' rather than 'users', as '[t]hey do not form a community of use in the same sense as the others ... they have target communities to aim to belong to but are not members of an existing L2 community outside the classroom' (p. 208).

12 The *critical period* is 'a period of time when learning a language is relatively easy and typically meets with a high degree of success. Once their period is over ... the average learner is less likely to achieve native-like ability in the target language' (Marinova-Todd, Marshall and Snow, 2000, p. 9, as cited by Liu, 2007a, p. 171). See our entry for the critical period in Chapter 5 for further information.

13 However, Tomlinson (1998) has also warned that designing materials based on localized culture, learning conditions, etc., might ignore the more fundamental need for materials to 'provide opportunities for learner choice' (p. 338) and to offer 'greater flexibility in decisions about content, order, pace and procedures' (p. 280).

14 The term 'polyfocal attention' has been used to refer to the ability to pay attention to various media and/or people at the same time (see Scollon, 1998, as cited by Cooke and Simpson, 2008).

15 In particular, Cooke and Simpson (2008) are writing about English learners who are migrants to traditionally English-dominant countries (ESOL); however, we believe these four themes of electronic literacy can relate to any language learner in the twenty-first century.

16 McEnery, Xiao and Tono (2006) define a *corpus* as 'a collection of sampled texts, written or spoken, in machine-readable form which may be annotated with various forms of linguistic information' (p. 4).

17 Lippi-Green (1997) considers these practices to be language discrimination, even though such discrimination is not often interpreted as discriminatory by judges and lawmakers.

Chapter 2

1 Please note that our discussion of endorsement certificates is primarily for readers living and working in the United States.

2 Also referred to as *practitioner knowledge* (Hiebert, Gallimore and Stigler, 2002) and the *content* of L2 teaching (Freeman and Johnson, 1998).

Chapter 3

1 For a detailed discussion of publication, please also refer to the section in Chapter 4 on professional development.

2 For the detailed research agenda (2004 version and 2014 version), please visit TESOL International website (http://www.tesol.org).

Chapter 4

1 Harold B. Allen, *A Survey of the Teaching of English to Non-English Speakers in the United States*. New York: Arno Press, 1978, *c.*1966, pp. 28–30.

References

Adler, P. (1974), Beyond cultural identity: Reflections on cultural and multicultural man. In R. W. Brislin (ed.), *Topics in Culture Learning*, Vol. 2 (pp. 23–40). Honolulu, HI: East-West Center.

Alderson, J. C. and Clapham, C. (1995), Assessing student performance in the ESL classroom. *TESOL Quarterly*, 29(1), 184–7.

Allen, H. B. (1966), *A Survey of the Teaching of English to Non-English Speakers in the United States*. New York: Arno Press.

Allwright, D. and Bailey, K. (1991), *Focus on the Language Classroom*. New York: Cambridge University Press.

Alptekin, C. (2002), Towards intercultural communicative competence in ELT. *ELT Journal*, 56(1), 5–64.

—(2010), Redefining multicompetence for bilingualism. *International Journal of Applied Linguistics*, 20(1), 95–110.

American Association for Applied Linguistics (2014), *2014 Conference Program*. Retrieved from https://app.box.com/s/2772oofxkg6jyzmd3l7j

Amin, N. (1997), Race and the identity of the nonnative ESL teacher. *TESOL Quarterly*, 31(3), 580–3.

Arizona Board of Regents, University of Arizona (2013), *Prospective Students*. Retrieved from http://slat.arizona.edu/prospective-students

—(2014), *Master of Arts in Teaching of English as a Second Language*. Retrieved from http://nau.edu/CAL/English/Degrees-Programs/Graduate/MA-TESL/

Armour, W. (2004), Becoming a Japanese language learner, user, and teacher: Revelations from life history research. *Journal of Language, Identity, and Education*, 3(2), 101–25.

Aronin, L. and Singleton, D. (2012), *Multilingualism*. Amsterdam: John Benjamins.

Bachman, L. F. and Palmer, A. S. (2010), Describing Language use and Language Ability. In L. F. Bachman and A. S. Palmer (eds), *Language Assessment in Practice* (pp. 33–58). Oxford: Oxford University Press.

Bailey, K. M. (1990), The use of Diary Studies in Teacher Education Programs. In J. C. Richards and D. Nunan (eds), *Second Language Teacher Education* (pp. 215–26). New York: Cambridge University Press.

Bailey, K. M. (ed.) (1998), *Learning about Language Assessment: Dilemmas, Decisions, and Directions*. Boston, MA: Heinle & Heinle.

Bambino, D. (2002), Critical friends. *Redesigning Professional Development*, 59(6), 25–7.

Barduhn, S. and Johnson, J. (2009), Certification and Professional Qualifications. In A. Burns and J. C. Richards (eds), *The Cambridge Guide to Second Language Teacher Education* (pp. 59–65). Cambridge: Cambridge University Press.

Batalova, J. F. and Fix, M. (2010), A profile of limited English proficient adult immigrants. *Peabody Journal of Education,* 85, 511–34.

Beatty, K. (2003), *Teaching and Researching CALL.* London: Longman.

Beck, C. and Kosnik, C. (2006), *Innovations in Teacher Education: A Social Constructivist Approach.* Albany, NY: State University of New York Press.

Belcher, D. (ed.) (2009), *English for Specific Purposes in Theory and Practice.* Ann Arbor, MI: University of Michigan Press.

Bell, N. (2009), *A Student's Guide to the MA TESOL.* Hampshire: Palgrave.

Benson, P. (2013), *Teaching and Researching Autonomy* (2nd edn). Abingdon: Routledge.

Berns, M. (2009), World Englishes and Communicative Competence. In B. Kachru, Y. Kachru and C. Nelson (eds), *The Handbook of World Englishes,* Vol. 48 (pp. 718–30). Oxford: Wiley-Blackwell.

Bhatia, T. K. and Ritchi, W. C. (eds) (2012), *The Handbook of Bilingualism and Multilingualism* (2nd edn). Chichester: Wiley-Blackwell.

Biber, D., Johansson, S., Leech, G., et al. (1999), *Longman Grammar of Spoken and Written English.* Harlow: Longman.

Blackledge, A. and Creese, A. (2010), *Multilingualism: A Critical Perspective.* London: Continuum.

Blake, R. (2011), Current trends in online language learning. *Annual Review of Applied Linguistics,* 31, 19–35.

Block, D. (2009), *Second Language Identities.* London: Continuum.

Bourke, J. M. (2006), Designing a topic-based syllabus for young learners. *ELT Journal,* 60(3), 279–86.

Braine, G. (2002), Academic literacy and the nonnative speaker graduate student. *Journal of English for Academic Purposes,* 1(1), 59–68.

—(2005), A Critical Review of the Research on Non-native Speaker English Teachers. In C. Gnutzman and F. Intemann (eds), *The Globalization of English and the English Language Classroom* (pp. 275–84). Tübingen: Gunther Narr.

—(2010), *Nonnative Speaker English Teachers: Research, Pedagogy, and Professional Growth.* New York: Routledge.

Braine, G. (ed.) (1999), *Non-Native Educators in English Language Teaching.* Mahwah, NJ: Lawrence Erlbaum.

Brandt, C. (2006a), Allowing for practice: A critical issue in TESOL teacher preparation. *ELT Journal,* 60(4), 355–64.

—(2006b), *Success in your Certificate Course in English Language Teaching: A Guide to Becoming a Teacher in ELT/TESOL.* London: Sage Publications.

Breen, M. P. and Candlin, C. (1980), The essentials of a communicative curriculum in language teaching. *Applied Linguistics,* 1(2), 89–112.

Brewster, J., Ellis, G. and Girard, D. (1992), *The Primary English Teacher's Guide.* Harmondsworth: Penguin.

Brinton, D. M., Kagan, O. and Bauckus, S. (eds) (2008), *Heritage Language Education: A New Field Emerging.* New York: Routledge.

Brock, M., Yu, B. and Wong, M. (1992), 'Journalling' Together: Collaborative Diary-keeping and Teacher Development. In J. Flowerdew, M. Brock and S. Hsia (eds), *Perspectives on Second Language Teacher Development* (pp. 295–307). Hong Kong: City University of Hong Kong.

Brodkey, D. and Young, R. (1981), Composition correctness scores. *TESOL Quarterly,* 15(2), 159–67.

Brophy, J. (1998), *Motivating Students to Learn*. New York: McGraw-Hill.

Brown, H. D. (1973), Affective variables in second language acquisition. *Language Learning*, 23(2), 231–44.

—(2007), *Teaching by Principles: An Interactive Approach to Language Pedagogy* (3rd edn). White Plains, NY: Pearson Education.

Brown, H. D. and Abeywickrama, P. (2010), *Language Assessment: Principles and Classroom Practices* (2nd edn). White Plains, NY: Longman.

Brown, J. D. (1998), *New Ways of Classroom Assessment*. New Ways in TESOL Series II: Innovative Classroom Techniques. Alexandria, VA: TESOL.

Brown, J. D. and Hudson, T. (1998), The alternatives in language assessment. *TESOL Quarterly*, 32(4), 653–75.

Brown, K. (1993), Second Language Teacher Education. *TESOL Quarterly*, 27(4), 753–6.

—(1995), World Englishes: To Teach or Not to Teach. *World Englishes*, 14(2), 233–45.

Brown, S., Armstrong, S. and Thompson, G. (1998), *Motivating Students*. London: Kogan Page.

Brumfit, C., Moon, J. and Tongue, R. (eds) (1991), *Teaching English to Children: From Practice to Principle*. London: Collins ELT.

Buck, G. (2001), *Assessing Listening*. Cambridge: Cambridge University Press.

Burns, A. (1999), *Collaborative Action Research for English Language Teachers*. New York: Cambridge University Press.

Burns, A. and Richards, J. C. (eds) (2009), *The Cambridge Guide to Second Language Teacher Education*. Cambridge: Cambridge University Press.

Burt, M. and Dulay, H. (1978), Some guidelines for the assessment of oral language proficiency and dominance. *TESOL Quarterly*, 12(2),177–92.

Burton, J. I. and Carroll, M. (eds) (2001), *Journal Writing*. Alexandria, VA: TESOL.

Butler, Y. G. (2007), How are nonnative English speaking teachers perceived by young learners? *TESOL Quarterly*, 41(4), 731–55.

Byram, M. (1997), *Teaching and Assessing Intercultural Communicative Competence*. Bristol: Multilingual Matters.

Cabrelli Amaro, J., Flynn, S. and Rothman, J. (eds) (2012), *Third Language Acquisition in Adulthood*. Amsterdam: John Benjamins.

Calderhead, J. and Gates, P. (eds) (2004), *Conceptualising Reflection in Teacher Development*. London: Routledge.

Cameron, L. (2001), *Teaching English to Young Learners*. Cambridge: Cambridge University Press.

—(2003), Challenges for ELT from the expansion in teaching children. *ELT Journal*, 57(2), 105–12.

Canagarajah, A. S. (1999), Interrogating the 'Native Speaker Fallacy': Non-linguistic roots, Non-pedagogical Results. In G. Braine (ed.), *Non-Native Educators in English Language Teaching* (pp. 77–92). Mahwah, NJ: Lawrence Erlbaum.

—(2006a), Changing communicative needs, revised assessment objectives: Testing English as an international language, *Language Assessment Quarterly*, 3(3), 229–42.

—(2006b), TESOL at Forty: What are the issues? *TESOL Quarterly*, 40(1), 9–34.

—(2006c), Negotiating the local in English as a lingua franca. *Annual Review of Applied Linguistics*, 26, 197–218.

Canagarajah, A. S. (ed.) (2005), *Reclaiming the Local in Language Policy and Practice*. Mahwah, NJ: Lawrence Erlbaum.

Canale, M. (1987), The measurement of communicative competence. *Annual Review of Applied Linguistics*, 8(1), 67–84.

Canale, M. and Swain, M. (1980), Theoretical bases of communicative approaches to second language teaching and testing. *Applied Linguistics*, 1(1), 1–47.

Canton, J. (2006), *The Extreme Future: The Top Trends That Will Reshape the World in the Next 20 Years*. New York: Plume.

Carless, D. and Walker, E. (2006), Effective team teaching between local and native-speaking English teachers. *Language and Education*, 20, 463–77.

Carrier, K. A. (2003), NNS teacher trainees in Western-based TESOL programs. *ELT Journal*, 57(3), 242–50.

Carroll, J. B. and Sapon, S. M. (1959), *Modern Language Aptitude Test (MLAT)*. San Antonio, TX: Psychological Corporation.

Carter, K. (1992), Toward a Cognitive Conception of Classroom Management: A Case of Teacher Comprehension. In J. H. Shulman (ed.), *Case Methods in Teacher Education* (pp. 111–30). New York: Teachers College Press.

Carter, R. and McCarthy, M. (2006), *Cambridge Grammar of English: A Comprehensive Guide to Spoken and Written Grammar and Usage*. Cambridge: Cambridge University Press.

Casanave, C. P. and Schecter, S. R. (eds) (1997), *On Becoming a Language Educator: Personal Essays on Professional Development*. Mahwah, NJ: Lawrence Erlbaum.

Casanave, C. and Vandrick, S. (2003), *Writing for Scholarly Publication: Behind the Scenes in Language Education*. Mahwah, NJ: Lawrence Erlbaum.

Celce-Murcia, M. (1995). The Elaboration of Sociolinguistic Competence: Implications for Teacher Education. In J. E. Alatis, C. A. Straehle and M. Ronkin (eds), *Linguistics and the Education of Language Teachers: Ethnolinguistic, Psycholinguistic, and Sociolinguistic Aspects.* Proceedings of the Georgetown University Round Table on Languages and Linguistics, 2005 (pp. 699–710). Washington DC: Georgetown University Press.

—(2007), Rethinking the Role of Communicative Competence in Language teaching. In E. A. Soler and M. Pilar Safont Jordà (eds), *Intercultural Language Use and Language Learning* (pp. 41–57). Dordrecht: Springer.

Celce-Murcia, M. and Larsen-Freeman, D. (1999), *The Grammar Book: An ESL/ EFL Teacher's Course* (2nd edn). Boston, MA: Heinle & Heinle.

Celce-Murcia, M., Dörnyei, Z. and Thurrell, S. (1995), A pedagogical framework for communicative competence: A pedagogically motivated model with content specifications. *Issues in Applied Linguistics* 6(2), 5–35.

Cenoz, J. (2013), Defining multilingualism. *Annual Review of Applied Linguistics*, 33, 3–18.

Cenoz, J., Hufeisen, B. and Jessner, U. (eds) (2001), *Cross-Linguistic Influence in Third Language Acquisition: Psycholinguistic Perspectives*. Bristol: Multilingual Matters.

Chalhoub-Deville, M. (2010), Technology in Standardized Language Assessments. In R. B. Kaplan (ed.), *The Oxford Handbook of Applied Linguistics* (2nd edn) (pp. 511–26). Oxford: Oxford University Press.

Chamberlin-Quinlisk, C. (2012), TESOL and media education: Navigating our screen-saturated worlds. *TESOL Quarterly*, 46(1), 152–64.

Chambers, G. (1999), *Motivating Language Learners*. Bristol: Multilingual Matters.

Chapelle, C. A. (1994), CALL activities: Are they all the same? *System,* 22(1), 33–45.

—(2001), *Computer Applications in Second Language Acquisition*. Cambridge: Cambridge University Press.

—(2003), *English Language Learning and Technology: Lectures on Applied Linguistics in the Age of Information and Communication Technology*, Vol. 7. Amsterdam: John Benjamins.

Charlesworth, A. (2009), *The Digital Revolution*. London: Dorling Kindersley.

Chinnery, G. M. (2006), Emerging technologies. Going to the mall: Mobile assisted language learning. *Language Learning & Technology,* 10(1), 9–16.

Chomsky, N. (1957), *Syntactic Structures*. Princeton, NJ: Mouton and Company.

—(1965), *Aspects of the Theory of Syntax*. Cambridge, MA: MIT Press.

Chun, D. M. (2011), Developing intercultural communicative competence through online exchanges. *CALICO Journal,* 28(2), 392–419.

Clark, E. and Paran, A. (2007), The employability of non-native-speaker teachers of EFL: A UK survey. *System,* 35(4), 407–30.

Clark, J. B. (2012), Introduction: Journeys of integration between multiple worlds: Reconceptualising multilingualism through complex transnational spaces. *International Journal of Multilingualism,* 9(2), 132–7.

Cohen, A. D. (1994), *Assessing Language Ability in the Classroom*. Boston, MA: Heinle & Heinle.

Cohen, M. and Dörnyei, Z. (2002), Focus on the language learner: Motivation, styles and strategies. In N. Schmidt (ed.), *An Introduction to Applied Linguistics* (pp. 170–90). London: Edward Arnold.

Collins, A. and Halverson, R. (2009), *Rethinking Education in the Age of Technology: The Digital Revolution and Schooling in America*. New York: Teachers College Press.

Conrad, S. (2000), Will corpus linguistics revolutionize grammar teaching in the 21st century? *TESOL Quarterly,* 34(3), 548–60.

Cook, V. J. (1991), The poverty-of-the-stimulus argument and multi-competence. *Second Language Research,* 7(2), 103–17.

—(1992), Evidence for multicompetence. *Language Learning,* 42, 557–91.

—(1999), Going beyond the native speaker in language teaching. *TESOL Quarterly,* 33(2), 185–209.

—(2002a), Background to the L2 User. In V. J. Cook (ed.), *Portraits of the L2 User*, Vol. 1 (pp. 1–28). Bristol: Multilingual Matters.

—(2007), 'The nature of the L2 user'. *Eurosla Yearbook,* 7(1), 205–20.

Cook, V. J. (ed.) (2002b), *Portraits of the L2 User*, Vol. 1. Bristol: Multilingual Matters.

Cook, V. J. and Bassetti, B. (eds) (2011), *Language and Bilingual Cognition*. Oxford: Psychology Press.

Cook, V. J., Bassetti, B., Kasai, C., et al. (2006), Do bilinguals have different concepts? The case of shape and material in Japanese L2 users of English. *International Journal of Bilingualism,* 10(2), 137–52.

Cook, V. J. and Newson, M. (2007), *Chomsky's Universal Grammar: An Introduction*. Malden, MA: Blackwell Publishing.

Cooke, M. and Simpson, J. (2008), *ESOL: A Critical Guide*. Oxford: Oxford University Press.

Coombe, C. A., Folse, K. S. and Hubley, N. J. (2007), *A Practical Guide to Assessing English Language Learners*. Ann Arbor, MI: University of Michigan Press/ESL.

Cortazzi, M. and Jin, L. (1999), Cultural Mirrors: Materials and Methods in the EFL classroom. In E. Hinkel (ed.), *Culture in Second Language Teaching and Learning* (pp. 196–219). Cambridge: Cambridge University Press.

Cosh, J. (1998), Peer Observation in Higher Education: A Reflective Approach. *Innovations in Education & Training International*, 35(2), 171.

—(1999), Peer observation: A reflective model. *English Language Teaching Journal*, 53(1), 22–7.

Crandall, J. (1993), *Improving the Quality of Adult ESL Programs: Building the Nation's Capacity to Meet the Educational and Occupational Needs of Adults with Limited English Proficiency*. Washington, DC: The Southport Institute for Policy Analysis (ERIC Document Reproduction Service No. ED375684).

—(2000), Language teacher education. *Annual Review of Applied Linguistics*, 20, 34–5.

Crandall, J., Ingersoll, G. and Lopez, J. (2010), *Adult ESL Teacher Credentialing and Certification Table*. Washington, DC: Center for Adult English Language Acquisition. Retrieved from http://www.cal.org/adultesl/pdfs/adult-esl-teacher-credentialing-and-certification-table.pdf/

Crandall, J. and Kaufman, D. (eds) (2002), *Content-Based Instruction in Higher Education Settings*. Alexandria, VA: TESOL.

Crookes, G. and Schmidt, R. W. (1991), Motivation: Reopening the research agenda. *Language Learning*, 41, 469–512.

Crossley, S. A. (2013), Advancing research in second language writing through computational tools and machine learning techniques: A research agenda. *Language Teaching*, 46(2), 256–71.

Cummins, J. (2000), *Language, Power, and Pedagogy: Bilingual Children in the Crossfire*. Bristol: Multilingual Matters.

—(2009), Multilingualism in the English-language classroom: Pedagogical considerations. *TESOL Quarterly*, 43(2), 317–21.

Dantas-Whitney, M. and Rilling, S. (2010), *Authenticity in the Language Classroom and Beyond: Children and Adolescent Learners. TESOL Classroom Practice Series*. Alexandria, VA: TESOL.

Davies, A. (2003), *The Native Speaker: Myth and Reality*. Bristol: Multilingual Matters.

Davies, P. (2000), *Success in English Teaching: A Complete Introduction to Teaching English at Secondary School Level and Above*. Oxford: Oxford University Press.

Davison, C. and Leung, C. (2009), Current issues in English language teacher-based assessment. *TESOL Quarterly*, 43(3), 393–415.

Day, R. R. (1990), Teacher observation in second language teacher education. *Second Language Teacher Education*, 43–61.

De Groot, A. M. B. (2011), *Language and Cognition in Bilinguals and Multilinguals: An Introduction*. New York: Psychology Press.

De Oliveira, L. C. (2011), Strategies for Nonnative-English-Speaking Teachers' continued development as professionals. *TESOL Journal*, 2(2), 229–38.

Deller, S. and Price, C. (2007), *Teaching Other Subjects through English*. Oxford: Oxford University Press.

Department of Linguistics, University of Illinois at Urbana-Champaign (2014), *MATESL Graduate Degree.* Retrieved from http://www.linguistics.illinois.edu/students/grad/matesl/

Department of Second Language Studies, University of Hawai'i (2014), *PhD in SLS.* Retrieved from http://www.hawaii.edu/sls/sls/programs/doctorate/

Derwing, T. M. and Munro, M. J. (2005), Second language accent and pronunciation teaching: A research-based approach. *TESOL Quarterly,* 39(3), 379–97.

Dörnyei, Z. (2001a), *Motivational Strategies in the Language Classroom.* Cambridge: Cambridge University Press.

—(2001b), *Teaching and Researching Motivation.* Harlow: Longman.

—(2003), Attitudes, orientations, and motivations in language learning: Advances in theory, research, and applications. *Language Learning,* 53(Supplement 1), 3–32.

— (2007), Creating a motivating classroom environment. In J. Cummins and C. Davison (eds), *International Handbook of English Language Teaching,* Vol. 2 (pp. 719–31). New York: Springer.

Dörnyei, Z. and Csizér, K. (1998), Ten commandments for motivating language learners: Results of an empirical study. *Language Teaching Research,* 2, 203–29.

—(2002), Some dynamics of language attitudes and motivation: Results of a longitudinal nationwide survey. *Applied Linguistics,* 23, 421–62.

Dörnyei, Z. and Murphey, T. (2003), *Group Dynamics in the Language Classroom.* Cambridge: Cambridge University Press.

Dörnyei, Z. and Skehan, P. (2003), Individual Differences in Second Language Learning. In C. J. Doughty and M. H. Long (eds), *The Handbook of Second Language Acquisition* (pp. 589–630). Malden, MA: Blackwell.

Douglas, D. (2000), *Assessing Languages for Specific Purposes.* Cambridge: Cambridge University Press.

Douglas, D. and Hegelheimer, V. (2007), Assessing language using computer technology. *Annual Review of Applied Linguistics,* 27, 115.

Dulay, H. C. and Burt, M. K. (1973), Should we teach children syntax? *Language Learning,* 23(2), 245–58.

Ducate, L. and Arnold, N. (eds) (2006), *Calling on CALL: From Theory and Research to new Directions in Foreign Language Teaching.* San Marcos, TX: CALICO Publications.

Dunne, F., Nave, B. and Lewis, A. (2000), Critical Friends Groups: Teachers helping teachers to improve student learning. *Phi Delta Kappa Research Bulletin,* 28, 9–12.

Egbert, J. and Hanson-Smith, E. (eds) (1999), *Computer-Enhanced Language Learning.* Alexandria, VA: TESOL.

Egbert, J. and Petrie, G. M. (2005), *Bridge to the Classroom: ESL Cases for Teacher Exploration,* Vol. 3. Alexandria, VA: TESOL.

Ehrman, M. (1996), An Exploration of Adult Language Learner Motivation, Self-efficacy, and Anxiety. In R. Oxford (ed.), *Language Learning Motivation: Pathways to the New Century* (pp. 81–103). Honolulu, HI: University of Hawai'i Press.

Ellis, E. (2004), The invisible multilingual teacher: The contribution of language background to Australian ESL teachers' professional knowledge and beliefs. *The International Journal of Multilingualism,* 1, 90–108.

Ellis, R. (2006), Current issues in the teaching of grammar: An SLA perspective. *TESOL Quarterly*, 40(1), 83–107.

Farrell, T. S. C. (2001), Tailoring reflection to individual needs: A TESOL case study. *Journal of Education for Teaching: International Research and Pedagogy*, 27(1), 23–8.

—(2008), Critical incidents in ELT initial teacher training. *ELT Journal*, 62(1), 3–10.

Farrell, T. S. C. (ed.) (2012), Special Issue: Novice Professionals in TESOL. *TESOL Quarterly*, 46(3), 435–604.

Ferris, D. R. (1999), The case for grammar correction in L2 writing classes: A response to Truscott (1996), *Journal of Second Language Writing*, 8(1), 1–11.

Fitzpatrick, A and O'Dowd, R. (2012), *English at Work: An Analysis of Case Reports about English Language Training for the 21-Century Workforce*. Monterey, CA: The International Research Foundation for English Language Education (TIRF).

Folse, K. (2009), *Keys to Teaching Grammar to English Language Learners: A Practical Handbook*. Ann Arbor, MI: University of Michigan Press.

Fotos, S. and Ellis, R. (1991), Communicating about grammar: A task-based approach. *TESOL Quarterly* 25(4), 605–28.

Franceschini, R. (2011), Multilingualism and multicompetence: A conceptual view. *The Modern Language Journal*, 95(3), 344–55.

Franzak, J. K. (2002), Developing a teacher identity: The impact of critical friends practice on the student teacher. *English Education,* 34(4), 258–70.

Frazier, S. and Phillabaum, S. (2011/2012), How TESOL educators teach nonnative English-speaking teachers. *CATESOL Journal*, 23(1), 155–81.

Freeman, D. (1989), Teacher training, development, and decision-making: A model of teaching and related strategies for language teacher education. *TESOL Quarterly*, 23(1), 27–45.

—(1998), *Doing Teacher Research: From Inquiry to Understanding*. Boston, MA: Heinle & Heinle.

—(2002), The hidden side of the work: Teacher knowledge and learning. *Language Teaching*, 35, 1–13.

Freeman, D. and Johnson, K. E. (1998), Reconceptualizing the knowledge-base of language teacher education. *TESOL Quarterly*, 32(3), 397–417.

Freeman, D. and Richards, J. (eds) (1996), *Teacher Learning in Language Teaching*. Cambridge: Cambridge University Press.

Fulcher, G. (2003), *Testing Second Language Speaking*. Harlow: Pearson Education.

—(2010), *Practical Language Testing*. Oxford: Oxford University Press.

Fulcher, G. and Davidson, F. (2007), *Language Testing and Assessment: An Advanced Resource Book*. London: Routledge.

García, O. (2009), Emergent Bilinguals and TESOL: What's in a Name? *TESOL Quarterly*, 43(2), 322–6.

Gardner, R. C. (1985), *Social Psychology and Second Language Learning: The Role of Attitude and Motivation*. London: Edward Arnold.

—(2001), Integrative motivation and second language acquisition. In Z. Dörnyei and R. Schmidt (eds), *Motivation and Language Acquisition* (pp. 1–19). Honolulu, HI: University of Hawai'i Press.

—(2010), *Motivation and Second Language Acquisition: The Socio-Educational Model*. New York: Peter Lang.

Gardner, R. C. and Lambert, W. E. (1959), Motivational variables in second language acquisition. *Canadian Journal of Psychology,* 13, 266–72.

—(1972), *Attitudes and Motivation in Second Language Learning.* Rowley, MA: Newbury House.

Gardner, R. C. and Tremblay, P. F. (1994), On motivation, research agendas, and theoretical frameworks. *The Modern Language Journal,* 78, 359–68.

Garvie, E. (1990), *Story as Vehicle: Teaching English to Young Children.* Bristol: Multilingual Matters.

Gebhard, J. G. (2009), The Practicum. In A. Burns and J. C. Richards (eds), *The Cambridge Guide to Second Language Teacher Education* (pp. 250–8). Cambridge: Cambridge University Press.

Gebhard, J. G. and Oprandy, R. (1999), *Language Teaching Awareness: A Guide to Exploring Beliefs and Practices.* New York: Cambridge University Press.

Georgia State University (2013), *PhD in Applied Linguistics.* Retrieved from http://www2.gsu.edu/~wwwesl/phd_applied_linguistics.html

Georgia TESOL (n.d.), *Adult Education Interest Section Hybrid Workshop.* Retrieved from GATESOL website: http://gatesol.org/event-645290

Gilmore, A. (2011), 'I prefer not text': Developing Japanese learners' communicative competence with authentic materials. *Language Learning,* 61(3), 786–819.

Glaser, B. G. (1978), *Theoretical Sensitivity: Advances in the Methodology of Grounded Theory,* Vol. 2. Mill Valley, CA: Sociology Press.

Glaser, B. G. and Strauss, A. L. (1967), T*he Discovery of Grounded Theory: Strategies for Qualitative Research.* London: Weidenfeld and Nicolson.

Godwin-Jones, R. (2009), Emerging technologies focusing on form: Tools and strategies. *Language Learning and Technology,* 13(1), 5–12.

Goldberg, A. E. (1995), *Constructions: A Construction Grammar Approach to Argument Structure.* Chicago, IL: Chicago University Press.

Goodman, J. (1991), Using a Methods Course to Promote Reflection and Inquiry among Preservice Teachers. In R. Tabachnick and K. Zeichner (eds), *Issues and Practices in Inquiry-Oriented Teacher Education* (pp. 56–76). London: Falmer Press.

Goulding, C. (2009), Grounded Theory Perspectives in Organizational Research. In D. A. Buchanan and A. Bryman (eds), *The SAGE Handbook of Organizational Research Methods* (pp. 381–94). London: SAGE.

Grabe, W. (2009), Motivation and Reading. In W. Grabe (ed.), *Reading in a Second Language: Moving from Theory to Practice* (pp. 175–93). New York: Cambridge University Press.

Graddol, D. (2006), *English Next,* Vol. 62. London: British Council.

Griswold, O. V. (2010), Narrating America: Socializing adult ESL learners into idealized views of the United States during citizenship preparation classes. *TESOL Quarterly,* 44(3), 488–516.

Grosjean, F. (1985), The bilingual as a competent but specific speaker–hearer. *Journal of Multilingual Multicultural Development,* 6, 467–77.

Grosse, C. U. (1991), The TESOL methods course. *TESOL Quarterly,* 25(1), 29–49.

Hadfield, J. (2013), A Second Self: Translating Motivation Theory into Practice. In T. Pattison (ed.), *IATEFL 2012: Glasgow Conference Selections* (pp. 44–7). Canterbury: IATEFL.

Hall, J. K., Cheng, A. and Carlson, M. T. (2006), Reconceptualizing multicompetence as a theory of language knowledge. *Applied Linguistics*, 27(2), 220–40.

Halliday, M. A., McIntosh, A. and Strevens, P. (1964), *The Linguistic Sciences and Language Teaching*. London: Longmans and Green.

Halliday, M. A. and Matthiessen, C. M. (2004), *An Introduction to Functional Grammar* (3rd edn). London: Edward Arnold.

Harding, K. (2007), *English for Specific Purposes*. Oxford: Oxford University Press.

Harmer, J. (1999), *How to Teach Grammar*. White Plains, NY: Pearson/Longman.

Hasselgreen, A. (2005), Assessing the language of young learners. *Language Testing*, 22(3), 337–54.

Hawkins, M. R. and Legler, L. L. (2004), Reflections on the impact of teacher–researcher collaboration. *TESOL Quarterly*, 38(2), 339–43.

Hawkins, M. R. and Norton, B. (2009), Critical Language Teacher Education. In A. Burns and J. C. Richards (eds), *The Cambridge Guide to Second Language Teacher Education* (pp. 144–52). Cambridge: Cambridge University Press.

He, D. and Zhang, Q. (2010), Native speaker norms and China English: From the perspective of learners and teachers in China. *TESOL Quarterly*, 44(4), 769–89.

Hedgcock, J. S. (2002), Toward a socioliterate approach to second language teacher education. *The Modern Language Journal*, 86(3), 299–317.

—(2009), Acquiring Knowledge of Discourse Conventions in Teacher Education. In A. Burns and J. C. Richards (eds), *The Cambridge Guide to Second Language Teacher Education* (pp. 144–52). Cambridge: Cambridge University Press.

Hiebert, J., Gallimore, R. and Stigler, J. W. (2002), A knowledge base for the teaching profession: What would it look like and how can we get one? *Educational Researcher*, 31(5), 3–15.

Higgins, C. (2003), 'Ownership' of English in the Outer Circle: An alternative to the NS–NNS dichotomy. *TESOL Quarterly*, 37(4), 615–44.

Hinkel, E. (ed.) (1999), *Culture in Second Language Teaching and Learning*. New York: Cambridge University Press.

Hinkel, E. (2010), Integrating the four skills: Current and historical perspectives. In R. B. Kaplan (ed.), *The Oxford Handbook of Applied Linguistics* (2nd edn). New York: Oxford University Press.

Hinkel, E. and Fotos, S. (eds) (2001), *New Perspectives on Grammar Teaching in Second Language Classrooms*. Mahwah, NJ: Lawrence Erlbaum.

Ho, B. and Richards, J. C. (1993), Reflective thinking through teacher journal writing: Myths and realities. *Prospect*, 8, 7–24.

Holliday, A. (2005), *The Struggle to Teach English as an International Language*. Oxford: Oxford University Press.

—(2013), 'Native Speaker' Teachers and Cultural Belief. In S. A. Houghton and D. J. Rivers (eds), *Native Speakerism in Japan: Intergroup Dynamics in Foreign Language Education* (pp. 17–26). Bristol: Multilingual Matters.

Hong, Y., Wan, C., No, S., et al. (2010), Multicultural Identities. In S. Kitayama and D. Kohen (eds), *Handbook of Cultural Psychology* (pp. 323–45). New York: Guilford Press.

Horwitz, E. K., Tallon, M. and Luo, H. (2009), Foreign language anxiety. In J. C. Cassady (ed.), *Anxiety in Schools: The Causes, Consequences, and Solutions for Academic Anxieties* (pp. 95–115). New York: Peter Lang.

House, J. (2003), English as a lingua franca: A threat to multilingualism? *Journal of Sociolinguistics,* 7(4), 556–78.

Huang, K. M. (2011), Motivating lessons: A classroom-oriented investigation of the effects of content-based instruction on EFL young learners' motivated behaviours and classroom verbal interaction. *System,* 39(2), 186–201.

Huling, L. and Resta, V. (2001), *Teacher Mentoring as Professional Development.* ERIC Digest, ED460125. Washington, DC: ERIC Clearinghouse on Language and Linguistics. Retrieved 31 May 2014, from http://www.ericdigests. org/2002-3/mentoring.htm

Hunston, S. and Francis, G. (2000), *Pattern Grammar: A Corpus-Driven Approach to the Lexical Grammar of English.* Amsterdam: John Benjamins.

Hyland, K. and Hamp-Lyons, L. (2002), EAP: Issues and directions. *Journal of English for Academic Purposes,* 1(1), 1–12.

Hymes, D. (1967), Models of the interaction of language and social setting. *Journal of Social Issues,* 23(2), 8–28.

—(1972), On Communicative Competence. In J. Pride and J. Holmes (eds), *Sociolinguistics* (pp. 269–83). Harmondsworth: Penguin Books.

Ilieva, R. (2010), Non-native English-speaking teachers' negotiations of program discourses in their construction of professional identities within a TESOL program. *The Canadian Modern Language Review/La Revue Canadienne des langues vivantes,* 66(3), 343–69.

Jamieson, J. (2005), Trends in computer-based second language assessment. *Annual Review of Applied Linguistics,* 25(1), 228–42.

Jamieson, J. and Chapelle, C. A. (1987), Working styles on computers as evidence of second language learning strategies. *Language Learning,* 37, 523–44.

Janzen, J. (2008), Teaching English language learners in the content areas. *Review of Educational Research,* 78(4), 1010–38.

Jenkins, J. (2000). *The Phonology of English as an International Language.* Oxford: Oxford University Press.

—(2002), A sociolinguistically based, empirically researched pronunciation syllabus for English as an International Language. *Applied Linguistics,* 23(1), 83–103.

—(2005a), Implementing an international approach to English pronunciation: The role of teacher attitudes and identity. *TESOL Quarterly,* 39(3), 535–43.

—(2006a), Current perspectives on teaching World Englishes and English as a Lingua Franca. *TESOL Quarterly,* 40(1), 157–81.

—(2006b), Points of view and blind spot: ELF and SLA. *International Journal of Applied Linguistics,* 16(2), 136–62.

—(2007), *English as a Lingua Franca: Attitude and Identity.* Oxford: Oxford University Press.

Jessner, U. (2007), Multicompetence Approaches to the Development of Language Proficiency in Multilingual Education. In J. Cummins (ed), *Bilingual Education* (pp. 91–103). New York: Springer.

Johnson, K. E. (2006), The sociocultural turn and its challenges for second language teacher education. *TESOL Quarterly,* 40(1), 235–57.

—(2009), Trends in Second Language Teacher Education. In A. Burns and J. C. Richards (eds), *The Cambridge Guide to Second Language Teacher Education* (pp. 20–9). Cambridge: Cambridge University Press.

Jonson, K. F. (2002), *Being an Effective Mentor: How to Help Beginning Teachers Succeed.* Thousand Oaks, CA: Corwin Press.

Judd, E. (2006), Turning 40: A midlife crisis for the profession? Presidential plenary at the TESOL Convention and Exhibit, Tampa Convention Center, Tampa, Florida, 17 March.

Kabilan, M. K., Adlina, W. F. W. and Embi, M. A. (2011), Online collaboration of English language teachers for meaningful professional development experiences. *English Teaching: Practice & Critique,* 10(4), 94–115.

Kachru, B. B. (1976), Models of English for the third world: White man's linguistic burden or language pragmatics? *TESOL Quarterly,* 10(2), 221–39.

—(1985), Standards, Codification, and Sociolinguistic Realism: The English Language in the Outer Circle. In R. Quirk and H. G. Widdowson (eds), *English in the World: Teaching and Learning the Language and the Literature* (pp. 11–30). Cambridge: Cambridge University Press.

—(1986), *The Alchemy of English: The Spread, Functions and Models of Non-Native Englishes.* Oxford: Pergamon.

—(1991), Liberation linguistics and the Quirk concern. *English Today,* 25, 3–13.

—(1992), World Englishes: Approaches, issues and resources. *Language Teaching: The International Abstracting Journal for Language Teachers and Applied Linguistics,* 25(1), 1–14.

Kachru, B., Kachru, Y. and Nelson, C. (eds) (2009), *The Handbook of World Englishes,* Vol. 48. Oxford: Wiley-Blackwell.

Kachru, Y. and Smith, L. E. (2008), *Cultures, Contexts, and World Englishes,* Vol. 10. London: Routledge.

Kamhi-Stein, L. D. (2006), *Learning and Teaching from Experience: Perspectives on Nonnative English-Speaking Professionals.* Ann Arbor, MI: University of Michigan Press.

—(2009), Teacher preparation and English-speaking educators. In A. Burns and J. C. Richards (eds), *The Cambridge Guide to Second Language Teacher Education* (pp. 91–101). Cambridge: Cambridge University Press.

—(2014), Non-native English-speaking Teachers in the Profession. In M. Celce-Murcia, D. Brinton and M. A. Snow (eds), *Teaching English as a Second or Foreign Language* (4th edn). Boston, MA: Heinle Cengage Learning.

Kang, O. (2010), Relative salience of suprasegmental features on judgments of L2 comprehensibility and accentedness. *System,* 38, 301–15.

Kaufman, D. and Crandall, J. (eds) (2005), *Content-Based Instruction in Primary and Secondary School Settings.* Alexandria, VA: TESOL.

Kemmis, S. and Henry, J. A. (1989), Action research. *IATEFL Newsletter,* 102, 2–3.

Kemmis, S. and McTaggart, R. (eds) (1988), *The Action Research Planner* (3rd edn). Geelong, Australia: Deakin University Press.

Kern, R. (2006), Perspectives on technology in learning and teaching languages. *TESOL Quarterly,* 40(1), 183–210.

Kern, R. and Kramsch, C. (2014), Communicative Grammar and Communicative Competence. In C. A. Chapelle (ed.), *The Encyclopedia of Applied Linguistics* (1–6). Malden, MA: Wiley.

Kirkpatrick, A. (2007), Linguistic Imperialism? English as a Global Language. In M. Hellinger and A. Pauwels (eds), *Handbook of Applied Linguistics: Language Diversity and Change*, Vol. 9 (pp. 331–65). Berlin: Mouton De Gruyter.

Koromilas, K. (2011), Obligation and motivation. *Cambridge ESOL Research Notes*, 44, 12–20.

Korthagen, F. A. J., Kessels, J., Koster, B., et al. (2001), *Linking Practice and Theory: The Pedagogy of Realistic Teacher Education*. Mahwah, NJ: Lawrence Erlbaum.

Kramsch, C. (1986), From language proficiency to interactional competence. *The Modern Language Journal*, 70(4), 366–72.

—(1993), *Context and Culture in Language Teaching*. Oxford: Oxford University Press.

—(2006a), From communicative competence to symbolic competence. *The Modern Language Journal*, 90(2), 249–52.

—(2006b), Preview Article: The multilingual subject. *International Journal of Applied Linguistics*, 16(1), 97–110.

—(2007), The uses of communicative competence in a global world. In J. Liu (ed.), *English Language Teaching in China: New Approaches, Perspectives, and Standards*. London: Continuum.

—(2009), *The Multilingual Subject: What Language Learners Say about Their Experience and Why it Matters*. Oxford: Oxford University Press.

Kramsch, C., A'Ness, F. and Lam, W. (2000), Authenticity and authorship in the computer-mediated acquisition of L2 literacy. *Language Learning and Technology*, 4(2), 78–104.

Krashen, S. D., Long, M. A. and Scarcella, R. C. (1979), Age, rate and eventual attainment in second language acquisition. *TESOL Quarterly*, 13(4), 573–82.

Kroll, J. F., Gullifer, J. W. and Rossi, E. (2013), The multilingual lexicon: The cognitive and neural basis of lexical comprehension and production in two or more languages. *Annual Review of Applied Linguistics*, 33, 102–27.

Kubota, R. and Lin, A. (2009), Race, Culture, and Identities in Second Language Education: Introduction to Research and Practice. In R. Kubota and A. Lin (eds), *Race, Culture, and Identities in Second Language Education: Exploring Critically Engaged Practice* (pp. 1–23). New York: Routledge.

Lamb, M. (2004), Integrative motivation in a globalizing world. *System*, 32, 3–19.

Lamb, T. (2009), Controlling Learning: Learners' Voices and Relationships Between Motivation and Learner Autonomy. In R. Pemberton, S. Toogood and A. Barfield (eds), *Maintaining Control: Autonomy and Language Learning* (pp. 67–86). Hong Kong: Hong Kong University Press.

Larsen-Freeman, D. (2003), *Teaching Language: From Grammar to Grammaring*. Boston, MA: Heinle & Heinle.

—(2006), The emergence of complexity, fluency, and accuracy in the oral and written production of five Chinese learners of English. *Applied Linguistics* 27(4), 560–619.

Larsen-Freeman, D. and Anderson, M. (2011), *Techniques and Principles in Language Teaching* (3rd edn). New York: Oxford University Press.

Lather, P. (1991), *Getting Smart: Feminist Research and Pedagogy with/in the Postmodern*. New York: Routledge.

Lave, J. and Wenger, E. (1991), Situating learning in communities of practice. *Perspectives on Socially Shared Cognition*, 2, 63–82.

LeBlanc, R. and Painchaud, G. (1985), Self-Assessment as a second language placement instrument. *TESOL Quarterly,* 19(4), 673–87.

Lenneberg, E. H. (1967), Biological foundations of language. Oxford: Wiley.

Leung, C. (2005), Convivial communication: Recontextualizing communicative competence. *International Journal of Applied Linguistics,* 15(2), 119–44.

—(2009), Second Language Teacher Professionalism. In A. Burns and J. C. Richards (eds), *The Cambridge Guide to Second Language Teacher Education* (pp. 49–58). Cambridge: Cambridge University Press.

Levy, M. (2009), Technologies in use for second language learning. *The Modern Language Journal,* 93, 769–82.

Lewin, K. (1946), Action research and minority problems. *Journal of Social Issues,* 2, 34–46.

Li, W. and Moyer, M. (eds) (2008), *The Blackwell Handbook of Research Methods on Bilingualism and Multilingualism.* Oxford: Blackwell.

Liao, P. (2007), Teachers' beliefs about teaching English to elementary school children. *English Teaching & Learning,* 31(1), 43–76.

Lier, L. van (1988), *The Classroom and the Language Learner.* New York: Longman.

Lippi-Green, R. (1997), *English with an Accent: Language, Ideology, and Discrimination in the United States.* Hove: Psychology Press.

Liu, D. (2014), *Describing and Explaining Grammar and Vocabulary in ELT: Key Theories and Effective Practices.* New York: Routledge.

Liu, J. (1988), Reflections on the experimental research on Suggestopedia. *English Teaching and Research Notes,* 4, 33–9.

—(1998), Peer Reviews with the Instructor: Seeking Alternatives. In J. C. Richards (ed.), *Teaching in Action: Case Studies from Second Language Classrooms* (pp. 236–40). Alexandria, VA: TESOL.

—(1999), Nonnative-English-speaking professionals in TESOL. *TESOL Quarterly,* 33(1), 85–102.

—(2000), The power of Readers' Theater: From reading to writing. *ELT Journal,* 54, 354–61.

—(2005), Promising Asia and Unlimited Boundaries. Keynote address presented at 27th ThaiTESOL Annual convention, Bangkok, Thailand, January.

—(2007a), Critical Period Hypothesis Retested: The Effects of Earlier English Education in China. In J. Liu (ed.), *English Language Teaching in China: New Approaches, Perspectives and Standards* (pp. 170–91). London: Continuum.

—(2007b), Empowering Non-native English-speaking Teachers through Collaboration with their Native English-speaking Colleagues in EFL Settings. In J. Liu (ed.), *English Language Teaching in China: New Approaches, Perspectives and Standards* (pp. 107–23). London: Continuum.

—(2007c), Epilogue: Beyond Communicative Competence: A Pedagogical Perspective. In Jun Liu (ed.), *English Language Teaching in China: New Approaches, Perspectives and Standards* (pp. 329–35). London: Continuum.

Liu, J. (ed.) (2007d), *English Language Teaching in China: New Approaches, Perspectives and Standards.* London: Continuum.

Liu, Yongbing (1997), A study of some conversational formulas – from a cross-cultural perspective. *Language, Society and Culture.* Retrieved from the Internet on 22 November 2009: http://www.educ.utas.edu.au/users/tle/JOURNAL/Articles/Yongbing/Yongbing.html/

Llurda, E. (ed.) (2005a), *Non-Native Language Teachers: Perceptions, Challenges and Contributions to the Profession*. New York: Springer.
Llurda, E. (2005b), Non-native TESOL Students as seen by Practicum Supervisors. In E. Llurda (ed.), *Non-Native Language Teachers: Perceptions, Challenges and Contributions to the Profession* (pp. 131–54). New York: Springer.
Lockhart, C. and Richards, J. C. (1994), *Reflective Teaching in Second Language Classrooms*. New York: Cambridge University Press.
Long Thanh, V. and Hoa Thi Mai, N. (2010), Critical friends group for EFL teacher professional development. *English Language Teachers Journal*, 64(2), 205.
Lorimer, C. and Schulte, J. (2011), Reimagining TESOL professionalism: The graduate student perspective. *CATESOL Journal*, 23(1), 31–44.
Lotherington, H. and Jenson, J. (2011), Teaching multimodal and digital literacy in second language settings: New literacies, new basics, new pedagogies. *Annual Review of Applied Linguistics*, 31, 226–46.
Louhiala-Salminen, L. and Kankaanranta, A. (2011), Professional communication in a global business context: The notion of global communicative competence. *Professional Communication*, 54(3), 244–62.
Lozanov, G. (1978), *Suggestology and Outlines of Suggestopedia*. New York: Gordon & Breach.
Lyons, J. (1996), On Competence and Performance and Related Notions. In G. Brown, K. Malmkjaer and J. Williams (eds), *Performance and Competence in Second Language Acquisition* (pp. 11–32). Cambridge: Cambridge University Press.
McArthur, T. (2002), *Oxford Guide to World English*. Oxford: Oxford University Press.
McEnery, A. (2006), *Corpus-Based Language Studies: An Advanced Resource Book*. London and New York: Routledge.
MacIntyre, P. D. (2002), Motivation, Anxiety and Emotion in Second Language Acquisition. In P. Robinson (ed.), *Individual Differences and Instructed Language Learning* (pp. 45–68). Amsterdam: John Benjamins.
MacIntyre, P. D., MacMaster, K. and Baker, S. C. (2001), The Convergence of Multiple Models of Motivation for Second Language Learning: Gardner, Pintrich, Kuhl, and McCroskey. In Z. Dörnyei and R. Schmidt (eds), *Motivation and Language Acquisition* (pp. 461–92). Honolulu, HI: University of Hawai'i Press.
McKay, S. L. (2002), *Teaching English as an International Language: Rethinking Goals and Approaches*. Oxford: Oxford University Press.
—(2009), Second Language Classroom Research. In A. Burns and J. C. Richards (eds), *The Cambridge Guide to Second Language Teacher Education* (pp. 281–8). Cambridge: Cambridge University Press.
McKay, S. L. and Bokhorst-Heng, W. D. (2008), *International English in its Sociolinguistic Contexts: Toward a Socially Sensitive EIL Pedagogy*. New York: Routledge.
McKenzie, M. and Carr-Reardon, A. M. (2003), Critical Friends Groups: FAQs about CFGs. Retrieved from http://www.city.waltham.ma.us/SCHOOL/WebPAge/cfg.htm/
McLean, A. C. (2012), Destroying the Teacher: The Need for Learner-centered Teaching. In *English Teaching Forum*, Vol. 50, No. 1 (pp. 32–5). Bureau of Educational and Cultural Affairs, US Department of State, Washington, DC.

McVeigh, J. (2012). *Try a Webinar!* [Web log post, 6 July]. Retrieved from http://blog.tesol.org/try-a-webinar/

Mahboob, A. (2005), Beyond the native speaker in TESOL. *Culture, Context, & Communication,* 30, 60–93.

Mahboob, A. (ed.) (2010), *The NNEST Lens: Non Native English Speakers in TESOL.* Newcastle upon Tyne: Cambridge Scholars Press.

Mahboob, A. and Tilakaratna, N. (2010), *A Principles-Based Approach for English Language Teaching Policies and Practices More: A TESOL White Paper.* TESOL International Association. Retrieved from http://s3.amazonaws.com/TESOLwebsite/docs/may_2012/TESOL_ Mahoob_Tilakaratna_whitepaperr.pdf/

Malderez, A. (2009), Mentoring. In A. Burns and J. C. Richards (eds), *The Cambridge Guide to Second Language Teacher Education* (pp. 259–68). Cambridge: Cambridge University Press.

Malderez, A. and Bodóczky, C. C. (1999), *Mentor Courses: A Resource Book for Teacher Trainers.* Cambridge: Cambridge University Press.

Mann, S. (2005), The language teacher's development. *Language Teaching,* 38, 103–18.

Marinova-Todd, A. H., Marshall, D. B. and Snow, C. E. (2000), Three misconceptions about age and L2 learning. *TESOL Quarterly,* 34(1), 9–34.

Markee, N. (1997), *Managing Curricular Innovation.* New York: Cambridge University Press.

—(1998), Second language acquisition research: A resource for changing teachers' professional cultures. *The Modern Language Journal,* 81, 81–93.

Marquardt, S. K. (2011), (Re)telling: A narrative inquiry into pre-service TESOL teachers' study abroad experiences. *Dissertation Abstracts International,* A: The Humanities and Social Sciences, 4426. Retrieved from http://ezproxy.gsu.edu/login?url=http://search.proquest.com/docview/1081897672?accountid=11226 (1081897672; 201212833)/.

Martin-Jones, M., Blackledge, A. and Creese, A. (eds) (2012), *The Routledge Handbook of Multilingualism.* London: Routledge.

Matsuda, A. (2003), Incorporating World Englishes in teaching English as an international language. *TESOL Quarterly,* 37(40), 719–29.

Mauranen, A., Hynninena, N. and Ranta, E. (2010), English as an academic lingua franca: The ELFA project. *English for Specific Purposes,* 29(3), 183–90.

May, S. (2013), *The Multilingual Turn: Implications for SLA, TESOL, and Bilingual Education.* New York: Routledge.

Medgyes, P. (1992), Native or nonnative: Who's worth more? *ELT Journal,* 46(4), 340–49.

—(1994), *The Non-Native Teacher.* London: Macmillan.

Medgyes, P. and Nikolov, M. (2010), Curriculum Development in Foreign Language Education: The Interface Between Political and Professional Decisions. In R. B. Kaplan (ed.), *The Oxford Handbook of Applied Linguistics* (pp. 263–74). Oxford: Oxford University Press.

Melvin, B. S. and Stout, D. S. (1987), Motivating Language Learners through Authentic Materials. In W. Rivers (ed.), *Interactive Language Teaching* (pp. 44–56). New York: Cambridge University Press.

Meskill, C. and Anthony, N. (2010), *Teaching Languages Online,* Vol. 6. Bristol: Multilingual Matters.

Messerschmitt, D. S. and Hafernik, J. J. (2009), *Dilemmas in Teaching English to Speakers of Other Languages: 40 Cases*. Ann Arbor, MI: University of Michigan Press.

Michigan State University College of Arts and Letters (2014), *M.A. TESOL (Teaching English to Speakers of Other Languages)*. Retrieved from http://linglang.msu.edu/tesol/

Moon, J. (2005), *Children Learning English*. Oxford: Macmillan.

Moussu, L. and Llurda, E. (2008), Non-native English-speaking English language teachers: History and research. *Language Teaching*, 41(3), 315–48.

Murphey, T. and Falout, J. (2013), Individual differences in the classroom. In C. A. Chappele (ed.), *The Encyclopedia of Applied Linguistics*. Oxford, UK: Blackwell Publishing Ltd. Retrieved from http://onlinelibrary.wiley.com/doi/10.1002/9781405198431.wbeal0533/full

Murphy, J. M. and Byrd, P. (eds) (2001), *Understanding the Courses We Teach: Local Perspectives on English Language Teaching*. Ann Arbor, MI: University of Michigan Press.

Murphy, J. M. (2014), Intelligible, comprehensible, non-native models in ESL/EFL pronunciation teaching. *System*, 42, 258–69.

Nagata, N. (1993), Intelligent computer feedback for second language instruction. *Modern Language Journal*, 77(3), 330–39.

Nation, P. (2013), *What Should Every EFL Teacher Know?* Seoul: Compass Media.

Nemtchinova, E., Mahboob, A., Eslami, Z., et al. (2010), Training Non-native English Speaking TESOL Professionals. In A. Mahboob (ed.), *The NNEST Lens: Non Native English Speakers in TESOL* (pp. 222–38). Newcastle upon Tyne: Cambridge Scholars Press.

Nickerson, C. (2005), English as a lingua franca in international business contexts. *English for Specific Purposes*, 24(4), 367–80.

Noels, K., Pelletier, L., Clement, R., et al. (2000), Why are you learning a second language? Motivational orientations and self-determination theory. *Language Learning*, 50(1), 57–85.

Norton, B. (1995), Social identity, investment, and language learning. *TESOL Quarterly*, 29(1), 9–31.

Nunan, D. (1992). *Research Methods in Language Learning*. Cambridge: Cambridge University Press.

—(1999), President's message: October/November 1999. *TESOL Matters*, 9(5), 1.

—(2011), *Teaching English to Young Learners*. Anaheim, CA: Anaheim University Press.

—(2013), Innovation in the Young Learner Classroom. In K. Hyland and L. L. C. Wong (eds), *Innovation and Change in English Language Education* (pp. 233–47). New York: Routledge.

O'Connor, A. and Sharkey, J. (2004), Defining the process of teacher–researcher collaboration. *TESOL Quarterly*, 38(2), 335–9.

O'Loughlin, J. B. (2011), Experience speaks: On coteaching and collaboration. *TESOL Connections*, 2 October 2011. Retrieved from http://newsmanager.commpartners.com/tesolc/print/2011–10–01/4.html/

Ortega, L. (2013), SLA for the 21st century: Disciplinary progress, transdisciplinary relevance, and the bi/multilingual turn. *Currents in Language Learning*, 63 (Supplement 1), 1–24.

Oscarson, M. (2004), Alternative forms of assessment and student participation. *Language Testing Update,* 36, 114–15.

Palfrey, J. G. and Gasser, U. (2008), *Born Digital: Understanding the First Generation of Digital Natives.* New York: Basic Books.

Paltridge, B. (2009), Afterword: Where have we come from and where are we now? In D. Belcher (ed.), *English for Specific Purposes in Theory and Practice* (pp. 289–96). Ann Arbor, MI: University of Michigan Press.

Paul, D. and Chan, M. (2010), *Teaching English to Children in Asia.* Hong Kong: Pearson Longman.

Pavlenko, A. (2005), *Emotions and Multilingualism.* New York: Cambridge University Press.

—(ed.) (2011), *Thinking and Speaking in Two Languages.* Bristol: Multilingual Matters.

Paulston, C. B. (1974), Linguistic and communicative competence. *TESOL Quarterly,* 8(4), 347–62.

Peacock, M. (1997), The effect of authentic materials on the motivation of EFL learners. *ELT Journal,* 51(2), 144–56.

Peirce, B. N. (1995), Social identity, investment, and language learning. *TESOL Quarterly,* 29(1), 9–31.

Penn Graduate School of Education (n.d.), *TESOL Workshop.* Retrieved from University of Pennsylvania TESOL Workshop website: http://www.dolphin.upenn.edu/pennelf/TESOL/Workshop.html

Pennington, M. C. (1992), Second class or economy? The status of the English language profession in tertiary education. *Prospect: An Australian Journal of TESOL,* 7(3), 7–19.

—(1995), The teacher change cycle. *TESOL Quarterly,* 29(4), 705–31.

Pennycook, A. (1994), *The Cultural Politics of English as an International Language.* London: Longman.

—(2001), *Critical Applied Linguistics: A Critical Introduction.* London: Lawrence Erlbaum.

Phillabaum, S and Frazier, S. (2012), Student perceptions of how TESOL educators teach nonnative English-speaking teachers. *CATESOL Journal,* 24(1), 245–71.

Phillipson, R. (1992), *Linguistic Imperialism.* Oxford: Oxford University Press.

—(1996), ELT: The Native Speaker's Burden. In T. Hedge and N. Whitney (eds), *Power, Pedagogy and Practice* (pp. 23–30). Oxford: Oxford University Press.

Pickering, L. (2006), Current research on intelligibility in English as a lingua franca. *Annual Review of Applied Linguistics,* 26, 219–33.

Pinter, A. (2006), *Teaching Young Language Learners.* Oxford: Oxford University Press.

Pitton, D. E. (2006), *Mentoring Novice Teachers: Fostering a Dialogue Process.* Thousand Oaks, CA: Corwin Press.

Polio, C. (ed.) (2013), *Annual Review of Applied Linguistics: Topics in Multilingualism,* Vol. 33.

Prabhu, N. S. (1990), There is no best method: Why? *TESOL Quarterly,* 24(2), 161–76.

Prensky, M. (2001), Digital natives, digital immigrants. *On the Horizon,* 9(5), 1–5.

Prodromou, L. (1997), Global English and the Octopus. *IATEFL Newsletter,* 137, 18–22.

Purpura, J. E. (2004), *Assessing Grammar*. Cambridge: Cambridge University Press.

Quirk, R. (1969), English today: A world view. *TESOL Quarterly,* 3(1), pp. 23–9.

Ramage, K. (1991), Motivational factors and persistence in second language learning. *Language Learning,* 40(2), 189–219.

Rampton, B. (1995), *Crossing: Language & Ethnicity among Adolescents*. London: Longman.

Read, J. (2000), *Assessing Vocabulary*. Cambridge: Cambridge University Press.

Reindeers, H. (2009), Technology and Second Language Teacher Education. In A. Burns and J. C. Richards (eds), *The Cambridge Guide to Second Language Teacher Education* (pp. 230–37). Cambridge: Cambridge University Press.

Reppen, R. (2010), *Using Corpora in the Language Classroom*. Cambridge: Cambridge University Press.

Richards, J. C. (1987), The dilemma of teacher education in TESOL. *TESOL Quarterly,* 21(2), 209–26.

—(1990a), Beyond training: Approaches to teacher education in language teaching. *The Language Teacher,* 14, 3– 8.

—(1990b), The Dilemma of Teacher Education in Second Language Teaching. In J. Richards and D. Nunan (eds), *Second Language Teacher Education* (pp. 3–15). Cambridge: Cambridge University Press.

—(1998), *Teaching in Action: Case Studies from Second Language Classrooms*. Alexandria, VA: TESOL.

Richards, J. C. and Crookes, G. (1988), The practicum in TESOL. *TESOL Quarterly,* 22(1), 9–27.

Richards, J. C. and Farrell, T. S. C. (2005), *Professional Development for Language Teachers: Strategies for Teacher Learning*. Cambridge: Cambridge University Press.

Richards, J. C. and Lockhart, C. (1996), *Reflective Teaching in Second Language Classrooms*. Cambridge: Cambridge University Press.

Richards, J. C. and Nunan, D. (eds) (1990), *Second Language Teacher Education*. Cambridge: Cambridge University Press.

Rivera-Mills, S. V. and Plonsky, L. (2007), Empowering students with language learning strategies: A critical review of current issues. *Foreign Language Annals,* 40, 535–48.

Roberts, J. (1998), *Language Teacher Education*. London: Edward Arnold.

Römer, U. (2011), Corpus research applications in second language teaching. *Annual Review of Applied Linguistics,* 31(1), 205–25.

Ross, S. J. (2008), Language testing in Asia: Evolution, innovation, and policy challenges. *Language Testing,* 25(1), 5–13.

Royce, T. D. (2007), Multimodal Communicative Competence in Second Language Contexts. In T. D. Royce and W. L. Bowcher (eds), *New Directions in the Analysis of Multimodal Discourse* (pp. 361–89). Mahwah, NJ: Lawrence Erlbaum.

Rubin, J. (1975), What the 'good language learner' can teach us. *TESOL Quarterly,* 9(1), 41–51.

Salaberry, M. R. (2001), The use of technology for second language learning and teaching: A retrospective. *The Modern Language Journal,* 85(1), 39–56.

Savignon, S. J. (1983), *Communicative Competence: Theory and Classroom Practice*. Reading, MA: Addison-Wesley.

—(2007), Beyond communicative language teaching: What's ahead? *Journal of Pragmatics*, 39(1), 207–20.

Schmidt, T. and Worner, K. (eds) (2012), *Multilingual Corpora and Multilingual Corpus Analysis*. Amsterdam: John Benjamins.

Schon, D. (1983), *The Reflective Practitioner: How Professionals Think in Action*. New York: Basic Books.

Schwartz, A. M. (2001), Preparing Teachers to Work with Heritage Language Learners. In J. K. Peyton, D. Ranard and S. McGinnis (eds), *Heritage Languages in America: Preserving a National Resource* (pp. 229–52). McHenry, IL: Center for Applied Linguistics.

Scott, W. and Ytreberg, L. (1990), *Teaching English to Children*. London: Longman.

Scovel, T. (1978), The effect of affect on foreign language learning: A review of the anxiety research. *Language Learning*, 28(1), 129–42.

—(2000), A critical review of the critical period research. *Annual Review of Applied Linguistics,* 20(1), 213–23.

Seargeant, P. (2010), The historical ontology of language. *Language Sciences,* 32, 1–13.

Seidlhofer, B. (2002), Closing a conceptual gap: The case for a description of English as a lingua franca. *International Journal of Applied Linguistics,* 11(2), 133–58.

—(2009), Common ground and different realities: World Englishes and English as a lingua franca. *World Englishes,* 8(2), 236–45.

Sengupta, S., Forey, G. and Hamp-Lyons, L. (1999), Supporting effective English communication within the context of teaching and research in a tertiary institute: Developing a genre model for consciousness raising. *English for Specific Purposes* 18, S7–S23.

Shaaban, K. (2001), Assessment of young learners. *English Teaching Forum,* 39(4), 16–23.

Shin, J. K. (2006), Ten helpful ideas for teaching English to young learners. *English Teaching Forum,* 44(2), 2–13.

Shin, J. K. and Crandall, J. (2014), *Teaching Young Learners English*. Boston, MA: National Geographic Learning/Cengage Learning.

Shohamy, E. (2004), Assessment in Multicultural Societies: Applying Democratic Principles and Practices to Language Testing. In B. Norton and K. Toohey (eds), *Critical Pedagogies and Language Learning* (pp. 72–92). Cambridge: Cambridge University Press.

Shulman, L. S. (1987), Knowledge and teaching: Foundations of the new reform. *Harvard Educational Review,* 57(1), 1–22.

Shvidko, E. (2014), *4 World Cup Writing Activities* [Web log post, 13 June]. Retrieved from http://blog.tesol.org/4-world-cup-writing-activities/#more-4135/

Sifakis, N. C. (2004), Teaching EIL – teaching international or intercultural English: What teachers should know. *System,* 32(2), 237–50.

Snow, D. (2006), *More than a Native Speaker: An Introduction to Teaching English Abroad* (2nd edn). Alexandria, VA: TESOL.

Snow, M. A., Kamhi-Stein, L. D. and Brinton, D. M. (2006), Teacher training for English as a lingua franca. *Annual Review of Applied Linguistics*, 26, 261–81.

Snyder, I. (ed.) (2002), *Silicon Literacies: Communication, Innovation and Education in the Electronic Age*. London: Routledge.

Soheili-Mehr, A. H. (2008), Native and non-native speakers of English: Recent perspectives on theory, research, and practice. *Language Teaching*, 41, 445–57.

Spada, N. and Tomita, Y. (2010), Interactions between type of instruction and type of language feature: A meta-analysis. *Language Learning*, 60(2), 263–308.

Stansfield, C. (ed.) (1986), *Technology and Language Testing*. Washington, DC: TESOL.

Stillwell, C. (2009), The collaborative development of teacher training skills. *English Language Teachers Journal*, 63(4), 353.

Strickland, D. S. (1988), The teacher as researcher: Towards the extended professional. *Language Arts*, 65, 754–64.

Swain, M. (1985), Communicative competence: Some roles of comprehensible input and comprehensible output in its development. *Input in Second Language Acquisition*, 15, 165–79.

Swales, J. M. and Feak, C. B. (2004), *Academic Writing for Graduate Students: Essential Tasks and Skills* (2nd edn). Ann Arbor, MI: University of Michigan Press.

Taylor, C., Jamieson, J. and Eignor, D. (2000), Trends in computer use among international students. *TESOL Quarterly*, 34(3), 575–85.

Taylor, L. L., Guiora, A. Z., Catford, J. C., et al. (1969), The role of personality variables in second language acquisition. *Language Learning*, 24, 23–35.

Tedick, D. J. (ed.) (2005), *Second Language Teacher Education: International Perspectives*. Mahwah, NJ: Lawrence Erlbaum.

Tedick, D. J. and Walker, C. L. (1994), Second language teacher education: The problems that plague us. *The Modern Language Journal*, 78(3), 300–12.

TESOL (2002), *TESOL Standards for P-12 ESL Teacher Education Programs*. Retrieved from http://www.udel.edu/ education/masters/tesl/standard-summaries.pdf/

—(2004), *TESOL Research Agenda*. August. www.tesol.org/docs/pdf/2937.

—(2008a), *Position Statement on English as a Global Language*. Retrieved from http://www.tesol.org/s_tesol/bin.asp?CID=32&DID=10884&DOC=FILE.PDF/

—(2008b), *TESOL Membership Statistics 2007*. 1 January. Retrieved from http://www.tesol.org/docs/pdf/10434.pdf?sfvrsn=2/

TESOL International Association (2012), *Membership Statistics: Grand Totals for Basic Membership, by Member Type*. October. Retrieved from http://www.tesol.org/docs/ membership/october-2012-membership-statistics.pdf?sfvrsn=0/

—(2014a), *CELTA Programs, TEFL Certificate Programs, and Distance Learning Programs*. Retrieved 12 April 2014, from http://www.tesol.org/enhance-your-career/career-development/beginning-your-career/celta-programs-tefl-certificate-programs-and-distance-learning-programs

—(2014b), *Common Qualifications for English Language Teachers*. Retrieved 12 April 2014, from http://www.tesol.org/enhance-your-career/career-development/beginning-your-career/common-qualifications-for-english-language-teachers/

—(2014c), *PreK-12 English Language Proficiency Standards*. Retrieved from http://www.tesol.org/advance-the-field/standards/prek-12-english-language-proficiency-standards/

—(2014d), *Social Responsibility.* Retrieved from http://www.tesol.org/connect/
interest-sections/social-responsibility/

—(2014e), *TESOL/NCATE Standards for P-12 Teacher Education Programs.*
Retrieved from http://www.tesol.org/advance-the-field/standards/
tesol-ncate-standards-for-p-12-teacher-education-programs/

—(2014f), *TESOL Standing Committees.* Retrieved from http://www.tesol.org/
about-tesol/association-governance/standing-committees/

—(2014g), *2014 Membership Statistics.* 13 May. Retrieved from http://www.
tesol.org/docs/default-source/membership/april-2014-membership-statistics.
pdf?sfvrsn=0/

—(2014 [n.d.1]), *Diversity Committee.* Retrieved from http://www.tesol.org/
about-tesol/association-governance/standing-committees/diversity-committee/

—(2014 [n.d.2]), *Mission and Values.* Retrieved from http://www.tesol. org/
about-tesol/association-governance/mission-and-values/

Thiel, T. (1999), Reflections on critical incidents. *Prospect,* 14(1), 44–52.

Thomas, J. (2006), Cross-cultural Pragmatic Failure. In Bolton, K. and
B. B. Kachru (eds), *World Englishes: Critical Concepts in Linguistics,* Vol. 4
(pp. 22–48). London and New York: Routledge.

Thomas, M. (2004), Book review of *Portraits of the L2 User,* by V. Cook (ed.).
The Modern Language Journal, 88, 141–2.

Thompson, G. (1996), Some misconceptions about communicative language
teaching. *ELT Journal,* 50(1), 9–15.

—(2014 [2004]), *Introducing Functional Grammar* (2nd edn). London: Edward
Arnold.

Thornbury, S. (2000), *How to Teach Grammar.* Harlow: Pearson Education.

Thorne, S. L., Black, R. W., and Sykes, J. M. (2009), Second language use,
socialization, and learning in Internet interest communities and online
gaming. *Modern Language Journal,* 93, 802–21.

Thumboo, E. (2009), Literary Creativity in World Englishes. In B. Kachru, Y.
Kachru and C. Nelson (eds), *The Handbook of World Englishes,* Vol. 48
(pp. 405–27). Oxford: Wiley-Blackwell.

Todeva, E. and Cenoz, J. (eds) (2009), *The Multiple Realities of Multilingualism:
Personal Narratives and Researchers' Perspectives.* Berlin: Mouton de Gruyter.

Tollefson, J. W. (2010), Perspectives on Language Policy and Planning. In
R. B. Kaplan (ed.), *The Oxford Handbook of Applied Linguistics* (2nd edn)
(pp. 463–72). Oxford: Oxford University Press.

Tomlinson, B. (1998), *Materials Development in Language Teaching.* Cambridge:
Cambridge University Press.

Toohey, K. and Norton, B. (2010), Language Learner Identities and Sociocultural
Worlds. In R. B. Kaplan (ed.), *The Oxford Handbook of Applied Linguistics*
(2nd edn) (pp. 178–99). Oxford: Oxford University Press.

Tripp, D. (1993), *Critical Incidents in Teaching.* London: Routledge.

Tsagari, C. (2004), Alternative assessment: Some considerations. *Language
Testing Update,* 36, 116–24.

Tsui, A. B. M. (2007), The complexities of identity formation: A narrative inquiry
of an EFL teacher. *TESOL Quarterly,* 41(4), 657–80.

Twomey, S. J. (2010), Facilitating 'gem moments' of learning: Reading research
as teacher professional development. *Journal of Teaching and Learning,* 7(1),
41–54.

Ushioda, E. (2008), Motivation and Good Language Learners. In C. Griffiths (ed.), *Lessons from Good Language Learners* (pp. 19–34). Cambridge: Cambridge University Press.

Van Duzer, C. and Florez, M. C. (2003), *Adult English Language Instruction in the 21st Century*. Issues in Preparing Adult English Language Learners for Success Series. Washington, DC: Center for Applied Linguistics.

Vo, L. T. and Nguyen, H. T. M. (2010), Critical friends group for EFL teacher professional development. *ELT Journal*, 64(2), 205–13.

Vygotsky, L. (1962), *Thought and Language*. Cambridge, MA: MIT Press.

—(2014 [1978]), *Mind in Society: The Development of Higher Psychological Processes*. Cambridge, MA: Harvard University Press.

Wachob, P. (2006), Methods and materials for motivation and learner autonomy. *Reflections on English Language Teaching*, 5(1), 93–122.

Wajnryb, R. (1992), *Classroom Observation Tasks: A Resource Book for Language Teachers and Trainers*. Cambridge: Cambridge University Press.

Wallace, M. J. (1998), *Action Research for Language Teachers*. New York: Cambridge University Press.

Wardbaugh, R. (1972), TESOL: Our common cause. *TESOL Quarterly*, 6(4), 291–303.

Warschauer, M. (1998), Researching technology in TESOL: Determinist, instrumental, and critical approaches. *TESOL Quarterly*, 32(4), 757–61.

—(2014 [2000]), The death of cyberspace and the rebirth of CALL. *English Teachers' Journal*, 53(1), 61–7.

—(2014 [2004]), *Technology and Social Inclusion: Rethinking the Digital Divide*. Cambridge, MA: MIT Press.

—(2014 [2007]), The paradoxical future of digital learning. *Learning Inquiry*, 1(1), 41–9.

Weigle, S. C. (2002), *Assessing Writing*. Cambridge: Cambridge University Press.

—(2014 [2007], Teaching writing teachers about assessment. *Journal of Second Language Writing*, 16(3), 194–209.

Wenger, E. (1998), Communities of practice: Learning as a social system. *Systems Thinker*, 9(5), 2–3.

Wesche, M. Bingham (2010), Content-based Second Language Instruction. In R. Kaplan (ed.), *The Oxford Handbook of Applied Linguistics* (2nd edn) (pp. 275–93). Oxford: Oxford University Press.

Widdowson, H. G. (1994), The ownership of English. *TESOL Quarterly*, 28(2), 377–89.

Wilhelm, K. H. (2005), Developmental and alternative assessment: Knowing what they know (and don't know!). *Crosslinks in English Language Teacher*, 2, 63–93.

Williams, M. (1991), A Framework for Teaching English to Young Learners. In C. Brumfit, J. Moon and R. Tongue (eds), *Teaching English to Children: From Practice to Principle* (pp. 203–12). London: Collins ELT.

Willis, D. (2003), *Rules, Patterns, and Words: Grammar and Lexis in English Language Teaching*. Cambridge: Cambridge University Press.

Wissot, J. (1970), A total approach to the high school English-as-a second-language program. *TESOL Quarterly*, 4(4), 361–4.

Wong, M. S. (2011), Fifty ways to develop professionally: What language educators need to succeed. *Language Education in Asia*, 2(1), 142–55.

Wright, T. (2010), Second language teacher education: Review of recent research on practice. *Language Teaching,* 43(3), 259–96.

Wu, X. (2003), Intrinsic motivation and young language learners: The impact of the classroom environment. *System,* 31, 501–17.

Xu, H. and Jiang, X. (2004), Achievement motivation, attributional beliefs, and EFL learning strategy use in China. *Asian Journal of English Language Teaching,* 14, 65–87.

Young, R. (1996), *Intercultural Communication: Pragmatics, Genealogy, Deconstruction.* Bristol: Multilingual Matters.

Yung, K. W. H. (2103), Bridging the gap: Motivation in year one EAP classrooms. *Hong Kong Journal of Applied Linguistics,* 14(2), 83–95.

Index